AD

"The Gottmans' *The New Marria~*
rigor and clinical wisdom by curating cutting-edge empirical finnings on iei....
health with what works in psychotherapy. This compendium of clinical brilliance is
both fun and funny, filled with insightful humor and offering a deeply enjoyable journey for any clinician seeking to help couples thrive. What a gift to our professional
world! *The New Marriage Clinic* will extend readers' current understandings into
new and exciting avenues for helping couples connect more deeply and learn how to
support each other in these challenging times."

—**Daniel J. Siegel, MD,** *New York Times* best-selling author of *Aware, IntraConnected,*
and *Personality and Wholeness in Therapy*

"Wow! What a ride. In *The New Marriage Clinic*, iconic researcher John Gottman,
partnering with brilliant couples therapist Julie Gottman, give us an updated and
revised encyclopedic compendium of research surrounding the phenomenon of marriage and the techniques and technologies of marriage therapy. From the theoretician looking for theory, to the researcher looking for facts, to the clinician looking
for effective therapeutic interventions, this book is for them all, and in abundance.
We recommend this book to everyone—from student to seasoned clinician—who is
involved in conversation, training, practice, research, and theory-building about marriage. This is an essential and primary source."

—**Harville Hendrix, PhD, and Helen LaKelly Hunt, PhD,** coauthors of
Doing Imago Relationship Therapy in the Space Between

"For decades, research on couple processes by John and Julie Gottman has yielded cutting-edge strategies for effective assessment and intervention. Now, with this updated
edition of *The New Marriage Clinic*, the Gottmans extend the legacy of their sci-
ence-based method of couples therapy with new and extensive findings underlying
their comprehensive approach to treating couple distress and promoting health and
resilience in intimate relationships. *The New Marriage Clinic* is filled with practical,
evidence-based, step-by-step strategies that should be part of every couple therapist's
toolkit. New contributions address effective strategies targeting couple violence, infidelity, and substance misuse. Especially compelling are specific techniques for helping
couples process those inevitable 'regrettable incidents' of everyday life and for restoring deep friendship and intimacy between partners who have drifted apart. *The New
Marriage Clinic* is an essential resource that every couple therapist should have on
their bookshelf and consult regularly."

—**Douglas K. Snyder, PhD,** professor of psychological and brain sciences,
Texas A&M University (College Station), and coeditor of
The Clinical Handbook of Couple Therapy

"In this truly remarkable book, John and Julie Gottman pour all their brilliant research, professional experience, and passion for understanding and helping couples into the authoritative text for future generations of couples therapists and the researchers who will work to inform them. This may be the capstone for the careers of perhaps the two most important clinician-researchers of the past fifty years. We owe them a great debt for their work and for the enormous effort of putting it all together in one volume, and for doing so with the highest level of scientific inquiry, which has produced the most effective clinical approaches to working with couples."

—**Richard G. Tedeschi, PhD,** professor emeritus, The University of North Carolina at Charlotte, and executive director of The Boulder Crest Institute for Posttraumatic Growth

THE
NEW MARRIAGE
CLINIC

THE
NEW MARRIAGE CLINIC

A Scientifically Based Marital Therapy
UPDATED

JOHN M. GOTTMAN
JULIE SCHWARTZ GOTTMAN

Norton Professional Books

An Imprint of W. W. Norton & Company
Independent Publishers Since 1923

Note to Readers: Standards of clinical practice and protocol change over time, and no technique or recommendation is guaranteed to be safe or effective in all circumstances. This volume is intended as a general information resource for professionals practicing in the field of psychotherapy and mental health; it is not a substitute for appropriate training, peer review, and/or clinical supervision. Likewise, any member of the general public who is not a professional practicing in the field of psychotherapy and mental health should regard the recommendations in this book as suggestions only and any such recommendations should not be seen as a substitute for obtaining professional advice. Neither the publisher nor the author(s) can guarantee the complete accuracy, efficacy, or appropriateness of any particular recommendation in every respect. As of press time, the URLs displayed in this book link or refer to existing sites. The publisher and author are not responsible for any content that appears on third-party websites.

Some identifying characteristics such as names, dialogue, and visual depictions have been changed.

For information about permission to reproduce selections from this book, write to Permissions, W. W. Norton & Company, Inc., 500 Fifth Avenue, New York, NY 10110

For information about special discounts for bulk purchases, please contact W. W. Norton Special Sales at specialsales@wwnorton.com or 800-233-4830

Manufacturing by Lakeside Book Company
Production manager: Gwen Cullen

ISBN: 978-1-324-01631-1

W. W. Norton & Company, Inc., 500 Fifth Avenue, New York, NY 10110
www.wwnorton.com

W. W. Norton & Company Ltd., 15 Carlisle Street, London W1D 3BS

1 2 3 4 5 6 7 8 9 0

*For our dear friends, Rafael Lisitsa,
Vladimir Brayman, and Ed Sargent.
Your combined vision has led
our way into the future.*

Contents

Acknowledgments

This book is a reworking of the original marriage clinic book after nearly 30 years of clinical work, clinical training, and subsequent research in The Relationships Research Institute's portable psychophysiology lab, SPAFF coding stations, and the new Gottman Institute Love Lab, run by Dr. Carrie Cole. We begin by acknowledging the essential, vital contributions of our great lifelong friend, Dr. Robert Levenson, of the University of California, Berkeley. Without Bob, none of this research and thinking would have ever seen the light of day. Despite the best advice from John and Bob's older colleagues, who firmly advised them to stop doing research together, and to stop the foolhardy practice of investigating two interacting people at once, Bob agreed to follow his and John's unstoppable curiosity about what makes love relationships succeed or fail. Bob and John began doing research together with almost no hypotheses, which is a definite violation of good research practice. Almost 50 years later, they can proudly claim that they began together happily in complete ignorance. Fortunately, still in complete ignorance, John and Bob both got lucky and met the loves of their lives in Dr. Julie Schwartz and Dr. Michelle (Lani) Shiota. This new Marriage Clinic book is guided by John and Julie's Sound Relationship House theoretical translation of our research findings discriminating the "masters" from the "disasters" of relationships, including same-sex couples as well as cross-sex couples. Our basic research was always longitudinal, and that led to some surprising findings; for example, that 69% of all relationship conflicts never get resolved.

Using all the vast time-series data that Bob and John generated, we want to acknowledge the enormous contributions of Dr. James Murray and his students for helping us create our first nonlinear dynamic mathematical models of couples' interaction, which resulted in many papers and the MIT Press book, *The Mathematics of Marriage*, in 2002. That mathematical work was extended by Dr. Vladimir Brayman and his world-class colleagues, Dr. Dmitriy Drusvyatskit and Dr. Yuriy Gulak. For the last six years, our close friend Rafael Lisitsa has been the valiant and endlessly persevering CEO, first at Affective Software, Inc. (ASI), and now that ASI and TGI have merged, Gottman Inc. (GI). He is a man of multidimensional vision and talented leadership in many areas of life and is far ahead of the curve in the new revolutionary world of artificial intelligence. We also want to thank Ed Sargent, past CEO of TGI and now current Chief of Learning for GI. Ed brings amazing skill, team building, and a profound understanding of our mission that has helped spread our work across the globe. Ed is also a dear, beloved friend, and endless supporter of our work. We also bow to the genius and hard work of Dr. Vladimir Brayman, who has served as our Chief Technology Officer, first at ASI, and now at GI. He has been the architect of all our algorithmic creations and programming, including our validated Trust Metric, and he has become a treasured friend besides. Dr. Brayman has pioneered all our ML and AI technological development as it carves out a never-before-achieved pathway into emotionally-intelligent AI assistance. Together, Rafael and Vladimir have created revolutionary new patent-winning innovations, and remarkable technological inventions. These include creating the online validated questionnaires of the Gottman Relationship Checkup, and using AI machine learning to create our online Love Lab, with its automated Specific Emotion Coding (SPAFF), automated heart rate detection for any skin tone using only videography, and the enormously powerful mathematics and software of GottmanConnect for assessing relationships. Brayman and his team have also integrated 37 modules and assessment recommendations to fine-tune assessment and interventions.

Our goal in creating a web-based platform has been to democratize help for couples, so that anyone—regardless of geography, sexual orientation, gender, or socioeconomics—can access the best, scientifically-based help for their relationships. We are proud to announce that it is now possible for any couple in the world to fully assess *and treat* their relationship issues on their phones, tablets, or computers in the comfort and privacy of their own home. We are hoping that in the future, younger clinicians will use these assessment and intervention tools in their own couples' work. We are also planning to reach out preventatively to individuals and couples with these same tools, but assisted by an automated emotionally-intelligent (and humble) computer advisor.

Rafael and Vladimir have had a great staff to assist them. Therefore, we also wish to acknowledge the contributions of Connor Eaton to our AI development, Steven Fan for the Gottman Coach videos as well as current ongoing videography projects, Dr. Dmitriy Drusvyatskit of the University of Washington for his mathematics, Alexander Elguren, for his brilliant leadership in content development, Inna Brayman, our calm and patient head of customer service, plus numerous others, including John Fantell, Dr. Yuriy Gulak of Rutgers University (for his mathematics), Sam Hage, Kendra Han, Sean Jeffries, Raleigh Keagan, Frans Keylard, Brianne Korthase, Alexander Miropolsky, Torsten Oberst, Letha Penhale, Vadim Popov, Philippe Post, Alexandra Spangler, Braeden Stamas, Janani Subramanian, and Lisa Tashjian. If we have neglected to mention any of our current dedicated staff, please forgive our error, which is solely our own.

For the last 30 years, we have benefitted from the contributions of many of our colleagues working at The Gottman Institute (TGI), The Relationships Research Institute (RRI), and Affective Software, Inc. (ASI), which has now been joined in one company, called Gottman, Inc. (GI). We wish to recognize our valiant cofounder of TGI, our dear friend, Etana Kunovsky, our highly esteemed prior CEO, and dear friend, Alan Kunovsky, and our current CEO of TGI, and also our dear friend, Ed Sargent—who is now also head of TGI and director of all online learning. We wish to acknowledge the huge contributions of Dr. Renay Bradley, who brilliantly led our nonprofit Relationships Research Institute for many years, conducting several critical clinical trials. We also want to acknowledge the invaluable contributions of Dr. Sybil Carrere, John's former lab director at the University of Washington, and the vast contributions of John's former students, Dr. Lynn Katz, Dr. Jim Coan, Dr. Janice Driver, Dr. Howard Markman, Dr. Cliff Notarius, Dr. Regina Rushe, Dr. Amber Tabares, and Dr. Dan Yoshimoto. We also want to recognize our late colleague, Dr. Neil Jacobson, and his widow, Dr. Virginia

Rutter, for their invaluable support, especially regarding the study of domestically violent couples.

Our TGI staff, past and present, have supported our mission to bring relationship help to over a million individuals. They include:

Erin Cox: professional development and tech support; Dr. Carrie Cole: our current Love Lab Research director; Dr. Don Cole: clinical director; Crystal Cressey: early couples department support; Emily Cripe: social media; Jen Dalby: early online learning; Caitlyn Donahue: marketing; Katelyn Ewen: graphic designer; Michael Fulwiler: former director of marketing; Beth Goss: master trainer of our worldwide Bringing Baby Home (BBH) program; Belinda Gray: early director of products department; Walter Guity: former head of customer service; Kendra Han: director of couples department; Laura Heck: early director of professional clinical development, Certified Gottman Trainer (CGT), and 7 Principles for Making Marriage Work Program; Stacy Hubbard: CGT, development of 7 Principles for Singles (with Dave Penner); Kennedy James: head of operations; Sean Jeffries: inventory management; Amy Loftis: director of professional development; Jennifer Luu: marketing; Vivian Lu: graphic design; Torsten Oberst: marketing director; Sadie Peterson: professional development, operations; Joni Parthemer: development and teaching of BBH; Dr. Dave Penner: clinical director and master trainer for 12 years, developer of the 7 Principles Program and 7 Principles for Singles (with Stacy Hubbard); Carolyn Pirak: development and teaching for BBH and Emotion Coaching programs; Katie Reynolds: public and media relations and GI; Becca Sangwin: marketing; Aziza Seykota: director of product development; Therese Soudant: couples department support; Janani Subramanian: head of finance and accounting; Weston Triemstra: website development and tech support; Keeley Trygstad: tech and operations support; and Linda Wright: early director of couples department.

We want to also express endless gratitude for the unique contributions of our housemates and wonderful friends, master trainers and clinicians, Dr. Don Cole, our esteemed clinical director, and Dr. Carrie Cole, our research director and the head of our new Seattle social psychophysiology Love Lab. Don and Carrie Cole courageously moved from Houston to Seattle to become the new clinical and research faces of The Gottman Institute, as John and Julie someday plan to recede into the sunset in their Seaward double kayak. Carrie Cole had to master so many things at once, including learning psychophysiology and how to run a very complex laboratory, while simultaneously getting her PhD. There is nothing that woman cannot do. We are forever grateful to Don and Carrie.

From our partners in doing-good-in-the-world (Tikkun Olam), and from the company Idea Architects, first we acknowledge our brilliant and visionary dear friend and literary agent, Doug Abrams, and our the incredibly gifted writing assistant, Alyssa Knickerbocker. With all her magic, Alyssa waved her wand to help create and perfect the book you now hold in your hands. Without brilliant Alyssa, this book would not exist. We also want to acknowledge Bella Roberts, our assistant literary editor, who helped with the proposal and scheduling, and executive assistant Mellisa Kim, who helped with the footnotes. We also wish to acknowledge Brockman Inc., particularly our agent Katinka Matson, who first shepherded our *New York Times* bestseller, *The Seven Principles for Making Marriage Work,* written with Nan Silver, as well as other subsequent books.

We could never have created this book without our stalwart friends, life stewards, and fellow journey men and women: Cara and Phillip Cohn, for their spiritual guidance and wisdom; Alison Shaw and Derk Jager, for their undying decades of love, support, and Alison's incredible cooking; and Mavis Tsai, for her enduring friendship both as a fellow researcher and creator, lifelong wise companion, and Julie's favorite partner in all things adventurous.

Last but not least, we thank our beloved and endlessly working almost-a-doctor daughter, her precious husband who is a long-sought son, and our most amazing grandchild, who they've thankfully brought into our lives. How can we thank you enough for wanting to raise your child in a multi-generational family? We are so profoundly honored. We love you so much.

Our work would not have been possible without the incredibly important help we've received from so many of our friends and colleagues. First, we begin by recognizing the nearly 100,000 couples to date who have voluntarily contributed to everything we know about love relationships. You courageously volunteered to reveal the most intimate part of your lives for our scientific review. Without you, we would have nothing to offer the world. Without all of you, we would have failed utterly. Therefore, to all these partners in our lifelong venture, we bow our heads in deeply heartfelt gratitude.

Preface

We have had the privilege of sharing in a great scientific and clinical adventure for over 50 years. It all started in 1972. John was an assistant professor at Indiana University, where he met two talented graduate students, Cliff Notarius and Howard Markman, who have become professors and brilliant clinicians in their own right. With their support, John, Howard, and Cliff created John's first lab to study relationships. John soon met Robert Levenson, another psychology professor at Indiana University who specialized in psychophysiological research. Bob became John's dearest friend and lifelong research collaborator. Over the decades, we have pursued further study in several labs: Bob and John's lab at Indiana University, John's lab at the University of Illinois, Bob's labs at UC San Francisco and UC Berkeley, John and Julie's labs at the University of Washington, including an "apartment lab" (later dubbed "Love Lab"), and more recently, our newest lab at the Gottman Institute in downtown Seattle, headed by Dr. Carrie Cole. In the interim, we have built two companies: (1) the Gottman Institute, Inc., led in turn by our three close friends Etana Kunovsky; her husband, Alan Kunovsky; and, today, Edward Sergeant; and (2) Affective Software. We have also built our clinical practices. Five years ago we formed our new sister company, Affective Software, Inc., led by our dear friends Rafael Lisitsa and Dr. Vladimir Brayman. This year (2023) these two companies have merged to form Gottman, Inc.

All along, we have been blessed with talented students, brilliant collaborators, dedicated clinicians, and terrific business leaders. We've also been gifted by the work of three superb colleagues: our clinical directors, Dr. David Penner and Dr. Don Cole, and our research director, Dr. Carrie Cole. None of this work could have been accomplished without them.

After these 50 years of work, we have decided it's time for *The Marriage Clinic 2.0*. A lot has changed since publishing our first Marriage Clinic book. We have integrated our research with clinical work, and interwoven mathematical modeling into theory building. We have developed dozens of therapeutic research-based interventions. We have created and led a couples workshop, The Art and Science of Love, for an estimated 50,000 couples overall. We and our institute master trainers have offered clinical training workshops to over 100,000 clinicians in 15 countries. And hundreds of therapists certified in our methods have seen many more couples in private practice. All the couples we've seen have served as a constant reminder to us that we've just scratched the surface about couples dynamics and therapy. There is so much more to learn! We've funded our own research for the past 12 years, hope to in the future, and we thank God for all our good fortune and the many people, too numerous to name, who have helped us every step of the way.

We are very proud to be able to share this scientific and clinical adventure with you. We hope you will find this book even more useful than our first edition in your studies and clinical work. And perhaps you, too, will feel inspired to conduct your own research in this field so that our understanding of love and relationships may only deepen in the decades to come.

CHAPTER 1

The Myths, Mistakes, and Promise of Couples Therapy

In this chapter we share the story of our Levenson-Gottmans' Love Lab and our scientific adventure of the past five decades. We also share our views of the current status of marital therapy and consider again the question of what is "dysfunctional" when a relationship is ailing or headed for dissolution. There are many myths and misconceptions about this question, and clearing up these misconceptions is critical in setting the goals of couples therapy.

Creating a Relationship Lab

Our research on marriage is based, in part, on a 48-year-long collaboration with John's best friend, Robert W. Levenson, who is now a psychology professor at the University of California, Berkeley. Bob and John met at Indiana University, taught Abnormal Psychology together using feature films, supervised group therapy of clinical grad students, and laughed a lot. They rapidly became good friends. They did a "trial collaboration" that turned out to be easy and conflict-free, so they decided it'd be fun and easy to work together. John had already been doing research on couples for a few years before Bob joined him.

When Bob and John began doing their research on divorce prediction in 1975, there were nearly 2,000 published studies on divorce, only six of which were longitudinal prospective studies, based mostly on self-report measurements of personality. These six studies did very poorly at prediction. The correlations were all around .25. The correlation coefficient measures the amount of association between two variables, and it ranges from −1 to +1. Its maximum, 1.0, means perfect directional predictability from one variable to another variable. To find out how strongly two variables are related, a common method is to determine the "percent of the variation" that is accounted for by the correlation. To get that percent-of-the-variation number, we square the correlation and then multiply by 100. A correlation of .25 means that these researchers could account for very little variance in their predictions because a correlation of .25 means that we square .25, which equals .0625, then multiply by 100, so we compute .0625 × 100%, which equals 6.25% of the variation that gets explained, a pretty poor prediction for anything calling itself a science. That's because the remaining *unexplained* variation is 100% minus 6.25%, or 93.75%. So, we are saying that close to 94% is error. That's just plain embarrassing.

Also, the results were not very interesting theoretically. For example, Newcomb and Bentler (1980) found that clothes-conscious women were less likely to divorce, while there was no such correlation for men. Imagine, as a humorous aside, a couple's therapy based on these two results. The therapist would tell Martha to go shopping but tell George that his wardrobe didn't matter—go ahead and wear sweatpants. There were also some weak results in the Kelly and Conley (1987) study that "neuroticism" predicted divorce. These results are hard to interpret for methodological reasons, and they are hard to use to design marital interventions. Are people neurotic because their marriages are unhappy, or are they unhappily married because they're neurotic, or both? It's also unclear in the Kelly and Conley study whether neuroticism and marital unhappiness are both measuring the same or different things. Since Kelly and Conley had each couple's friends fill out the self-report personality inventory in that study, the friends may have used characteristics like their friends' depression to rate their friends' marital unhappiness. We just didn't know what was being measured. So, the previous research wasn't very useful for building a couples therapy.

John and Bob were doing their research in the mid-1970s. Here's what was going on at the time in their world. It's part of their context. A famous Stanford psychologist, Walter Mischel, had just written a very influential book titled *Personality and Assessment*, in which he challenged the whole field of psychology. He said that our best measures of personality were really quite terrible at predicting whether a person would wind up being a productive citizen, a mental patient, or a homicidal killer. The best measures predicted human behavior with, at most, correlations in the .30s. As we've noted, the correlation coefficient measures how good a prediction is. The biggest a correlation can get is 1.0, and the smallest is zero. It can also be negative, such as if some measure like "neuroticism" correlated negatively with something good, like staying married. That negative correlation would mean that more neurotic people are less likely to stay married. As we noted, to evaluate the strength of prediction, one had to square the correlation coefficient and multiply the result by 100 to get the percentage of predictability. That number would tell you how much variation in the criterion variable (like marital stability) was accounted for by the predictor variable of neuroticism. So, in Mischel's book a correlation of .3 would account for $.3 \times .3 \times 100 = 9\%$ of the variation. So that meant that 91% was error, and Mischel said, basically, that stinks, that's not much of a science. We have got to do much better than that.

So, with Mischel's challenge in mind, what were Bob and John supposed to measure about a marriage? They had no idea, but they were both strongly affected by Paul Ekman's powerful research on emotion in the human face. Paul had studied facial expressions and emotional experiences cross-culturally. He'd demonstrated that the human face was not a "researcher's nightmare," as the famous psychologist Jerome Bruner had claimed. Paul also studied the face anatomically, detailing how to measure its 46 muscle groups, some of which, some of the time, conveyed reliable emotional information. Much later, Bob and Paul did their own cross-cultural research on the autonomic signatures of specific emotions. But at that time, in the mid-1970s,

Bob and John thought, "Maybe we'll just try to *measure emotions* as a couple talked to one another." Seemed like a good idea at the time.

Also at that time, everyone thought they knew that emotion was all about three components: "emotional" behavior (as displayed in words, emotions in the voice, the face, and the body), physiology (heart rate, respiration, blood velocity, and so on), and the internal personal subjective experiences of emotion (which were usually called "feelings"). Almost all research on emotion agreed that there were those three components, and agreed that the most important dimension in the personal subjective component was how positive or negative the emotions felt. With these components in mind, we settled on videotaping faces, words, bodies, and voices for the emotional behavior component (we'd later "code" behavior into broad emotion categories second by second); measuring physiology (part of Bob's expertise); and using a video-recall method to measure internal subjective experiences. With this method, each partner watched video replays of their conversations, and privately turned a dial that ranged from *very negative* to *very positive* to match how they felt during moments of their conversation. With these variables agreed upon, Bob and John were all set to begin their studies.

There was another context to Bob and John's life back then. They were both assistant professors, without tenure. That meant that 7 years after getting hired, the faculty in their psychology department would either give them tenure, which would mean a secure job and a promotion from "assistant" to "associate" professor, or just fire them. Terrifying, especially since they'd each already spent about 7 years getting their PhDs. By the way, in Europe in the late Middle Ages and Renaissance, when universities first began, all professors were expected to be male, stay unmarried (that's where the "bachelor's degree" comes from), declare their dedication to Christianity and the Trinity, and give horoscope readings to both royalty and clergy. Every professor had to know how to read the stars and predict the future by casting horoscopes. "Tenure" started in the Renaissance as a way to protect faculty from both the church and the state. What if a professor made the wrong predictions, or predicted in favor of the state against the church? If he took sides against either the church or the state, he had to have a way to literally avoid execution. So, tenure was originally invented to prevent the slaughter of professors. Nowadays it's just their job security.

Bob and John each had a separate committee evaluating their work for an eventual terrifying up-or-out tenure decision. As they undertook this work on relationships, their committees both said to them:

> *Here's our advice: Number 1, we don't like assistant professors working together because how do we evaluate each individual for tenure? How do we know who to credit, or who to not credit? So, don't work together if you want to get tenure. Number 2, if we can't predict the behavior of one person, how do you expect to predict the behavior of two people? You'll never discover anything. You will never get a research grant. Number 3, psychology is the study of the individual, not the study of groups. A couple is a group. That's sociology, or anthropology, not psychology. So, study something else instead of couples, study something more reasonable, something more psychological.*

That didn't seem very friendly or encouraging to Bob and John.

They talked it over, and decided that if they were going to get fired in 7 years, they might as well get fired for doing what they wanted to do. That's called academic freedom. You get fired, maybe, but you get to decide what you're going to study and what you're maybe going to fail at. So why change study topics, be bored, and maybe fail anyway? And they liked each other. So they decided to defy all three suggestions their committees made and to study their chosen topics anyway.

They had another big problem to solve. How could they synchronize the data they collected with the video time code, so that they could know exactly when something occurred in a partner's physiology, and link it to both the emotional behavior of each person and that person's video-recall dial ratings? Luckily, Bob is a very talented man, including being a computer programmer. He also once had a job repairing kitchen appliances, so he could build electronics and do things like soldering, which John couldn't do. Also, the psychology department had a great shop, and Bob had some seed money available for building his psychophysiology lab, in which he was studying psychosomatic illness.

As to computing, you need to know that in the mid-1970s every university had just *one* computer, a big monster mainframe. Professors would take their data in very heavy boxes of IBM punch cards to a little window of the computing center and come back several hours later to get the results of their analyses. Personal computers weren't invented until the early 1980s. But Bob's lab actually had its own computer, called a PDP-11. It was the size of three refrigerators, but Bob knew how to program that monster so it could synchronize the physiology of two people and the video-recall rating dial data to the video time code.

Bob and John's lab also contained two cameras, one focused on each partner's face. The videos from both cameras could be merged into one split-screen picture. John would provide the observational system for scoring the couple's emotions. Bob and John also learned from Paul Ekman and his colleague Wallace Friesen how to score facial expressions of emotion using Ekman and Friesen's Facial Action Coding System (abbreviated FACS). But to earn Paul's trust and help, Bob and John had to learn "how to speak FACS," which involved learning how to read and score 46 "facial actions"; otherwise, Paul wouldn't take them seriously. John later worked out how an observer could reliably code emotion not just in the face but also in the words, voice tones, and gestures a person might make, using his Specific Affect Coding System (abbreviated SPAFF). For SPAFF to achieve reliability, SPAFF had to meet a very strict criterion: two independent observers had to agree on the right codes over 85% of the time, a tall order. But observing is fun for John, who had been an amateur actor in community theater. Actors have to display emotions as actions, and coders have to infer emotions from people's actions. Same thing, in a way, because actors have to know how to display emotions and do so well, so they have to be able to know what emotions look and sound like. So do reliable emotion coders. (As Shakespeare said, all the world's a stage.)

Back to the couple. What should the couple talk about? Bob and John settled on three 15-minute conversations. Is that long enough to describe an entire relationship? Who knew? They decided that couples would have an "events-of-the-day" conversation after they'd been apart at least 8 hours, then a "conflict" conversation in which they were asked to solve their biggest area of controversy, and finally a "positive topic" conversation they'd select from a list of topics (like "Plan your next vacation"). Their conversations would be videotaped and later coded, using SPAFF. A 5-minute silent baseline time period would precede each conversation. The partners' physiology would be collected during all three conversations and while each partner turned the rating dial as they watched video replays of their conversations. That was our standard protocol. We were all set to go. We recruited 30 married couples for our first study.

In summary, Bob and John brought this "multimethod" approach to the measurement of emotion in marital processes as they manifested in three domains:

1. *Interactive behavior:* coding partners' behaviors and emotions as they interacted in various contexts;
2. *Perception:* ascertaining each partner's perceptions of both themself and their partner by using questionnaires, video-recall procedures, attributional methods, and interviews; and
3. *Physiology:* measuring autonomic, endocrine, and immune system responses.

In grad school Bob's and John's professors had told them not to do research unless they had a hypothesis and a good theory. They had neither. Both Bob and John as young men were actually pretty clueless about relationships. Their own relationships with women were not going so well—just one disaster after another. After all these years, that's no longer the case; they're both happily married to wonderful women. But early on, being fairly dumb about relationships, John and Bob could come up with only one hypothesis after going to the library and examining all the research literature. And back then there was almost no research on physiology, or emotion, or relationships. Luckily, in 1964, three researchers, Kaplan, Burch, and Bloom, had measured the "linkage" of skin conductance (sweating from the eccrine glands of the hand) of roommate nurses talking to one another. Skin conductance is what lie detectors measure, and "linkage" just meant that over time you could predict one nurse's hand sweating in the next second by knowing how much the other nurse's hand had just sweat right now. What was really so cool about their work was that, unexpectedly, these three scientists found evidence of linkage only for nurses who *disliked* one another.

So, Bob and John speculated that the physiological linkage was probably due to negative rather than positive emotions that the two nurses felt toward one another. They imagined that the nurses who disliked one another probably had nastier conversations that were full of negative affect (like tension, irritability, disgust, contempt, and sadness), whereas the nurses who liked one another probably were more interested in each other, were affectionate, and laughed a lot. That was, of course, just a guess, because Kaplan, Burch, and Bloom hadn't made videotapes or coded the nurses' emotions.

Would that physiological linkage prove true for unhappily married couples but not happily married ones? They were dying to know. They also wondered whether they could do actual prediction of the future of the relationship over time, so they recontacted the couples, who came into the new lab 3 years later, to see whether they could predict their changes. They did nothing to try to help these couples because, basically, they knew nothing then about how to help couples. They also wondered, if they found differences in the three domains between husbands and wives over time, would they also see those same kinds of differences if they studied gay male and lesbian couples? They thought that would be a pretty cool study to do someday (which they later did, for 12 years). Bob and John oversampled both happily and unhappily married couples, so, rather than having the usual bell curve of distribution in relative happiness, they had a rectangular distribution. That meant their samples included a greater number of unhappy couples and a greater number of happy couples than you would see in a normal distribution. They also always insisted on studying representative samples of every ethnic and racial group living in the places they worked.

Bob and John were astounded and delighted to discover that they could use all three domains of measurement to understand *current* variation in marital happiness, and they could also actually *predict* the longitudinal future course of a marriage. They were dumbfounded to discover how powerful their correlations were: in the .90s, meaning they could account for over 81% of the variance! Bob called John and asked him whether he'd ever found correlations in the .90s before (remember, the highest a correlation can be is 1.0), and John said absolutely not. And the predictions weren't hard to understand.

The First Studies

Over the course of the first 25 years of their studies, John and Bob conducted seven studies of over 700 couples. What did they find? First of all, physiological linkage occurred only for the unhappily married couples, echoing the findings of Kaplan, Burch, and Bloom for the nurses. However, more recent research by Bob and Barbara Fredrickson has found physiological linkage for happily married couples during moments of positive affect, like shared humor. Furthermore, Bob and John found that the more physiologically aroused people were, the more their marriages deteriorated over the 3-year period, regardless of their initial marital happiness. A sweet finding (though sad for the couple). While partners talked, if their hearts beat faster, their blood flowed faster, they sweat more, breathed more often and more shallowly, and jiggled around more in their seats, their marriages got worse over 3 years, regardless of how happy or unhappy they were when they started. This physiological arousal, commonly called "fight-flight-or-freeze," was diffuse, meaning that many neurotransmitter systems were activated. These findings implied that physiological arousal in all systems was harmful for relationships, while calmness was predictive of relationships that got better over time. That made sense, because other research had shown that people in fight-flight-or-freeze physiological activation are somewhat impaired cognitively and emotionally. They can't process new information very well; their hearing narrows into "tunnel hearing," and their vision, into "tunnel seeing." In these conversations, everything a physiologically aroused partner sees or hears alarms them, making them think their partner is attacking them. Rather than being with their partner, they feel like they're facing a saber-toothed tiger. They want only to survive this great danger. They certainly cannot listen very well, empathize well, or engage in creative problem-solving. So if couples are physiologically in fight-flight-or-freeze during their interactions, their discussions are bound to be unsatisfying, thus leading to greater relationship unhappiness later.

The "disasters" of marriage, meaning the studied couples who were unhappily married but stayed together, or ended up divorced, 6 years later were really different from the "masters" of marriage, the couples who were happily married and stayed together. Also, all couples whose rating dials were more negative were in more trouble 6 years later than if their rating dials were more positive. Bob and John also computed the ratio of the number of seconds couples' emotions were positive versus negative during a 15-minute conflict discussion. Positive emotions included expressing interest, shared humor, affection, joy, validation, and empathy; negative emotions conveyed anger, sadness, tension, fear, disgust, and contempt. If that ratio averaged less than 5 to 1 during conflict, that is, fewer than 5 positives for every 1 negative—the couple was in trouble. If it averaged 5 to 1 or higher, they were OK. Unhappy or unstable couples (the disasters of relationship) averaged a 0.8-to-1 ratio, whereas the masters of relationship averaged a 5-to-1 ratio, a huge difference.

The masters and disasters were dramatically different during conflict, but they were also different even on the events-of-the-day conversation. During this conversation, the masters showed a lot of interest in their partner's day, but the disasters seemed to go out of their way to communicate disinterest and boredom, what the late Erving Goffman called "away" behaviors. Away behaviors communicate "I am really not here" or "This ceiling is a lot more interesting than you are." People were usually enthusiastic when talking about their day, but when listening, the disaster couples were far less enthusiastic and more "away" than the masters.

It turned out that not all negatives were equally negative. Four behaviors on the SPAFF coding system stood out as the most predictive of relationship demise. John wound up calling them the "Four Horsemen of the Apocalypse," named after the Four Horsemen in the New Testament Book of Revelations that spell out the end of the world. These four behaviors—criticism, defensiveness, contempt, and stonewalling—were first spelled out and named by John in his 1994 book *What Predicts Divorce?*

What are these Four Horsemen of the Apocalypse? In the conflict discussions the disasters often began the conversation by using the first of the Four Horseman: criticism. One partner would say something like "I don't understand why you're so lazy and selfish. What's wrong with you? Why do you always leave me to clean up the kitchen after you?" To be fair, these critics were actually hoping that their partner would take this kind of harsh startup as "constructive" criticism, and respond with gratitude, saying something like "Oh, dear, thank you so much for telling me what's wrong with me. You are so intelligent and insightful. Let's have lunch next week so you can tell me more about how I've been failing you." However, we can safely say that there is no such thing as constructive criticism in a love relationship. Of course, gratitude was not the typical response to criticism at all; it was usually the second Horseman, defensiveness, expressed either through escalated counterattack (e.g., "You think you're so perfect, well, let me tell you a thing or two about what's wrong with *you* . . . ") or speaking like an innocent victim (e.g., "Why are you always picking on me? I can't do anything right to please you. None of the things I do in this relationship ever get appreciated. You're just never going to be happy with me").

The third Horseman, contempt, was similar to criticism but expressed from a superior position, which came from feeling better than the partner on any dimension, like punctuality or neatness. With a hint of disgust, the criticism became a snide put-down, with a superior, snobby tone or a scoffing sound. Some partners also used a universal facial expression of contempt, first described by Paul Ekman. In that expression people pull the left lip corner to the side, creating an unflattering dimple; usually it's accompanied by an eye roll and often the scoffing sound. People also nailed their partner with mockery, insults, abrasive sarcasm, nasty name-calling, and (John's favorite) correcting someone's grammar when they were angry. That's professorial contempt. For example, if Julie angrily said to John, "I could care less," John's contemptuous response might sound like "Julie, the proper way of saying that is 'I couldn't care less.' Now what's your point?"

The fourth Horseman, stonewalling, turned out to be very intriguing: It contained a secret. Normally while one partner is speaking, the listening partner will signal that they are interested and tracking the conversation. Listening signals include facial movement, nonverbal brief "assent" vocalizations (like "huh," "mm-hmm," "oh"), eye contact, and an open body posture. In stonewalling, however, there are none of these cues for minutes at a time. There's no facial movement, no brief assent vocalizations, no eye contact, and a closed body posture (like looking down and away, arms akimbo across the chest). In effect, the listener becomes a stone wall. We discovered that 85% of the time stonewallers were men. We really wondered whether lesbians would stonewall. (They do.)

Now here's the secret: We learned from Bob's physiological measures that people who stonewalled were anything but still internally. We found that while a partner was simply sitting in a chair, 10 seconds before they stonewalled, it was more likely than baseline that their heart rate was exceeding 100 beats a minute, the rate at which we start secreting the stress hormones adrenaline and cortisol. In short, our stonewallers were in a state of fight-flight-or-freeze. We reasoned that during those earlier 10 seconds, they were probably feeling attacked and were turning inward in an attempt to shut out any more stimuli, thus transforming into a stone wall on the outside while mentally running for the hills on the inside.

A further finding: Some negatives turned out to be more destructive for relationships than others. Contempt was the worst, like sulfuric acid for a relationship, making it our best predictor of divorce. Criticism, defensiveness, and stonewalling also spelled potential doom. In contrast, when emotions were expressed without the Four Horsemen, anger and sadness weren't so bad. That came as a big surprise too.

What did the masters do instead of the Four Horsemen of the Apocalypse? The masters of relationship were very different from the disasters. They mostly used what we now call "softened startup" to begin a conflict discussion. Often, they reassured their partner that everything was basically OK between them. Then they expressed their emotions about a specific topic, and stated a need (or a preference, a desire, or a wish), usually what we call a "positive need"—in other words, what they *did* want, not what they didn't want. For example, they might say, "I get so angry when you're on your cell phone during dinner. Could we please have conversation at dinner with no phones or email?" In effect, they were proposing a very specific recipe for how their partner could succeed with them and shine for them. However, it was *not* the case that the masters of relationship were *never* critical; they were just critical less often than the disaster couples. Also, during those few times when there was criticism, the master partner's response was different. Defensiveness sometimes occurred, but less often than for the disaster couples. Instead of defensiveness, the more common master response was taking responsibility, even for a part of the problem.

Our hero in this regard was a lawyer who was helping his wife specify what in his way of speaking irritated her the most. He said, "Is it the way I phrase things?" "Yes," she said. "Do I sound, what, authoritative?" he asked. "No, you sound *authoritarian*," she said. "Yeah, I can be that way," he responded; "how does that sound to you?" "Like 'I have spoken!,' the King has spoken," she replied. He laughed and said, "I guess I do get that way. It works in the courtroom." "But it fails at home," she replied. Then they both laughed. That guy is one of our heroes. A real master at down-regulating his defensiveness.

In the 1990s, Julie and John built an apartment laboratory at the University of Washington. We had 130 newlywed couples live there for 24-hour periods (the cameras turned on at 9 a.m. and off at 9 p.m.). We asked only that they do what they would normally do on a Sunday at home. We also videotaped each couple's behavior as in Bob and John's standard lab. The British Broadcasting Corporation heard about our apartment lab, did a special show on it, and dubbed the new lab the "Love Lab." The name stuck. In the apartment part of the lab, we used Holter monitors from Spacelabs (who conducted the physiological measurements of NASA astronauts) and their beat-to-beat computer program for analyzing the couple's electrocardiograms. We also assayed the partners' urinary stress hormones, and in collaboration with an immunology professor, Dr. Hans Ochs, we took blood samples for standard immunological assays.

With the couples who came to our apartment lab, instead of displaying contempt, which essentially occurred zero times for the masters, we noticed the master newlyweds displayed many small moments of unsolicited compliments, small appreciations, and words of admiration or respect. We attribute this to a *habit of mind* in which masters scan their social environment looking for what their partner is doing right, and then say something about it. They can't be like the strong-and-silent guy who loved his wife so much that one day he almost told her. It has to come out of the mouth. This contrasts with a habit of mind of disaster couples in which they are scanning their social environment looking for their partner's mistakes, and then saying something, which is often a criticism, to correct them. Research shows that this negative habit of mind makes one partner miss a full 50% of the positive things that their partner is actually expressing or doing (Robinson & Price, 1980).

Instead of stonewalling, when masters were physiologically aroused, they tended to remain engaged with the conversation as listeners, they continued using nonverbal assents, and they used shared humor or affection to lower their own physiological arousal. It's important to point out that we couldn't have predicted what the masters would do differently by merely studying the disasters and thinking, "Just don't do that." The masters were adding some new valuable information, which is why John and Bob needed to have adequate statistical power to describe couples across the whole spectrum of happiness-to-misery.

The table below summarizes some of these initial findings.

The Disasters (positive–negative ratio 5 to 1, or more): "The Four Horsemen of the Apocalypse"	The Masters (positive–negative ratio .8 to 1, or less)
Criticism	Use softened startup
Defensiveness	Take responsibility
Contempt	Say what you need, and express appreciation and respect in small moments, often
Stonewalling	Share humor or affection

Our Venerable Rating Dial

After many years of study, we'd come to have quite a lot of respect for the numbers we got out of our rating dial. For example, Bob added a second rating dial pass-through, where he also asked people to use the rating dial to guess what their partner was feeling. These people pretended to be their partner and tried to guess at what their partner was feeling. As usual, he also recorded physiology during the rating dial procedure. Bob and his student Anna Ruef measured how closely the physiologies of the two people paralleled one another. While they were watching the videotape, those people whose physiology more closely resembled their partner's during the interaction itself had rating dial data that closely matched their partner's. If, instead, their physiology (while watching the tape) matched their own physiology in the interaction, they were bad at guessing how their partner felt during the interaction. Bob and Anna thought that some people physically experienced their partner's physiology by mirroring the partner's emotional reactions. Incredibly, Bob and Anna had thus discovered a physiological way of defining empathy. No one had ever done that before. That was a pretty amazing accomplishment for our lowly video-recall rating dial.

Bob later did a now-classic study with his student Rachel Ebling to see how well other professionals could do this prediction of divorce that had brought fame to our lab. Dr. Sybil Carrère, who ran our lab, had discovered that SPAFF coding of only the first 3 minutes of a conflict discussion could predict better than chance whether a couple would divorce or stay married years down the road. Bob wondered whether that level of prediction was easy or difficult for professionals to do without SPAFF coding. He selected the first 3 minutes of 10 couples' conflict discussions; 5 couples had later divorced, and 5 had stayed married. Then he asked professional therapists and relationship researchers to guess who would and who wouldn't eventually divorce. Every professional group he studied did no better than chance. He also asked regular people who had no professional credentials to perform the same task. Everyone was bad at making accurate predictions, except for people who had just gone through a divorce. Those people were just a smidgen better than chance, but not by much. But John's SPAFF observational coding of emotions did just fine. In fact, this study became so famous that the California Academy of Sciences in San Francisco created a display asking people to watch these tapes and predict each couple's outcome. It became one of the most popular exhibits the museum ever had. We are pleased that the use of our video-recall rating dial procedure has now become pretty standard in many current social psychology studies.

Specific-Moments Interviews

Sometimes we also selected specific moments from videotapes that related to some salient dimension, such as ratings, behavior, or physiology. Then we interviewed couples about their perceptions of those particular moments. We asked them how they were feeling, how they thought their partner was feeling, and what their goals were during that moment. They also filled out a questionnaire about each moment. From their answers we learned that there were two basic categories of negative reactions they were experiencing: feeling like an "innocent victim," which was expressed through whining and defensiveness; and "righteous indignation," expressed with anger, disgust, and contempt.

In this way we also learned what heterosexual men were thinking when they were stonewalling. When we brought these stonewalling guys back into the lab, and asked them what they were feeling, they told us their internal dialogue went something like this:

Stonewalling Internal Monologue

Just don't say anything. You always make it worse when you talk. How long can she go on like this? I'm gonna time her. No, don't do that. That'll just get her madder. The woman's gonna give herself a heart attack, she gets so worked up. Oh, I could say something now, that happened 6 years ago. No, don't say anything. You always make it worse when you talk. I can endure this. This too shall pass. Hey, it's 10 minutes until the game. She can't touch me then.

So, these brief interviews and questionnaires about specific moments helped us to better understand interactions and our SPAFF emotion codes.

Our Oral History Interview

We wondered how people thought about their entire relationship. Did they have great or bad memories, or no memories at all? Did that matter? Did they share a philosophy about what love is, or should be? Did their ways of thinking matter at all? Did they vary with culture, with social class, with ethnicity? What if partners came from different cultures, countries, races, or ethnicities? To answer questions like these, we developed interviews to ascertain spouses' perceptions of the history of their marriage, their parents' marriages, their philosophies of being married, and their levels of comfort or discomfort with the basic emotions. We also developed an interview for the purpose of eliciting the rituals, roles, life dreams, goals, symbols, and myths that had guided their search for meaning. With John's talented grad student Lowell Krokoff at the University of Illinois, we also tried to understand how their answers might vary with social class. In that large study we had a survey research company actually draw our representative sample at random from the many phone calls they made in the Champaign–Urbana area and surrounding rural area.

Then, at the University of Washington, with our creative staff member Kim Buehlman, we developed a coding system to determine dimensions and numbers on these recorded Oral History Interviews. We coded spouses' behavior from the videotapes using objective coding systems and trained observers. They noted facial expressions, voice tone, gestures, body positions and movements, the distance between partners, and so on. And then, just as Bob and John had done, Julie and John followed the couples for many years. The Buehlman coding of the Oral History Interview predicted, over a 6-year period, whether newlyweds would stay married or divorce—with 94% accuracy! That's been our best prediction result to date. So these overall narratives about the relationships proved to be very revealing. Parts of the Oral History Interview are now standard in our first therapy session assessment of a relationship's strengths and challenges.

We have now studied newlyweds, couples in the first 7 years of marriage, violent marriages (with Neil Jacobson), and (with Bob) long-term couples in their 40s and in their 60s. We have followed couples becoming parents and interacting with their babies, their preschoolers, and their teenagers. We have followed kids from ages 4 to 15, and started following a total of over 700 couples in five different longitudinal studies. Our database comes from seven longitudinal studies, including both Four Horsemen couples and devitalized couples. The longest we have followed couples (in Bob's lab) is 20 years. Our studies have ranged across the life course, from the newlywed stage through the transitions to retirement, and across sexual orientations.

Bob and John were also interested in studying physical health. For example, they discovered that contempt was a great predictor not just of divorce but also of the number of infectious illnesses the recipient of contempt would have during the next 4 years. A very interesting finding. But what was the mechanism for such a result? A new field emerged to answer that question.

Psychoneuroimmunology

Just the name of this new field is a mouthful, and it is reflective of the powerful integration of three fields of study. In fact, the field of immunology has undergone a revolution in recent decades. Part of that immense set of discoveries is the connection between the nervous system and the immune system, and a second part is the connection of both systems to stress, and the potentially protective or destructive factor of relationship quality and stability (see Davis, 2013; Richtel, 2019). Bob and John were the first scientists to tie together and predict health or illness, divorce or stability, and relationship happiness or unhappiness. Now other researchers have repeated these findings. Rand Conger's lab at Iowa, Tom Bradbury's lab at UCLA, and Jan Kiecolt-Glaser and her husband Ron Glaser's lab at Ohio State University have also successfully predicted which couples wind up stable but unhappily married, and which couples eventually divorce. In Chapter 2 we will describe Kiecolt-Glaser and Glaser's amazing findings that reveal the biological mechanisms underlying these strong predictions.

Dean Ornish has also written about the connection between interpersonal closeness and physical health in his important book *Love and Survival.* Ornish reviewed research that demonstrated the protective power of close emotional connection in families. For example, in the longitudinal Harvard study, male college students were asked to describe their relationship with their parents. Their responses were scored to suggest that their relationship with their parents was either cold and aloof, or warm and engaged. Thirty-five years later, when these men were middle aged, the study assessed their physical health. The findings were dramatic. People who described their parents as cold and aloof had many serious, chronic, life-threatening illnesses in middle age, whereas those who had described their parents as warm and engaged were generally healthy in middle age. These findings don't demonstrate causality, of course, but they are very interesting. And, of course, Harvard students are a select bunch, but the research was later extended to include women, and to include children of working-class families in Boston. The general predictive results held true, and a strong genetic component has also been revealed as part of these predictions. See also Wilkinson and Pickett's excellent 2019 book, *The Inner Level*.

But Let's Step Back. Why Should We Care About Relationships and Marriages?

A New Field Called "Social Epidemiology"

In the past 50 years a new and incredibly fruitful field of study has emerged from epidemiology. The new field is called social epidemiology. It emerged initially from the work of a UC Berkeley professor named Leonard Syme. Syme started studying longevity and mortality in immigrant populations in the United States. He initially thought that the food Chinese Americans ate would be lower in cholesterol and would account for this population's higher longevity compared to Euro-Americans. Instead, he discovered the surprising fact that longevity and health are mostly determined in today's America not by diet, exercise, or cholesterol in the blood but instead by the presence of and the quality of people's closest relationships. Those findings held worldwide.

Len Syme and his student Lisa Berkman launched the now-classic Alameda County study, with over 9,000 people. They discovered that living or dying was predicted over time by people having or not having close friends and intimate lovers. Remarkably, later research showed that for both men and women it was the *quality* of these close relationships that predicted health, the speed of recovery from illness, lifetime accumulated wealth, and also the quality of outcomes for the children of these relationships (Berkman et al., 2014; Holt-Lunstad et al., 2010; Verbrugge, 1979, 1986). This was a spectacular set of results, some of which are summarized in Lydia Denworth's recent book, *Friendship* (2020). There's also a great book now that is titled

Social Epidemiology, written by Lisa Berkman, Ichiro Kawachi, and M. Maria Glymour. In that book there is a chapter by Laura Kubzansky, Ashley Winning, and Kawachi reviewing research that shows that in happy relationships people may be aging more slowly than in ailing relationships.

The Emergence of the "Gottman Trust Metric"

There's more to this emerging story of how important relationships are. An entire body of research arose called "social capital" research, which demonstrated the importance of **trust**. In that research, the proportion of people in a geographic region who generally trust others was found to predict the health of entire sections of the country, and even the well-being of states, whole countries, and their economies. This "social capital" field was started by a landmark book by Robert Putnam called *Bowling Alone*. Putnam documented the dramatic decline of community in the United States starting around 1960.

In this new field, researchers would survey people and ask them whether they generally trusted others, or not. It turned out that the proportion of the population that trusts others varies enormously from region to region within the United States, and also across countries. In general, trust has declined in North America since 1960. Trust also lowers the more one heads south from Canada. Similar results were also obtained across countries: Trust percentages vary enormously. For example, in Brazil, 2% of people trust others, whereas in Norway 69% of the people do. Why are these trust percentages important?

Startlingly, these trust percentages predict the amount and nature of local philanthropy, the amount of social participation in communities, whether people vote or not, the amount of violent crime, the amount of poverty, a region's economic well-being, children's school achievement, people's physical health and longevity, and a host of other variables that index people's well-being in a region. The trust percentage turns out to be strongly related to the income discrepancy between the richest and poorest people in that region. Lower trust in people accompanies larger income discrepancies.

So, it turns out that the quality of people's closest relationships, and the nature of interpersonal **trust** in these relationships, taps something vital for the health and prosperity of our clients. It likewise also generally affects people, communities, and countries in our current climate of decreasing trust.

But what is "trust" within a relationship? How can one define trust? Furthermore, how does a couple naturally build or erode trust? How can we help a couple build or rebuild trust? These critical questions remained unasked and unanswered.

John's Trust Metric

Because of these powerful results about trust, it became vital to ask how relationship therapists could understand and utilize this new knowledge. So, one day the two of us were watching an unusual TV show called *Numb3rs*, in which a math professor teams up with his brother, who is an FBI agent, to solve crimes. The show ran for five seasons. It caught John's attention because it is so very rare for a mathematician to be a hero in fiction. John started life as a mathematician, and he still loves to read math books. In 2002 John and the mathematician James Murray and his students published a book titled *The Mathematics of Marriage*. In that book John and James and their students applied the math of difference equations to model marital interaction. John was especially interested in the TV show's "trust metric." Also, because of mathematician Stephen Wolfram, all the math in the *Numb3rs* show was actually correct math. All except for the one show that talked about cracking a dangerous terrorist cell using this "trust metric." After the show, John looked up the Wolfram commentary and, unfortunately, there was actually no such mathematical creature as a trust metric.

Game Theory. John thought that maybe he could create a trust metric using a branch of math called "game theory." Game theory was created and described in 1949 in a breakthrough book by John von Neumann and Oskar Morgenstern called *Theory of Games and Economic Behavior*. That book introduced a new form of mathematics into economic theory, and a decade later two social psychologists, John Thibaut and Harold Kelley, brought game theory into the psychological study of relationships. In two-person game theory an exchange of strategies or actions is viewed in a payoff table (also called a "payoff matrix") of possible strategic moves for each person. In each cell of the table there is the "payoff" (cost or benefit) of each possible move, exchange, or strategy, for each person. In competitive win–lose, or "zero-sum," games (like tic-tac-toe, chess, or checkers), all the positive payoff goes to the winner and all the cost (or negative payoff) to the loser. Adding together the positive and negative numbers in a win–lose scenario, the sum-total payoff to both players is zero. In more cooperative games, there is some cost and benefit to each person playing the "game." Games are presumed to have rules, which can be inferred, in part, by this payoff matrix.

The idea was to view a relationship like a game. In a real relationship two people interact, choosing behaviors from their repertoire, and they exchange these behaviors over time, and each possible exchange has a certain cost or benefit for each person. For example, John may smile at Julie and Julie smiles back at John. They both enjoy this exchange and would rate it as very positive using the rating dial. In a more complex view, long *sequences* of exchanges (i.e., entire strategies) can have a certain cost or benefit for each person. Using Bob and John's video-recall rating dial to rate the positivity or negativity of their emotions on a 9-point scale, John had a potential "payoff" variable. He also had the SPAFF coding of the couple's interactions.

Using game theory, John was able to create a husband-by-wife table summarizing a couple's 15-minute conversation into positive, neutral, and negative SPAFF exchanges as assessed by the lab SPAFF observers. Then John would fill in each square of the table (one square for Partner 1 and one for Partner 2) with each partner's rating dial number averaged over the time taken for each SPAFF-coded exchange. In this configuration, with the measures John and Bob computed, John could define high "trust" as each partner acting at various times (during the exchanges noted by the SPAFF observers) in ways that would maximize each partner's rating dial number for that exchange. When added together, the sum of both partners' payoffs would yield a total payoff score for each behavior exchange. The idea was "I trust you because you behave as if you have my best interests at heart, not just your own." A table for a trusting couple like this will contain maximum payoff sums. A mutually trusting couple cannot improve on their behavior-exchange payoffs. They've already achieved their highest payoff sums. In other words, during their conversation, this couple has accomplished a series of best-possible-emotion behavior exchanges, an "equilibrium point" that is known as the "Nash equilibrium." John Nash won the 1994 Nobel Prize in economics for his work on the Nash equilibrium. This work was made into a wonderful 2001 biographical movie of John Nash called *A Beautiful Mind*, starring Russell Crowe.

John created and validated his trust metric. This breakthrough metric makes it possible to quantify the amount of trust that exists in any conversation. It is described in the book John wrote titled *The Science of Trust* (2011) and in the 2012 book by Gottman and Silver titled *What Makes Love Last? How to Build Trust and Avoid Betrayal*. It also turns out that in low-trust relationships, people have higher baseline resting blood velocity to the ear. This means that in low-trust relationships, the heart is, unfortunately, contracting much harder and thus working much harder with every heartbeat, compared to the healthier, lower baseline blood velocity found in high-trust couples. This may explain some of the lowered longevity associated with low trust. The good news, however, is that the trust metric can be altered. Dan Yoshimoto's doctoral research revealed a promising finding that a process we call "attunement" can build the trust metric. Attunement is a special kind of daily reflective listening, when negative and positive emotions are being discussed, that creates emotional connection and greater trust.

Understanding and Predicting Divorce

No one could fail to notice that the divorce rate has remained high in the United States and that, in general, the remainder of the world is not far behind. Current estimates of the chances of first marriages in the United States ending in divorce (within a 40-year period) are a bit below 50%. A peak rate of 67% was reported in 1989 by Martin and Bumpass. Since then, most scholars agree that the rate has fallen. The data suggest that failure rates for second marriages are either about the same (Martin & Bumpass, 1989) or about 10% *higher* than for first marriages. Cherlin (1981) presented data that show that this trend is not new in the United States. The divorce data back to the 1890s can be well fitted with an exponential function. That means that the increases in divorce are proportional to the divorce rate itself. Thankfully, though still high, divorce rates have stabilized a bit in the past 20 years.

There still remain serious consequences of marital dissolution for the mental and physical health of both spouses and their children. These negative effects include increased risk of psychopathology; increased rates of automobile accidents, including fatalities (Bloom et al., 1978); increased incidence of physical illness, suicide, violence, and homicide (Bloom et al., 1978; Burman & Margolin, 1992); decreased longevity (Berkman & Breslow, 1983; Berkman & Syme, 1979; Friedman et al., 1995); significant immunosuppression (e.g., Kiecolt-Glaser et al., 1987, 1994); and increased mortality from diseases (Bloom et al., 1978; Burman & Margolin, 1992).

Also, there is now convincing evidence to suggest that marital distress, conflict, and disruption are associated with a wide range of deleterious effects on children, including depression, withdrawal, poor social competence, health problems, poor academic performance, a variety of conduct-related difficulties, and—believe it or not—markedly decreased child longevity in the Terman longitudinal study of gifted children. This is not to say that spouses in ailing marriages should stay together for the sake of the children. In our own laboratory we have discovered that the same consequences are experienced by children when parents remain in hostile marriages (Gottman & Katz, 1989). However, we have now discovered that the active ingredient that hurts children in divorce appears to be continued marital hostility between the parents, particularly if the child is used as a pawn by parents to hurt one another (Buchanan et al., 1991; Hetherington & Clingempeel, 1992). Fortunately, this alienation of affection by a separated or divorced parent against the co-parent has become a felony crime in many states as a result of these discoveries.

It clearly seems that we are still in a crisis in the United States today in terms of the dissolution of families. Everyday American families and children reap the negative consequences of this crisis. These consequences are now very well researched. We marital therapists are supposed to help solve this problem. Unfortunately, in our view, we still do not have the tools adequate to eliminate these consequences. But we can begin to help. Our own research has discovered that if even just one parent uses *emotion coaching* with their children, these negative effects of divorce can be greatly reduced (see Gottman & DeClaire, 1997; and the Gottman Institute's downloadable video and manualized *Emotion Coaching Workshop*). The positive effects of emotion coaching have now been documented in research done in the United States, Australia, South Korea, and the UK. In Chapter 2 of this book we will review our work on a concept we call "meta-emotion," which refers to people's feelings and thoughts about emotion. That research led to the discovery of emotion coaching in parenting, work that was later extended to couples by Dan Yoshimoto's doctoral dissertation in his discovery of the process of attunement.

Not all marriages end in divorce, and among those couples who remain married there is a wide range of marital happiness. What predicts divorce and eventual marital happiness has been the subject of surprisingly little prospective research. This kind of research is important for designing a marital therapy, because it pinpoints what may be "dysfunctional" in marriages that are ailing.

Let's take a moment and ask a question: Is divorce prediction easy? One claim, made by Laurie Abraham in her 2010 book, *The Husbands and Wives Club*, is that if one predicted that 100% of the newlyweds in our study would get divorced, given that the U.S. national divorce rate was then about 50%, one would be right half the time. So, the argument goes, predicting who will divorce and who will stay married at 94% accuracy isn't such a great feat. However, this argument has a logical error. The U.S. divorce rate has indeed been estimated by sociologists to be approximately 50%, *but only over the course of as many as 40 years of marriage* (Cherlin, 1992). In a short-term longitudinal study, in just 6 years of marriage, only 13% of the couples in our newlywed sample divorced, so if one guessed they would *all* divorce, one would be wrong 87% of the time. Tom Bradbury at UCLA found a divorce rate of only 7.6% over 4 years in his sample of newlyweds. So, if one guessed everyone would divorce in Bradbury's sample, one would be wrong 92.4% of the time. In fact, the problem of guessing which newlyweds in our lab would divorce and which would not within 6 years after the wedding, even at 90% accuracy by chance alone (90% is our average accuracy across our seven separate longitudinal studies), is exactly like trying to randomly pick out, while blindfolded, 15 of 17 red balls from a bowl that also contains 113 white balls. The probability of picking 15 out of 17 red balls correctly by chance alone (that's with 90% accuracy) can be computed as approximately 2.5 in 10^{15}. To spell that out, the chance of picking 15 out of 17 divorces out of 130 couples by chance alone is about one in 2,500,000,000,000,000, or one in two and a half quadrillion (a quadrillion is 10^{15}). So, therefore, our 90% prediction accuracy in 6 years is actually quite unlikely.

The prediction of divorce or stability is no easy feat.

More importantly, identifying what is "dysfunctional" when a marriage is not going well essentially tells us only a part of what is broken and what needs fixing. Some clinicians have suggested that this knowledge alone could determine the goals of couples therapy. However, we suggest that this is wrong. We also need to know *what is going well* when a relationship is working well to fully define the real goals of couples therapy. It is simply not the case that the masters of relationship have eliminated what the disasters of relationship are doing. There is new and very important knowledge in what the masters do right, as well as what the disasters do wrong. Later in this chapter we will address the many myths that abound in our field, and discuss what we actually do know.

Marital Therapy Effects: Early Disappointing Results and More Promising Recent Results

When we (John and Julie) began working together, we assumed that John and Bob's research had to be the foundation for creating an effective couples therapy. The natural ways that the competent people in our studies coped with difficult issues would help us to create interventions that would more likely "stick" and be adopted as natural by ailing couples. Otherwise, we'd be groping in the dark, making the mistake of knowing only what didn't work and telling couples, "Don't do this."

After moving to the University of Washington in the mid-1980s, John and his colleagues took the first steps to study the effects of brief interventions on marital interaction. These brief interventions included eight experiments with approximately 500 couples. They were based on our observations of successful couples and were designed to simply change one distressing conversation into a better one. The ones that worked, we kept. The ones that didn't, we discarded.

Early Results

More people seek therapy for marital problems than for any other type of problem (Veroff et al., 1981). In the 1970s behavioral approaches to couples therapy flourished. How effective were these early therapies? The largest effect sizes found in meta-analyses were those for behavioral marital therapy (for a review of these meta-analyses of early behavioral marital therapies, see Bray & Jouriles, 1995). There are two ways to get a large effect size in a meta-analysis. One is by having large experimental group effects. The other is by having large deterioration in no-treatment control groups. Indeed, when Jacobson (1984) reanalyzed data from four of his behavioral marital studies (which had among the largest effects), he reported that, although 55% of the couples improved after treatment, only 35% were in the nondistressed range at the end of therapy. He concluded that significant effect sizes in controlled marital therapy studies may exist largely because people tend to deteriorate in the waiting-list control groups. Jacobson and Addis (1993) wrote, "The success that investigators have had establishing these effects for their preferred treatments is not as impressive as first thought. The lack of improvement given the absence of treatment means that even small improvements in an experimental treatment are likely to be statistically significant" (p. 85).

Furthermore, a pervasive problem existed for almost all these early marital therapies that have been systematically evaluated using long-term follow-up (and this is a minority of studies): It is a ubiquitous *relapse* effect. Of the couples that make some initial gains in marital therapy a sizable percentage of these couples, about 30%–50%, relapse in 2 years (Jacobson & Addis, 1993). Something like a second law of thermodynamics seems to function in marriage—that is, when marital distress exists, things usually deteriorate (entropy increases). The therapeutic effects of the therapies that have been scientifically evaluated are generally weak, and there is a very high relapse rate.

What effects, in general, does marital therapy have as it is usually practiced? In our longitudinal research we have typically found a strong positive correlation (about .50) between having been in marital therapy and getting divorced. Is our result representative? The best study we have available on what therapy is "out there"—that is, non-university-based therapy—was done by Cookerly (1980). Cookerly conducted a 5-year follow-up of 326 clients treated using a wide variety of marital therapies in the United States. The separation/divorce rate was 43.6% after 5 years. The highest separation/divorce rate occurred in the first year after therapy. These rates are considerably higher than base rates would lead one to predict. *So marital therapy as it is practiced appears to reliably drive couples over the cliff and into divorce!*

Recent Results

In the past 45 or so years we have seen the emergence of Jacobson and Christensen's "acceptance-based" couples therapy (ABCT) and Susan Johnson's emotionally focused therapy (EFT). In the early studies, as we've noted, after taking a hard look at relapse rates, our best estimate was that for about 35% of couples, marital therapy was producing clinically significant, immediate changes, but after a year, about 30%–50% of the lucky couples who made the initial gains relapsed. So all we could claim was that, in the best studies, conducted in universities with careful supervision, only 11%–18% of couples maintained clinically meaningful initial gains when treated with our best marital therapies.

Recent results are far more encouraging. Using marital satisfaction as the major outcome measure, we can conclude that effects last in both ABCT and EFT, at least after 1 year post-treatment. That is a huge improvement! However, the studies that have been done so far have primarily screened out most subjects with comorbidities, plus the initial relationship satisfaction of couples in most studies is quite high, within half a standard deviation (which is about 7 points) below the mean of 100. Also, the effect sizes of therapy vary from half a standard deviation to 1.2 standard deviations.

The Challenge

Are those effect sizes acceptable? Not for us. We conducted a recent international study (Gottman et al., 2019) with over 40,000 couples (both heterosexual and same sex) about to start therapy. They averaged 2.5 standard deviations below the mean in marital satisfaction, with a range up to six standard deviations below the mean. So, the best therapies available wouldn't do much good for most of our sample.

In that large study conducted before beginning therapy, all couples were assessed using the Gottman Relationship Checkup (RCU) scales. These scales had been previously validated against multimethod data gathered from our coded Oral History Interview and our SPAFF emotion coding of couples' conflict interactions. The RCU scales proved valid and reliable for couples of all sexual orientations.

The overall conclusion of the 2019 paper is that the couples we clinicians see every day are far more disturbed than the samples recruited in typical university studies of couples therapy. Previous studies usually screened out comorbidities, and tended to recruit happier and generally healthier couples. As we mentioned, in our study the couple scores on relationship satisfaction averaged 2.5 standard deviations below the mean. This compares with an average of 0.5 standard deviations below the mean for most other therapy outcome studies. Also, comorbidities were commonplace among our samples, whereas these are usually screened out of most couples therapy outcome studies. For example, over 60% of our couples presented with some form of domestic violence, 32% of heterosexual couples presented with an affair, 26% with addiction, and 45.9% with clinical depression. There were also stable and significant differences across sexual orientation. When compared to heterosexual couples starting couples therapy, same-sex couples were better on friendship variables, but worse on past trauma harkening back to their primary family. The online RCU data collection continues to this day, with over 15,000 therapists having contributed data on over 150,000 couples about to begin couples therapy as of winter 2020. We can also now process repeated checkups to monitor change in therapy. (See www.GottmanConnect.com.)

If we ask the question Jacobson and Revenstorf (1988) asked about whether the observed changes in marital satisfaction are clinically meaningful, the results of most marital therapies turn out to be quite unimpressive. As we noted, in our longitudinal research we have consistently found significant correlations between going for marriage counseling and getting a divorce. *Consumer Reports* (1995; see also Seligman, 1995) published a survey of its readers who had undergone some form of psychotherapy from various types of professionals. Despite many flaws in the design of this study, therapy generally got reasonable marks for customer satisfaction. However, if one makes the (probably large) assumption that most of the marital therapy in this study was done by marriage counselors, the number of couples showing major improvement in their presenting symptoms constituted only 22% of the sample. These couples saw their counselors for less than 6 months. For those who saw their counselors for longer than 6 months, the percentage showing improvement was 37%. Other research (Simmons & Doherty, 1995) shows that couples attend, typically, 11 sessions, meaning that, for whatever reason, they leave after a little less than 3 months.

In this area of marital and family therapy we have discovered that any-thing we do will work to some degree, as long as the therapist is highly active and the intervention has some clear rationale that is explained to the clients. Otherwise, people terminate, against professional advice. That is a perva-sive finding in our field: Nondirective approaches lead people to quit family therapy. So it seems that in the family therapy field, anything that makes sense will have some degree of effectiveness if the therapist is directive and active—at least it will be considered "effective" in terms of customer satis-faction and therapists' ratings.

Unfortunately, therapists' ratings are biased, and customer satisfaction ratings evaluating treatment in child, family, and marital therapies have proved to be invalid as indicators of real change. This was one of the basic findings of the researchers at the Oregon Social Learning Center when they first started doing interventions. The parents reported that everything was now fine, even when the target children had not changed at all, as deter-mined by observation or teacher reports. The parents simply wanted to say "thank you" to the therapists for trying, and they did so on the self-report measures of change (Patterson, 1982). So, in such research on change, we cannot rely on studies that limit their assessment to self-report variables to measure therapeutic outcomes.

How general is this Oregon Social Learning Center result that would lead us to doubt self-report data alone as outcome data? Jacobson et al. (1987) conducted a 2-year follow-up of two groups of couples post-therapy: "main-tainers," who retained their therapeutic gains, and "relapsers," whose gains deteriorated. They wrote that "both sets of couples were unanimous in their positive feeling expressions about therapy: 80% of the maintainers and 100%

of the relapsers expressed the belief that therapy had a positive impact on them, while only 6% of couples, across groups, insisted that therapy had not been useful" (p. 193). Our conclusion is this: We cannot rely on "customer satisfaction" data to evaluate our interventions. We must insist on harder data that assess the outcome of our interventions.

Giving Science a Chance

Our hypothesis is that couples therapy still needs a major fix. Past therapies have not been based on solid empirical knowledge of what is actually predictive of marital dissolution (what is "dysfunctional") and what real couples do to keep their marriages happy and stable (what is "functional"). Instead, couples therapy programs have mostly been devised by the imagination of their creators. We can't know how to design intervention programs for target populations by *imagining* what they need, or even by designing them according to some theory. About 30 years ago, we decided we needed to give descriptive science a chance. First, we had to do the hard work of description and prediction to find out how couples who are doing well with particular problems manage to do the tasks competently. It just meant giving science a chance.

Of course, we were assuming in this approach that if we learned how couples normally go about the business of being married, staying married, and doing so happily, then we would discover a set of principles that could be used to help marriages that are ailing. That was our hope.

We figured that one set of empirically based principles was what we needed. Research evidence does suggest that all marriages, happy or unhappy, seem to have to deal with the same "tasks" of being married. For example, it is well-known that the rank-order correlation of problems by their severity across happy and unhappy couples is very high, in the .90s (the maximum correlation is 1.0). But interestingly, when we consider the predictors of divorce, we don't find that these NEVER occur in marriages that are stable and happy—they just occur less often. That is why, as you'll see later, part of our focus is on repair mechanisms. Every couple in their daily life together mess up communication, and every marriage has a "dark side." It seems that what may matter most is *the ability to repair things when they go wrong rather than trying to be perfect in communicating.*

Nonetheless, the basic assumption of our approach, laid bare, is that we need real theory of how marriages succeed and fail, and that theory ought to emerge from a study of what real couples do to accomplish the everyday "tasks" of being married.

Dispelling Myths and Mistakes in Marital Therapy

Caveat. Let us first say that our goal in dispelling these myths is not to insult anyone or to make us look good. Many of the people we will refer to have made important contributions to our thinking in the area of marriage. We respect their contributions and try to build upon them. It is absolutely critical, however, in the interests of science, that the ideas we propose be capable of rejection—which means they have to be testable.

For this reason, we will not comment about ideas that have not been researched. We can't evaluate ideas without studies that meet reasonable standards of measurement and experimental control. All we will be able to say is that, in our opinion, these are good ideas. We prefer to hold everyone to these standards of scientific inquiry, including ourselves. In the intervention section of this book we comment on some of the major orientations that have influenced our thinking, and we recommend a basic bookshelf on couples therapy for clinicians.

We want to emphasize that the search for what we will call "myths" is purely in the service of relentless pursuit of truth. We need to take a hard look at what beliefs are embedded in the literature and carefully examine what, if anything, we can trust enough to "hang our hats on it." What we identify as "dysfunctional" greatly influences what we recognize as the goals of therapeutic intervention.

In this field writers do a great service by clearly articulating hypotheses. You don't have to be right to make a significant contribution. You just have to be interesting. Sometimes a great service to knowledge is rendered by being totally wrong but clear. John kept careful track of his own hypotheses once and found that he was wrong 60% of the time. It turns out that 40%

right isn't bad. But if he had not done the research, he would have believed he was right 100% of the time—a fallacy.

The Myth of Active Listening

Perhaps the most influential theory of marital therapy is the "active listening model." This model forms the basis of most marital treatments (e.g., see Gottman et al., 1998; Jacobson & Margolin, 1979). The hypothesis is that stable, happy marriages are characterized by active, empathic listening during conflict resolution, and that ailing marriages are characterized by the absence of this quality. That is, in order to have a happy, lasting marriage, partners need to be able to be nondefensive and empathic listeners, even when they feel they are being attacked by their partner. In most couples therapies this assumption is translated into some form of the listener–speaker exercise. For example, let's say the wife starts as the speaker, wording her complaints as "I-statements." She complains she is hurt about the way her husband relates to their youngest child. She hates the way he ignores the boy and criticizes him. Then he is asked to paraphrase both the content and feelings of his wife's message and to verify that he has heard her accurately. Next he is asked to validate her feelings, to suspend judgment, and to respond nondefensively.

This hypothesis has formed a central core in couples therapies from all schools of thought. The behavioral school has referred to active listening as social skill training (e.g., see Jacobson & Margolin, 1979). The systems orientation has referred to active listening as a mechanism for introducing feedback in message systems of communication (e.g., see Gottman et al., 1976). The psychoanalytic school has also included active listening as a way of increasing empathy, which is believed to facilitate developmental change and also help decrease narcissism (e.g., see Siegel, 1992, chap. 16).

Where does this "knowledge" that the active listening pattern is basic to a good marriage come from? When we teach couples this method, we are teaching them what Carl Rogers trained therapists to do: provide unconditional acceptance and empathy. Rogers's approach inspired Bernard Guerney (Guerney, 1977; Guerney & Guerney, 1985) to develop empathy training for couples. Eventually, all the other marital therapies followed his lead. In fact, they expanded the idea of active listening into "communication skill training components." But what was the scientific justification for teaching these communication skills? How did the active listening creators decide that "I-statements" are better than "you-statements"? How was *any* of it decided? By the way, the original Thompson I-statement followed the format: "When you do X, in situation Y, I feel X." As you will see, this form of I-statement is still what we call a "harsh startup," because it is designed to elicit defensiveness in the partner. Our form of I-statement, instead, will be of the form: "In situation X, I feel Y, and my positive need is Z." We will explain why this form of I-statement is superior to the earlier form.

It may come as a surprise that even in psychotherapy research the original Truax therapist process variables of accurate empathy, warmth, and genuineness were never shown to relate consistently to therapeutic outcome. In fact, a great deal of doubt about this hypothesis was raised in studies by Bergin and Garfield (e.g., Bergin & Jasper, 1969) in the late 1960s and early 1970s. But even if these variables had been shown to be effective in individual therapy, it is an enormous leap to apply an individual therapy model to dyadic relationships like marriages. The therapist in Rogerian therapy does indeed empathize with the client, but the client is usually complaining about *someone else*, a third person. Once the client starts complaining about the *therapist*, it is usually called *resistance*, and the usual recommended intervention is no longer one of empathizing with the client.

Later we suggest that, in marriages, the easiest starting place for empathy is when the partner is complaining about a *third person*, in the context of the stress-reducing conversation. Then empathy is a matter of colluding against a third party, for which there appears to be no more satisfying way of engendering a couple's solidarity and we-ness. It is extremely common in marital interactions, and it is very soothing. The late Dan Wile (1988) stated the problem of making I-statements quite effectively and pragmatically: "It is impossible to make 'I-statements' when you are in a 'hating-my-partner, wanting revenge, feeling-stung-and-needing-to-sting-back' state of mind. At such a moment you cannot remember what an 'I-statement' is, and frankly you do not care" (p. 2). Wile's statement rings a gut-level bell, but we sought empirical data for it as well. Perhaps active listening can work only when we also consider what the speaker may be saying. This requires looking at sequences of interaction.

That's precisely what we did. The usual way to operationalize active listening sequences would be to look for a pattern in which one partner expresses negative affect and the other partner validates it, a kind of two-step dance. In our research paradigm we cast a wider net than the usual definition of active listening, examining all exchanges in which one partner expressed low- or high-intensity negative affect that was followed by either interest, affection, humor, or direct validation by the partner. In the stability analyses, all the statistics were nonsignificant because these sequences occurred very infrequently for all couples, approximately 4 seconds out of 900 seconds. In the satisfaction analyses, the statistics were again all nonsignificant. Hence, what we found empirically was that these *active listening exchanges hardly ever occurred (only 4.4% of the time) and they did not predict greater marital happiness.* We were quite surprised by these results on the active listening model. In past writings John had also recommended this intervention (e.g., Gottman, 1994; Gottman et al., 1976, 1977). To be more sure about this, John conducted a series of qualitative analyses on the data from this study and on another longitudinal cohort we had been following for the past 14 years. He examined every videotape and transcript of every stable, happy couple in detail. It turned out that happily married people were not paraphrasing their spouse very often, nor were they summarizing their partner's feelings (e.g., "Sounds like this makes you pretty mad"), nor even summarizing the *content* of their spouse's statements (e.g., "You'd like it if we saved more money each month"). Furthermore, they almost never validated their spouse's feelings (e.g., "I can understand why this would make you upset"). In short, what John discovered was that couples were not doing much direct processing of emotion and not much empathizing after negative affect had been expressed. People said what they thought about an issue, they got angry or sad, but their partner's response was never anything like what we were training people to do in the listener–speaker exercise, not even close.

When people feel attacked, they tend to respond negatively; usually, in stable, happy marriages, they respond in kind (anger is met with anger), while in unstable and unhappy marriages, they *escalate the negativity* (anger is met with criticism, defensiveness, or contempt). Our data suggest that asking people to be accepting, nondefensive, active listeners toward their spouse when they feel they are being attacked may go against the natural grain of interaction, even in the best of marriages. Perhaps teaching people to be empathic when they are feeling attacked is like trying to teach couples a form of *emotional gymnastics*, when, in fact, they are feeling emotionally crippled and are even having trouble walking, so to speak. If, indeed, we are trying to teach emotional gymnastics to the emotionally lame, it is no wonder our therapies stop working when the therapist is no longer on the scene.

Given the data that do not support active listening as characteristic of happily married couples, are we suggesting that couples stop being empathic with one another or that empathy is a bad thing? No, but it may be asking people to do something that is not natural, that has too great a psychological cost. In turn, expecting too much from our couples may be related to our major relapse problem in couples therapy. So, let's take a look at the hypothesis that active listening, even if it isn't naturally something happily married couples do, might still be effective if unhappily married couples did it more often. Just because couples do not naturally do anything like active listening does not mean it isn't an effective intervention for distressed marriages.

Is there any direct research on this question? The answer is yes. There is a superbly conducted study by the Munich group, Hahlweg et al. (1984). They followed Guerney's method precisely, comparing his active listening with a behavioral treatment that combined behavior exchange plus problem-solving training. To their credit they also used observational methods, and they had follow-ups at 6 months and a year. They reported that, in the short term:

- Active listening showed decreases in negative interaction but no increases in positive interaction (observational data).
- Behavioral intervention showed both decreases in negativity and increases in positivity (observational data).

In the long term, Hahlweg et al. wrote, couples in the behavioral couples therapy group reported significant and stable decreases of quarreling behavior compared to couples in the active listening group, who eventually returned to pre-treatment levels. On their communication self-report scale, couples in the behavioral group remained stable, whereas couples in the active listening group relapsed to pre-treatment levels. In assessing the clinical significance (not just statistical significance) of results, the typical couple in the behavioral group scored within the "happy" ranges of marital quality, whereas the typical couple in the active listening group was within the "unhappy" range. The conclusion? Active listening *does not work*.

Ultimately this discussion of the issue about active listening need not be a polemic. Clearly people in marriages need to listen to one another and listen empathetically. The issue is probably more about *how* this needs to be accomplished, which we now address.

Fixing the Problems With Active Listening

Here's what we think: The first real problem with active listening is that the listener needs to be physiologically calm in order to be able to absorb any information at all. When people are in physiological fight-or-flight, in contrast, they simply cannot take in any new information (see Chapter 2 on flooding). They also distort their partner's statements and see them as negative. They cannot be good listeners, nor can they be empathetic. The second real problem with active listening is that the speaker needs to be in self-disclosure mode rather than in attack–defend mode. Only when *the speaker* is regulated in this way and uses what we call "gentle startup" can active listening work. The third real problem with active listening is that each person must listen and be able to state—to their partner's satisfaction— their partner's *entire position*, not just the very last thing the partner said. Furthermore, they need to be able to understand their partner's entire position empathetically and summarize both the emotions and the content of their partner's position with sincere compassion. The fourth problem with active listening is that the couple needs to *postpone persuasion* until they first achieve mutual understanding. The fifth problem with active listening is that, once mutual understanding is reached, the couple needs to be guided carefully toward problem-solving and compromise. Once mutual understanding is reached, work on persuasion, problem-solving, and compromise can begin. These modifications of active listening are based, in part, on the work of Anatol Rapoport in his classic book, *Fights, Games, and Debates* (1960/1974). We will introduce these modifications of active listening as our Gottman–Rapoport Conflict Blueprint. We've named this new kind of listening "reflective listening," which we introduce in Chapter 10. Thus, we alter active listening into reflective listening in what we call the Gottman–Rapoport Conflict Blueprint.

The Myth That Emotional Closeness and Eroticism Cannot Coexist in Love Relationships: The Coolidge Effect

This myth surfaces periodically, and it often has a large contingency that believe it. There are two claims in this myth. First is the claim that while emotional closeness or emotional security may be a great thing, it militates against a hot erotic relationship. Second, the claim continues, arguing that eroticism requires mystery, novelty, and not familiarity, and that emotional security breeds familiarity, security, and boredom. Third, this myth also claims that affairs are often about a search for desire in order to feel truly alive within the context of a dull relationship in which desire has died.

The second claim is also known as "the Coolidge effect." The story behind that label is that President Calvin Coolidge and the first lady were once separately touring a government farm, and the tour guide proudly mentioned that a particular rooster had sex dozens of times a day. The first lady was then quoted as saying, "Tell that to the president." When the president was told that the first lady had said that, he asked, "Dozens of times with the same hen?" and he was told, "Oh no, sir, always with a different hen." Coolidge then reportedly said, "Tell *that* to the first lady." That's now called the Coolidge effect: Familiarity breeds sexual desire, but desire only for a new, different partner.

As David Buss reviews in his excellent book *The Evolution of Desire*, men in many cultures confirm the validity of the Coolidge effect. But the effect holds only *in the context of casual sex, exploration,* or *seeking novelty*, as in dating. There is no question that novelty enhances sexual desire. Where our lab comes in is in the context of established relationships, in which the Coolidge effect is often given by some professional therapists as the reason people have affairs. The claim is that people have affairs in search of "hot" sexual novelty. However, the data suggest that affairs are not the result of the Coolidge effect—that is, the search for sexual novelty. In our review of research in established relationships, we have reached exactly the opposite conclusion about why people have affairs. Instead, affairs are primarily an answer to loneliness, which is caused by the *lack* of emotional connection, and also (as Shirley Glass discovered) by the presence of conflict and self-disclosure avoidance. In fact, research has shown that most (but not all) affairs are *not* about sex at all, but about finding someone who likes you and finds you interesting, within the context of an emotionally distant and lonely relationship.

The oft-cited suggestion for solving the Coolidge effect is for all couples to consider having a relationship that permits nonmonogamy, which is the practice, presumably, for a large percentage of gay men. With nonmonogamy, the argument goes, emotional safety and erotic sex can coexist, because having sex with novel partners is permitted. This idea has had great appeal to many people. At the least it offers a justification of betrayal. The Coolidge effect is stated as the hypothesis that a monogamous relationship becomes a safe haven when a couple become friends and are emotionally close. However, that kind of relationship kills off erotic sex. Is that conclusion supported by real data?

Once again, within close relationships, a great deal of research suggests that actually quite the opposite of this hypothesis is true. That is, that one cannot have a hot erotic relationship *unless* there is emotional closeness. The data support the contention that the solution to sexual boredom is to create enhanced emotional connection. In fact, boredom with sex results from emptiness, precisely from emotional disconnection, from a life together that has, in effect, ignored the relationship. Instead of building an intimate connection, the relationship has become managerial. Partners lead parallel lives, and ignore romance, play, and adventure, in favor of a life steeped in infinite to-dos. The need to feel emotionally close in order to feel erotic and have sex may be especially true for women; safety is a precondition for feeling erotically interested. For a review, see Emily Nagoski's excellent 2021 book on sex, beautifully titled *Come as You Are*.

Women tie together feeling sexual with feeling safe. Why? Because women experience much more fear, in general, day to day, than men. The world is a far more dangerous place for women than for men. The national probability in the United States that a woman will be seriously attacked physically or sexually in her lifetime is 49%, while the comparable figure for a man is 9%. Sexual assault is clearly underreported in the military, but it is still reported by 50% of military women. In Tokyo there is a pink train for women only, so that they can avoid the prevalent groping women experience on ordinary Tokyo trains. Twenty-five percent of girls have experienced sexual abuse by the age of 18, and that percentage includes only girls who have reported their abuse. If we include the girls who have been too ashamed to report their abuse, the number is likely much higher. In our ancient history, women evolved to be caretakers of the young, keeping them safe. Anthropologists have observed that nonhuman primates and hunter-gatherer women who are nursing infants together tend to sit in a circle so they will have a 360-degree view of potential predators. In addition, for most women, emotional *safety* first requires emotional *closeness and trust*. As Emily Nagoski points out, the data show that there are generally three prerequisites for a woman to feel turned on erotically: (1) feeling emotionally close and safe with her partner, (2) not facing a long list of undone tasks (like the dog needing to be fed, which is why partners who help with the housework have more sex than partners who do not help), and (3) having a situational context that is clearly erotic. In sum, women have more prerequisites for sex than men. As comedian Billy Crystal once said, "Women need a reason for sex. Men only need a place." Bancroft et al. (2011) conducted a U.S. national study of women ages 20–65. They reported that only 29.1% rated orgasm as very or extremely important for their sexual satisfaction. In contrast, 83.2% of women rated feeling emotionally close to their partner as extremely important for their sexual satisfaction.

Pornography is the ultimate in impersonal sex. It is also the ultimate in disconnection. It's possible to plug in anyone when viewing porn and still have a masturbatory orgasm. No communication is necessary. On the other hand, in a committed love relationship sex is highly personal. The person you love is not replaceable. No one else will do, because with this person there is love, trust, commitment, friendship, and romance. This is the person with whom you have built an entire life together. Furthermore, the truth is that impersonal sex actually creates greater loneliness. Loneliness is often the reason people seek an affair. A case in point: When sociologists asked high-priced escorts about their male customers' most prominent fantasy, these women said their customers wanted "the girlfriend experience." That is, they wanted the escorts to pretend that they loved them, that they had *chosen* them just for themselves and not for the money. A new partner may provide novelty, but not the personal sex these customers are seeking, sex melded together with love, affection, trust, communication, and commitment.

One exception where the Coolidge effect may actually hold true is the relationships of insecure avoidantly attached people, studied by DeWall et al. (2011). The avoidant insecure attachment classification involves denying and suppressing one's needs for emotional security and comfort. The insecurely attached avoidant baby in the famous "Ainsworth strange situation" continues playing and ignores the mother when she returns. The reunion with Mom only *appears* to be a nonevent for the avoidantly attached baby, however. Many avoidantly attached babies have higher activated physiology when the mom returns, but they don't show their distress behaviorally. On the other hand, the insecure, anxiously attached baby is both clingy and hard for Mom to comfort during reunion. DeWall et al. discovered, in eight separate studies, that insecure, avoidantly attached adults have more trouble with commitment in romantic relationships, and are more likely to succumb to the temptations of sexual involvement with others. Since insecurely attached, avoidant people are unable to trust the comfort of a committed, emotionally close, monogamous marriage, having a nonmonogamous "partner in the wings" may make sense as a reproductive strategy. Of course, it can be terrifying for anyone to become vulnerable and fully committed to another person. Fear of commitment is not a pathology. It makes sense to not trust someone with your life, unless they have proved themselves to be trustworthy. However, it appears to be the case that a relationship *lacking* trust and commitment does not confer any of the great potential benefits reviewed above that love can offer. Please note that we are not saying that having a nonmonogamous relationship is only for the insecurely attached.

There is a need for all relationships to discuss the prospect of nonmonogamy; it may very well work for some couples. The data are just not available yet for knowing when, for whom, and under what conditions nonmonogamy is a great idea for avoiding the Coolidge effect.

The Myth That Anger Is the Dangerous Emotion

A pervasive marital therapy model is based on the hypothesis that anger destroys marital relationships. For example, Hendrix (1988), in a section titled "The Destructive Power of Anger" in his best-selling book on marriage, wrote:

> Anger is destructive to a relationship, no matter what its form. When anger is expressed, the person on the receiving end of the attack feels brutalized, whether or not there has been any physical violence; the old brain does not distinguish between choice of weapons. Further, because of the strange workings of the unconscious, the person who unleashes the anger feels equally assaulted, because on a deep level the old brain perceives all action as inner-directed. (p. 147)

This view of anger was also expressed by Parrott and Parrott (1995), who, in a chapter titled "The Deadly Emotion of Anger," wrote:

> It would be tough to find another emotion that has caused married couples more difficulty than anger. Why do we get angry at the person we love the most? Why do we allow ourselves to get angry when we know in advance that we will need to apologize? Why do we raise our voices when it does no good? (p. 78)

This negative view of anger is quite pervasive in most theories of marital therapies. In Greenberg and Johnson's (1988) emotionally focused marital therapy, one of the central tenets of the therapy is to always reframe anger into the "more vulnerable" emotions believed to underlie anger. Writing from an attachment theory perspective, they suggest that those vulnerable emotions involve fear and insecurity. This point of view is emphasized by Jacobson and Christensen (1996) as well as by Lewis's (1997) marital therapy.

Where does this attitude toward anger come from?

We suspect it is a culturally biased view toward anger, probably not shared by cultures that highly value emotional expression and discourse. Winkler and Doherty (1983) studied Israeli Jewish couples and compared them to American Jewish couples. The couples in the United States linked the expression of anger with marital unhappiness. No such link existed for the Israeli couples. These researchers also found in U.S. couples over-all that *suppressing* anger was correlated with physical violence. If these results are generally true, it follows that a more favorable attitude toward anger may reduce violence in marriages. This contrasts with the emphasis on anger control as a treatment for violent marriages, an emphasis Jacobson and Gottman (1998) found to be misplaced. They discovered that the real accelerant in violent marriages is the rejection of influence, not uncontrolled anger.

Research suggests that anger is hardwired as an approach emotion that has adaptive value (see Davidson & Begley, 2012a), meaning it leads individuals toward others rather than away from them. (The latter is called a withdrawal emotion.) Anger is an adaptive reaction to injustice, unfairness, or a blocked goal. In contrast to these negative views on anger, Gottman and Krokoff (1989) reported that, although the expression of anger was associated with lower concurrent marital satisfaction, it was also associated with increases in marital satisfaction over time. In two longitudinal studies Gottman (1994) reported that anger in marital interaction did not predict divorce, whereas *contempt* and *defensiveness* did so reliably. This finding was replicated in a longitudinal study of newlyweds (Gottman et al., 1998).

If a therapy method is rooted in the belief that anger is a dangerous emotion, the therapist will probably work on "softening" the anger, or perhaps suggest that "beneath" the anger is a more vulnerable emotion like fear or sadness. Imago couples therapy and emotionally focused couples therapy both highlight this goal. However, modern cognitive neuroscience has found that anger issues primarily arise from a goal being blocked (see Ortony et al., 1988). A person's anger can actually convey important information. One partner may express anger if they think their partner is treating them unfairly, unjustly, or disrespectfully. Rather than responding defensively or with counterattack, the listening partner can reply respectfully by asking, "What are your concerns?" and then taking notes, reflecting back, and validating. This nondefensive response is possible only if the angry speaker does not use criticism or contempt to express their emotion. These two Horsemen often get mixed up with the expression of anger. Anger may also escalate if it's dismissed, minimized, or otherwise disrespected. Anger expressed purely, that is, as one's own emotion, works far better to improve the quality of a relationship.

The Myth of the Quid Pro Quo—Reciprocal Contingency Contracts

Lederer and Jackson's (1968) *Mirages of Marriage* was a bold and daring book. These pioneers spelled out what they believed is dysfunctional about ailing marriages and how therapists ought to go about fixing them. Their book was an important contribution to the study of marriage. It charted lots of ideas about romanticism, trust, and so on. One of the most important was that the "sine qua non" of marriage is its "quid pro quo," which means that in good marriages, there is a reciprocal exchange of positive behaviors, and that in bad marriages, for various reasons (like romanticism), there is a breakdown of these agreements, these implicit contracts. This point of view was consistent with an economically based behavior exchange theory recommended 10 years earlier in social psychology by Thibaut and Kelley (1959). The Lederer and Jackson book had an enormous impact. In marital behavior therapy alone, it led to the marital therapy method of "contingency contracting" (Azrin et al., 1973).

Unfortunately, it turned out that this quid pro quo idea was totally wrong. Not only are happy marriages *not* characterized by the quid pro quo; the quid pro quo actually characterizes *unhappy* marriages! Unhappy couples are the ones who keep tabs on marital positives given and received, whereas happy couples are positive unconditionally. Yet the erroneous and untested quid pro quo assumption not only spawned a new marital therapy but also spread as a major ingredient of other marital therapies, despite being disproved by Murstein and his associates (Murstein et al., 1977).

It is really amazing that contingency contracting carried on, despite

Murstein et al.'s (1997) findings. Imagine if, in trying to battle AIDS, we recommended a biochemical treatment process that was related to patients' deteriorating from the disease. Wouldn't you think that something was wrong here?

Yet, nothing seems to die in the areas of psychological treatment. In fact, no one is ever even willing to say that the emperor has no clothes on, that a therapy method seems to be ineffective. It's not that the people who write the books we read aren't smart or well-intentioned. It's just that very smart people working on very tough problems can often be wrong. Interesting ideas are capable of disconfirmation. Often, more is learned by *disconfirming* an interesting hypothesis than from any other outcome of a study.

The Myth of Contingent Positivity

The supposed value of reciprocating positive behavior led to a great debate in the behavioral literature. As a result, behavior exchange interventions have changed or evolved over time (since the early 1970s), in part due to experience with Stuart's (1980) "love days" and the use of the Weiss Spouse Observation Checklist (Weiss, 1975). The modification introduced by Stuart led to questioning the philosophy of "give to get" that formed the basis of behavior exchange intervention, especially during couples' conflict. Eventually, the intervention expanded into an attempt to create, overall, greater positivity, kindness, and love in people's everyday interactions (not just during conflict). Furthermore, the interventions became noncontingent. Therapists were training people to be nicer to their spouses regardless of what they got back.

Perception wound up playing an important role in this equation of behavior exchange. Therapists had clients discuss whether they noticed the positivity or failed to see it. This was a fascinating modification of behavior exchange, and it led to an interest in modifying cognitions. Robinson and Price (1980) did a very clever study. They had observers count the number of positive acts one partner did with or for the other. They also trained the couple to do this coding of their own partner at the same time. They discovered that, compared to what objective observers detected in the couples, unhappily married couples underestimated the amount of positivity by a factor of 50%! The happily married couples were totally in line with the outside observers.

Behavior therapy using contracting assumed *without evidence* that unhappily married people were not at all positive toward one another. They therefore needed the love days. But perhaps the big problem with the behavior exchange therapy was not about getting people to be more positive toward their partner, but getting people to *notice* the positivity that was actually already there. Yet, even with this, a problem remained. Robinson and Price (1980) reported that only happily married couples, and not unhappy couples, were happier after attending to their positive interactions. So, increasing a couple's awareness of positivity may not be a very effective intervention with distressed couples.

Why would this be the case? The answer probably has to do with the nature of the *attributional processes*, in which negative attributions become a non-disconfirmable hypothesis. In other words, people who make negative attributions about their spouse simply discard counterexamples. The research of Donald Baucom (Baucom & Epstein, 1990) has informed us about the difficulty of trying directly to alter these negative cognitions.

The Harmony Myth

The harmony myth essentially posits that couples who argue and bicker cannot be happy, because only couples who are "harmonious" with one another can have happy marriages. Harmonious couples are those that rarely fight and never bicker. A man we admire a lot, Harold Raush (Raush et al., 1974), published the first study of couples experiencing the transition to parenthood. Raush gave couples a variety of scripted marital arguments to read, and then asked them to decide, together, who was most at fault in each vignette. Based on *how* the partners discussed their answers, he observed that his sample included three types of couples. One type was not harmonious, because, in deciding who was at fault, they argued and bickered over everything, even the most trivial details. For example, regarding one vignette's fault assignment, they might end up arguing over how to load glasses in the dishwasher. Raush identified a second group of couples who were not harmonious because they minimized the differences in these vignettes and totally avoided conflicts, and seemed to have little psychological insight. Raush decided that a third group was "harmonious." They disagreed, but very politely and logically. Raush decided that the bickerers were dysfunctional. No one could be so passionate about such trivia! The avoiders, he decided, were also dysfunctional, with "brittle" psychological defenses. So, the two hypotheses suggested by Harold Raush were:

- Conflict avoidance is dysfunctional. *Wrong*
- Bickering about trivial issues is also dysfunctional. *Wrong*

Raush was wrong on both counts. John discovered that both conflict-avoiding and volatile, bickering couples can have stable, happy marriages, *but only if* they maintain a positive-to-negative ratio during conflict that is 5 to 1 or larger. In fact, John discovered that the bickering, passionate couples were the only ones to still have a romantic marriage after 35 years (Gottman, 1994). So "harmony" is a myth. Having real conflicts and bickering can be quite characteristic of happily married couples. That fact may be a part of why untrained observers see dysfunction in marital conflict when, actually, no dysfunction exists at all.

More Myths, and Some Truths

Superb examples of the confusion and resulting lack of efficacy in both marital therapy and research are the conflicting views on the benefits versus the disadvantages of *dominance* in marital relationships. There is actually research evidence to support both of the following hypotheses, so which one is actually true?

- A dominance structure is dysfunctional. *Correct*
- The lack of dominance structure is dysfunctional. *Wrong*

The data on power and dominance in marriages are very confusing, because it is difficult to operationalize and measure the power variable in the concept of dominance. Power may vary depending on what aspect of a marriage one studies, such as who wins in decisions, who gets greatest access to resources, and to resources in which specific areas of the relationship. A complete review of these hypotheses would take us too far afield. Broderick's (1993) book on family process discusses power in terms of the "regulation of vertical space," which is an intriguing idea. Gottman (1979) defined dominance as an asymmetry in predictability in interactive behavior. This means that if one can predict the wife's subsequent behavior from her husband's immediate past behavior better than the converse (predicting the husband's behavior from his wife's most recent past behavior), then the husband is dominant. Statistical tests exist to make this determination. The concept is that in an egalitarian marriage there is no such asymmetry. What do the data say? Gottman found that the predictability of one spouse's behavior from the other's behavior was greater in distressed marriages than in nondistressed marriages. However, there is a caveat. On low-conflict tasks both distressed and nondistressed couples showed an egalitarian dominance pattern. But on high-conflict tasks, the husband was dominant only in distressed marriages. Our research has thus shown that sharing power, in terms of what we call "acceptance of influence" (particularly the husband's acceptance of his wife's influence), is critically important for the stability of marriages, even among newlyweds, and it is also critically important in understanding spouse abuse.

Another hypothesis, but this one is somewhat true.

- A "female-demand/male-withdraw" pattern (also called "female-pursuer/male-distancer" pattern) is dysfunctional. *This one is correct!*

The best work on this hypothesis has been done by Andrew Christensen and his students (Christensen, 1987, 1988; Christensen & Heavey, 1990; Cohen & Christensen, 1980; Heavey et al., 1993). However, there's also a caveat here. The demand–withdraw pattern is not consistently descriptive of distressed marriages, for two reasons. First, the demand–withdraw pattern is actually characteristic of *all* marriages. We have actually found this pattern even in our study of happy, long-term, stable marriages. Second, Christensen and his associates discovered that the pattern can be changed greatly when the issue under discussion is the *husband's* issue versus the wife's issue. However, and here's the important point: Even if this pattern is generally true of all marriages, Christensen and his associates have shown conclusively that the pattern does indeed become *exacerbated* when the marriage is ailing. So, the female-demand/male-withdraw pattern turns out to be one of the more reliable findings in the area of marriage. It is, however, important to understand the *etiology* of the pattern, because otherwise women might get blamed for starting the conflicts in marriages. The totally inaccurate stereotype is that women are so terribly demanding that the poor men just can't take it, so they withdraw. The person who wants the change comes off as demanding, and the defensiveness of the other partner gets coded as withdrawal. So, we have to be very careful with how we use and understand this pattern. In emotionally focused couples therapy, this demand–withdraw pattern has been taken as *the* major relationship dysfunction, and that is just simply a mistake. The data do not support that conclusion.

Here is an early behavioral view, to our knowledge advocated primarily by Neil Jacobson:

• Changing one another's behavior is essential to a happy marriage. *Wrong*

To the early behavioral marital therapists this almost seemed like a tautology. It is interesting that this hypothesis was never empirically established by behavioral marital therapists, and even more interesting that more recently, Jacobson and Christensen (1996) claim that the goal of marital therapy ought to be first to get people to accept one another and *not* try to change behavior. The truth, as Jacobson and Christensen actually suggested, must lie somewhere between the two positions in an interesting dialectic, which seems to be "Accepting one another is the only proper context in which change can be requested." That makes a lot of sense because this is what we have observed the masters of relationship do, especially when it comes to their perpetual problems.

The next hypothesis will expand on this idea of perpetual problems.

The following popular mythical hypothesis has formed the cornerstone of nearly all marital therapies:

• Poor problem-solving skills are dysfunctional. *Wrong*

Our research suggests that this hypothesis, in its simplest form, is essentially wrong. Instead, the role of problem-solving has been greatly exaggerated in marital therapy. In fact, even in the best marriages, while some minor fraction of marital problems does get solved, over time most marital problems (69%) *do not ever get solved at all*; instead, they become what we call "perpetual" issues. What turns out to be important is the *affect* that surrounds the way people talk about (but do not really solve) these perpetual marital problems. They either establish a "dialogue" with these problems, or they go into a state of "gridlock." Later, we will discuss that what matters is the affect with which people don't solve their perpetual problems. In fact, it turns out that most gridlocked perpetual issues actually have an underlying hidden agenda within which lies a dream or a core existential position that must be brought out using our Dreams Within Conflict intervention. That discovery requires that couples therapy must be an existential therapy. However, we point out that 31% of couples' issues do, in fact, get solved over time. This fact led us to identify six critical social skills that make it more likely that solvable problems will get solved. These six skills are (1) practicing physiological self-soothing, (2) using softened startup, (3) repairing and de-escalating, (4) listening to one's partner's underlying feelings and dreams, (5) accepting influence, and (6) compromising.

The Sequential Two-Step

In testing some of the myths it became necessary to use the mathematics of information theory to do a "two-step" sequential analysis of our interaction codes over time. We needed to be able to identify *sequences* of interaction. How does one do this? The answer is that a sequence "Partner 1 does emotion code A" followed by "Partner 2 does emotion code B" occurs when the uncertainty in the occurrence of B is significantly reduced by knowing that A has just occurred. For example, we can establish the sequence "Wife Angry → Husband Contemptuous" if the husband is contemptuous 10% of the time overall, but when the wife has expressed anger, he is then subsequently contemptuous 25% of the time. The knowledge of the wife's anger has increased our prediction of his contempt from 10% to 25%. The math of information theory provides the statistical test of whether 25% versus 10% is significant beyond chance.

Using these mathematics, our lab was able to do a "two-step" sequential analysis to examine the actual function of specific behaviors like "mind reading" and "meta-communication," which we will now discuss. Later, we used new analyses designed by the late brilliant primatologist, John's friend Gene Sackett, to do "lag-sequential analysis" to identify longer sequences. To learn more about the mathematics of information theory, see Bakeman and Gottman's 1997 book, *Observing Interaction: An Introduction to Sequential Analysis*; Bakeman and Quera's 2011 book, *Sequential Analysis and Observational Methods for the Behavioral Sciences*; and Gottman and Roy's 1990 book, *Sequential Analysis*. The two-step and more helped to finally test some important hypotheses.

An influential hypothesis we can test with our two-step sequential analysis:

- Mind reading is dysfunctional. *Wrong*

Mind reading is attributing thoughts and feelings or motives to the other person. Instead of asking what one's partner is feeling, people mind read and assume they know what their partner is thinking and feeling—and this is dysfunctional (e.g., a statement like "You always get tense at my mother's house"). Watzlawick's great rationalist's hope (Watzlawick et al., 1967) was that people's relationships would be fine if only they communicated clearly. For this reason concepts like "feedback" mechanisms were so appealing.

The assumption was that if people could give one another feedback, then communication would become clearer and pathology would just vanish. This was a very good idea. Unfortunately, it just wasn't usually true. What turned out to be true is that:

IN AILING MARRIAGES PEOPLE GENERALLY
COMMUNICATE VERY CLEARLY, BUT WHAT THEY
COMMUNICATE IS MOSTLY NEGATIVE.

We believe this dysfunctional, mind-reading myth came from the fact that the early systems therapists worked primarily with very disturbed families. Recall that family process was initially proposed as the cause and the cure for individual psychopathology. It is only recently that its goals have changed to improving family relationships. Probably the only consistent finding to emerge from studies of interactions in families with severe psychopathology was that the communication in these families was negative, and sometimes unclear, confusing, and hard to follow (for a review, see Jacob, 1987). Hence, it was natural to suggest that if one could provide feedback loops that could just *clarify* messages (and discrepancies in their component parts), a cure could be achieved. Unfortunately, in distressed marriages the communication is often quite clear but, unfortunately, also quite hostile. So improved clarity does little to help distressed couples.

What did the two-step analysis discover about mind reading? People do, indeed, mind read a lot in marriages (see Gottman, 1979). Instead of saying, "How do you feel at my mother's house?" they say, "You hate going to my mother's house." That's because they usually already know this from past conversations. It isn't bad communication; it is usually based on real knowledge. Actually, it turns out that whether mind reading is dysfunctional or not depends entirely on the *affect* with which it is delivered. We used our sequential two-step to examine this question. Mind reading with positive affect acts as a "feeling probe"; it is the major way people in marriages generally ask about feelings. We examined the second step of a mind reading by one partner. An example: "I've noticed that you always get tense at my mother's house." Nodding in agreement, the spouse answers, "Yes, I do. Maybe if the two of you didn't gang up on me, I'd be more relaxed." So, mind reading with positive affect has the consequence that the partner agrees and elaborates a feeling and need.

Mind reading with negative affect has the same effect as blaming. An example: "You *always* get tense at my mother's house." Bristling, the spouse retorts, "I don't *always* get tense there. Will you just shut up?" It turns out that spouses don't tend to ask questions about each other's feelings; they much more typically mind read! They do not say, "How do you feel about my recent purchase?" Instead, they say, "You think I'm a spendthrift." So, mind reading had a different meaning than Watzlawick thought it did. The two-step showed that mind reading with negative affect resulted in the partner disagreeing and escalating the negativity of the interaction.

This knowledge could be gained only by doing basic descriptive research on marital interaction—a step many theorists tend to skip—and adding the two-step sequential analysis. Deborah Tannen, who is a keen observer of linguistic styles of speech, has made similar observations. For example, she noticed that New Yorkers allow far less time after they think a speaker is done, before they take a speaking turn, than Californians, who wait longer. New Yorkers also think that they are "speaking along with" a speaker, which they think shows support and interest, whereas Californians see speaking along with as interruption. Julie is from Oregon, John is from New York City; we have a similar perpetual conflict in interpreting our different speech patterns.

Here is a very popular hypothesis about happy couples, one first suggested as part of the famous "double-bind" hypothesis put forward by the very original thinker Gregory Bateson.

- Engaging in "meta-communication" characterizes well-adjusted couples. Dysfunctional couples can't meta-communicate. *Wrong*

"Meta-communication" is any statement about the *process* of the communication. An example would be "We are getting off the topic." In the original classic paper on the double-bind hypothesis of schizophrenia, early communication general systems theorists Bateson et al. (1956) targeted the confusing message of a schizophrenic patient's mother, who approaches him for a hug and then stiffens when he hugs her. She is sending two contradictory messages, which puts him in a double bind. He is damned if he does (hugs her), and damned if he doesn't (she feels rejected and lets him know it). There is an old Jewish joke that Sigmund Freud cited: The mother gives her son two ties for a gift. The next time she sees him he is wearing one of the ties. The mother says, "What's the matter? You didn't like the other tie?" Once again, this is an example of being damned if you do, and damned if you don't.

But what did the general systems theorists suggest the schizophrenic son *do* to escape this double bind? They suggested that he comment on the *process*. Indeed, commenting on the process became the main tool of the systems approach to therapy. The sine qua non of good communication became *meta-communication* for the general systems theorists. They suggested that it surely ought to characterize the problem-focused conversations of well-adjusted couples, but not those of distressed couples. Good hypothesis. Just wrong. We again used the two-step. This hypothesis was simply not true.

Furthermore, we now know that meta-communication is part of *repair processes*. Again, what is most salient is *how the meta-communication is responded to*, not whether it occurs or how it is delivered. Happily married couples have short chains of meta-communication followed by agreement, and they use these often as repair mechanisms, but unhappily married couples have long meta-communication chains in which the affect transfers to the "meta" level, and also escalates negatively. This is a pattern of "cross meta-communication." The meta-communication doesn't work, and it doesn't change anything. In distressed marriages one meta-communication tends to be countered with another meta-communication (Gottman, 1979). These repair processes occur naturally in marital interaction even in the most distressed marriages, and they occur more frequently the more distressed the couple. They are also likely to be occurring when the interaction is negative affectively, so that they are often made with some irritability or sadness. When they work, they may sound like this: "Will you shut up and let me finish?" followed by "All right, damn it, finish!" That's an effective repair, because it usually takes the couple out of the negative affect chain. However, a more polite meta-communication is more likely to be seen as collaborative rather than adversarial (Wile, personal communication, 1998).

Here is a fascinating hypothesis proposed by Lederer and Jackson (1968):

• High expectations for marriage cause divorce. *Wrong*

They suggested that people's unreasonably high and usually romantic expectations for marriage were destructive. If people had more reasonable expectations, they proposed, they wouldn't get so disappointed. Donald Baucom has systematically investigated this hypothesis (e.g., Baucom et al., 1996) and has found exactly the opposite to be true. People who have higher standards and higher expectations for their marriage (including romantic ones) have the best marriages, not the worst. Therapist Dan Wile (1992) anticipated these results and recommended that people hold on to romantic ideals rather than compromising them.

Another hypothesis that has been put forward:

- We are all the products of very poor parenting, and for this reason we have a lot of unfinished psychological business to attend to. We search for this healing by pairing with someone who has the potential to heal us. *Wrong*

This is a fascinating hypothesis. Unfortunately, the mate-selection process is not so purposeful, orderly, or deterministic. It appears to be a much more random process, with some "similarity filters" put in place to ensure that people of similar social class meet one another. In fact, research has actually been totally unable to measure anything in two individuals that will predict whether they will like one another once they meet (Joel et al., 2017). All the matching algorithms in dating websites are wrong, because they are searching for similarity. For example, in Christian Rudder's 2014 book, *Dataclysm*, on matching on the site OkCupid, it took 50,000 matches to find two people who liked meeting one another. In fact, random pairing does way better than any matching algorithm in coming up with the largest number of people who will like one another once they meet. Similarity in desires, wishes for particular traits, personality characteristics—all of these fail to get a happy match.

There is, in fact, some evidence that it is *diversity* that determines mate selection, to some degree. In the now famous "T-shirt study" of Claus Wedekind, heterosexual women smelled T-shirts worn for 2 days by a variety of men. It turned out that the T-shirts women preferred were worn by men who were most different from the women in genes of the immune system, called the major histocompatibility complex. Women, perhaps unconsciously, were seeking men of major diversity from them genetically. The question remained as to whether they would like these men once they met them. That study has now actually been done, and the answer was yes, they did. For a scholarly review of this research see Daniel Davis's 2013 *The Compatibility Gene*. However, random pairing in dating seems to do best—in random pairing, 30% of people say they liked one another. Therefore, mate selection is still a great unsolved mystery. We seem to be looking for someone very different from us; we're not seeking our clone. But relationships with significant differences between partners go awry when we subsequently try to change that partner into us. At least, that's what our data say.

Here is a hypothesis that was first countered in the 1930s by Nathan Ackerman (1966):

- Healthy marriage is not possible unless personality issues and wounds from one's family of origin are resolved. *Wrong*

The above is yet another myth. Ackerman earned a lot of disapproval and rejection from practitioners of the predominant therapy mode of that time (psychoanalysis) when he suggested that two neurotics could have a happy marriage. It was almost a heresy, given the time he suggested it. The psychoanalytic lore was that happy marriage was possible only for two non-neurotic, mature people. Ackerman also contended that the expectation that childhood issues needed to be resolved before one could have a happy marriage was not helpful. The modern version of this hypothesis can be found in object relations theory and, more popularly, in the writings of Harville Hendrix (1988). He contends that most marital conflict stems from childhood wounds resulting from bad parenting. A goal of Hendrix's treatment is to help the couple develop what he calls "X-ray vision" so that they can see the wound behind the hostility. The argument goes that, if the perceived hostility or insecurity could only be expressed as a "vulnerable affect," then these marital conflicts would simply dissipate. But it takes the therapist to convince the couple of that, and once treatment is terminated, hostility just seems like . . . hostility. Likewise, Greenberg and Johnson's (1988) emotion-focused therapy, based on attachment theory, claims that all marital hostility comes from insecure attachment, so they also train their clients to see the fear or vulnerability "behind" the anger. In these approaches the therapy essentially softens any negative affect by providing a personality theory that "explains it away"; it is really something else, and if that is the case, then the receiver of the hostile message should not be so upset.

The problem with *the therapy* softening the issues for the couple is that, once the therapist leaves the scene, it may be difficult for the couple to apply the concepts to the hostility that continues to surface. We have found in our research that *reciprocated negative affect in marriages is quite natural*—anger is met with anger—and that is *not* dysfunctional. Nevertheless, we *do* need to teach couples soothing skills to modulate negative interchanges.

Let's think about whether we really need these personality concepts in our marital therapy. What is the evidence that the individual's personality actually is important in our understanding of and ability to predict marital outcomes? In Howard Markman's dissertation (1977), the prediction of marital happiness two and a half years after the period of engagement was predicted by the *perceived* similarity between partners, not the actual personality traits. In an ailing marriage, lasting negative attributions are made about the spouse's perceived negative personality traits—but the *traits themselves* were not very predictive. There is some evidence that measures of agreeability and neuroticism predict later marital dissatisfaction and even divorce, but the predictions are quite weak, with correlations of about .25, which is about the level of uninformed prediction of marital satisfaction itself. In addition, the measures of neuroticism are confounded with distress assessments, and the statistics also have the problem of common method variance with the assessment of marital satisfaction.

In fact, many complex variations of the personality hypothesis have been explored in the marital literature. Probably the best known one is the Winch (1958; see also Tharp, 1963, for a review of research) hypothesis of "need complementarity." This theory was originally embraced but was then abandoned by psychoanalytic therapists. The idea was that if one person has a need (say, the need to dominate), they will be happily married if they marry someone with the complementary need (the need to be dominated). Winch's theory was abandoned when it received absolutely no empirical support.

Furthermore, research has shown that personality traits do not discriminate distressed from nondistressed couples, because people's interactions with their spouses are not predictive of their interactions with other people. Birchler et al. (1975) studied the interactions of distressed and nondistressed couples with each other and with strangers while engaging in a conflict-resolution task (the Inventory of Marital Conflict, a set of vignettes in which husband and wife get different stories and have to decide who is most at fault in each vignette, husband or wife). Distressed spouses were significantly more negative and less positive with one another than nondistressed spouses, but the interactions of a distressed spouse with a stranger were no different from that of a nondistressed spouse with a stranger.

In a study John did with Albert Porterfield (Gottman & Porterfield, 1981) on sending and receiving the nonverbal component of messages, distressed husbands were poor receivers of their *wives'* nonverbal behaviors, but they were fine at receiving the nonverbal behaviors of married female strangers. This result was actually perfectly replicated by a completely independent study conducted by Pat Noller (1980, 1984) with Australian couples. Based on interviews, we suggested that this inability to receive their wives' nonverbal messages was the result of their emotional withdrawal in their marriages, and that these men had not always been so withdrawn.

Although the evidence for the contribution of individual personality traits to the predictability of marriage is not compelling, the area of violence may be an exception. Here we found that *highly antisocial men were violent not only to their wives but also to coworkers, friends, family, and strangers.* Here— and only for this subgroup of men—the aggression seems trait related. So, at extremes of personality and psychopathology we may find it useful to consider personality, but in general it adds very little.

So why do marital therapy theorists such as Hendrix and Greenberg and Johnson use these concepts? The answer, we think, is that it can be very appealing to therapists to do a lot of the work that the couple should be doing in learning how to de-escalate and soften their conflicts. The bottom line is that, when a marriage is not going well, *then* people perceive their partner's personality as a problem. It is generally the *perception of personality differences* that is related to marital unhappiness (and perhaps the result of unhappiness), not *actual* personality differences. Rather, as issues arise and become implacable and painful to talk about, people try to explain them in terms of their partner's perceived personality inadequacies. In a sense, the apparent personality change is *an artifact of declining marital satisfaction*, not the cause of it.

We think it's best to view a relationship as you would the music a jazz quartet makes when the musicians come together. The marital interaction is the music. As they interact, the two people create a third element, just as the music of the jazz quartet is a brand-new entity, the fifth element produced by the four musicians. It is the *music* we must study. The temporal forms that spouses create and the way they feel about what they create when they are together are the essence of marriage. The "temporal forms" are like music; they are the repeated *sequential* patterns or themes of the marriage. They can be measured quantitatively (see Gottman, 1979). As the spouses interact, they improvise around these central marital themes. To understand the music of the quartet, it helps very little to describe the personalities of the players. Even the solo work of the musicians will often not predict how much a particular quartet is, or is not, "in the groove"—that is, making beautiful music together.

The other possibility may be that we have not studied personality very well, because the field has relied primarily on self-report measurement. Perhaps if personality were studied using a multimethod perspective, we might find that it would, indeed, make some contribution to our understanding of marriages. However, Terman's (Terman et al., 1938) original hope that there would be some ideal or optimal personality structure for successful marriage does not seem likely to be borne out.

We are not claiming that the past is unimportant. Later in this book we will suggest that discovering the origins of marital patterns is very useful in diagnosis and prediction. In the intervention section we will discuss the importance of how triggers from past traumas need to be understood in processing past regrettable incidents. Also, resistance to change can reveal a person's internal working model about salient marital processes.

Marital conflict is shared by both happy and unhappy couples, and, in fact, the rank-order correlation of severity of problems is about .94 across these two groups. (The maximum value is 1.00, so this is extraordinarily high.) The result is very important. It means that, for example, all spouses argue about finances and sex. It essentially means that in all marriages there are tasks that need to be accomplished. Conflict is endemic to marriages because people have different ideas about how to go about accomplishing these tasks. The presence of marital conflict does not imply that our parents have failed in raising us. Conflict goes with the territory of marriage.

The following hypothesis is primarily the work of Jacobson and Margolin (1979):

- Marriages start off happy—newlyweds are highly important and reinforcing for one another—but this pattern of spouses supplying each other with positive reinforcement erodes over time. "Reinforcement erosion" is the source of marital dysfunction and divorce. *Wrong*

Empirical work has also shown this idea to be wrong. The idea is that during courtship we find a large number of things our partner does that are wonderful, exciting, and rewarding. After a while, however, this positive glow fades and our partner loses the ability to charm and delight us. We know the old stories, jokes, and behaviors, and they no longer ignite excitement. Though this is a rather cynical hypothesis, there appears, at first glance, to be some support for this idea. For example, the first longitudinal study of 1,000 engaged couples by Burgess and Wallin (1953) reported that, over time, the marital satisfaction of couples declined. After 15 years the couples reported communicating less, being less in love, doing fewer things together, having less sex, and not being sure they would marry the same person if they had it all to do over again.

But many couples followed the opposite pattern, growing closer over time. In long-term happy couples, people become generally more mellow and accepting of one another as they stay married, rather than less. The relationship seems to get better and better, so we can actually contend that there is a reinforcement *gain* that occurs over time. In marriages that do not work very well the positive things don't erode; they are just done less and less over time, as people turn away from one another.

In our 20-year longitudinal research on older couples (those couples in midlife or facing retirement) who had been married a long time, the modal pattern was quite the opposite of reinforcement erosion. These partners wanted to spend more time with each other, and affection increased with the length of time married. These data are somewhat biased, however, because we were studying a sample of couples whose marriages had survived. Carstensen (Carstensen, 1992, 1995; Carstensen & Turk-Charles, 1994) proposed a "selectivity theory" of aging. Typically, as people age they become more selective about whom they prefer to spend time with, and spouses rank high on the preferred list. The reinforcement value of these special, close relationships appears to *increase* with time, not decrease. That is part of the good news—as it endures, the modal relationship generally gets better. What might have been different about those marriages that did "erode" and those that did not? An analysis of Burgess and Wallin's data by Dizzard (1968) revealed that those couples who became disenchanted moved toward less power sharing and toward a traditional division of labor, with less joint decision-making. In addition, researchers who have investigated the early formation of relationships (see Bradbury, 1998), have found no such period of "bliss," when everything works well and partners are highly reinforcing of one another. Rather, it seems that patterns are established very early in a relationship, and then they only stabilize further over time.

We conclude that this cynical hypothesis of reinforcement erosion is simply not true.

Here is another interesting hypothesis:

- Similarity between spouses is the basis of marital stability and happiness. *Wrong*

On the surface, this idea appeared to be true, until later research discovered it was a myth, too. Newcomb and Bentler (1980) found that similarity was indeed a predictor of marital stability. Fowers and Olson (1986) base their "PREPARE" program of premarital counseling on helping couples explore their similarities in 11 different areas of the marriage. There are also consistent findings that spouses who are similar to one another in interests (Huston & Houts, 1998) or who share similar religiously conservative values are less likely to be unhappy or to divorce (Kahn & London,

1991). However, similarity is, at best, a weak predictor of marital outcomes, for two reasons. The first is that measuring the similar variables often taps the degree of community support that the couple receives. This is especially true when the sample population shares conservative religious values. Being part of a supportive community turns out to be somewhat helpful for couples in trying times and accounts for martial stability in cultures that still arrange marriages (e.g., countries like Kuwait). Les and Leslie Parrott (1995) and Mike McManus (1995) are now trying to rec-reate these results in less cohesive communities by using couple-mentor programs. Still, similarity of values and interests is not a strong predictor of marital stability. The divorce rate is only slightly lower among Catholics than among non-Catholics, for example. In addition, the presence of a sim-ilarity does not tell us anything about *process*, about how partners relate to each other in their sharing of beliefs and interests. An example: I love to canoe. I don't know how many times I have seen spouses canoeing down a river screaming contemptuously at each other, "That's not how you do a J-stroke, you idiot!" Yes, they have this interest in common, but being crit-ical and contemptuous toward one another while they share the interest will carry greater weight—in the negative direction. Similarity is a weak predictor because it does not tap the processes that matter in maintaining, or destroying, a marriage.

Still more reasonable hypotheses could be generated, such as that nonegalitarian marriages are dysfunctional, and so on. The question is, are any of these contentions true? If not, then what *is* true? What should a mar-ital therapist select as a goal? What should a therapist decide needs fixing in an ailing marriage? My fundamental point is that we benefit from solid empirical knowledge about what may be "dysfunctional" and "functional" in terms of predicting what happens to marriages. A marital therapy needs to be developed that has *a process mode that is based on empirical findings*. One way to think about developing a marital therapy is by asking what factors are predictive of whether couples stay married or get divorced. In the context of this question, let's consider another area dappled by the misleading hypoth-eses that pervade our field.

Myths Specifically About What Predicts Divorce

Myth: Affairs Cause Most Divorces. Wrong

The most common myth is that extramarital affairs cause divorce. There are some writers—for example, Pittman (1989)—who have strongly suggested that the root cause of divorce is extramarital affairs. It is indeed true that about 25% of all marital therapy cases report a revealed extramarital affair as the major presenting issue. So, we do have to know how to help these couples.

However, it is very difficult to obtain reliable data on extramarital affairs, in part because the issue is so explosive, and deception and secrecy are part of the phenomenon. Collecting representative data is as difficult as attempting to do a quick survey on whether 17-year-old boys are virgins, and asking the question when their friends are present. In one large and important study done on sex in the United States (Michael et al., 1995), interviewers asked about extramarital affairs while the spouse was in the house, even sometimes in the same room. As you might expect, they reported a very low rate!

The most reliable information we know of comes from work published in 1992 by Lynn Gigy and Joan Kelly of the California Divorce Mediation Project. I believe that, within this careful context of helping both spouses reach a less rancorous solution to dissolving the marriage, it is reasonable to trust the honesty of people's self-reports of the causes for divorcing. The major reasons for divorcing given by close to 80% of all men and women? They said it was how they had been gradually growing apart and losing a sense of closeness, and they did not feel loved and appreciated. Extramarital affairs were endorsed as a cause of the divorce by only 20%–27% of all the couples. Severe and intense fighting was indicated by 40% of the couples—44% of females and 35% of males.

This omission of affairs as the reported cause of marital dissolution is not a recent phenomenon. In William Goode's 1948 study (1956/1969), the major reasons mentioned for divorcing were nonsupport and neglect (also heavy drinking by the man). Probably associated with increasing divorce rates and the shift of women into the workplace, Kitson and Sussman (1982) reported that women's most frequent complaints had shifted from specific negative behaviors to affective or emotional deficiencies in the marriage. Thurner et al. (1983) also reported a decline in citing economic problems and alcoholism as reasons for divorce. Cleek and Pearson (1985) found that communication problems, basic unhappiness, and incompatibility were the reasons given. In a Danish sample (Koch-Nielsen & Gundlach, 1985) "growing apart" was the major reason given by both men and women.

Furthermore, many clinicians, including Pittman, who have worked with couples in attempting to repair the damage caused by an extramarital affair have been quick to point out that "affairs involve sex, but sex is usually not the purpose of the affair" (Pittman & Wagers, 1995, p. 298). In fact, most clinicians who have written in this area report that affairs are usually about outwardly seeking friendship, support, understanding, and validation. In Jacobson and Christensen's (1996) terms, the spouses who have affairs are trying to gain acceptance that is missing in the marriage.

Gigy and Kelly (1993) concluded that loss of feelings of closeness and rising feelings of emotional barrenness, boredom with the marriage, and serious differences in lifestyle were the prevalent reasons given for divorce. The majority of respondents in their mediation project reported high levels of conflict and/or tension in their marriages. Also, 65% of men and 64% of women reported sexual intimacy problems as an important factor in the breakdown of their relationships.

In summarizing these research projects, "feeling unloved" was the most commonly cited reason for wanting a divorce (67% of the women in the California study and 75% in the Danish study), and sensitivity to being belittled has apparently increased over the past 15 years: 59% of both men and women in the Danish study cite this factor, and American men show an increase in citing it since the early 1970s, from 0% to 37% in Gigy and Kelly's study. We must conclude that most marriages end with a whimper, the result of people gradually drifting apart and not feeling liked, loved, and respected.

The slow slide toward divorce, in what we call the "distance and isolation cascade," suggests that the final stage of loneliness makes people vulnerable to relationships outside the marriage. This means that the interactions of couples in treatment are often *not* characterized by intense fighting but by emotional distance and the absence of affect. We have found that this is especially the case for couples divorcing later in the course of the marriage, in midlife, after being married for 16 to 20 years. It is not easy working with couples who are already at this stage of emotional disengagement. Intervening with this type of couple is one of the major clinical problems we will consider.

Myth: Monogamy Is Good, but Just for Women. Wrong

Let us also lay to rest the spurious sociobiological theories that men do not need monogamy, that men need to philander but women do not, and that monogamous marriage is a "female thing." This view has been promulgated in part by Helen Fisher (1993) in her book *The Anatomy of Love*. This is the general view that men need to philander and that women just have to get used to this fact. The argument is that this behavior is basically biological, part of male evolutionary heritage. There is, in fact, some truth to the argument that philandering by both genders has actually been a part of our reproductive strategies throughout our history as a species. It has been estimated that up to 20% of offspring are unrelated to the putative father of these children.

But portraying men as philanderers due to evolutionary factors? There is a fair amount of data to show that men actually benefit more from a committed marriage than women do! In a classic longitudinal study of longevity by Berkman and Syme (1979), being married predicted longevity for men but not for women (friendships were more important for women). In a famous analysis of this concept, Jessie Bernard (1982) also made this point, that marriages are more protective of men's health than women's. We believe that the sociobiological argument is overstated, and that the evidence supports the idea that a high-quality marriage is beneficial for *both* men and women. In fact, for many men, whose social support systems tend to be inferior to women's, marriage may provide the only close and supportive relationship they have. So, it is not the case that monogamy is just for women. Furthermore, historically it is men who have tried to enforce having exclusive rights to their wives!

Scientific analysis shows that the early data on gender differences in the frequency of extramarital affairs have been confounded by *opportunity*. Lawson (1988) found that, as women have entered the workplace in massive numbers, where they've had access to men other than their husbands, the number of extramarital affairs of young women has exceeded those of men (for a review, see Brown, 1991). According to Lawson, affairs now occur sooner in the marriage than in the past. Two thirds of the women and half of the men who were having affairs were in their first 5 years of marriage. Twenty years ago the comparable figure was 20%. The summary finding is that "social background does not significantly influence a person's tendency to have an affair. Affairs, however, are significantly associated with dissatisfaction with marital intercourse, and with personal readiness!" (Lawson, 1988, p. 6).

Myth: Gender Differences Cause Divorce. Wrong

This notion has become quite popular with the publication of John Gray's (1989) Mars–Venus books. However, a moment's reflection will show the logical fallacy in some of his writing.

Gender difference cannot explain divorce, because there is a male and a female both in couples divorcing and in those couples who may stay married—and all the males are "from Mars" and all the females are "from Venus." End of case. If gender differences are going to predict divorce, there has to be an *interaction* of gender differences with something (like marital conflict) that does the job of prediction.

There are, indeed, some reliable gender differences that do, in fact, manifest themselves only when there is intense marital conflict and the "vigilance system" of males is activated. These gender differences, in interaction with intense marital conflict, are differences in *attributional processes, physiological reactivity*, and *physiological recovery*. Later we propose why and how these differences are part of the evolutionary heritage of our species.

Relationship Satisfaction in Same-Sex Couples

We've conducted years of research on gay male and lesbian relationships. Levenson and Gottman conducted a 12-year longitudinal study of gay and lesbian couples (Gottman et al., 2003a). Using observational methods, that study revealed that in many ways gay male and lesbian couples' relationships were stronger than comparable heterosexual relationships. For example, gay male and lesbian couples were gentler in presenting issues, less defensive, and had a better sense of shared humor in responding to their partner during conflict discussions. Our mathematical modeling of their interaction confirmed this superiority (Gottman et al., 2003b). In our large-N RCU study we found significant and stable differences between same-sex and heterosexual couples when they presented for couples therapy. Same-sex couples starting couples therapy had stronger friendships than heterosexual couples, but had experienced more past trauma in their primary families. Lesbian couples were less likely and gay male couples more likely than heterosexual couples to present with an affair. In an uncontrolled outcome study done in collaboration with the Gay Couples Institute of San Francisco, we reported that Gottman method couples therapy was highly effective in treating both gay and lesbian couples, with a 2 standard deviation effect size (Garanzini et al., 2017). A weekend workshop (taught by our gay and lesbian therapists) was specifically designed to help same-sex couples.

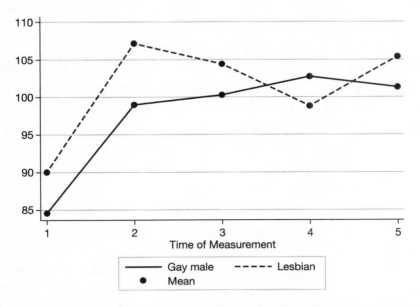

FIGURE 1.1: Relationship Satisfaction (MAT) for Gay and Lesbian Couples in Therapy Over Time

The Real Hope: Prevention

Recently, two intervention studies were conducted in Iran, one showing that Gottman method couples therapy was effective compared to a control group (Davoodvandi et al., 2018), and a second study showing that Gottman method couples therapy was more effective than emotion-focused couples therapy (Haavasi et al., 2018). The effect sizes of these interventions are promising, but they still need to be increased. There is much better news when it comes to preventing relationship problems. Take Markman and Stanley's PREP program. It works for people who aren't too unhappily married, but not for couples who are unhappily married.

In the 1990s we had two labs. One was our standard lab, just like the one Levenson and John had at Indiana University, and like the one John had at the University of Illinois. In that lab we started doing intervention research, trying to change couples' interaction with small exercises that would test our Sound Relationship House theory. The other lab was an apartment lab in which we saw 130 newlyweds. It was on the University of Washington medical school campus facing the beautiful Montlake Cut, in which boats moved from the salt water of Lake Union to the clear water of Lake Washington. It was a beautiful setting, made possible by the Center for Developmental Disabilities. They had their own shop, with engineers who built and fixed equipment for us. The apartment lab had a room for our standard method of the couple sitting down, facing one another, and having a conflict conversation for 15 minutes. That conversation had our usual array of physiological measures (respiration, heart rate, blood velocity to the middle finger of the nondominant hand, skin conductance, and gross motor movement). There was also the rating dial. We added our Oral History Interview, which we could now code from videos using the system Kim Buehlman and I developed. That system was able to predict which newlyweds would divorce and which would stay married with 94% accuracy. We also had this studio apartment in which a couple would spend 24 hours, free to move around with no instructions whatsoever. They each wore Holter monitors to record their electrocardiograms, and whenever they urinated we took a urine sample to measure stress hormones. There were three cameras bolted to the walls with remote pan, tilt, and zoom. The three cameras got merged into a split screen of only two cameras at a time. The lab was run by an enormously talented undergraduate, Jim Coan, who later became famous for his hand-holding brain relationship and research at the University of Virginia. The camera operators quickly noticed these frequent moments when one partner was trying to engage the other, which we called a "bid" for emotional connection. In these moments the control-room camera operator would find another camera that would get a headshot of the partner's response. If there was no response, we coded that exchange "turning away"; if there was any kind of response, even a grunt, we called that exchange "turning toward"; if there was a grumpy response (like "Will you be quiet, I'm trying to read"), we called the exchange "turning against" (which didn't happen very often). Later my student Janice Driver discovered that of the newlywed couples who later divorced (6 years later) they had only turned toward their partner's bids an average of 33% of the time. The newlywed couples who stayed together 6 years after their wedding had turned toward their partner's bids a whopping 86% of the time on average.

We followed the couples as many became pregnant, and John learned how to study baby–parent interaction from his old and illustrious friend Edward Tronick, a world expert on the subject, and infant physiology from his illustrious friend Steve Porges, who studied vagal tone in babies. Steve had discovered that he could measure the functioning of the vagus nerve (it's our 10th cranial nerve) using baby heart rate. Babies high in vagal tone could self-soothe when upset, focused attention better, cried less and laughed more, and were more responsive and healthier (less inflammation) than babies low in vagal tone. John collaborated with the Swiss psychologist Elisabeth Fivaz-Depeursinge, from Lausanne. Elisabeth had perfected analyzing the microanalytic structure of parent–infant interaction. With his student Alyson Shapiro, John followed the couples through pregnancy and again studied the interaction with their 3-month-old infant.

The results of this longitudinal study of newlyweds were remarkable. A full 67% of couples experienced a significant drop in relationship happiness after the birth of their first baby, and relationship satisfaction didn't ever recover 3 years after the baby's birth. Furthermore, a pregnancy Oral History Interview showed that some husbands changed philosophically with their wives during this transition to becoming a parent. They and their wives underwent major changes in their identity and thinking about their relationship and their future. They became a family unit. The husbands thought their pregnant wives were beautiful and they had sex often. Other husbands resisted these changes that their wives underwent. They distanced themselves from the pregnancy. They would engage in athletics (like skiing) without their wives, and do many things separately from their wives. They didn't become a comfortable family unit. In the pregnancy Oral History Interview these husbands thought their pregnant wives were unattractive and they had sex rarely during the pregnancy. One of these husbands said, "She's fat as a whale." Alyson also discovered that the SPAFF codes of the couple's conflict conversation in the lab a few months after their wedding significantly predicted which couples would have a hard time going through the transition to parenthood and which couples would have an easy time. The positive-to-negative ratio below 5.0 and the presence of the Four Horsemen predicted a difficult transition to parenthood.

Alyson discovered that the SPAFF coding of couples' conflict conversations in their last trimester could strongly predict the vagal tone of their 3-month-old baby, and predict how much their baby would laugh and cry. SPAFF codes accounted for half the variance in the baby's vagal tone, for example. Those couples whose relationship happiness dropped also had a lot of hostility in their post-baby marital interaction (coded double blind so that the coders didn't know which couples had had a baby and which hadn't). These couples' interactions with the baby were more uncoordinated and competitive, which made their baby cry, compared to couples whose relationship happiness didn't drop. The couples whose relationship happiness dropped had significant problems with sexual satisfaction 3 years after the baby's birth.

Nonetheless, one third of the couples sailed through the transition to parenthood and their babies were doing better than the other two thirds of the couples. Could we design an intervention, a 2-day preventive workshop for couples in their last trimester that would reverse this drop in relationship happiness and also avoid the couple's problematic interaction with their baby?

During this time Jay Belsky at the Pennsylvania State University and Philip and Carolyn Cowan at Berkeley were getting similar results about how hard this transition to parenthood was for most couples having a baby. The Cowans designed a couples' group intervention, but 6 years after baby the control and experimental groups were no different.

Our results were different, and our intervention was easy for nurse practitioners to do on their own. Working with two nurse practitioners, Joanie Parthemer and Carolyn Pirak, who specialized in giving birthing classes at Swedish Medical Center, Alyson, Julie, and John designed a workshop called Bringing Baby Home. The workshop had three components: (1) the importance of fathers and of keeping dads involved with the baby (for lesbian couples taking this workshop, we discussed what dads usually uniquely contribute in baby play, which can also be done by anyone else); (2) information about the social–emotional development of babies; and (3) skills in conflict management, maintaining friendship and intimacy, and the importance of the changing shared meaning system once people become parents. We then conducted a randomized clinical trial of our intervention, with a no-treatment control group. For 77% of the couples who attended the workshop there was no drop in relationship happiness, whereas the no-drop rate in the control group was again around 33%. Also, without intervention 62.5% of the new mothers developed symptoms of postpartum depression, whereas that figure was 23.5% for the workshop group. The average increase in relationship happiness in the workshop group compared to the control group was 60 points, which is a 4 standard deviation effect size. Based on the results of that study, we (John and Julie) wrote our first book together, titled *And Baby Makes Three*. We also noticed (Figure 1.2) that the workshop had a big effect on observed marital hostility, scored from videotapes (double blind—observers didn't know which group or time point they were scoring), and changes in indices of postpartum depression (Figure 1.3).

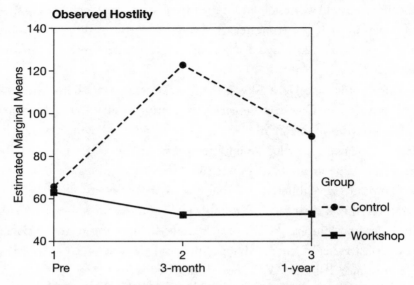

FIGURE 1.2: Changes in SPAFF-Scored Observed Hostility in the Two Groups Over Time

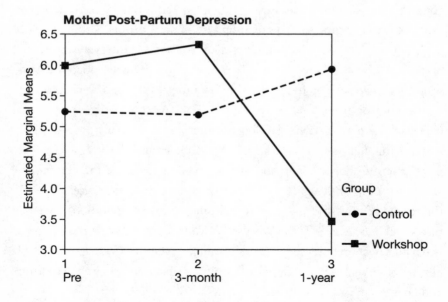

FIGURE 1.3: Changes in Maternal Postpartum Depression Over Time

Hostility in marital interaction increased in the control group over the course of a year and decreased in the control group. We later conducted a study on a version of Bringing Baby Home for the Administration of Children and Families called Loving Couples Loving Children. That intervention was tested with low-income married and unmarried couples about to have a baby. Results were mixed and hard to understand, in part because the evaluators of that intervention study used only an unreliable one-item measure of relationship happiness. However, the intervention did work best for African American couples, compared to Caucasian couples. Later that same program was extended slightly by adding biofeedback and employed with a sample of couples in a randomized clinical trial treating situational domestic violence. With a far more extensive and thorough measurement network used in our lab, that same intervention proved highly effective (see Chapter 18).

Our New Technology: Objective Video Replay

In this book we'll acquaint you with the technology we've developed recently that puts our Levenson–Gottman Love Lab at your fingertips. Since the COVID-19 pandemic we've developed this technology for using teletherapy as well as for live couples therapy. What this technology can now do is:

- Automate detecting partners' heart rates from video for any skin tone.
- Automate our specific affect (SPAFF) emotion coding; using machine learning, the automation does as well as the best human coders and can make that information rapidly available to the therapist.
- Integrate that information with the video-recall rating dial data, giving the therapist positive-to-negative ratios, and the trust metric.

One way for a therapist to use this information is to be able to offer a couple a dynamic portrait of them at their best and at their worst. In this way the algorithms guide video playback so the therapist and the couple can use actual objective and subjective data to understand where their interaction goes well and where it needs improvement. This technology offers the therapist a dynamic tool for incisive video playback.

To illustrate the potential of this technology, we will summarize a 2-minute events-of-the-day conversation a couple had on Gottman Connect. In the first 45 seconds of their conversation they were doing very well, sharing a great deal of positive affect. The couple had this conversation, and then did the video-recall rating dial task. In minutes the therapist had these data to discuss with the couple. Here's a transcript of the positive 45 seconds of their events-of-the-day conversation:

(Both laughing)
Wife (W): A lot going on.
Husband (H): You had a long day yesterday.
W: (laughing) I did, yeah, yeah.
H: Long.
W: I'm recovering. I mean, yeah, it was long. I'm (sigh) looking forward to a couple of days of rest.
H: Mmm-hmm.
W: I mean I can't wait until . . .
H: Before this weekend?
W: Before this weekend, well, no, this weekend will be restful, I . . .
H: Sure, sure . . . sure.
W: Parents gonna come, and take care of us, and uh (big sigh), yeah, relax and just . . .
H: Right.
W: So . . .
H: Well, good.
W: (nods) How are you feeling about work lately, and are you feeling a little busy with this weekend?
H: Well, yeah good, I'm, uh, work's good, I just got two more weeks and, uh, kind of wrapping things up and so it feels like light at the end of the tunnel.

The automated emotion codes show sequences of neutral affect to interest; that sequence is typical of a very nice interaction. There is a fair amount of laughter as well. The figure below is an automated summary of the software's analysis of their positive 45 seconds of interaction, showing them at their best. As you can see, their rating dial is high, the positive-to-negative ratios are nearly 5.0, which is very good, their heart rates are low, and their trust metrics are at 95%.

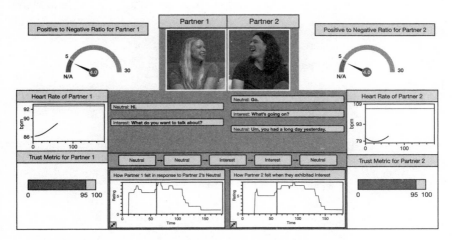

Reproduced with permission from Gottman Inc., www.gottman.com. Copyright Gottman Inc.

The conversation then takes a turn for the negative. Here is the transcript.

W: Oh, ah, I told my parents that they could stay in our room this weekend, so we're just gonna go on the couch, is that, are you good with that?

H: You already told them?

W: Yeah! I mean whatever, they're my parents, right?

H: (scoffs).

W: They're coming from so far away, like . . . it's—

H: It's just that you know I don't sleep well out there . . .

W: (frowns, disgust face) It's for the weekend, what's the big deal?

H: (shrugs) Well I wanna be like, you know, at my best with your parents, I don't want to be like, you know, grumpy because I didn't sleep . . .

W: Ohhh, (contempt face) it's not like you're at your best with my parents anyway, so . . .

H: Ohh . . . kay (scoffing laugh).

W: Well why are you making that face? It's just—

H: Well because, like I'm saying, I'm making an effort with your parents and I'm—

W: OK, well why has it taken three years to do that? Why is it just the weekend?

H: Three years, you don't think I've made an effort for . . .

W: No, you literally made my dad cry last weekend.

H: I didn't . . .

W: Like over the phone.

H: I wouldn't make him cry, what?

W: I was wishing him a happy birthday last weekend and you just had to say a snide comment?

H: I wouldn't . . . I was trying to be . . . funny and . . .

W: (looks away, rolls her eyes).

H: And I . . . how was I supposed to know your dad like . . .

W: You think, oh my God, OK just (shrugs) forget it.

Both: (stop talking).

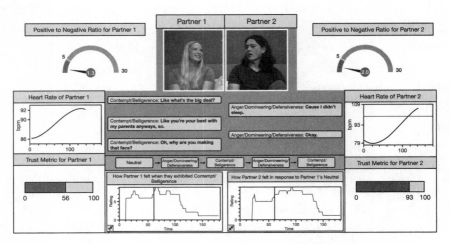

Reproduced with permission from Gottman Inc., www.gottman.com. Copyright Gottman Inc.

In contrast, this figure shows a summary of the software's automated analysis of their negative 75 seconds of interaction, showing them at their worst. Their rating dial plummets, the positive-to-negative ratios drop well below 5.0, into the red zone (seen as the dark gray area to the left of the dial in the reproductions in this book), which is very bad; their heart rates become elevated, his exceeding the cutoff of 100 beats a minute, and her trust metric plummets to 56%. Their specific affect sequences show the escalation from anger to contempt/belligerence. All of this playback and automated analysis is available to the couple and the therapist using this new technology.

In the next chapter we will specifically explore the implications of each partner's physiology on their relationship as we discuss flooding.

The Effects of Income Inequality

Strongly related to trust percentages, with low trust there are much bigger differences in the earnings of the richest and poorest people in a country or in a region within a country. With income inequality the entire region or country becomes more socially hierarchical. We want to alert you to the breakthrough work of British sociologists Richard Wilkinson and Kate Pickett in their first landmark book, from 2010, *The Spirit Level: Why Greater Equality Makes Societies Stronger*, and in their 2019 landmark book, *The Inner Level: How More Equal Societies Reduce Stress, Restore Sanity, and Improve Everyone's Well-Being*. In addition to their own work, they review an enormous amount of research literature by others in their books.

In the United States this vastly growing income gap between the richest 1% and the rest of the people—since about 1980—has become a huge area of political controversy in our time. One index is American CEO salaries, which had gone from 20 times the average worker's salary in 1960 to 400 times greater by 2010. The results of the research on income inequality are truly breathtaking. For example, in a now-classic work, Sir Michael Marmot's *The Health Gap*, in two regions of Glasgow a short bus ride apart there is a huge 20-year difference in longevity! Small earnings gaps even across neighboring levels in the UK civil-servant system also tracked gaps in health. The health-gap results of income inequality held throughout the world.

These are not small effects! Furthermore, their importance for the health

and well-being of individuals and entire communities and countries was unde-
niable. Let us briefly summarize some of the results of income inequality worldwide. There are many indices of income inequality, including comparing the
average incomes of the top and bottom 20% of the population in a region, and
the famous "Gini index." Here is a brief summary of these astounding results:

- Today's wealthy societies with income inequality have the following char-
  acteristics (compared to countries with less income inequality):
  – Worse physical health, and lower longevity. The effect is approximately
    the same as for smoking (meaning it's a large effect), about 10 to 17
    years less life. This effect also holds across states within the United
    States, and regions within the UK. The evidence is that people age
    more rapidly in income-unequal countries. These effects are present for
    all income levels in income-unequal countries.
  – Higher infant mortality and teenage births.
  – Greater incidence of mental illness, especially anxiety, depression, sui-
    cide, and alcohol and drug abuse. These differences are also true for
    manic-depressive disorder and schizophrenia.
  – Much higher crime and violence, with accompanying greater incarcera-
    tion rates, severely punitive sentencing in courts, more severely punitive
    prisons, and higher recidivism.
  – Increased marital hostility, higher divorce rates, and higher incidence of
    domestic violence.
  – Lower child achievement, lower adult literacy and academic achieve-
    ment, and higher child bullying, at 10 times the rate of more income-
    equal countries. These effects are present for all income levels in
    income-unequal countries.
  – Lower social mobility.
  – Poorer social relationships, less community participation, and less
    voting. There were also two experimental studies relating health
    to social relationship quality. In one experimental study by the
    Kiecolt–Glaser group, they induced wounds in volunteers, and
    found that marital hostility was related to slower wound healing. In
    a second experimental study, they gave volunteers a cold virus and

discovered that volunteers with fewer friends were more likely to get cold symptoms.

– It is important to point out that these are not just true of the poorest people in these unequal countries. *Everyone does worse in income-unequal countries!*

* There are vast *physiological* effects of income inequality. These include higher chronic stress levels in everyone, including:

  – Higher daily cortisol secretion. Cortisol is one of our major stress hormones.

  – Higher blood clotting factor (fibrinogen). Blood clotting is a useful result when the sympathetic nervous system is acutely activated in danger, in the event of hemorrhage. It is not helpful when it is chronically activated.

  – Higher systolic blood pressure (about 15 to 25 points). Also, in income-unequal countries blood pressure increases with increasing age, but it does not in more income-equal countries.

  – These physiological effects are present not just for the lowest social class levels. In the classic Whitehall studies of the British civil service, the effects were observable at *every* rank.

* There are also vast *psychological* effects of income inequality. These are best characterized by Susan Fiske, who wrote the book *Envy Up, Scorn Down*. Those at a lower income level envy those who are close to them but wealthier, and they have scorn and contempt for those close to them and less wealthy. These psychological effects include:

  – The *myth of meritocracy* abounds in income-unequal countries. Both the wealthier and the less well-off people in these counties falsely believe that wealthy people are somehow smarter, more talented, and more knowledgeable than less well-off people. That myth is false. Talented people come from everywhere.

  – People's self-worth tends more to be evaluated by social class and money.

  – People become much more materialistic with greater income inequality. We really love our stuff a lot more and stuff comes to represent self-worth.

  – Most people feel an omnipresent social evaluative pressure in social

interactions, resulting in greater shame the poorer one is. Poorer people at all levels of unequal countries feel more like failures, and they
respond to their enhanced social anxiety in one of two ways: (1) they
become depressed and withdrawn, becoming more socially isolated and
lonely, or (2) they become more self-aggrandizing and narcissistic, and
feel that they have to scrabble and compete to survive.

– Corporations in income-unequal countries become more competitive,
psychopathic, and narcissistic. The successful managers in these corporations tend to become more psychopathic and narcissistic. In fact,
in one study in the UK, 39 senior business managers were compared to
psychopathic criminals in a high-security prison. The business leaders
were higher on superficial charm, insincerity, egocentrism, manipula-
tiveness, exploitativeness, rigidity, stubbornness, dictatorial features,
and less on empathy than the criminals.

– Richer people in more income-unequal countries are less generous, less
likely to help old people or the disabled, more likely to cheat, and more
contemptuous and hostile toward others than in more income-equal
countries.

• Here is the important bottom line for us therapists: The quality of our clients' friendships and the quality of their love relationships matter hugely
in income-unequal countries. There is a much greater need to create better love relationships and trusting friendship networks in income-unequal
countries and regions. The effects of helping people make these changes
are powerful. We will also see many couples where a career focus has created emotion-dismissing behavior in one partner and great loneliness in
the other partner. According to the UCLA Sloan Center study of dual-
career couples in Los Angeles, these effects are even more serious if both
partners are overly career focused and are both emotion dismissing. They
tend to lead parallel lives with increasing emotional distance over time.

In 1994, we decided we had to do more—to take this research out of the ivory
tower and into the world. We wanted to try to create happier and healthier
relationships and provide more help to the clinicians, including ourselves,
who supported them. Together with our dear friend Etana Kunovsky, we

formed TGI to do systematic intervention research, workshops for couples, and training for therapists.

Our newest TGI lab, in downtown Seattle (with wireless physiology), is now run by our director of research, Carrie Cole. The new lab has seen 100 couples, who come in for the express purpose of getting their relationships evaluated and receiving our new manualized "marathon" couples therapy, in which we see a couple for 3 consecutive days for 5 hours a day. With our "Relationship Checkup," an online couples assessment, we have gathered questionnaire data from 150,000 couples to date. We have been doing weekend couples workshops with over 15,000 couples to date. We have also created workshops for therapists that have included about 50,000 therapists so far. We also now add 6 follow-up sessions to maintain gains and prevent relapse.

"Gottman Connect"

Four years ago, with our dear friends Rafael Lisitsa and Vladimir Brayman, we formed Affective Software (ASI) as a sister company to TGI. We designed it to create software and create the new 87 Gottman Relationship Coach videos to democratize couples therapy and bring the Levenson–Gottmans' Love Lab to every interested clinician's office in person (using an iPad or computer) or via teletherapy using a platform called GottmanConnect.com. We will be talking more about Gottman Connect in this book. With ASI's new, and HIPAA-compliant, platform and app and Gottman Connect, we have produced a version of our Love Lab that is now available for use in every therapist's office.

A validated and reliable set of questionnaires that we created (called the RCU) is available for partners to separately take online before their first visit to the therapist. The questionnaires take less than 1 hour to complete. Detailed analyses and treatment recommendations are available after the couple's RCU. If a clinician decides to add the Love Lab assessment to the RCU, an even more detailed assessment is created in a therapist's and couple's report.

Physiology can be assessed with Gottman Connect using inexpensive wireless pulse oximeters (which the couple purchase for their assessment). The physiological data are synchronized to the video. Pulse oximeters measure heart rate and percentage oxygen for every second of any videotaped interaction. If pulse oximeters are not selected by the therapist, an innovation that ASI has just patented allows us to read heart rate from the video for any skin tone. It turns out that the arrival of a bolus of blood pumped by the heart changes the face enough for a machine to read, even if these changes are invisible to a human observer. That information will eventually be made available to the therapist.

In Gottman Connect, the strengths and challenges in a particular relationship get assessed quantitatively with recommendations for treatment. During therapy it will eventually be possible to videotape any interaction the therapist chooses to record and have the couple rate for video playback. The software will then be able to select short video clips of the couple at "their best" and at "their worst" for viewing during a therapy session. "Best" and "worst" can be defined using either rating dial, SPAFF codes, or physiology.

Gottman Connect also can help direct a therapist to use any of our printed materials and handouts for intervention, including those recent 87 brief videos (arranged into 37 treatment modules) that form our Relationship Coach. A therapist can access all these videos for office use in couples therapy, or teletherapy. The therapist can also assign video modules as homework that couples can access on their cell phones; the app, together with videos, can be used by a couple in either "homework mode" or "crisis-intervention mode" between sessions. We hope that will help make the therapy last all week. The hardware and software of Gottman Connect are part of our new patent (U.S. Patent Office Patent No. 10,681,311). Coming soon in the Gottman Connect suite of programs is the automatic machine learning–based coding of specific emotions of the SPAFF (a new subpatent), time-synchronized to the video and rating dials, and all this information will be available to the therapist. This provides a new way of doing video playback, by presenting to a couple a video and analysis of themselves at their best and at their worst, using actual data for feedback. We are also now releasing an inexpensive app that couples can use on their cell phones to get automated help, without a therapist but with access to therapists, should they need help with the app. Our experience indicates that having such an app available makes it more rather than less likely that couples will seek out therapeutic help. The app will hopefully drive more distressed couples to therapy. Currently, we estimate that only 10% of all distressed couples ever see a therapist, and, of the ones who do, they wait an average of 6 years after significant problems develop before they ever talk to any professional.

CHAPTER 2

Physiological and Psychological Flooding

Why are our clients at times so mean to the people they love? In this chapter we explain one reason why conflicts escalate, why we therapists need to assess the couple's physiology during their interactions, and why taking breaks, self-soothing, and helping our clients create high "vagal tone" are so essential as potential goals of couples therapy. Furthermore, the resilience suggested by these findings is something we therapists can actually help our clients build in therapy.

Why do so many couple interactions become awful fights and regrettable incidents? How can we become so mean to the person we love? Why do so many conflicts become screaming matches where we are at our worst, and the Four Horsemen of the Apocalypse emerge from what seem like the smallest of issues?

In this chapter we will explore one major reason why lovers become enemies; one we call physiological and psychological "flooding." At the time of this writing, we are still the only major couples therapeutic method that includes this very important aspect of living with another person.

Our research over the past 50 years on couples and relationships has demonstrated that nearly all couples need to deal with elevated and diffuse physiological arousal and what we call flooding. John and Bob discovered that what predicted the deterioration of couples' relationships over time was the amount that their physiology became overly activated during couples' conversations. The faster their hearts beat, the faster their blood flowed, the more rapidly they breathed, the more their hands sweat, and the more they jiggled around, the more their relationships deteriorated over time. These were not very complex findings, but they were powerful predictors of relationship demise. Bob and John also discovered that chronic physiological arousal could even predict couples' future health.

First, let's discuss the *physical* aspect of flooding. The body has two stress axes. One is involved with the secretion of adrenaline and the other, with the secretion of cortisol. We start secreting these two stress hormones when our heart rate exceeds 100 beats a minute. The latter is called the "intrinsic" heart rate, the usual rate of our pacemakers. Our heart doesn't usually beat at this rate because the vagus nerve slows our heart down (Rowell, 1993). The vagus nerve acts as a brake on heart rate, but when we feel threatened, the vagus removes its inhibitory effect. Then our heart rate increases rapidly. To increase beyond 100 beats a minute, our sympathetic nervous system—which is our accelerator—starts increasing the heart's rate and also increasing the heart's contractility. The heart starts beating faster and contracting harder at each beat.

Why would this physiological arousal matter so much when it comes to understanding relationships? The reason is that when our body becomes physiologically aroused, or flooded, as described above, there are huge psychological effects that change the nature of our interaction with our partner, which we will explain later. But historically, through evolution, this adaptive mechanism has helped us deal with acute danger. When physiologically flooded, we sharply focus our attention on surviving and preparing to either fight or flee. For example, if we're facing a saber-toothed tiger, our ramped-up heart rate will turbocharge our efforts at fighting the tiger or running for our lives.

Here's a more current example: John and Julie were once driving from Seattle to Portland when an elderly woman entered the freeway going the wrong way. She had ignored the "Do Not Enter" signs, and both she and we were in the HOV lane rapidly bearing down on each other. John immediately moved to the next right lane over, and she sped by. Later, at the end of a workshop in which John told this story, a man in the audience came up and told him that it was his aunt. Turns out, fortunately, she didn't kill herself or anyone else that day. She just drifted into the median and fell asleep. The police took her back to her nursing home. What happened in John's body during this incident? When something like this happens to us, a cascade of physiological events occurs, all without us having control over them. This cascade includes the following:

Cascade of the Physical Effects of Flooding

What happens in our body when we are physiologically flooded? Here is some of what happens:

- We shut off blood supply to "nonessential" functions. This includes stopping blood to the gut to digest food, which is now unimportant; stopping blood to the kidneys to purify blood, which is now unimportant; stopping blood to the genitals, which are now unimportant; constricting arteries; pumping angiotensin into our blood to increase blood volume in the event of hemorrhage; and drawing blood from the arms and legs into the trunk to reduce the damage of hemorrhage.
- We secrete adrenaline and cortisol into the blood, to speed up metabolism.
- We convert glycogen in the liver into glucose to increase available energy.
- We maintain blood flow to the brain by keeping the carotid artery open.
- We increase blood clotting factor (fibrinogen) so our blood will clot faster in case of hemorrhage.

Two pioneering scientists, Jan Kiecolt-Glaser, a psychologist, and her husband, Ron Glaser, an immunologist, discovered the link between physiological arousal during marital conflict, and physical illness. They studied newlyweds in their first year of marriage. They used a unique procedure in which they took very small quantities of blood from the couple as the couple discussed an area of conflict. In other words, they measured the couple's hormones and neurotransmitters in their blood in real time, as they argued. Then they followed these newlyweds for 10 years. They found that those couples that eventually divorced years later, secreted 34% higher adrenaline during their conflict discussion in their first year of marriage than the couples who remained married—24% more adrenaline during the day, and 17% more adrenaline at night. Note that they were predicting the fate of these newlywed couples 10 years later, just by measuring adrenaline and noradrenaline in their blood during their first year of marriage! They examined another stress hormone, called adrenocorticotropic hormone (ACTH), which is responsible for releasing cortisol from the adrenal cortex. Cortisol is a stress hormone that has been related to sadness, depression, excessive rumination, separation panic in babies, resignation, giving up, and helplessness. In the newlywed women, ACTH was twice as high in those women whose marriages eventually wound up troubled. These results are also quite stable across laboratories (Kiecolt-Glaser et al., 2003). Effective prediction of the eventual fate of romantic relationships using physiology, observational data, and self-report data is now a well-established fact. That is very good news for the premise that assessment can and should precede intervention in couples therapy. The Glasers also studied the immune system and discovered that immunosuppression accompanied escalated conflict and the secretion of stress hormones. There was a marked decrease in the ability of T and B cells to fight an antigen and in the cytoxicity (killing ability) of natural killer cells in these newlyweds, even during one escalated conflict discussion. Because of this great research, we now know the mechanism linking some forms of hostile marital conflict with ill health.

In addition to this cascade of physical events, an entire cascade of *psychological* events also occurs, without our awareness. Here's a summary of these psychological effects. The amazing thing is that these things can happen to a couple even when they are sitting in our lab having a conversation and neither partner is physically in real danger. However, when flooded, they *perceive* themselves to be in danger.

The Psychological Effects of Flooding

There are huge psychological effects of being flooded. Here's a partial list:

- We feel very stressed out.
- We hate the way our body feels right now.

- We totally lose access to our sense of humor.
- We feel overwhelmed and disorganized.
- We can't take one more thing right now.
- It feels like all this came out of nowhere. It makes no sense.
- We feel attacked, unsafe, and in real danger.
- It is harder for us to think logically.
- We are more likely to see our partner as the enemy.
- We cannot take in, or process, any new information. Therefore, we become terrible listeners.
- We tend to "shut down" psychologically. We are no longer open-minded.
- We get a kind of "tunnel vision" because our peripheral vision is compromised.
- We literally cannot hear as well. John had no memory of Julie having said anything to him, because he couldn't hear very well at the moment of flooding.
- We get ready to act, usually to fight, or flee, or freeze, or otherwise withdraw.
- We would rather be anywhere in the universe other than here.
- If we're talking, we tend to repeat ourselves.
- We mistakenly believe that repeating ourselves will make our partner more agreeable.
- We believe if we repeat ourselves louder, we'll be more persuasive.
- We become less creative.
- It is harder for us to be effective problem solvers.
- It is harder for us to see things from our partner's perspective.
- It is harder for us to empathize with our partner.
- It is harder for us to be polite.
- It is hard to recall why we're with this person at all.
- We do not have very much access to newly acquired skills we've just learned in therapy.

Furthermore, over time a form of purely *psychological* flooding can arise, due to prior conditioning. Remember conditioning from your introductory psychology course? Place a rat in a box with a floor that can be electrified and that can deliver a very unpleasant electric shock to the rat. Turn on a white light in the box, and there's no response from the rat. Why should there be? But now pair the white light with the electric shock a few times, and the next time that just the white light comes on, the rat responds with total fear. The white light has become a conditioned stimulus for fear. In the same way, every escalated argument in which we get flooded is the equivalent of the electric shock. The equivalent of the white light can be just a raised voice, or a little irritability, and a full or partial physiological *sense* or memory of being physiologically flooded can then emerge, at an even earlier time than before. And even prior to actual physiological flooding, the argument can now escalate. In this way, conditioning can make conflict discussions progressively more aversive, and also more likely to occur sooner. Over time the relationship can become filled with regrettable incidents. Flooding can even potentially spill over into every interaction the couple has. So psychological flooding can also be a state of mind, and not necessarily a state of the body, just by the association with physiological flooding. That's why physiological flooding and psychological flooding may not always go together. Either one, however, is bad news for relationships. Here's why.

The Marital Standoff: The Zero-Sum Game

Flooded people feel fundamentally threatened and under attack during a conversation, and their state of mind makes cooperation and flexibility very difficult. This is because their primary way of thinking is inherently selfish, and it ought to be selfish, since survival of the self is the number one goal when feeling threatened. They think that they need to push their point of view forward by any means, even tyrannically. This implies that physiologically or psychologically flooded people are in a win–lose mentality, a zero-sum game. In a zero-sum game there is but one winner and one loser. The partner necessarily becomes one's adversary. Therefore, for the flooded person, stubbornness prevails, we get the standoff, and the power struggle becomes the modus operandi. There may be other reasons for the standoff, but being threatened is one of the major reasons we see in our data. Another major reason is what we call "triggers," in which people's enduring vulnerabilities become activated, and they feel threatened because they are actually in a post-trauma state. We will talk about how we deal with triggers when we discuss how to process regrettable incidents (in Chapter 13). Daniel Siegel calls flooding "flipping one's lid" because the frontal cortex goes "off-line" and rational thought and cooperation become less accessible.

Assessing Flooding: The Pulse Oximeter

As part of our pre-intervention assessment, we use two pulse oximeters when a couple have their two 10-minute conversations, the events-of-the-past-week and conflict conversations. These little devices are used in every operating room in the world. They are reliable and inexpensive. They became very popular during the COVID pandemic. Every couples therapist should get two of them to use in couples therapy. It may also be a good idea to have your clients buy two of them to use at home. The pulse oximeter gives us two measures every second: (1) the heart rate in beats per minute, and (2) the percentage of oxygen in the blood. Some pulse oximeters come with an audible alarm. We set that alarm to go off if the heart rate exceeds 100 bpm, or the percentage of oxygen becomes less than 95% (which means the person is not breathing deeply and is depriving the brain of oxygen). We use the pulse oximeters so we'll know if people become flooded during these two conversations. We now have a patent that makes it possible to get heart rate reliably directly from video, for any skin color. That's possible because the

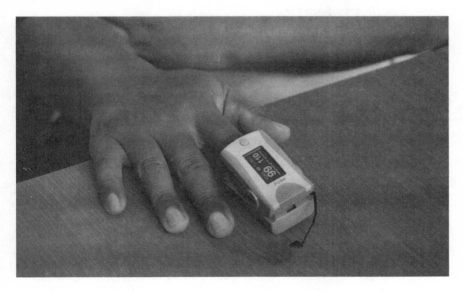

face darkens a bit when the pulse pressure wave from the heart arrives in the face. It is not visible to the human eye, but a machine-learning algorithm can detect it reliably, assuming the video is not overly corrupted.

The Good News

The good news is that after just a *real* 30-minute break (one without rumi-nations), access to our communication skills and more normal states of mind more or less returns. Why do we italicize the word "real" in the last sentence? Because it takes at least 30 minutes for the stress hormones to metabolize out of our bloodstream and into our bladder, where they are no longer having an effect. After getting flooded, then taking a real break and returning to the conversation, it looks like we've had a brain transplant. Our ability to listen comes back. Our ability to empathize comes back. We can now take in new information. We have access to newly acquired skills. Our sense of humor comes back. Our rational mind comes back. We can now be fully present and pay attention. We have done this experiment in our lab and learned that taking a break actually works to interrupt flooding and stop it from derailing a conversation.

Experimental Verification of Taking a Break
From Conflict as Soothing

In a randomized clinical trial, we interrupted the conflict discussion of cou-ples with one of two breaks in which the couple read magazines for 20 min-utes without talking to one another before resuming the conflict discussion. There were 20 couples in each condition. In one condition we had them do the video-recall rating dial procedure before they took the break, and in another condition, we postponed the video-recall rating until after the sec-ond conflict discussion. The first break condition was designed to simulate a "damaged break," with rumination about what had happened during the previous conflict discussion. The second condition was designed to simulate a real break, with non-rumination and relaxation, then returning to the conversation. Both conditions were successful in significantly lowering both partners' heart rates. However, only in the second relaxation break did the reduction in heart rate also result in significantly less of the Four Horsemen and more neutral affect when the conflict discussion resumed. Furthermore, the effect was obtained only for husbands, not for wives, to explain which we hypothesized on the basis of a consistent finding that women ruminate more about conflict than men.

Therefore, a break has to be a *real* break. Here are the essential points of a real break.

- First, in calling for a break, couples have to stop on a dime, stop talking immediately, and not finish what they were about to say. They can't try to get in the last word.
- Also, during the break couples cannot ruminate about the conversation they just had. Rumination will just maintain physiological or psychological flooding.
- Couples also have to physically get away from one another. Couples shouldn't stay in the same room, if they can avoid it.
- Couples cannot plan what to say when they return. They cannot keep feeling righteously indignant, or feeling like an innocent victim. They can't be having a pity party for themselves. They also can't be nursing a grudge.
- Couples have to totally distract themselves during the break. They have to breathe deeply and slowly. They can do whatever is calming. Do systematic muscle relaxation, tensing and relaxing muscle groups (see relaxation instructions in the appendix of this book). They can go for a walk, listen to music, read magazines, play an instrument, work out if they enjoy exercise, take a bath or shower, play a video game if it isn't an aggressive one, or do anything that is fun and takes their mind off the previous interaction.

Vagal Tone

We have mostly been talking about the "accelerator" pedal on our metabolism, the automatic actions of the sympathetic branch of our autonomic (or automatic) nervous system. It's a system that has evolved in mammals to keep us safe. There is another branch of that automatic system that acts like a "brake" on physiological arousal, and it can restore calm to our body after the real or imagined danger has passed. That branch is called the "parasympathetic" nervous system.

Now here's what's interesting. Unlike the sympathetic, the parasympathetic has one major nerve. It happens to be the largest nerve in our body. Because it's so large the Latin form of its name was the "vagabond nerve," or, in Latin, the *vagus* nerve. It starts in the brain stem as one of our 12 cranial nerves. It's number 10. It then extends from the brain stem to innervate the lungs, heart, gut, kidneys, and genitals.

This nerve is really important. A great deal of research on the vagus nerve was conducted by John's friend Steven Porges and discussed in his landmark 2011 book, *The Polyvagal Theory*. It turns out that when this nerve is functioning well, which is called having "high vagal tone," a number of very good things happen. We are more and not less responsive to emotion. We return more rapidly to being calm after we're flooded. Therefore, we're both more reactive and more resilient. With high vagal tone, we tend to smile and laugh more often. We are ready to interact cooperatively. We tend to notice more, so we're more apt to see attempts our partner is making to emotionally connect with us (which we call bids for connection). We are also less likely to be the victims of inflammation, and we have fewer stomach and bowel disorders. We're calmer and healthier. We can focus our attention more easily. We can also shift attention more rapidly when we have to.

And, most important, with high vagal tone we can wait at least two beats before we respond to our partner. Waiting two beats reduces our reactivity. It gives us a chance to say something helpful like "I can see you're upset. I'm listening." It can help down-regulate our own defensiveness, which we believe is, in fact, the major "work" we need to do to make relationships work well.

Now here's the *really* good news. You can actually help *build* your own vagal tone, or the vagal tones of your clients. The evidence is that high vagal tone can be built by mindful meditation. It can also be built with a small biofeedback device called the emWave2, made by a company called Heart-Math. We've used the emWave2 in our clinical work for the past 15 years, and we've done research with it with situationally violent couples. The emWave2 works through a fascinating phenomenon in our bodies. That phenomenon is called RSA, which stands for respiratory sinus arrhythmia. Let us explain. The time between two large spikes of the electrocardiogram (called the R-wave) decreases when we inhale and increases when we exhale. That means that in the time between beats there is a respiratory rhythm. It measures how much controlling our breathing also controls our heart rate. That RSA is a measure of vagal tone, and a very useful one. With the emWave2 you put a clip on your earlobe. If there's very little vagal tone in your body at the moment, then a light on the device goes red. If there's a bit more vagal tone, that same light will turn blue. If there's a high vagal tone, that same light turns green. While you use the device and "get into the green zone," you are instructed to think purely positive thoughts, perhaps about something you love unequivocally or something you feel grateful for. It can be a favorite walk in the woods, a favorite place, a pet, or a person. The HeartMath company has data showing that if you get into the green zone 10 minutes in the morning and 10 minutes at night, and do this every day for a year, your vagal tone will significantly increase. You'll also probably become less angry and less anxious, be able to self-soothe more easily, be able to focus attention better, and maybe even sleep better.

In our clinical practices for the past 15 years, we have been using the emWave2 to have each partner get into the green zone for 5 minutes before the couple have their next conversation. We have also used the emWave2 in research on effectively treating situational domestic violence. People can use the emWave2 during their breaks and use it to get into and stay in the green zone. It can also facilitate meditation.

© HeartMath Inc. Reproduced with permission.

Summary: Flooding and Taking Breaks

What Exactly Is Being "Flooded"?

It's mostly a state of *mind,* and often it is also a state of physiological arousal. Ask your clients the following questions:

- Do you feel like you'd rather be anywhere on the planet than in this room talking to this person?
- Do you feel attacked or unsafe?
- Did this attack seem to come out of nowhere?
- Do you feel overwhelmed and disorganized by all the negativity?
- Does this feel like your partner is being unkind or selfish?
- Do you want to leave?
- Do you feel unappreciated?
- Do you feel blamed?
- Do you feel picked on?
- Does this all feel totally unfair?
- Do you feel like right now your partner doesn't even like you?
- Do you hate the way your body feels right now?

If your client answers yes, then they are probably flooded.

What's Happening in Your Physiology?

Sometimes physiological arousal does accompany flooding. Sometimes it doesn't, but prior conditioning takes over. Your **state of mind** is the most important clue. We also know that if your heart rate is above 100 beats a minute—if you're an Olympic athlete make that 80 beats a minute—you are probably flooded. Above that heart rate your body has started secreting adrenaline, and lots of systems are firing (e.g., the heart is pumping more rapidly, contracting harder, and arteries are constricting). That research was spearheaded by Loring Rowell, the world's expert on the cardiovascular system's response to stress (Rowell's book is called *Human Cardiovascular Control.*) Remember, in flooding we will get "tunnel vision," so that we cannot process information very well, we actually cannot hear as well, our peripheral vision is compromised, we lose our sense of humor, we lose philosophical perspective, we can't be creative problem solvers, we can't empathize, and we will want to withdraw or become more aggressive, because we want to shut down all that negativity and attack coming from out of nowhere at us. That means we can't listen very well when we're flooded. We will want to withdraw, or we'll want to get mean. We have exceeded our "carrying capacity" for our partner's negative affect. So we should not keep talking when we are flooded!

A sure sign—we keep repeating ourselves. When people become flooded they often repeat themselves, which we call the "summarizing yourself syndrome." We will find ourselves actually thinking something like "If I repeat my point of view I just know that my partner will respond by saying something like 'Oh, now I get what you're saying. I now totally agree with you. Now let's have sex.'" There was a couple John was once working with. The wife said to her husband, "I don't think you're listening to me." John could tell he was flooded because he next said, "OK, then, let me repeat my position." John then said, "OK, you're flooded." He replied, "No, I'm not." John said, "I can tell you are flooded because what you just said was illogical and you're usually a very logical person." The husband thought for a moment and said, "Oh, I should ask *her* to repeat *her* position!" John said, "Right!" It was time for a break using the emWave2. The bad news here is that most people cannot tell when they are flooded. A lot of that research was done by a psychologist named Ed Katkin. We encourage people to just say "I'm flooded. I need a break." During the actual break we can engage in paced breathing at 10 breaths a minute, which will relax us.

Tried and Tested Solutions (Tested in Levenson–Gottmans' Lab) When Clients Are Flooded

1. Whenever the pulse oximeter beeps, say, "I'm flooded, I need a break." Stop talking immediately. Stop on a dime, do not try to finish your point. Immediately take a break. Repeat: Stop talking if one of you is flooded (or feeling flooded). Go to separate rooms. Be out of acoustic contact.

2. Make this an OK neutral ritual in your relationship. Add a hand signal you agree on when your pulse oximeter tells you that you're flooded. (Don't use the rude hand signal you're probably thinking of.) Always let your partner take a break if you see this hand signal from your partner.

3. The break must last at least 30 minutes. You can't be thinking thoughts that maintain physiological arousal, like thoughts of getting even, or righteous indignation. Listen to music, or take a walk, or a hot bath. Or work out.

4. To avoid feelings of abandonment, make an appointment to come together again and talk. Don't wait too long. Even if you're still flooded, check in with each other. If you're still flooded, give it another 30 minutes. Check in again. And so on.

5. Remember, the break must involve you doing something very relaxing, like taking a walk or a bath. If possible, try to do things that put you in a positive affective state (e.g.: interest, affection, humor, empathy, peacefulness, loving thoughts).

6. During the break you cannot be rehearsing thoughts that maintain your distress. These are usually thoughts of your own righteous indignation or feeling like an innocent victim. Do not *ruminate* over the details of your last conversation.

7. Go through the following steps of relaxation (see our appendix materials for specific instructions to use):
   – Deep abdominal breathing, about 10 breaths a minute. The emWave2 will help you do it.
   – Tense each muscle group, and first hold the tension (for 4 seconds) in that major muscle group, then let it go. Relax.
   – After each muscle group is tightened, then relaxed, notice how this muscle group feels heavy, and warm.
   – Take yourself to a special peaceful place in your mind.

In the next chapter we talk about our focus on interaction *process* as we talk about Dan Wile's approach to "solving the moment" as part of his collaborative couples therapy.

CHAPTER 3

Solving the Moment, or "Doing a Dan Wile"

*In this chapter we discuss one method we use in many sessions.
It is called "doing a Dan Wile." This method highlights how our
therapy is experiential and emotion focused. We are often just
solving the moment. Here's how we do it.*

We use many of Dan Wile's methods within our own work. So . . .

Who Was Dan Wile?

Dan was a great therapist who lived in Oakland, California. Dan was our very good friend. Unfortunately, Dan died in 2021 of a fatal heart condition. He and his wife, Dorothy Kaufmann, had completed his last book, titled *Solving the Moment*. We suggest that you get that book and memorize it. We have.

Dan also wrote three other wonderful books: *After the Honeymoon*; *Couples Therapy*; and *After the Fight*. Please read them. All of them. You will really enjoy his legacy, we're sure of it. John studied with Dan Wile. He sat in Dan's basement and watched videos of Dan's work with couples. It was very enlightening. We want to share his work with you, because it is so very useful.

We have always honored Dan Wile's approach to couples therapy, which he called "collaborative couples therapy." We also honor Dan because he alone intuitively anticipated many of our research findings. For example, he intuitively knew that most relationship problems are perpetual. In a remarkably insightful book, *After the Honeymoon*, Dan Wile (1988/2008) wrote, "Choosing a partner is choosing a set of problems" (p. 12). He wrote that problems are a part of any relationship, and that a particular person would have some set of problems no matter who that person married. The perpetual problems may be different in a different relationship. Presciently, Dan wrote:

> *Paul married Alice and Alice gets loud at parties and Paul, who is shy, hates that. But if Paul had married Susan, he and Susan would have gotten into a fight before they even got to the party. That's because Paul is always late, and Susan hates to be kept waiting. She would feel taken for granted, which she is very sensitive about. Paul would see her complaining about this as her attempt to dominate him, which he is very sensitive about. If Paul had married Gail, they wouldn't have even gone to the party because they would still be upset about an argument they had the day before about Paul's not helping with the housework. To Gail, when Paul does not help she feels abandoned, which she is sensitive about, and to Paul, Gail's complaining is an attempt at domination, which he is sensitive about. The same is true about Alice. If she had married Steve, she would have the opposite problem, because Steve gets drunk at parties and she would get so angry at his drinking that they would get into a fight about it. If she had married Lou, she and Lou would have enjoyed the party but then when they got home the trouble would begin when Lou wanted sex because he always wants sex when he wants to feel closer, but sex is something Alice only wants when she already feels close. (p. 13)*

Wile also wrote:

> *There is value, when choosing a long-term partner, in realizing that you will inevitably be choosing a particular set of unsolvable problems that you'll be grappling with for the next ten, twenty, or fifty years. (p. 13)*

So, Dan thought, instead of solving the whole relationship, let's work on just **solving the moment**. We also honor Dan because his approach to couples' communication makes so much sense to us. Many of our faculty at TGI trained with Dan.

The Collaborative Conversation

Dan viewed a therapy session as a search for collaboration instead of the conversation turning into one of two "fallback positions": attack or withdrawal. In the fallback position of attack, the couple enters the "adversarial cycle." In the adversarial cycle the partner is cast as the enemy ("You're not for me, you're against me"). In the fallback position of withdrawal, the couple enters the "withdrawal cycle." In the withdrawal cycle the partner is cast as the stranger ("I don't know who you are right now"). There is also a third fallback position, in which one person attacks and the other withdraws. The psychologist Andrew Christensen at UCLA has intensively studied this position. It's not a myth. It actually characterizes many unhappily married couples. This third fallback position was first noticed by psychologist Virginia Satir, who called it the "pursuer–distancer" fallback position. In that fallback position, one partner seeks greater emotional connection and the response of the partner is to create greater emotional distance. The goal in Dan Wile's therapy is to get the couple to enter the collaborative cycle.

In these three fallback positions, Dan wrote, there is always a "leading-edge feeling." In these fallback positions the emotions people have often also include a loss of voice, so it can be helpful if the therapist speaks for them in that moment, using empathy to reflect their emotions, or at least guessing what they are actually feeling, much of it unsaid. The leading-edge feeling may be anger, sadness, disappointment, hurt, disgust, or fear. Or it can even be some blend of the emotions. However, most of the time people actually feel a complex constellation of emotions, including some unsaid positive emotions and some unsaid negative emotions.

Doubling

In moving a couple from attack, defend, withdraw, or attack–withdraw the therapist helps the couple create a platform from which they can self-disclose what they are feeling and thinking. To facilitate the collaborative conversation the therapist uses a tool called **doubling**. In doubling the therapist speaks as if they were one of the partners. Let's say Rose is the partner for whom the therapist is doubling. The therapist is speaking *for* Rose—as well as *to* Rose—saying something like "Let me see if I can speak for you, Rose, and correct me if I get this wrong." Dan Wile generally moved out of his chair and squatted or knelt beside the person he was speaking for, but he said that tactic is not absolutely necessary, although he did say that it made doubling more powerful. We've done that less often as our knees have given us more trouble. In doubling for a partner, the therapist uses the following principles:

- *Principle 1:* The therapist changes the tone. The therapist softens an attack tone of voice, or facial expression, making the same feelings neutral, or more gentle, sometimes talking *about* the feelings rather than talking *from* the feelings. When the therapist encounters anger, the therapist talks about the anger.
- *Principle 2:* The therapist adds more vulnerable feelings (but not denying anger if it is there). The therapist can recast complaints as wishes or fears. The therapist may also add positive feelings that haven't been expressed.
- *Principle 3:* The therapist makes acknowledgments of what the therapist thinks are the *other partner's* feelings and needs. At times this may require scanning hard for acknowledgments. Sometimes the acknowledgment can be just reporting the partner's state of mind.
- *Principle 4:* The therapist reports the couple's predicament right now. At times the therapist can turn a partner's monologue into a dialogue by appending a question that that person hasn't yet asked, or can ask a speaker to respond to a sentence completion (e.g., adding "and you would need . . . ?").

We suggested to Dan that he add another step: Once the therapist checks with the partner to make sure their words have accurately represented the partner spoken for, the therapist then adds, "Rose, can you please now try to say that in your own words?" In that way, the therapist is facilitating an actual collaborative conversation in which vulnerability in self-disclosure mode is substituted for attack–defend or withdraw. This process is called "solving the moment." Eventually, and hopefully, the couple will do this solving the moment on their own.

Example. This is just one brief example of how solving the moment can work. The therapist can get creative and poetic to make these interventions more powerful.

Herb: Sheila, I hate the fact that you are drinking again. Yesterday you attacked our daughter Vera at dinner, and I think that was just uncalled for. As I get closer to Vera I can see how domineering you are and I am now thinking of leaving you.

Sheila: Go ahead and leave, Herb, it's what you always do. You're good at leaving, just like you left as a father all those years, and I had to totally raise Vera on my own, like a single parent, so I know her far better than you do. What I said to her was perfect, but you just cannot see it.

Therapist doubling for Herb: Herb, let's see if I can speak for you, and correct me if I get this wrong. Sheila, I know that I left you to do most of the child rearing, and I regret that now that I'm getting closer to Vera. I can see why you're angry with me. I know you are a great mother. I should appreciate you more as a great mom. But I get worried about Vera, and I get scared about you putting her down, which only happens when you're drinking. I know I said I was thinking of leaving, but I really don't want to do that. I just get desperate to help Vera now that I'm starting to try to be a better dad to her. Does that come close to what you're feeling, Herb? In what way was I wrong, and in what way was I right in capturing how you feel?

Herb: Yes, that's exactly what I said.

Therapist: Hmm.

Herb: Or what I meant to say.

Therapist: Right. Can you now put this in your own words, Herb?

Herb: Sure. Sheila, you've done all the parenting. I know that and I haven't been much of a helper to you, or much of a good dad to Vera. I know that. But since my heart attack last year I decided to be a better father to her and a better husband too. So I started noticing that she needs more self-confidence. How do you think I can help her without putting you down?

Sheila: Well, Herb, you can start by showing me some respect. Try helping me around the house. I'm not going to live this way, doing everything myself, and taking care of Vera, and taking care of you too, since you're a cardiac patient. I am not your nurse!

Therapist: Let me see if I can speak for you, Sheila, and correct me if I get this wrong.

Therapist doubling for Sheila: Herb, I am glad that you have made these vows to become a better dad and a better husband since your heart attack. And I applaud you trying to get closer to Vera. I'm having a little trouble, though, getting over my own anger at you for being gone so long. You criticizing how I talk to Vera and blaming me for drinking a few glasses of wine at dinner is just making me feel very defensive. I am going to need a lot more appreciations from you, and more respect from you about how hard I work at making our home beautiful and being a mother. Please join in, and help out. It would go a long way with me. Sheila, in what way was I wrong, and in what way was I right in capturing how you feel?

Sheila: Well, you got it mostly. I just would add that he expects me to take care of him now too, and I'm just unwilling to do that.

Therapist: OK, that makes sense. Can you tell him how you feel in your own words?

Sheila: I'll try. Herb, it's good news you want to improve. He's right about that. I'll cheer you on. But for God's sake take some direction from me. I really know our daughter. And don't align with her *against* me. Try to support me in front of her. If you disagree with me, talk to me about it privately. I'll listen. I will. And I am *not* drinking, Herb. I'm just not. And I need to talk to you about your needs for nursing support. I don't want to take that on too.

And so on ...

In addition to Dan Wile's doubling method for solving the moment to maximize collaboration, we believe that a couple also needs blueprints and specific communication skills that also facilitate collaboration. To accomplish that, we need a theory. The next chapter talks about our theory, the Sound Relationship House.

CHAPTER 4

The Sound Relationship House Theory

In this chapter we describe our theory of what makes relationships succeed or fail. The Sound Relationship House (SRH) theory is the basis of all our assessments and all our interventions.

Prediction isn't the same as understanding. The fact that Bob and John were able to predict the future of a relationship with high accuracy did not imply that we understood how to help couples. For example, we discovered that, among newlyweds, shared humor during conflict reduced physiological arousal, and it predicted good things over time for a relationship. How could we use that to actually help people? Could we just tell a couple to laugh more the next time they had a conflict discussion? Believe it or not, that intervention was actually tried (not by us). It didn't work. However, later in this chapter we will tell you the secret of getting a couple to laugh together more during conflict. The finding may surprise you. It did surprise us.

We quickly realized that to help couples we needed a theory. We also wanted to build a theory that could be proved wrong, a disconfirmable theory, one in which we could measure every concept in the theory reliably and accurately in our lab. We thought that if we could measure it, maybe we could build it. We also wanted to extend that measurement to therapists, with the idea that assessment ought to precede intervention.

The figure below is our theory of what makes relationships succeed or fail, the SRH theory. The figure is drawn as a house with each floor and wall representing a component of our theory. When working with clients, we often move from one floor or wall to another, but in no particular order. We choose what interventions to apply at any given moment, depending on what the couple presents at that moment. In other words, we follow the couple's lead.

The first three levels of the house describe how to strengthen friendship in relationships. Now here's part of the great thing about being scientists. We can't just say, "Friendship is important in relationships." We have to be able to define what we mean, which automatically gives us a potential recipe for success. Our research points to these three important builders of relationship friendship: (1) building love maps, (2) sharing fondness and admiration, and (3) turning toward instead of away. Let's talk about each of these three in turn.

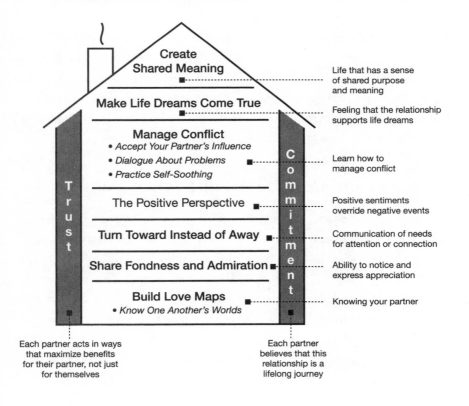

The Sound Relationship House

Create Shared Meaning — Life that has a sense of shared purpose and meaning

Make Life Dreams Come True — Feeling that the relationship supports life dreams

Manage Conflict
• Accept Your Partner's Influence
• Dialogue About Problems
• Practice Self-Soothing
— Learn how to manage conflict

The Positive Perspective — Positive sentiments override negative events

Turn Toward Instead of Away — Communication of needs for attention or connection

Share Fondness and Admiration — Ability to notice and express appreciation

Build Love Maps
• Know One Another's Worlds
— Knowing your partner

Trust

Commitment

Each partner acts in ways that maximize benefits for their partner, not just for themselves

Each partner believes that this relationship is a lifelong journey

1. Build Love Maps

A love map is a road map you create in your mind of your partner's inner psychological world. It is the most basic level of friendship. It's about knowing your partner well, and feeling known by your partner in the relationship. And that interest doesn't shut down over time. What are your partner's worries and stresses at the moment? Do you know? What are some of your partner's hopes and aspirations, what are some of your partner's dreams, values, and goals in life? What is your partner's mission in life that guides their actions? How do you learn answers to questions like these? By asking questions, open-ended questions that you want to know the answer to. Not closed-ended questions like "Did you call the plumber?" During courtship and dating, it's common to ask each other questions just to get to know one another. But then life gets busy, and the questions drop off. Still, we all evolve over time, and as we change, our answers will change, too, as we grow. That's why it's so important for partners to build in time to ask each other questions like these, and listen well to the answers. When people ask open-ended questions, it's an invitation, another way of saying, "I'm still interested in who you are—your feelings, needs, values, and dreams." To build love maps for a relationship: (1) ask questions you're interested in, (2) remember the answers, and (3) keep asking new questions. One can't have a deep friendship without knowing the kind of person your partner is.

2. Share Fondness and Admiration

This level of the Sound Relationship House refers to both partners feeling and expressing affection and respect for one another. There are two parts. First, individuals need a habit of mind that guides them to look for characteristics to love, admire, and be proud of in their partner. Second, the love, admiration, and pride in their partner needs to be expressed—in other words, the feelings need to come out of the mouth in words, or be expressed non-verbally and affectionately, not just tucked away. Most people don't always feel loved and worthy of respect on a daily basis. It's easy for people to begin doubting there's love if it's not shown. Partners need to hear the words and feel the affection throughout their relationship, not just during the dating or honeymoon phase. They also need to watch for their partner's beloved qualities. Then say words like "I saw how you handled that, and I was so proud of you," or "I love how generous you are." In this way couples actively build a culture of love and respect together that nourishes their friendship.

3. Turn Toward Instead of Away

When people are just hanging out together, they actually are often letting their needs be known to one another in small ways, either nonverbally or verbally. We call this making bids for connection. A bid is the most fundamental unit of emotional connection. Bids for connection unfold in two steps: first the bid, and then the response to the bid. In a bid, partners verbally or nonverbally signal that they need attention, interest, and conversation; or shared humor, affection, warmth, and empathy; or help and assistance, support, and so on. These tiny two-step moments of emotional connection really form a kind of bank account, what we call an "emotional bank account," that gets built over time. It's important in the relationship that each partner make bids, rather than presuming that their partner is a mind reader and magically knows what they need. Needs can be hard to express, especially when they're big asks. Many people have been shamed in the past for having any needs at all. Being too "needy" is an often-heard criticism, aimed at women especially. However, it's important to remember, we humans are pack animals—we never could have survived throughout history without gathering in pairs and in groups to help one other in all kinds of ways. Relationships function best when both partners are clear about what their needs are, and are not afraid to convey them. Remember, too, that a person who expresses their needs is giving their partner an opportunity to feel trusted, needed, and possessing strengths of value. Thus, making bids for connection functions as a gift for both giver and receiver.

Now, how about the response to a bid for connection? In a study of newlyweds who spent 24 hours in our apartment lab, it took 7 years to spot what couples were doing that differentiated the ones who, 6 years down the road, will have stayed together happily from those that will have separated and divorced. We saw that couples responded to each other's bids for connection in one of three ways: (1) turning away, (2) turning against, or (3) turning toward. Here's what each of these responses looks like: (1) Partners who turn away from bids for connection simply ignore their partner's bid, and act as if nothing has been said. In other words, they leave the person making the bid feel ignored, unimportant, invisible, and devalued. Here's a simple example: One partner gazes out the window, and says, "There's a pretty boat . . . " The other partner does nothing and says nothing, effectively giving no response—that's turning away. (2) Partners who turn against a bid respond with hostility and negativity, often hurting the feelings of the person who's made the bid, which in turn discourages them from making future bids. Picture a sea anemone that has opened its many arms to reach out. Poke it, and what happens? It closes up and shrinks away. That's the effect of turning against the bidding partner. In the above example, "There's a pretty boat," a turning-against response would sound like "Will you be quiet? I am trying to read!" Ouch. (3) A turning-toward response is the one we want to see. It's as simple as "There's a pretty boat . . . " and the responder says (while looking out the window), "Huh." That's all that turning toward takes. A simple utterance the responder makes that signals to the bidder that they've been listened to and the responding partner is interested in what they've just said. Good enough. That makes all the difference between a couple whose relationship lasts and a couple whose relationship later falls apart. Of course, there are also the champion responders who turn toward their partner's bids *enthusiastically*. Here's what that response looks like: The same bid . . . "There's a pretty boat," and the response, "Wow, that *is* a beautiful boat. Hey, baby, let's quit our jobs and get a boat like that and sail away together, what do you say?" But, bottom line, any kind of turning-toward response builds up the emotional bank account. And with a sizable account, there's plenty of good feelings left over even when a bad fight takes a big chunk of change out of the account. In our research, when we looked back at the apartment-lab videos of our newlywed couples, we saw that couples who 6 years later divorced turned toward each other's bids only 33% of the time. But the couples who 6 years later remained happily together turned toward each other's bids 86% of the time. That's a huge difference.

A fundamental process of helping couples increase turning toward is for each partner to increase their awareness of how their partner makes bids. Sometimes a partner's bids may be a bit negative or unclear. Types of bids and responses extend beyond the five love languages commonly mentioned (Chapman, 2015). For example, here's a story from our marriage: Once Julie was taking laundry out of the dryer and grumbling (her bid), so John asked Julie what was the matter, and Julie said she didn't mind doing the laundry, but she didn't much like folding it. So John volunteered to fold it. John always does housework in a self-indulgent manner, so he put on Bill Evans playing the piano, sat down on the bed, and started folding. Evans is a master jazz pianist. Julie gradually drifted over and sat down on the bed, and at that moment John could read Julie's mind. He was sure she was thinking, "I bet he's going to ask me to help." So John faked her out and didn't ask her to help, and she relaxed and listened to the music. They started reminiscing about how often they used to go to Dimitriou's Jazz Alley in Seattle before they became parents. Gradually, after this event, they found themselves doing the laundry more and more frequently so Julie could watch John fold the laundry (his action of turning toward) and listen to jazz. Our daughter stayed away because she didn't want to be asked to help, so we had some moments of gloriously peaceful time together.

John's former student Janice Driver discovered that newlywed couples who had higher levels of turning toward used lots of shared humor and affection during conflict discussions, compared to couples who didn't use humor and affection during conflict. Here's our earlier question: How do you get your clients to laugh more during conflict? We did an experiment, and it turns out that increasing turning toward produced higher levels of using shared humor and affection during conflict. Another bonus attributable to turning toward. That's the finding that surprised us.

And finally, here's a fundamental law of bids and turning toward: We discovered that turning toward leads to more turning toward. There is a positive feedback loop. So, in therapy we can start small. We don't have to have high standards. Turning toward will build over time. It's like kayaking down a river—you have the current at your back.

The Benefits of a Strong Friendship (as Defined by the First Three SRH Levels)

Let's return now to the test of a good theory. First, it ought to be disconfirmable—and that's how we designed the SRH theory. Second, it ought to be supported by experiments. We did many of these to test our hypotheses. And third, it ought to make unexpected new predictions that turn out to be true. These three criteria were met, as we made another surprising discovery. Love maps, fondness and admiration, and turning toward turned out to be the basis for more romance, passion, and great sex. An added bonus!

To convince yourself of the truth of this discovery, try this thought experiment. Ask yourself, "How would I try to make John and Julie's relationship more romantic in the next 2 weeks? What would I advise them to do?" Perhaps you'd consult a book, like one called *1001 Ways to Be Romantic* by Gregory Godek. Number 24 is addressed to guys: "What could be more romantic than getting your wife a golden locket with your picture in it?" Now imagine this: (1) John hasn't asked Julie a question in 10 years, so, strike one, he fails love maps. (2) Next consider fondness and admiration: Last night they went out to a dinner party, and as she was telling a story John said, "Don't tell that story. You don't know how to tell a story. Let me tell it." So, strike two, John fails fondness and admiration. And then (3) in turning toward versus away, John doesn't notice her bids, so strike three, he's out, he fails turning toward. And then he gets her a golden locket with his picture in it. And we ask you, "Is that going to be a romantic event in our marriage?" We don't think so. Julie will probably drive the SUV over it a few times, really flatten out that locket. But that isn't the case in our marriage. Julie knows that John finds her very interesting and updates his love maps, and that he expresses affection and respect often, and tries to turn toward her bids most of the time. So, any of those 1,001 romantic acts will work, *provided those first three levels of the SRH are working well.* He can even write a bad but heartfelt poem about how much he loves her and read it to her on their anniversary dinner at their favorite restaurant and John will choke up as he reads it, and her eyes will fill with tears. (This last part has happened.)

A further discovery: In our research, we also discovered that when couples had a fight that was not going well, and one of the partners tried to repair its downward spiral, the repair worked only when the first three levels of the SRH were strong. Repairs failed when those levels were weak. We realized that the basis for effective repairs is not how you make the repair but how much emotional money in the bank you have in the relationship, which predicts how the repair will be received. These three components of friendship also affect the way people behave when they disagree. Those with strong friendships actually have much more access to their humor, their affection, and other positive energies that facilitate their ability to have disagreements or to live with them in a much more constructive and creative way. In short, most important are the efforts a couple make to build up their emotional bank account.

4. Positive Sentiment Override, or the Positive Perspective

What happens when friendship isn't working? In his study of couples, our friend Robert Weiss in 1980 suggested that couples are in one of the following two states: negative or positive sentiment override. Weiss hypothesized that couples whose friendships are failing are in negative sentiment override. When we tested this idea, Weiss turned out to be totally right. Brilliant man. Let's explore the characteristics of these states.

Negative Sentiment Override
Negative sentiment override means that both the negative feelings and expectations we have of our partner override anything positive our partner might say or do. We are hypervigilant for put-downs. Even if our partner compliments us, we suspect a hidden agenda beneath their compliment—are

they trying to manipulate us with flattery? We hear criticism in everything our partner says, no matter what the words are. Even if our partner is talking about some neutral topic, we imagine they are somehow saying something negative about us. We also don't notice many of the positive actions our partner does for us. As we mentioned earlier, Robinson and Price in 1980 discovered that unhappy couples don't see or hear 50% of the positive things done or said by their partners that objective observers see. Instead, almost everything is viewed through a negative filter.

Positive Sentiment Override

Here, the opposite is true. The positive sentiments or feelings and expectations we have about the relationship and our partner override most of the negative things our partner might do or say. We don't take our partner's negativity or irritability personally. Instead, we view our partner's negative words or actions as evidence that our partner is either very stressed, in a bad mood that day, or perhaps unusually fatigued. In other words, we perceive negative events in the relationship, but we don't take them very seriously. On the other hand, we perceive most of our partner's positive actions and words the way objective observers do: very few are missed. And we appreciate them.

Implication

We've observed that people are in negative sentiment override for good reason—the friendship with their partner isn't working, and, as we later discovered, their conflict management is a nasty "absorbing state." An absorbing state of negative affect means that it is easier for partners to enter into that state of negativity than it is to exit from it. In that state, we tend to see our partner as our adversary, or as a stranger, and not as our momentarily annoying friend. Our SRH theory suggests that cognitive behavior modification will not work to change people's thinking from negative to positive sentiment override. And our research also suggests that it doesn't work. Instead, our theory suggests that only by strengthening their friendship and conflict management can couples gradually shift from negative sentiment override to positive sentiment override. Friendship and conflict-management dynamics shape this part of the SRH.

5. Manage Conflict

We use the phrase "manage" conflict rather than "resolve" conflict because relationship conflict is inevitable and natural. And contrary to many people's beliefs, conflict serves several positive functions. Conflict helps us to achieve an important goal: mutual understanding. Conflict also helps us learn how to better love and feel compassion for our partner, how to deal with change in our relationship, and how to renew courtship over time. We need to work on managing conflict rather than trying to eliminate it.

First Research Finding

We observed that when they were first introducing a conflict issue to discuss, the MASTERS of relationship spoke gently to one another. Using what we call "SOFTENED STARTUP," they raised an issue by describing their own feelings about a situation and what they needed from their partner in order to feel better about that situation. These couples omitted criticism and blame from their initial statements. The masters also ACCEPTED INFLUENCE from each other, they SELF-SOOTHED in order to avoid an escalated loud argument, they made REPAIRS TO DE-ESCALATE the discussion, and they each COMPROMISED when creating a conflict resolution together. This is the opposite of George Bach's *The Intimate Enemy*. Bach had couples take turns airing resentments. In his therapy, partners hit each other with foam-rubber bats called "batakas." This actually resulted in magnifying resentment, not diminishing it. There is no catharsis in anger. But this doesn't mean expurgate anger, it means make it constructive from the outset (see Carol Tavris's book *Anger: The Misunderstood Emotion*).

Second Finding—Not All Conflict in Relationships Is the Same

All relationships contain perpetual problems as well as solvable ones.

Our research revealed that 69% of the time when couples were asked to talk about an area of continuing disagreement, the issue they selected to discuss was a perpetual issue. Perpetual problems are ones that never go away. They keep popping up throughout the lifetime of the relationship, like a gopher digging holes in an otherwise immaculate lawn. These are problems that have to do with fundamental differences between a couple, such as differences in personality, lifestyle preferences, desires, or needs that are fundamental to their core definitions of self. These issues have no clear resolution. Couples just repeatedly talk about them. Occasionally they may make some progress, or perhaps the situation may improve for a short time, but then later on, the problem reemerges again. Thus couples end up simply having an off-and-on continuous dialogue about the problem over years of time. When we collected longitudinal follow-up data on our couples, the only thing that changed when they returned to the lab annually to again discuss a conflict were their hairstyles and outfits. Otherwise, the same problem, the same discussion.

Most Relational Conflict Is Not Resolvable
We maintain that:

> RELATIONSHIPS WORK TO THE EXTENT THAT YOU BOTH
> HAVE WOUND UP WITH A SET OF PERPETUAL PROBLEMS
> THAT YOU CAN LEARN TO LIVE WITH.

When a problem is a perpetual problem, instead of *solving it*, a couple needs to learn how to *dialogue* calmly about their different subjective realities. For the most part, the masters of relationship accept their partner's position while maintaining their own. Often their dialogues are brightened with amusement, respect, and affection. They can simultaneously communicate full-on acceptance of their partner but also the desire to improve this problem. That acceptance is an *existential* understanding of what their partner's position *means* to them. And that understanding makes all the difference.

> THE MASTERS OF RELATIONSHIP KNOW HOW TO
> MOVE FROM GRIDLOCK TO DIALOGUE ON THEIR
> PERPETUAL PROBLEMS.

If couples cannot establish such a dialogue, the conflict may become *gridlocked*. Gridlocked conflict is exactly what it sounds like. Partners get locked into a bitter struggle that gets stuck and goes nowhere. The conflict issue can be about anything. To an outsider it may seem trivial. But within the relationship it feels huge. Imagine two clenched fists pushing against each other—hard, locked into struggle and trying to win, not lose. There, you have gridlocked conflict. Both partners end up feeling fundamentally rejected, disliked, and unappreciated. Couples have the same conversation over and over and over again, but it seems like they're just spinning their wheels, and not making any headway. Compromise feels impossible. Over time people become more and more entrenched in their positions and even more polarized. Their conversations lead only to frustration and hurt. There's very little shared humor or amusement or affection or appreciation. Over time, they become even more polarized, and they often vilify their partner. The most common vilification we hear in the lab is "My partner is *selfish*." In a way that attribution makes sense, because in gridlock, each partner is thinking only of themselves. Eventually, gridlocked conflict results in conflict avoidance and, worse still, emotional disengagement. Unfortunately, trust erodes.

Gridlocked Conflict

Here's an example of a gridlocked conflict that ended in divorce. He wasn't even that committed to getting married, but she insisted that either they marry or the relationship was over, so he eventually proposed to her, and they married.

She wanted a dog, and her husband said no. To her, getting a dog meant that she would be safe when he traveled. It also meant they'd be loving the same creature together, kind of like a dry run for having a baby. But he wasn't so sure he wanted to even be a father. So the conflict about getting a dog was symbolic of issues involving divided views on parenting of any kind, baby or puppy. Then, one birthday, she happily bought him a puppy as a "present." She thought that he'd find the puppy irresistible and they'd settle this issue once and for all. He didn't fall in love with the puppy. In fact, he was furious with her for getting it. So, one day the puppy took a dump under his desk. He said that he'd never clean it up. No one cleaned that pile up until they had the house cleaned as they divorced and prepared to sell it. The gridlocked issue about getting a dog or not getting a dog had deep symbolic meaning for both of them, but their discussion never dove further down than the surface: to "puppy-up" or not to puppy-up.

Our research revealed that there is a very good reason most people cannot yield on gridlocked problems. Behind each person's position lies something deep and meaningful—something **core** to that person's belief system, core need, or personality. It might be a strongly held value or perhaps a dream not yet lived. But when a relationship is safe enough and one partner clearly communicates that they want to know what's underlying their partner's position, both partners can open up and talk about their deeper feelings, dreams, and needs, then slowly work on developing a compromise.

6. Make Life Dreams Come True

A crucial aspect of any relationship is the creation of a safe and nurturing atmosphere that encourages each person to talk honestly about their dreams, values, convictions, and aspirations, and to feel that the relationship supports each partner's life dreams. We are back to love maps in a deeper way here, in which partners learn all about each other's inner dreams. One of our favorite films is *Don Juan DeMarco*. In that film Johnny Depp plays a mental patient who thinks he is Don Juan. Marlon Brando plays his doctor, and Faye Dunaway plays the doctor's wife. In the end, the patient transforms the doctor's life, rather than the other way around. The doctor is about to retire. One day, after Don Juan talks to him about women, the doctor converses with his wife in their garden. He asks her what her life dreams are. After a long silence she says, "I thought you'd never ask."

Often, differing positions on a gridlocked conflict embody each partner's underlying dream, one that remains belowground when the atmosphere between partners is too toxic to unearth it. Dreams are fragile. In the past the dreams may have been pooh-poohed as trivial or unattainable and thus were buried even deeper. The masters of relationship excel at sharing their own individual dreams, and creating shared dreams for themselves as a couple. This is because the masters never shame one another for the dreams they harbor. They've built enough trust with each other to know that their partner will work hard to understand the other's dream and support the partner to fulfill it.

Here's a case in point from our own marriage. Julie was approaching her 50th birthday. She'd always dreamed of returning to the Himalayas, where she'd lived for months in the late '70s. This time she wanted to hike to the base camp of Mt. Everest, and perhaps climb higher. But when she and John had had their daughter, she had tabled this dream, since she didn't want to leave her little girl for weeks at a time when she was so young. But now her daughter was going on 9. Julie figured she was old enough to stay home with Daddy for the 4 weeks the trip would take. Julie approached John with the idea. His first question was *"Why?"* John considers himself a consummate "indoorsman." Camping outdoors was definitely not his favorite activity, let alone walking uphill for mile after mile. Julie explained what the dream meant to her: achieving a goal that superseded the polio she'd had as a kid, her loving mountains deeply, and her desire to go on a grand adventure before she got too old. John asked whether men would travel with her. "Not necessarily . . . " With the exception of the guide and a few porters, Julie agreed to take with her 10 women only. After much discussion, John agreed to support Julie's trip, despite Julie's dream being his nightmare. Julie went and John learned how to braid their daughter's hair. Their reunion afterward was full of joy and gratitude—for a husband who indeed supported Julie's dreams, and for a wife who didn't demand that John accompany her.

7. Create Shared Meaning

A relationship is about building a life together, a life that has a sense of shared purpose and meaning. Victor Frankl said that the mere pursuit of happiness and pleasure leaves a person empty. He suggested that, for a fulfilling life, we pursue deeper meanings in life, and find happiness along the way. It's in "the attic" of the SRH where we build a sense of shared purpose and meaning. We believe that everyone is a philosopher, trying to make some sense out of this brief journey we take through life. Couples can intentionally build shared meaning in four ways: (1) by creating rituals of connection that give meaning to the way they move through time together. Rituals of connection are specific ways to spend time together that the couple co-creates and can predictably count on. These can include ways to share formal events (like birthdays, anniversaries, graduations, confirmations, bar/bat mitzvahs, funerals, weddings, births, yearly holiday celebrations, etc.) and informal events (how each partner wants to be treated when sick, how to initiate sex, how to talk about sex, how to separate at the start of the day and reunite at the end of the day, how to spend weekends together, meals together, etc.); (2) by each partner supporting the many roles their partner may play in life (e.g., son, daughter, friend, worker, father, mother); (3) by creating shared goals, missions, legacies, community actions, and so forth; and (4) by creating shared values, symbols, religious/spiritual belief systems, or shared ethical, moral, and political views.

Creating shared meaning, however, doesn't mean only having identical views, goals, and ideas. This level also includes partners talking at length and sharing with one another their own individual ideas on what gives their lives meaning. This is the shared existential part of couples' lives together. We either build this part of our relationship INTENTIONALLY, or we fail to do so, and so risk living within an existential vacuum.

So, here, again, we return to BUILD LOVE MAPS, because this level requires knowledge of our partner's deeper self. Thus, the seventh level of the House loops back to the first level.

The Two Weight-Bearing Walls of SRH Theory

WALL 1. TRUST: Build Trust Instead of Distrust

People build trust in their relationship by discovering the answer to many forms of the same question: "Will you be there for me when I need you?" Remember our mentioning the trust metric in Chapter 1? Essentially, calculating a couple's trust metric means assessing whether one's partner is behaving in a way that supports and adds to their partner's welfare and maximizes their partner's payoffs as well as their own.

A strong correlate of the trust metric is a process we call **attunement**. Attunement means listening to one's partner nondefensively, with understanding and empathy for even their negative emotions (even if we are the target of them). Attunement is a major component of emotional connection and intimacy. Over time, when trust is established, often after the first or honeymoon phase of the relationship, the relationship becomes a safe haven. Our therapy, as well as the emotionally focused attachment couples therapy of Susan Johnson, seeks to accomplish this very important goal.

To attune to one's partner, it is essential to build one's ability to have intimate conversations. That means frequently asking our partner, "How are you doing, baby?" and really being interested in the answer. It also means, when our partner is experiencing a negative emotion, stepping up to the plate by being a great listener, and empathizing with the partner's feelings. The art of intimate conversation may be dying in the United States. Sherry Turkle's book *Alone Together* is about the declining art of close conversations in young people today, many of whom seem to prefer texting one another rather than having face-to-face conversation. Yet close conversations are not very difficult. They entail four skills.

The first skill of intimate conversation is being able to express one's feelings in words that fit what one is experiencing emotionally in one's body. Fortunately for us, Eugene Gendlin developed a program called *focusing*, which teaches people how to put their feelings into words, and then to check out with one's body that these words fit. The second skill of intimate conversation is to ask questions that help our partner explore their own emotions in a supportive manner. The third skill is to make statements that help our partner explore their own emotions in a supportive manner. And the fourth skill of intimate conversation is empathy. The Gottman Institute website has a small booklet that can help, called *How to Be a Great Listener*. There we list the tools for Skill 4, emotional attunement, which we've found builds trust.

Reminder: How to get people to do shared humor during conflict conversations. In developing our theory we also learned, through the work of John's graduate student Janice Driver, what can be done to get people to use more shared humor during conflict and to build more trust with each other. The answer is to increase turning toward. At first, this was a simple correlation. But it turned out to actually be an effective intervention. What's great about encouraging couples to turn toward each other more is that it is not very difficult to get people to do it, since the moments when turning toward works usually happen when the couple is not engaged in conflict. Trust building through turning-toward moments typically occurs during everyday neutral moments. Moments that, it turns out, have a great deal of meaning.

EXPRESS TOLERANCE, EMPATHY, AND UNDERSTANDING DURING AN ATTUNEMENT CONVERSATION.

Samples below:

Empathic Statements	More Empathic Statements
1. You're making total sense.	24. That must have annoyed you.
2. I understand how you feel.	25. That would make me mad too.
3. You must feel so hopeless.	26. That sounds infuriating.
4. I just feel such despair in you when you talk about this.	27. That sounds very frustrating.
5. You're in a tough spot here.	28. That is very scary.
6. I can feel the pain you feel.	29. Well, I agree with most of what you're saying.
7. The world needs to stop when you're in this much pain.	30. I would have also been disappointed by that.
8. I wish you didn't have to go through that.	31. That would have hurt my feelings also.
9. I'm on your side here.	32. That would make me sad too.
10. I wish I could have been with you in that moment.	33. POOR BABY!!!
11. Oh, wow, that sounds terrible.	34. Wow! That must have hurt.
12. You must feel so helpless.	35. I understand what you are feeling.
13. That hurts me to hear that.	36. You are making a lot of sense to me.
14. I support your position here.	37. I totally understand what you are feeling.
15. I totally agree with you.	38. OK, I think I get it. So what you are feeling is . . .
16. You are feeling so trapped!	39. Let me try to paraphrase and summarize what you're saying. You're saying . . .
17. That sounds like you felt really disgusted!	40. I would have trouble coping with that.
18. No wonder you're upset.	41. What I admire most about what you're doing is . . .
19. I'd feel the same way you do in your situation.	42. That would make me feel insecure.
20. I think you're right.	43. That sounds a little frightening.
21. I see. Let me summarize: What you're thinking here is . . .	44. Tell me what you see as your choices here.
22. You are in a lot of pain here. I can feel it.	
23. It would be great to be free of this.	

WALL 2. COMMITMENT:
Build Commitment and Loyalty Instead of Betrayal

Building commitment and loyalty are the goals of the third phase of love, the stage when people pledge their allegiance and dedication to living their journeys through life together. John found that his "betrayal metric" could be described and measured by following Caryl Rusbult's model, called the "investment and commitment" model. According to Rusbult, committed people do not make negative comparisons between their current relationship and an alternative real or imagined relationship (called "negative comps"). This means they do not view their partner negatively when comparing them to another, allegedly better "potential partner." They invest more in their here-and-now relationship. They sacrifice for it, nurture positive thoughts about it, and to get their needs met and to voice complaints they turn to their partner, not someone else. They encircle their relationship with a wide fence to guard it from intrusions by other potential partners. In John's study he found that commitment is fed by cherishing one's partner, minimizing the partner's shortcomings while valuing the partner's positive attributes, and above all, nurturing gratitude for the special qualities and gifts one's partner contributes to the relationship. These are the actions that sustain commitment.

Betrayal is created by opposite thoughts and actions. The partner will mentally trash their partner and harbor grudges and bitter resentment for what they think is missing. They will also downplay the partner's positive qualities, magnify the partner's shortcomings, and complain about the relationship to others (such as the one who participates in the betrayal later) rather than to the partner directly. The betrayal metric works by assessing the extent to which a couple's interactions during conflict are a zero-sum game. That is, where one partner's benefit is the other's loss, and the relationship is tormented by win–lose power struggles. The partners negotiate to get what they want, but regardless of the costs to the partner.

Commitment infers that this relationship is sacred and central to one's final life journey. Think of it this way: Alice in Wonderland follows the rabbit right down the rabbit hole, diving in headfirst. She doesn't wait to see whether another rabbit may come along tomorrow. This is her journey to Wonderland, which is full of enchantment but also terror (like facing the Red Queen, who cuts everyone's head off). Alice is fully committed to her wild and magical journey. Commitment means making a moral choice that this is your journey. There is an old Scottish wedding vow, "I plight thee my troth," which has two meanings. One meaning is "I offer you my truth," meaning there are no secrets or deception in our relationship. The second meaning is "I offer you all my worldly goods, and thus I have nothing to offer anyone else." Combined, commitment means "You have my whole heart for my whole life, and all my wealth as well." Which now leads us to the motto:

LOYALTY IS BUILT IN A LOVE RELATIONSHIP THROUGH COMMITMENT AND CHERISHING THIS PERSON AS UNIQUE AND IRREPLACEABLE.

Our research has shown that these seven levels and two walls of the Sound Relationship House are the building blocks of a lasting and fulfilling relationship. And each component can be directly or indirectly strengthened through careful interventions. And our interventions, as you'll see later, are modeled after the skills that thousands of successful couples similarly employ to make their relationships work. We owe them our deepest gratitude for all they have taught us.

CHAPTER 5

Our Relationship Checkup Questionnaires

In this chapter we will present our Relationship Checkup (RCU) scales: their scope, their reliabilities, and their validities. The importance of the RCU is that it makes it possible to do reliable and valid assessment before intervention, in order to obtain a coherent profile of a relationship. This profile is composed of a set of scores designed to pinpoint challenges the couple faces, strengths the couple possesses, and specific conflict issues and comorbidities that trouble the couple. With this knowledge specified first, the therapist can fine-tune the couple's therapy with interventions specifically designed to transform a couple's particular challenges into strengths while further expanding and deepening the couple's strengths. In this chapter we will also note the differences and similarities between same-sex and heterosexual couples who are starting therapy.

In actual clinical practice, the idea of thoroughly and quantitatively assessing a relationship *before intervening* is still a foreign concept for many couples therapists. We have to change that. Here are two examples of the dangers of ignoring assessment while prematurely diving into a couple's therapy:

- In one example, Péloquin et al. (2019) recently argued for the importance of the therapist creating a complete sexual portrait of couples seeking relationship therapy. In their study of 298 couples seeking couples therapy, they reported that a full 30% of couples had a significant sexual problem. If you don't assess, you won't know that.
- In a second example, O'Leary and colleagues (e.g., Rosenbaum & O'Leary, 1981) reported that a very high percentage of couples entering into couples therapy at a Stony Brook clinic were physically violent, as assessed by the Straus Conflict Tactics Scale (CTS; Straus, 1979). Their paper served as a dire warning, because, as they noted, couples therapists rarely assess for domestic violence before beginning relationship treatment. See also Froer et al. (2012), who confirm this point with even more data.

Think of what you might miss as a therapist if you launch into the work while remaining ignorant of these two vital problems in your couple's relationship. And these two concerns are only part of why we need assessment. Individual interviews are another imperative in assessment. The example below comes from *The Orchid and the Dandelion* by W. Thomas Boyce (2019):

[The case of] . . . a ten-year-old boy (call him Joe) from a distant county who was sent for hospitalization by his family doctor, to be evaluated for a gastric ulcer. As his attending pediatrician, I was among the first to hear his story and examine his troubled belly. His pain was crampy and severe, and lay directly over his stomach in the left upper quadrant of his abdomen. He had no other symptoms and specifically denied any change or blood in his stool, any vomiting, or any alteration of the pain before or following a meal. His diagnostic workup, including X-rays, tests for blood in his stool or urine, and blood measures of inflammation or anemia, was entirely unremarkable. Thinking that these must be episodes of psychosomatic pain brought on by difficulties in the family, I launched a full-bore search for the family or school dysfunction that was surely a root contributor to young Joe's disabling pain. All was well at school, and though Joe frequently stayed home as a consequence of his pain, there was no history

to suggest experiences of social or academic stress in his school life. He had good friends, was a talented student with good grades, and got along well with his teacher. I then interviewed Joe at length, on multiple occasions, about how life was going at home, about his parents' relationship, about any possible abuse from one or both of his parents, about any worries or troubles his family had. The result was a definitive zero: no history of anything unusual or suspicious in his report. So I then turned to the parents—both of them present and attentive during the entire hospitalization. Was there any worry or concern on Joe's part about either of the parents? How was their marital relationship? Any exposures to violence or conflict? Did they have any hunches about the origin of their son's pain? Nothing. The parents, in perhaps three or four serial interviews, turned up not a single psychological or relational issue that we could deem implicated in the genesis of Joe's pain. So we started him, despite absolutely no evidence for a gastric or duodenal ulcer, on an acid-blocking medication, and his pain began to subside. After several days in the hospital and with Joe's pain receding, we discharged the boy back home to the care of his primary care physician. That was all I heard of Joe or his family until three months later when I got a call from the district attorney's office in their home county. Did I have any reason to suspect violence or maltreatment from Joe's dad? Because "last night after supper" his mom had gone to the bedroom, retrieved a hidden handgun, and put a bullet through her husband's forehead, precisely between his eyes. Months later, a jury acquitted the mother, ruling justifiable homicide stemming from the father's chronic, relentless psychological and physical abuse of mother and child. The mom had finally reached a point of no return, when her only recourse, it seemed to her at the time, was to put an end to the husband who had tormented her and her son, Joe, for years. I had missed this crucial piece of family history by virtue of never interviewing the parents separately, only at the same time. There were no visible stigmata of child abuse on physical examination, and Joe and his mom, terrified of retribution that would surely follow a revelation of abuse, had been unable, with the dad constantly present, to provide me with that essential detail of their family's plight.

That's quite a dramatic story, highlighting why we need to do a thorough assessment before starting therapy.

Another point we want to make is that in the examples above, the sample sizes of couples seeking therapy were relatively small. There is clearly a need for an epidemiologically sized sample so that we can have confidence in our data. Therefore, we created and analyzed such a database. Also, over the past three decades we created and validated a set of questionnaires that produce a reliable and valid *profile* of a relationship's strengths and challenges. We have made that set of questionnaires available online on our software platform, Gottman Connect, together with nearly instantaneous automated scoring that produces a clinical report for the therapist, related recommendations for treatment, and a summary report for the couple.

Recently we reported our analyses of our first 40,682 gay, lesbian, and heterosexual couples worldwide that took the RCU questionnaires online as their first step before beginning treatment. We included same-sex couples seeking relationship therapy in order to compare their data to that of heterosexual couples. Many other scientists have called for this kind of data (Alonzo, 2018; Scott et al., 2018).

We also know very little about same-sex couples. In a series of systematic studies the late Lawrence Kurdek, using questionnaires, reported that same-sex couples were in most ways very similar to heterosexual married couples (Kurdek, 2004) but also, in other ways, far less troubled than heterosexual couples (Kurdek, 2005). In an *observational* longitudinal study of gay and lesbian committed couples, Gottman et al. (2003a) and Gottman et al. (2003b) reported that same-sex couples during conflict interactions were far less defensive, more egalitarian, and used humor more effectively than a group of married heterosexual couples equal in relationship satisfaction and length of relationship. In a thorough review of literature comparing heterosexual to same-sex relationships in the United States from 2000 to 2016, Rostosky and Riggle (2017) concluded that there were far more similarities than differences; they also suggested that questionnaires be tested and validated specifically for same-sex couples. Our study accomplished that goal. Garanzini et al. (2017), in an uncontrolled treatment outcome study, reported successful results in treating gay and lesbian couples with Gottman method couples therapy. Therefore, in our epidemiologically sized sample we compared the relationship and individual issues that gay male, lesbian, and heterosexual couples bring to couples therapy, and also, in supplemental tables for the *Journal of Marital and Family Therapy*, we present separate reliability data for same-sex and heterosexual couples.

History of Our Online RCU, a Part of Gottman Connect

The first step in creating the RCU was to design and validate a set of reliable questionnaires that correlated significantly with standard self-report questionnaires and also with *multimethod, non-self-report* predictors of relationship functioning within a particular multimethod paradigm of couples assessment (e.g., Levenson & Gottman, 1983). To give you some idea of why "multimethod" validation of our assessment methods was so important to us, consider a paper Thomas Bradbury wrote, titled "Why Do Happily Married Couples Divorce?" The answer to this question turned out to be that our assessments of marital happiness, used alone, are sometimes not very good indicators of what is actually going on in the relationship. Using observational methods, researchers assessed as happily married some couples who actually turned out to be quite troubled. This exemplifies why we can't rely on just one type of measurement process to validly assess the quality of a relationship. It's a good start, but it needs to be supplemented. That's why we did two things. First, we validated our questionnaires against observational and interview data. Second, we created Gottman Connect, which enables every clinician to assess their couples using a version of our Love Lab. On Gottman Connect, we examine the couple's relationship *dynamics*, using (1) the couple's video-recall data; (2) heart rate, obtained from their videos; and (3) our patented automated SPAFF coding of two 10-minute interactions, in which couples discuss events of the week and a conflict issue.

The creation of potentially valid items was predicated on our theory of relationship functioning, the SRH theory (Gottman, 1999; Gottman &

Gottman, 2018; Chapter 4 in this book). To briefly summarize, the SRH questionnaires assess functioning in these related domains: (1) friendship and intimacy, (2) the management of conflict, (3) fulfillment of individual dreams, (4) the shared meaning system, (4) trust, and (5) commitment.

Our multimethod validation included our scored Oral History Interview (Buehlman et al., 1992) and SPAFF emotion coding of conflict emotional interaction (Gottman & Levenson, 1985, 1986; Levenson & Gottman, 1985). It also included established criterion self-report scales of relationship functioning, such as the Locke–Wallace Marital Adjustment Test (Locke & Wallace, 1959), and the Weiss–Cerreto Marital Status Inventory, which assesses thoughts and plans to separate or divorce (Weiss & Cerreto, 1980). Following item analyses, the best items were then selected to reduce the size of the questionnaires, and empirically establish item cutoffs.

Validation of the SRH Reduced Scales

Two validation studies formed the basis for instrument development, reducing the number of items, and the establishment of cutoff scores. Study 1 recruited 51 couples taking a two-day workshop in marital communication. They filled out the larger 20-item SRH questionnaires, the Locke–Wallace, the Symptom Checklist SCL-90 (Derogatis et al., 1973), and the Weiss–Cerreto Marital Status Inventory (which assesses divorce proneness through items tapping persistent thoughts and actions about separation and divorce; Weiss & Cerreto, 1980). Results showed that the SRH scales correlated significantly with marital satisfaction, divorce proneness, and the SCL-90. Cronbach alphas for all scales varied between .62 and .92.

The second study was designed for multimethod validation and item analyses to reduce the number of items per scale from 20 to 5. A two-stage sampling procedure was utilized to draw a sample of 133 newlywed couples from the Puget Sound area in Washington. Couples were initially recruited using newspaper advertisements and flyers posted in the Puget Sound area. Couples interested were administered a screening phone interview that included the telephone version of the Marital Adjustment Test (MAT), a telephone scale measuring marital satisfaction (Locke & Wallace, 1959). The sample was selected so that there was an even rectangular distribution of marital satisfaction among the couples' scores on the telephone version of the MAT, thus oversampling the tails of the normal curve to have adequate power throughout the marital satisfaction range. By a rectangular distribution we mean that we had roughly equal numbers of couples at each point of the marital satisfaction distribution. This is in contrast to a bell-shaped distribution that has greater numbers of subjects in the middle of the distribution. This even distribution was chosen to oversample both very happy and very distressed couples. The sample was also selected to match the racial and ethnic demographics of the Seattle metropolitan area (City of Seattle Planning Commission Report, 1990).

Oral History Interview (OHI)

Couples were conjointly interviewed and asked questions about the history of their relationship and their philosophy of relationships. The dimensions tapped by the Buehlman Oral History coding system were *Positive reminiscences*: (1) cognitive room for the partner and the relationship, called their "love map"; (2) fondness and admiration expressed toward the partner during the interview; (3) we-ness, meaning do they finish each other's sentences, do they emphasize words like "we," "us," and "our," rather than "I," "me," and "mine," and do they emphasize their common ground in the marriage; (4) their philosophy of marriage, especially glorifying the struggle, or couple efficacy, which is the belief that they have gotten through past difficulties, and can get through any adversity together; (5) negative reminiscences, meaning negativity expressed toward the partner and the relationship; and (6) disappointment in the partner and the relationship. A prior study using the Buehlman coding of the OHI found that the OHI variables were able to predict, with 94% accuracy over a 4-year period, the divorce or stability of another sample of couples (Buehlman et al., 1992).

Study 2: Two-Factor Analysis of the Buehlman Oral History Scales

In the second multimethod validation study, for each partner the positive reminiscences scales of the OHI coding system (fondness and admiration, we-ness versus me-ness, expansiveness or love maps, expressed extensive knowledge about the relationship and one's partner's inner world, and glorifying the struggle) were subjected to a principal components analysis. We did the same analysis for the quality of the negative reminiscences, which is assessed with two scales: (1) expressed negativity about or toward the partner and the relationship; and (2) expressed disappointment with the partner, with the marriage, or with marriage in general. The first component of the husband-as-friend analysis accounted for 77.63% of the variance, and the first component of the wife-as-friend analysis accounted for 76.08% of the variance. The first component of the husband-as-adversary analysis accounted for 87.09% of the variance, and the first component of the wife-as-adversary analysis accounted for 86.95% of the variance. Thus, we were left with two general factors for each partner. The Cronbach alpha for the husband-as-friend component was .89, for the wife-as-friend component was .87, for the husband-as-adversary component was .83, and for the wife-as-adversary component was .84.

Couples Conflict Discussion

After couples filled out a Problem Inventory, an interviewer discussed their areas of contention in their relationship and helped the couples pick the most emotionally salient issue as a topic for them to discuss and attempt to resolve for the next 15 minutes.

Observational Coding of the Couples Conflict Discussion. Split-screen videotapes of the marital interactions were coded by independent observers using the Specific Affect Coding System–Version 4.0 (SPAFF-V4; Gottman, 1996). The SPAFF draws on facial expression (Ekman & Friesen, 1978), voice tone, and speech content to characterize the emotions expressed by the couple. Emotions are coded separately for each person and are coded in real time. We computed a negative affect variable, which was the total number of seconds each person displayed anger, belligerence, contempt, criticism, disgust, defensiveness, domineering, sadness, stonewalling (i.e., an observable withdrawing from the interaction), tension, tense humor, or whining. The positive affect variable was the total number of seconds of affection, interest, excitement/joy, low and high validation (low validation involves listener tracking the speaker; high validation involves expressions of understanding, empathy, and acceptance), and shared humor during conflict. The neutral affect variable, which has been shown to be constructive in conflict discussions (e.g., Gottman, 1994), was the absence of either positive or negative affect during conflict. Two independent observers coded each interaction and Cohen's kappas and free marginal kappas were computed for each partner's set of affects. Only those interactions with .61 or higher Cohen's kappa statistic were used for analyses. Free marginal kappa statistics across the marital interaction SPAFF categories in Study 2 averaged .84.

Validities. For validity computations we computed the friendship scales correlations with the OHI scales. Cross-method validation studies are rare, but we wanted to know that the scales could replace the more expensive measures obtained from coding an interview or observational coding of videotaped interactions. In general, cross-method correlations tend to be low (see Campbell & Fiske, 1959). For coded OHI Love Maps, the husband and wife OHI Love Map interview scores, respectively, were correlated with questionnaire Love Maps. For the husband, these correlations were .28, $p < .001$, and .47, $p < .001$; for the wife, these correlations were .24, $p < .01$, and .32, $p < .001$. For OHI Fondness and Admiration husband and wife variables, respectively, we computed the correlations with questionnaire Fondness and Admiration. These correlations for the husband were, respectively, .38, $p < .001$, and .36, $p < .001$, and for the wife they were .49, $p < .001$, and .44, $p < .001$. For OHI We-ness husband and wife variables, respectively, we correlated for questionnaire Turning Toward. For the husband, these correlations were .48, $p < .001$, .49, $p < .001$, and for the wife, .49, $p < .001$, and .51, $p < .001$. For the questionnaire Emotional Distance and Loneliness scale, we computed correlations with OHI Overall Negativity for husband and wife, respectively. For the husband, these correlations were .37, $p < .001$, and .39, $p < .001$, and for the wife, they were .39, $p < .001$, and .43, $p < .001$. These correlations could be termed moderate in size.

For conflict validity computations we computed the conflict scale correlations with the SPAFF coding of conflict discussions, starting with the husband and wife positive-to-negative ratios. For the husband questionnaire of Harsh Startup, the correlations with SPAFF positive-to-negative ratios were .18, $p < .05$, and .24, $p < .01$, and for the wife, .20, $p < .05$, and .32, $p < .001$. For the validity of the questionnaire Four Horsemen, we were able to compute correlations with *specific* SPAFF-coded husband and wife behaviors for the codes Criticism, Defensiveness, Contempt, and Stonewalling for husband and wife, respectively. For the husband Four Horsemen questionnaire, correlations were for husband SPAFF Criticism, Defensiveness, Contempt, and Stonewalling, respectively, .44, $p < .001$, .29, $p < .001$, .36, $p < .001$, and .30, $p < .001$. For the wife Four Horsemen questionnaire, the correlations with the wife SPAFF Criticism, Defensiveness, Contempt, and Stonewalling were, respectively, .35, $p < .001$, .24, $p < .01$, .22, $p < .001$, and .32, $p < .001$. For the Gridlock questionnaire, we also correlated this score with the SPAFF Four Horsemen. For the husband Gridlock questionnaire, these correlations with husband SPAFF Criticism, Defensiveness, Contempt, and Stonewalling were, respectively, .36, $p < .001$, .24, $p < .01$, .43, $p < .001$, and .14, n.s. For the wife Gridlock questionnaire, these correlations with wife SPAFF Criticism, Defensiveness, Contempt, and Stonewalling, respectively, were .30, $p < .001$, .32, $p < .001$, .12, n.s., and .15, n.s. For the questionnaire Accepting Influence, we again used the SPAFF positive-to-negative ratio. The husband Accepting Influence scale correlated with husband SPAFF positive-to-negative ratio $-.25$, $p < .01$. The wife Accepting Influence scale correlated with wife SPAFF positive-to-negative ratio $-.40$, $p < .001$. The husband Compromise scale correlated with the husband SPAFF positive-to-negative ratio $-.15$, n.s. The wife Compromise scale correlated with husband SPAFF positive-to-negative ratio $-.26$, $p < .01$. The husband Flooding scale correlated with husband SPAFF positive-to-negative ratio $-.32$, $p < .001$. The wife Flooding scale correlated with the wife SPAFF positive-to-negative ratio .31, $p < .001$. The husband Negative Sentiment Override scale correlated with husband SPAFF positive-to-negative ratio .27, $p < .01$. The wife Negative Sentiment Override scale correlated with wife SPAFF positive-to-negative ratio .30, $p < .001$. The husband Repair scale correlated with husband SPAFF positive-to-negative ratio

−.15, n.s. The wife Repair scale correlated with the wife SPAFF positive-to-negative ratio −.41, $p < .001$.

For Shared Meaning validity computations we correlated the SRH questionnaire scales with the conceptually opposite OHI scale of Chaos. For questionnaire husband Rituals of Connection, this correlation was −.42, $p < .001$. For questionnaire wife Rituals of Connection, the correlation was −.33, $p < .001$. For questionnaire husband Supporting Roles, the correlation was −.26, $p < .01$. For questionnaire wife Supporting Roles, the correlation was −.38, $p < .001$. For questionnaire husband Shared Goals, the correlation was −.37, $p < .001$. For questionnaire wife Shared Goals, the correlation was −.35, $p < .001$. For questionnaire husband Shared Symbols, the correlation was −.33, $p < .001$. For questionnaire wife Shared Symbols, the correlation was −.36, $p < .001$. In addition to considering Chaos as the conceptual opposite of Shared Meaning, we tested whether the Shared Meaning scales might be negatively related to SPAFF codes of Anger and Sadness during the conflict discussion. These correlations show that higher scores on the Shared Meaning scales are generally correlated with less anger and sadness during conflict, particularly for wives. Overall, we conclude that the SRH scales demonstrated their validity across multiple methods of measurement as low to moderate in size. In Table 5.1 we present summary correlations with our Shared Meaning scales and SPAFF Anger and Sadness coding.

Cutoffs and Reliabilities for the Reduced Scales

Longitudinal research from our laboratory and the laboratory of Robert Levenson at UC Berkeley have established that the positive-to-negative ratios in observer-coded conflict discussions using our SPAFF coding system predicted later divorce or marital stability, with an average ratio of 5 to 1 for couples who were eventually found to be stable, versus a ratio of 0.8 to 1 for couples who eventually divorced, with approximately 88% accuracy (Gottman, 1994). As we noted, very similar ratios of positive-to-negative statements during our lab's OHL (coded with the Buehlman coding system) predicted divorce versus stability with 94% accuracy over a 4-year period (Buehlman et al., 1992). Study 1 employed 20-item questionnaires, and the second study used item analysis to reduce these scales to just 5-item scales. In the interest of time and brevity for couples taking the online Relationship Checkup, smaller Cronbach alphas, on the order of .60, were considered acceptable for the reduced 5-item scales. Median splits were used to divide positive-to-negative ratios on both the SPAFF and OHI measures. Discriminant function analysis was then used to determine the *best cutoff scores* for each scale, the goal being the accurate prediction of the lower half of the SPAFF and OHI positive-to-negative ratios. This analysis produced empirically validated cutoff scores for *the reduced* 5-item scales. Cronbach alphas for the 5-item scales were as follows in validation Study 2: (1) Friendship and Intimacy Love Maps (Ha = .52; Wa = .68), Fondness and Admiration (Ha = .83; Wa = .87), Turning Toward or Away (Ha = .83; Wa = .87), Emotional Distance and Loneliness (Ha = .81; Wa = .88); (2) Conflict: Harsh Startup (Ha = .90; Wa = .91), The Four Horsemen of the Apocalypse (Ha = .92; Wa = .94), Gridlock on Perpetual Issues (Ha = .87; Wa = .91), Accepting Influence (Ha = .75; Wa = .75), Compromise (Ha = .75; Wa = .73), Flooding (Ha = .88; Wa = .90), Negative Sentiment Override (Ha = .92; Wa = .93), Effective Repair Attempts (Ha = .85; Wa = .82); and (3) Shared Meaning: Shared Meaning Rituals (Ha = .60; Wa = .74), Shared Meaning Roles (Ha = .49; Wa = .68), Shared Meaning Goals (Ha = .70; Wa = .85), Shared Meaning Symbols (Ha = .80; Wa = .87), Overall Meaning Scales (Ha = .87; Wa = .93).

The Relationship Checkup Scales of Gottman Connect

The resultant RCU website has been designed for couples therapists of any orientation to assess their clients before beginning therapy. The RCU is currently available only in English. Once the therapist joins the Gottman Connect website, and the therapist designates a couple, each partner is invited by the site to separately and privately fill out the questionnaires; a separate email address for each partner is required. The therapist gets a final summary report plus recommendations for treatment only if both partners independently complete every item of every questionnaire. Thus there were no missing data in our international sample. The entire procedure takes between 1.0 and 1.5 hours for each person to complete the RCU scales; they may return multiple times, since their work is saved upon exit. The summary report to only the therapist provides, for each partner, for each scale, two columns, with scores for each scale either inside a green circle for "a strength," or inside a red box for "a challenge." Therapists, if they wish, can zoom into the summary report data to view specific responses to all items by each partner, as well as viewing client written comments. Data on the website are encrypted for HIPAA protection. The partners' questionnaire answers are algorithmically analyzed to yield an automated summary report that is electronically sent to the therapist. The therapist is thus provided with a detailed summary assessment of the strengths and challenges the couple is facing, an analysis of the dynamics of the couple's functioning, and treatment recommendations. No demographic data were collected for this sample because we wanted to maximize the chances that a couple would fill out the scales without worrying about their demographic data not being private. We found that couples are much more sensitive about providing data to their therapist on socioeconomic data than data about more intimate psychological aspects of their lives. Approximately 12,000 therapists currently use the RCU, and about 3,800 couples a month currently take the questionnaires. There are never any missing data for the RCU. The current version of the RCU includes the possibility for repeated use, in order to evaluate a client couple's progress in therapy, and provide a balanced and functional report that the therapist can give directly to the clients.

Replication Sample

The failure to replicate results in psychology has recently become a major methodological issue (Killeen, 2019). A recent search we did on the term "failure to replicate" on PsychNet produced 809 papers. Therefore, for testing the replicability of our results, we used a random number generator to *randomly* divide the total sample in half so that all analyses could be carried out twice: once for testing, and once to assess whether results replicated or not. As is well-known, randomization precludes matching the two halves of our total sample. All analyses were carried out twice. Across both randomly selected subsamples, 93% of our results were stable.

Demographic Data

In our initial version of the RCU we did not collect demographic data because we wanted to avoid discouraging couples from completing the questionnaires. However, more recently we included demographic information, but made it optional—that is, a couple could avoid filling out this information and the therapist would still receive a full report. We were pleased to be able to report summary demographic data for an additional 25,014 individuals probably comparable with our sample who have now taken the RCU since our initial sample. These individuals are out of the 40,681 couples in the current sample. A brief summary:

- The mean ages of the couples were Heterosexual Wife 40.1 (SD = 10.0), Husband 42.3 (SD = 10.5); averaged across partners: Lesbian 40.6 (SD = 10.5), Gay male 39.5 (SD = 10.8), Transgender/Other 38.5 (SD = 11.5). The "Transgender/Other" category is new, and is part of the new optional demographic data we now collect.
- The percentage of couples married were Heterosexual 78.94, Lesbian 65.80, Gay male 41.78, Transgender/Other 63.77. The mean combined incomes were Heterosexual 134,989 (SD = 59,841), Lesbian 129,917 (SD = 54,236), Gay male 145,769 (SD = 53,179), Transgender/Other 148,418 (SD = 65,392).
- The percentages of couples who completed college or higher were Heterosexual 71.0, Lesbian 68.7, Gay male 73.1, Transgender/Other 68.1. Clearly these data suggest that our sample of couples seeking couples therapy are an educated and economically advantaged segment of the population.

Reliabilities

The Cronbach alphas are available *separately* for heterosexual, gay male, and lesbian couples in three supplemental files (1, 2, and 3) of the *Journal of Marital and Family Therapy* online; in summary, the reliabilities were quite comparable across subsamples, and quite comparable across sexual orientations.

Overall Static Relationship Functioning

There were five scales to assess the couples' overall functioning: (1) *Global happiness*. (GH, 15 items, 5-point scale; sample item: "I think my partner really cares about me.") This global scale was designed to measure relationship happiness, since other traditional measures of dyadic adjustment unfortunately confound happiness with conflict avoidance. For example, on the Locke–Wallace MAT, a couple gets higher scores if they report that they do not disagree on a set of issues. This would be the case either if they had resolved these issues or if they had never discussed these issues (that is, if they avoided conflict). The regression equation (Studies 1 and 2) between Locke–Wallace scores (LW) and GH scores is: $LW = 2GH - 39.0$. For the current sample, the Cronbach alphas for each partner were, respectively, (.93, .93); for heterosexual couples, Partner 1 was the wife and Partner 2 was the husband; for same-sex couples partners are not distinguished. (2) *Divorce potential*. (15 items, true/false; sample item: "I have made specific plans to discuss separation or divorce with my partner.") This scale, created by Weiss and Cerreto (1980), was used to measure divorce potential (alphas .84, .96). (3) *Chaos*. (5 items, true/false; sample item: "Do major unplanned negative events keep happening to the two of you?") This scale, designed in our laboratory, assesses the extent to which the couple feel that their lives are chaotic and subject to external events that they cannot control (alphas .73, .72). (4) *Trust issues*. (10 items, 5-point scale; sample item: "There were important times when my partner has not been there for me when I was really in need.") This scale, designed in our laboratory, assesses the extent to which each partner can count on and trust that their partner is emotionally "there for them" under any circumstance (alphas .89, .80). (5) *Commitment*. (10 items, 5-point scale; sample item: "After an argument I am not thinking I could be happier with someone else.") This scale, designed in our laboratory, assesses the extent to which each person is committed to staying in this relationship, for better or for worse (alphas .73, .75).

Dynamic Functioning—Sound Relationship House Theory

The following variables of the Sound Relationship House theory were designed to assess the *dynamics* of the relationship. In addition to trust and commitment, the SRH theory also assesses the relationship in three domains: friendship and intimacy, conflict management, and shared meaning. Cronbach alphas are for each partner for the *entire* current sample, for each sexual orientation, presented in the following order: heterosexual couples, lesbian couples, and then gay male couples. For heterosexual couples the husband alpha precedes the wife alpha: *Friendship and intimacy.* There were seven friendship/intimacy questionnaires (5 items per scale, true/false) that included 1. *Love maps.* This scale assesses how well the partners know one another's internal psychological worlds (sample item: "I know my partner's current worries"; alphas .69, .66); 2. *Fondness and admiration.* This scale assesses expressions of love, affection, and respect (sample item: "I am really proud of my partner"; alphas .77, .79); 3. *Turning toward or away.* This scale assesses the extent to which each partner responds positively to bids to connect emotionally (sample item: "My partner is usually interested in hearing my views on things"; alphas .75, .73); 4. *Satisfaction with romance, passion, and the quality of sex.* This scale assesses whether each partner still feels actively courted romantically (sample item: "The fire has gone out of this relationship"; alphas .82, .86); (e) *Satisfaction with the frequency of sex.* This scale assesses whether each partner is happy with how often sex occurs (sample item: "One problem is the amount of love in our lovemaking"; alphas .80, .81); and 6. *Loneliness.* This scale assesses the extent to which people feel lonely in the relationship (sample item: "I will at times find myself quite lonely in this relationship"; alphas .81, .80).

Conflict Management. Seven conflict questionnaires were designed and tested in our laboratory. They were 1. *Harsh startup.* This scale assesses the extent to which conflict discussion starts harshly with criticism, blame, or contempt, or gently by self-description (sample item: "Arguments often seem to come out of nowhere"; alphas .72, .74); 2. *The Four Horsemen of the Apocalypse.* This scale assesses the extent to which the Four Horsemen of the Apocalypse—criticism, defensiveness, contempt, and stonewalling—are present during conflict discussions (sample item: "I have to defend myself because the charges against me are so unfair"; alphas .68, .70); 3. *Psychological or physiological flooding*. This scale assesses the extent to which people feel overwhelmed and in physiological fight-or-flight during conflict conversations. It should be noted that there is not always a significant correlation between psychological flooding and physiological flooding (10 items, 5-point scale; sample item: "I feel attacked when my partner gets angry"; alphas .84, .85); 4. *Partner accepts influence*. This scale assesses the extent to which *the partner* thinks that the other partner accepts influence (5 items, true/false; sample item: "My partner has a lot of basic common sense"; alphas .67, .62); 5. *Compromise*. This scale assesses the extent to which the couple can arrive at compromise (5 items, true/false; sample item: "In discussing issues we can usually find our common ground of agreement"; alphas .72, .71); (f) *Negative sentiment override*. This scale assesses the extent to which the overall cost–benefit assessment of the relationship and the partner's character is tilted toward cost versus benefit (5 items, true/false; sample item: "I just want the negativity to stop"; alphas .70, .71); 6. *Repair attempts*. This scale assesses the extent to which the couple can make repairs to get the conversation back on track when the conversation is moving into negativity (5 items, true/false; sample item: "We are good at taking breaks when we need them"; alphas .75, .75).

Specific Conflict Areas—Sound Relationship House Theory. The following scales to assess perceived specific problem severity were designed in our laboratory to assess the extent to which the couple report that they argue about each specific issue. An important part of specific problem assessment online is the *comment section* for each problem, in which people can provide a history or a further explanation. An example will help illustrate how important this comment section is for the therapist. One woman, who described a problem with basic values and life goals, explained that her husband had recently converted to another religion and most of her conversations with him were now about his proselytizing to convert her. For each specific problem area the first question is whether there is a problem with the area. If the subject answers yes, five other true/false questions are asked. The specific problem areas assessed were (1) *Problems handling stress* (sample item: "We can reduce our stress by talking together"; alphas .74, .76); (2) *Problems with relatives and extended family* (sample item: "I feel unaccepted by my partner's family"; alphas .74, .77); (3) *Problems with jealousy* (sample item: "I can't deal with the lies"; alphas .92, .92); (4) *Presenting with an emotional or sexual affair(s)* (sample item: "I feel that our relationship has been violated")—we did not discriminate between them because in treatment an emotional affair often morphs into a sexual affair (alphas .90, .96); (5) *Problems with basic values and life goals* (sample item: "We seem to want different things out of life"; alphas .73, .80); (6) *Problems with housework and child care* (sample item: "We used to share more in the family's workload"; alphas .81, .75); (7) *Problems with financial issues* (sample item: "We are not united in managing our finances"; alphas .82, .82); (8) *Problems having fun together* (sample item: "We don't seem to have much time for fun"; alphas .77, .77); (9) *Problems with spirituality, religion, ethics* (sample item: "We have problems sharing the same beliefs"; alphas .86, .85); (10) *Problems with children* (sample item: "We have very different points of view about goals for our children"; alphas .86, .85); (11) *Problems with recent distressing events* (these could be incidents of domestic violence, or drug/alcohol use, or other traumatic events; sample item: "This is turning into a relationship I hadn't bargained for"; alphas .75, .69); and (12) *Gridlock on perpetual issues* (5 items, true/false; sample item: "My partner has a long list of basically unreasonable demands"; alphas .72, .74).

Shared Meaning—Sound Relationship House Theory. Four scales were designed and tested in our laboratory to assess the extent to which the couple have established a sense of shared meaning in their relationship. They were each five-item true/false scales: (1) *Rituals of connection.* This scale measures the extent to which the couple have created traditions in their relationship in which they can count on connection (sample item: "Reunions at the end of each day in our home are generally special times in my day"; alphas .75, .72); (2) *Supporting roles in life.* This scale measures the extent to which the couple feel that they are supported in the various roles they play in life: mother, father, friend, sibling, worker, and so on (sample item: "My partner and I have similar philosophies about balancing work and family life"; alphas .72, .71); (3) *Shared goals*. This scale measures the extent to which the couple have shared goals (sample item: "We have very similar financial goals"; alphas .71, .71); and (4) *Shared fundamental symbols*. This scale measures the extent to which the couple have shared values on fundamental symbols, such as defining what a home is, and what the importance of love is (sample item: "We see eye to eye about what a 'home' means"; alphas .63, .63).

Comorbidities and Individual Issues. The following scales measured a broad range of comorbidities, with sample items provided only for our scales: (1) *Emotionally difficult or traumatic primary family history—SRH theory* (sample item: "I was physically abused by my parents"; alphas .94, .94); (2) *Drug and alcohol abuse* (CAGE-AID, reliabilities in the .90s; current sample alphas .76, .78); (3) *Michigan drug and alcohol frequency screening* (b-MAST; reliabilities in the .90s; Zung, 1982; alphas .70, .68); (4) *Suicide potential*, designed in our laboratory (alphas .74, .61); (5) *Situational domestic violence—SRH theory*. "Situational" domestic violence refers to relatively minor violence that is symmetric between partners so that there is no perpetrator or victim, both partners take responsibility for the violence, there is no mental control (or "gaslighting"), and there is no fear of the partner (alphas .83, .84); (6) *Characterological domestic violence—SRH theory* is measured by three scales, designed in our laboratory: (a) *Fear of partner* (sample item: "Are you afraid of your partner?"), (b) *Social control by partner* (sample item: "In the past six months did your partner try to control your every move by making you ask for permission?"), and (c) The nature and *severity of injuries* sustained from the violence (sample item: "In the past six months have you sustained a broken bone by fighting with your partner?"; the combined alphas across the three scales were .91, .86). Friend et al. (2011) reported that these three scales successfully discriminated situational from characterological domestic violence in two separate samples, so that situational and characterological domestic violence are mutually exclusive and exhaustive categories of domestic violence. These scales were used to first successfully screen out characterologically violent couples, and then in a randomized clinical trial to successfully treat couples suffering from situational domestic violence (Bradley & Gottman, 2012; Bradley et al., 2014; Friend et al., 2011, 2017); (7) *Gottman Emotional Abuse Scale—SRH theory* (Emotional Abuse Questionnaire [EAQ], 10 items per scale, 4-point ratings)—via *Social isolation* (sample item: "My partner tries to control who I spend time with"; alphas .92, .91); (8) EAQ—via *Degradation and public humiliation* (sample item: "My partner tries to convince people that I'm crazy"; alphas .81, .81); (9) EAQ—via *Sexual coercion* (sample item: "In bed my partner makes me do things I find repulsive"; alphas .66, .38); (10) EAQ—via *Threats to harm partner or children*, or actual property damage (sample item: "My partner intentionally damages things I care about"; alphas .78, .80); and (11) the *Derogatis SCL-90 Symptom List (unrevised)*, which has consistently demonstrated both high internal consistency reliability and the ability to discriminate patient populations (Derogatis & Cleary, 1977). Reliabilities in the current sample, for Partner 1 and Partner 2 respectively, were *Somatization* (.86, .85), *Obsessive compulsive* (.90, .89), *Interpersonal sensitivity* (.88, .87), *Depression* (.92, .92), *Anxiety* (.91, .90), *Anger–hostility* (.84, .83), *Phobic anxiety* (.83, .79), *Paranoid ideation* (.81, .81), and *Psychoticism* (.78, .78).

Analyses

Computations

We computed the number and percentages of couples for whom one partner was flagged for a problem, both partners were flagged for a problem, or neither was flagged for a problem. Therefore, analyses were done at the dyad level, and the data have no interdependence issues (see Kenny et al., 2006, p. 15). Our tables present data only for Subsample 1, for each sexual orientation group. We present: (1) the percentage of couples for whom only one partner was flagged for a problem, (2) the percentage of couples for whom both partners were flagged for a problem, (3) chi-square results comparing the three sexual orientations, and, finally, (4) whether or not the analyses replicated for Subsample 2. We also compared husbands and wives for heterosexual couples.

Results

Reliability

The Cronbach alphas for all subjects is in Supplemental Files 1, 2, and 3; they are available online for each of the three groups of couples from the *Journal of Marital and Family Therapy*. Reliabilities were comparable across groups. Our conclusions are (1) reliability does not differ across heterosexual, lesbian, or gay male couples; and (2) all the scales have acceptable reliabilities.

Frequencies of Issues Couples Bring to Therapy

From 3 × 3 tables of groups-by-frequency of problems that either one partner, both partners, or neither partner had, we computed the overall $c^2(4)$ analyses. The groups were also then compared in subsequent c^2s. The c^2s are computed from frequencies, but, for clarity in comparison, in Table 5.3 we present these data as percentages. Only those variables where either the significance or nonsignificance of the global 3 × 3 $c^2(4)$s replicated across samples were included in Table 5.3; failure of a *specific* comparison c^2 to replicate is indicated in Table 5.3 by a dashed line. We found that 91.5% of the time the two samples yielded similarly significant or nonsignificant results across the sexual orientation groups, so that one would have to conclude that the two samples essentially gave replicable results. That result speaks to the current crisis in psychology about replicability. This kind of analysis is rarely done because it requires a large sample size.

Probably the most striking overall result of Table 5.3 is the *very* high percentage of couples where at least one partner is above cutoffs for important presenting problems. Although not quite the same scales—for example, 83% of our heterosexual couples reported serious problems with romance and sex, compared to 30% reported by Péloquin et al. (2019). Another example is that a full 97.4% of heterosexual couples reported being flooded during conflict, with no significant differences across sexual orientation in flooding. We were surprised by these results. In general, same-sex couples starting therapy were in much better shape than heterosexual couples. A greater percentage of same-sex couples were happier, and a smaller percentage had problems with love maps, fondness and admiration, turning toward, satisfaction with romance, satisfaction with the frequency of sex, emotion dismissing, and shared meaning (rituals of connection and supporting roles). A smaller percentage of same-sex couples had problems with stress, with values and goals, with having fun, with issues about spirituality/religion/ethics, and with issues related to children.

However, we did find that trust was a more common issue for gay male couples than for heterosexual couples, and trust was also a more common issue for heterosexual couples than for lesbian couples; a similar pattern held for the percentages of couples presenting with an affair. A greater percentage of same-sex couples compared to heterosexual couples also reported primary family trauma, serious problems with abusing drugs and alcohol, and on the SCL-90 problems with somatization, anxiety, and phobic anxiety. These considerations suggest some added issues therapists need to consider in couples therapy with same-sex couples. Table 5.4 is a summary of problems across both samples.

Differences Between Heterosexual Husbands and Wives. Table 5.5 is a summary of the paired t-tests between wives and husbands for heterosexual couples, for Sample 1. In these analyses we followed the recommendations of Kenny et al. (2006, pp. 62–67). Examining all the t-tests, one would conclude that wives coming to couples therapy were *overwhelmingly* more distressed than their husbands. They were significantly less happily married, more divorce prone, lower on love maps, lower in fondness and admiration, lower in turning toward, lower in romantic satisfaction, lower in the quality of sex, less satisfied with the frequency of sex, more lonely, lower in trust, lower in commitment, and less emotion dismissing. Wives, compared to their husbands, reported more of the Four Horsemen (criticism, defensiveness, contempt, and stonewalling), were more flooded, accepted influence less, compromised less, were more likely to be in negative sentiment override, and less likely to repair; wives reported a more traumatic family history, greater severity of *every* specific conflict area, less shared meaning (rituals, roles, goals, and symbols), less severity but greater frequency of abuse of alcohol and drugs, more emotional abuse (sexual coercion, more threats and property damage), and were higher on every scale of the Derogatis SCL-90. However, on a few scales husbands were significantly more distressed than their wives. Husbands reported harsher startup in conflict, more situational domestic violence, and greater emotional abuse in two areas—social isolation and public humiliation—than their wives. All wife-husband differences replicated with comparably sized t-ratios.

Conclusions

We can have confidence in these data because results replicated across two random samples of the large sample of couples about to begin couples therapy. It is clear from these data that over 80% of all couples about to enter couples therapy have serious problems dealing with both *conflict* and *intimacy*. Among heterosexual couples wives were far more distressed than husbands. Couples about to begin couples therapy are also far more troubled than the couples in the majority of studies in the literature that evaluate the effectiveness of couples therapy. This is probably because some university-based studies on the effectiveness of couples therapy have screened out many comorbidities that are commonly found in our sample. For example, a 5-year follow-up study of traditional versus integrative couples therapy excluded any couples with Axis I disorders of substance abuse or dependence, or bipolar disorder; Axis II disorders of borderline schizotypal personality disorder or antisocial personality disorder; and moderate to severe domestic violence (Baucom et al., 2009; Christensen et al., 2010). Our data suggest that *comorbidities are the norm*, not the exception, for couples seeking couples therapy. Twenty percent to 30% of our couples were flagged for the therapist to consider whether one of their clients was currently at risk for suicide. In some ways, this is not surprising. A recent study (Stulz et al., 2017) found that in 54.5% of a sample of people who had attempted suicide, interpersonal conflict was the trigger for their suicide attempts. Today, rather than screening out comorbidities, we need to learn which couples with which comorbidities we can help with a couples therapy approach. The therapy needs to fit the clinical population. Based on our data, we cannot currently claim that it does fit.

In a similar point, we need to study therapy effectiveness for couples that have much lower scores on industry-standard measures of relationship satisfaction than those commonly studied up to now. Two such scales used in these studies are the Dyadic Adjustment Scale (DAS; Spanier, 1988) and the Locke–Wallace (Locke & Wallace, 1959). Like the IQ test, the mean of both scales was designed to be 100.0 with a standard deviation of 15.0. In many couples therapy studies, pre-treatment scores were less than half of a standard deviation below the mean. For example, in the Johnson and Greenberg (1985) study, the pre-treatment DAS group mean was 93.5, or 0.4 standard deviations below the mean, and in Jacobson and Christensen's study of acceptance-behavioral couples therapy (Baucom et al., 2009; Christensen et al., 2010; Jacobson et al., 2000), the pre-treatment DAS group mean was 90.3, or 0.6 standard deviations below the mean. These pre-treatment averages are far higher than our overall sample's pre-treatment average of 63.0, *which is 2.5 standard deviations below the mean.* In other words, our data suggest that couples who are entering couples therapy are considerably more problem-ridden and distressed than the couples in many university-based studies that have evaluated couples therapy. Not only are they much more unhappy, they also have many more comorbidities than couples in university-based studies. Based on our data, we must come to the startling conclusion that *we cannot claim that our couples therapies are effective for the actual clinical population our therapists face every day.*

Furthermore, there may also be an additional serious problem with most university-based studies on the *effect sizes* of couples therapy. Based on thorough prior reviews, the effect size of most evidence-based couples therapies hovers between 0.5 and 1.2 standard deviations on the Spanier DAS (Pinsof & Wynne, 1995; Pinsof et al., 1996). That effect size is fine if couples are within a standard deviation below the mean in marital satisfaction, or reasonably close to the mean, as they have been in many couples therapy outcome studies. However, even at best, if we raise marital satisfaction post-treatment by 1.2 standard deviations, given the pre-treatment average we found of 2.5 standard deviations below the mean, our therapeutic interventions still leave couples post-treatment at 1.3 standard deviations below the mean. That is unacceptable. Therefore, we suggest that as a field we need to develop interventions that are far more powerful than current interventions, perhaps with effect sizes from 2 to 4 standard deviations (see Gottman & Gottman, 2018).

Our data suggest that same-sex couples were in *most ways* in better shape than heterosexual couples who were about to begin therapy. However, the data on trust issues for gay male couples provide interesting challenges for the couples therapist. These results are consistent with the classic McWhirter and Mattison (1984) study, which reported that not a single gay male pair was able to maintain fidelity in their relationship for more than 5 years. However, outside affairs, these researchers concluded, were not damaging to the relationship's endurance, but were essential to it. Based on our sample, an opposite pattern holds for lesbian couples, who are more monogamous than both gay male and heterosexual couples about to begin therapy.

Our sample was an educated and prosperous group. If our findings are representative, this means that couples therapy is not reaching the vast majority of couples who have lower income and education than the couples in our sample. Based on our clinical experience, these couples may be in worse shape than the couples in our sample. Because our online checkup requires both partners to complete all items, we may have biased the sample by eliminating those clients who might refuse to complete the questionnaires. Our intuition suggests, however, that the people eliminated by the minimal burden of assessment would probably be worse off rather than better off than our sample. Therefore, if anything, we may be *underestimating* the severity of problems confronting therapists every day.

The RCU offers the possibility of doing assessment and effectiveness research on couples therapy that is far more detailed and specific than relying only on one gross relationship satisfaction score as the gold standard for outcome evaluation. Hopefully, detail and specificity can inform the construction of more powerful couples therapies in the future. The field of couples therapy research has previously been characterized by small samples. The internet offers the possibility of large-N epidemiological and representative international samples. The current international sample was limited to English-literate couples, but that limitation could be remedied in the future.

Tables

TABLE 5.1 Correlations of Reduced Shared Meaning Scales With SPAFF-Coded Conflict Discussion Anger and Sadness (H = Husband, W = Wife).

Meaning Scale	SPAFF H Anger	SPAFF H Sadness	SPAFF W Anger	SPAFF W Sadness
H Rituals	−.12	.01	−21*	−.24**
W Rituals	.04	.01	−.04	−.38***
H Roles	−.08	.02	−.07	−.38***
W Roles	−.06	.00	−.22**	−.45***
H Goals	−.41***	−.07	−.31***	−21*
W Goals	.01	.00	−.16	−.01
H Symbols	−23**	−.03	−.16	−.01
W Symbols	−.15	.00	−26**	−.31***

*$p < .05$
**$p < .01$
***$p < .0001$

Table 5.2

This table is available only online at the *Journal of Marital and Family Therapy* (Supplemental Files 1, 2, and 3). Cronbach alphas for heterosexual, lesbian, and gay male couples. Reliabilities are high and comparable across sexual-preference types of couples.

Table 5.3

Percentage of couples in Sample 1 where one or two (both) partners were problematic for each variable (subtract total of both sums from 100 to determine percentage of couples with no problems). $C^2(4)$ refers to the 3 × 3 table (sexual orientation by proportion with one, both, or neither), $c^2(2)$ H/L to the reduced table comparing heterosexual with lesbian (L) couples, $c^2(2)$ H/G

TABLE 5.3 Paired t-Tests Between Wives and Husbands for Heterosexual Couples

Scale	Het One	Het Two	Les One	Les Two	Gay One	Gay Two	$c^2(4)$ 3×3	$c^2(2)$ H/L	$c^2(2)$ H/G	$c^2(2)$ L/G	$c^2(2)$ S/H
Global Happiness	32.0	36.1	25.2	30.6	34.8	28.1	41.5a	35.5a	6.4c	7.3c	34.2a
Friendship/Intimacy											
Love Maps	23.6	4.1	18.1	2.3	19.5	2.7	17.8a	14.4a	v3.6	0.3	17.5a
Fondness	30.3	29.3	27.1	19.2	25.3	21.3	56.2a	41.3a	15.8a	0.5	55.8a
Turn Toward	29.8	30.3	25.2	19.6	27.6	22.2	61.5a	51.6a	10.8b	1.6	60.0a
Romance Problems	20.7	62.3	23.5	54.0	23.5	56.6	---	---	---	0.7	18.6a
Quality Sex Problems	27.5	27.6	26.9	23.7	23.1	31.2	7.8	5.2	---	---	3.3
Frequency Sex Problems	24.3	24.3	17.9	19.4	19.9	19.5	33.3a	26.3a	7.5c	0.4	32.9a
Lonely	30.5	51.6	30.8	44.2	34.8	39.4	34.4a	19.7a	15.4a	---	32.8a
Trust Problems	29.7	4.4	22.1	3.1	35.3	2.7	22.6a	18.2a	4.2	14.0a	9.6b
Commitment Problems	20.8	4.6	14.8	2.5	18.6	7.2	21.8a	17.7a	4.0	11.7b	11.6b
Partner Emotion Dismissing	55.3	27.2	48.7	24.2	47.5	25.8	43.7a	31.7a	12.9b	0.2	43.5a
Conflict											
Harsh Startup	26.3	64.1	24.4	65.1	31.7	60.1	4.6	1.1	3.4	4.5	0.1
Flooding	9.7	87.7	9.4	88.1	8.6	89.1	0.4	0.1	0.4	0.2	0.3
Negative Sentiment Override	24.4	70.4	20.4	71.5	23.5	71.0	5.2	---	0.2	2.2	2.8
Prior Family Trauma	48.3	22.1	44.6	34.4	48.9	24.0	48.7a	48.2a	---	---	38.6a

TABLE 5.3 Continued

Scale	Het One	Het Two	Les One	Les Two	Gay One	Gay Two	c2(4) 3 × 3	c2(2) H/L	c2(2) H/G	c2(2) L/G	c2(2) S/H
Specific Problems											
Stress	32.8	44.7	38.1	33.7	34.4	32.6	43.5a	25.9a	18.3a	1.8	41.2a
Relatives	29.1	41.3	29.2	45.4	32.1	32.6	12.4c	5.1	7.1c	---	0.7
Affairs	12.4	18.6	9.6	13.3	17.2	24.4	27.8a	15.6a	11.7b	26.8a	2.3
Values/Goals	34.3	35.2	32.3	26.7	38.5	26.7	35.8a	29.1a	---	3.2	39.2a
Finances	26.5	49.0	27.7	47.1	22.2	52.9	3.0	0.7	2.2	2.9	0.1
Fun	21.3	64.3	24.6	53.2	22.2	50.2	64.0a	32.7a	32.8a	---	60.2a
Spirituality, Religion, Ethics	33.1	21.5	31.2	15.2	29.9	14.5	27.9a	17.6a	10.7b	0.3	27.6a
Children	27.5	24.7	22.1	25.0	21.7	11.8	40.9a	8.0c	33.3a	18.0a	23.9a
Shared Meaning											
Rituals of Connection	33.7	29.5	29.4	21.4	30.8	19.0	54.3a	35.7a	19.6a	0.5	53.9a
Supporting Roles	34.4	20.3	32.2	15.8	34.4	13.6	17.4b	---	7.0c	0.7	16.8a
Shared Goals	32.9	17.0	30.6	11.0	32.6	10.0	27.2a	18.8a	8.8c	0.4	26.9a
Individual Issues											
Drug/Alcohol Amount	19.7	2.4	26.2	4.0	23.1	3.2	22.8a	20.8a	---	1.2	21.3a
Suicide Potential	23.4	3.3	31.7	7.9	33.0	5.9	73.1a	57.3a	17.3a	0.9	71.2a

Situational Domestic Violence	18.3	10.0	15.8	13.3	19.0	12.7	9.23c	7.32c	2.04	1.17	8.14c
Characterological Domestic Violence	22.2	7.6	20.2	8.3	19.0	6.8	2.9	1.3	1.6	0.7	2.2
Emotional Abuse											
Social Isolation of Partner	33.9	6.2	30.2	8.3	29.9	8.6	8.7	5.7	---	0.3	---
Public Humiliation	11.6	2.7	11.0	1.4	12.2	2.3	4.3	4.1	0.3	1.1	3.5
Sexual Coercion	9.4	0.4	7.7	1.0	7.7	1.4	9.9c	---	5.2	0.2	9.4b
Threats	4.4	0.4	3.3	0.8	5.0	0.0	4.2	3.0	1.0	---	0.9
SCL-90: Psychopathology											
Somatization	22.8	2.7	25.8	6.5	16.7	2.3	38.0a	32.9a	4.8	14.7a	18.5a
Obsessive Compulsive	41.2	12.1	41.2	14.6	46.6	10.0	6.2	3.2	2.9	3.6	2.3
Interpersonal Sensitivity	42.0	13.2	39.6	16.0	41.2	14.9	4.0	3.5	0.5	0.2	3.8
Depression	37.1	9.4	35.2	12.3	38.0	6.8	6.9	5.0	1.8	0.5	1.4
Anxiety	24.7	2.8	30.2	5.6	23.1	1.8	25.8a	24.4a	---	---	12.5b
Anger–Hostility	41.0	15.7	37.9	18.9	38.0	13.1	7.4	4.5	---	4.0	3.0
Phobic Anxiety	13.3	0.8	16.5	2.9	13.6	0.9	32.2a	32.2a	0.6	4.0	23.5a
Paranoid Ideation	24.9	3.5	22.1	4.4	27.2	5.4	6.3	3.1	---	2.8	3.5

comparing heterosexual with gay (G) male couples, $c^2(2)$ L/G comparing lesbian with gay male couples, $c^2(2)$ S/H comparing same-sex with heterosexual couples. Chi-square cell left blank (---) if $c^2(4)$ did not replicate across the two samples; a $= p < .001$, b $= p < .01$, c $= p < .05$, no letter = not significant. Variables were presented *only when results (either significant, or nonsignificant) replicated across samples.*

TABLE 5.4 Percentage of Couples Beyond Cutoffs for Problems. (Sample 1 and Sample 2 are randomly selected subsamples from the total sample.)

Variable	Het % one partner	Het % both partners	Gay % one partner	Gay % both partners	Les % one partner	Les % both partners
Low Satisfaction	68.5	57.7	62.6	67.9	60.1	54.8
Divorce/Separation Potential	66.0	61.3	68.5	65.7	61.3	63.0
Romance Problems	83.2	80.6	80.4	82.9	80.2	83.6
Sex Frequency Problems	48.8	43.5	44.3	48.7	39.1	37.9
Lonely	82.4	75.5	76.7	82.4	76.9	71.7
Affair(s)	32.6	24.9	43.4	31.7	25.4	42.9
Drug Abuse Severe	26.1	32.5	26.9	26.2	25.8	27.4
Drug Abuse Frequency Severe	24.4	21.5	28.8	24.5	22.3	30.1
Domestic Violence Situational	28.6	27.0	29.2	30.1	29.6	25.6
Domestic Violence Characterological	30.1	27.0	29.2	30.1	29.6	25.6
Suicide Potential	20.7	26.8	28.3	20.7	30.7	30.1
Social Isolation	41.6	40.1	47.5	41.1	39.5	43.8
Humiliation	14.6	12.3	12.3	14.6	14.3	13.3

Variable	Het % one partner	Het % both partners	Gay % one partner	Gay % both partners	Les % one partner	Les % both partners
Sexual Coercion	10.5	6.9	9.6	10.7	7.8	11.4
Threats & Damage to Property	25.8	4.1	2.3	25.5	3.9	5.0
Traumatic Family History	69.8	77.9	76.3	69.7	80.6	74.0
Low Love Maps	27.9	19.3	23.3	27.9	18.6	20.6
Low Fondness & Admiration	66.5	47.8	49.8	60.3	46.6	44.8
Low Turning Toward	60.8	47.8	51.6	60.2	44.2	44.8
Chaos	58.8	54.2	50.2	59.0	55.6	49.8
Low Trust	35.2	25.8	37.4	35.1	26.8	32.9
Low Commitment	25.6	19.8	23.3	25.5	14.8	21.5
Harsh Startup	90.2	90.2	90.9	90.9	90.8	87.7
Four Horsemen	82.1	80.8	81.7	82.1	81.0	76.3
Flooding	97.5	97.8	97.3	97.6	96.7	95.9
Doesn't Accept Influence	50.4	42.7	46.6	50.7	45.8	40.2
No Compromise	83.4	80.4	77.2	83.6	82.0	78.1
Negative Sentiment Override	93.7	93.5	93.6	94.0	93.2	90.9
Repair Fails	83.7	82.2	77.2	83.5	83.0	77.2
Stress Problems	77.6	71.6	70.8	77.5	71.0	67.6
Relatives Problems	71.0	73.0	66.2	70.3	71.4	60.7
Jealousy Problems	71.0	73.0	66.2	70.3	71.4	60.7

Variable	Het % one partner	Het % both partners	Gay % one partner	Gay % both partners	Les % one partner	Les % both partners
Affair(s)	32.6	24.9	43.4	31.7	25.4	42.9
Goals Problems	70.0	61.8	66.7	70.1	61.3	62.1
Housework Problems	67.4	64.4	58.9	68.5	64.2	63.5
Financial Problems	75.8	76.7	75.4	75.8	73.8	75.8
Problems With Fun	75.8	76.7	75.4	75.8	73.8	75.8
Spirituality Problems	55.3	48.9	49.8	55.4	44.2	44.8
Problems With Children	52.0	45.6	30.1	52.3	46.4	28.3
Distressing Events	49.5	48.7	48.9	49.7	46.4	43.8
Rituals of Connection	55.1	46.4	43.8	55.7	50.3	47.0
Supporting Roles in Life	55.1	46.4	43.8	54.7	50.4	47.0
Shared Goals	50.1	41.7	46.1	49.8	42.9	35.6
Shared Symbols	71.5	66.0	63.9	71.1	64.4	69.9
Somatization	25.8	30.5	20.6	25.5	31.3	22.8
Obsessive–Compulsive	52.6	56.2	53.0	52.5	57.3	58.0
Interpersonal Sensitivity	54.5	53.6	56.2	54.4	57.3	58.5
Depression	45.7	46.4	42.9	46.0	49.3	43.8
Anxiety	26.4	33.7	23.8	26.9	34.6	32.4
Anger–Hostility	56.9	59.5	53.9	57.9	62.4	46.6
Phobic Anxiety	13.1	16.4	14.6	13.8	21.3	17.8
Paranoid Ideation	28.4	27.8	32.0	28.0	26.6	32.9
Psychoticism	16.1	15.5	16.4	16.0	19.0	19.6

TABLE 5.5 Wife–Husband Differences for Heterosexual Couples, Sample 1

Variable	Wife Mean	Husband Mean	*t ratio* (*df* = 19,528)
Global Satisfaction	51.40	54.64	−41.11***
Divorce Proneness	4.25	3.29	37.65***
Love Maps	3.86	4.00	−11.90***
Fondness & Admiration	2.61	2.88	−21.25***
Turning Toward	2.66	2.74	−6.96***
Satisfaction With Romance	2.82	2.94	−6.85***
Satisfaction With Sex Quality	2.85	2.91	−6.30***
Satisfaction With Sex Frequency	2.62	2.75	−6.30***
Loneliness	3.53	2.88	47.79***
Chaos	2.18	2.18	0.19 n.s.
Distrust	29.10	24.04	64.19***
Commitment	37.92	38.49	−14.27***
Partner Is Emotion Dismissing	34.87	29.95	77.96***
Harsh Startup	2.84	3.16	−22.57***
Four Horsemen	2.42	2.30	8.41***
Flooding	31.55	30.97	16.65***
Partner Accepts Influence	3.08	3.28	−15.91***
Compromise	2.28	2.59	−24.26***
Negative Sentiment Override	3.32	3.24	5.27***
Effective Repair	1.66	1.73	−5.81***
Traumatic Family History	8.61	6.61	25.33***
Specific Problems			
Stress	3.43	3.17	15.37***
Relatives	2.48	2.26	15.60***
Jealousy	2.72	2.40	19.81***
Affair(s)	2.16	1.80	16.54***
Goals, Values	2.42	2.15	15.49***
Housework–Child Care	2.44	1.81	37.90***
Finances	3.24	2.89	20.22***

Variable	Wife Mean	Husband Mean	t ratio (df = 19,528)
Fun Together	3.37	3.27	7.01***
Spirituality-Religion	2.12	1.55	30.28***
Children	1.88	1.51	24.64***
Distressing Events	1.33	0.96	34.78***
Gridlock	2.59	2.30	22.70***
Low Shared Rituals	3.21	3.45	−19.81***
Low Support Roles	3.55	3.77	−17.72***
Low Shared Goals	3.74	3.31	−7.66***
Low Shared Symbols	3.15	3.31	−12.59***
Drugs/Alcohol Intensity	0.90	2.00	−29.13***
Drug/Alcohol Frequency	1.71	1.17	39.53***
Suicide Potential	0.28	0.21	10.64***
Domestic Violence Situational	1.23	2.03	−18.04***
Domestic Violence Characterological	0.49	0.46	2.71**
Emotional Abuse			
Social Isolation	16.20	19.81	−40.52***
Public Humiliation	15.20	15.56	−7.75***
Sexual Coercion	8.86	8.08	33.21***
Threats, Property Damage	7.78	7.70	4.29***
SCL-90			
Somatization	8.89	6.51	38.14***
Obsessive–compulsive disorder	10.28	9.06	17.14***
Interpersonal Sensitivity	8.18	6.68	25.08***
Depression	16.51	12.44	42.53***
Anxiety	7.26	5.39	29.05***
Anger–Hostility	4.39	3.91	13.37***
Phobic Anxiety	1.46	0.86	23.97***
Paranoid Ideation	3.79	3.93	−3.74**
Psychoticism	2.56	2.59	−0.88 n.s.

**$p < .01$, ***$p < .001$; every t-test replicated for Sample 2

CHAPTER 6

The Levenson–Gottman Love Lab in Your Office: Emotion Dynamics

In this chapter we present our "Love Lab" analysis of a relation-ship, based on actual interaction. We discuss emotion measured in three ways: (1) emotion behavior coding, (2) perception using the rating dial, and (3) physiology.

Gottman Connect can be used to do a complete assessment of your couple that yields, once the data are collected, two detailed reports: one for the therapist and one for the couple. (Our technical manual—information for signing on to Gottman Connect, getting a summary of the RCU, videotap-ing the events-of-the-week and conflict conversations, and filling out the Brief Clinician's Checklist—is available on the Gottman Connect website.) By requesting each partner to fill out the RCU individually, you can print out a one-page summary report of how the couple responded to the RCU before your first session. It may influence the kinds of questions you initially ask.

We always supplement our RCU static snapshot with a moving picture of the dynamics the couple experience over time, as they converse. We ask the couple to have two videotaped 10-minute conversations with each other while we act like a fly on the wall, stay quiet, and do not intervene: (1) a discussion about their events of the week, and (2) a conflict conversation in which the couple addresses one of their unsolved problems. Each partner's individual heart and breathing rates are also recorded during their conversations. Then the couple is instructed on how to replay their videotapes and privately perform the video-recall rating dial task. It will take each partner only about 25 minutes to complete it. We recommend that one partner does the rating dial task in a private, separate space outside your meeting room, while inside the room, you conduct an individual interview with the second partner; then the partners switch places, with the second partner completing the video ratings while you interview the first partner. Once they each complete their ratings, the Gottman Connect software algorithms can now automatically combine and analyze the couple's conversations and rating dial data from three sources: (1) their specific affect codes (SPAFF; performed by two independent observers or, more recently, findings analyzed by machine learning; that feature will be available in the future), (2) what the partners each see using their video-recall ratings, and (3) their physiology (also available in the future). We now have a portrait of their interpersonal "dynamics" that describes their changing interactions over time, moment by moment.

Your final step is to complete a Brief Clinician's Checklist, that is, your subjective impressions of the couple. Now all of these data can be compiled into a printable therapist's report and couple's report. In essence, you have just completed a thorough evaluation of this couple's strengths and challenges, using methods that come straight out of our research lab. With these reports in hand, you can review the couple's report with them, being careful to focus on their interpersonal dynamics rather than their individual scores and ratings. (Your therapist's report will give you more individual details for each partner that can help you fine-tune your interventions.) This review can facilitate the next step: jointly agreeing on goals for therapy.

Dimensions of the Couple's 10-Minute Conversations

1. Emotion Dynamics: Codes Over Time—Observations Made by Either Human Observers or a Computer

The first part of our dynamic description of a relationship focuses on what we can objectively see as a couple interacts during each of two conversations: the events-of-the-week conversation and the conflict conversation. In our lab we use our observational coding system, called the Specific Affect Coding System (SPAFF). John developed this system to describe how couples interact with one another, moment by moment. The system was used to detect specific affects, or emotions, expressed during any conversation two partners might have. The SPAFF focuses solely on the affects that are expressed. The system draws on the emotional content in the words, facial expressions (based on Ekman and Friesen's [1978] Facial Action Coding System [FACS]), vocal tone, paralinguistic features (like stress), gestures, and other nonverbal cues, to characterize the emotions displayed. SPAFF has several versions, with up to 20 codes. The SPAFF numbers have repeatedly demonstrated their validity by being able to predict how a relationship changes over time. There are manuals that are used to train observers in SPAFF. A recent result we've had is that by using machine learning and a superfast computer (now inexpensively available), we can now do a 10-code SPAFF coding very quickly and automatically with a computer program that closely matches human observers. That feature will be available in the future for clinicians.

In one 16-code version of the SPAFF, coders categorize the emotions displayed using 5 positive affect codes (interest, validation, affection, humor, excitement/joy), 10 negative affect codes (disgust, contempt, belligerence, domineering, anger, fear/tension, defensiveness, whining, sadness, stonewalling), and 1 neutral affect code. For some purposes, we also weight the codes by their strength in predicting relationship breakup or stability. In that weighted SPAFF, for example, contempt receives a heavy negative weight of minus four (–4) because it was very good at predicting breakups, while humor receives a heavy positive weight of plus four (+4) because it was very good at predicting stability.

There's a great paper we want to tell you about, which appeared recently in the journal *Emotion*. The paper was written by Boiger et al. and it's titled "Different Bumps in the Road: The Emotional Dynamics of Couple Disagreements in Belgium and Japan." These scientists argued that culturally they expected to see more shame and guilt in the Japanese couples and more irritability in the Belgian couples. So, they created this highly imaginative figure. They plotted the couple's dynamics on a male-by-female graph very much like our phase space diagrams. Only, in their case, they arrayed their categorical emotion codes on each axis in a scale that ranged from calm to hurt. We won't go into too much detail describing their emotion codes, but you can get the gist of it from the figure. They then plotted points at each time point in the conflict conversation where they saw a combination of codes, such as female partner annoyed and male partner annoyed in the same 30-second segment. And then they connected the dots. They also shaded the pathways that were most frequent. That gave them a diagram summarizing the most frequent emotional pathways, or trajectories, of these conflict conversations. As you can see from the figure, the shaded, most frequent pathways for Belgian couples tended to be in the strong-annoyed regions of the phase plane. The most frequent pathways for the Japanese couples tended to be in the embarrassed-empathy region of the phase plane. Gottman Connect will be creating these Boiger et al. types of maps in the near future using our SPAFF codes.

For our mathematical modeling we went in a slightly different direction from that of Boiger et al. We created a *weighting* scheme derived from previous prediction research (Gottman, 1994), because some codes were better single predictors of breakup or stability of a relationship than other codes. A numerical value was calculated for the SPAFF codes for each 6-second time block separately for each partner by taking the sum of positive codes minus the negative codes, using the following weights: Disgust = -3, Contempt = -4, Belligerence = -2, Domineering = -1, Anger = -1, Fear = 0, Defensiveness = -2, Whining = -1, Sadness = -1, Stonewalling = -2, Neutral = $+0.1$, Interest = $+2$, Validation = $+4$, Affection = $+4$, Humor = $+4$, and Excitement/Joy = $+4$. This weighting yields a potential score range of about -25 to $+25$. For each couple two time series were created, kind of like the familiar stock

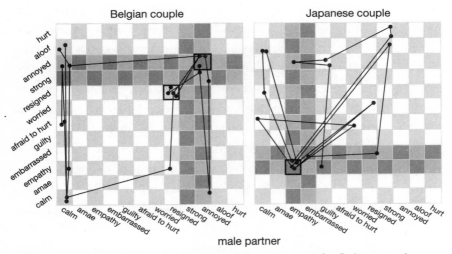

STATE SPACE GRID (SSG) of the Emotional Experience of a Belgian and a Japanese Couple During a 10-Minute Disagreement Interaction

NOTE: Each dot represents the emotional maxima (person-centered) experienced by the couple during a 30-s segment. Regions in the SSG that the authors had predicted to be relatively more central in the respective culture are highlighted with shaded bars. The inductively derived attractor states for each couple are indicated with a bold frame. Amae = like my partner would indulge any of my requests; empathy = empathy for my partner; afraid to hurt = afraid to hurt my partner. See the online article for the color version of this figure. *Copyright © 2022, American Psychological Association*

market Dow Jones average, one set of data over time for the husband and one for the wife, each with 100 data points. The interobserver correlations for these weighted data for married couples in one study was .90 ($p < .001$) during the conflict discussion. This weighting scheme was used in our 2002 book, *The Mathematics of Marriage*.

2. Video-Recall Rating Dial Emotion Dynamics: Observations Made by Each Partner

It is not enough to use observers' data to describe relationship dynamics. We need some way to also determine what the partners themselves actually see and feel. Perception can be very different from an objective coding of emotion. The second part of our description of the dynamics of a relationship moment by moment is to ask the partners to tell us what they recall having felt during the interaction. Why do we need this? A study by Robinson and Price (1980) found that unhappily married couples saw only 50% of the positivity that their partners were actually doing (as seen by outside observers). On the other hand, happily married couples were in line with outside observers in seeing all their partners' positivity. As you see, perception may not be in agreement with coded behavior. Therefore, John and Robert Levenson devised a "video-recall perception" for couples to use in scoring a videotape after their interaction. They asked people to turn a dial of numbers ranging from 1 to 10 to indicate what emotions they were feeling during the interaction. (Initially, the dial ranged from *very negative* to *very positive*.) The perception numbers have also demonstrated their validity by being able to predict how a relationship changes over time. Recently, we've helped couples in their ratings by attaching emotion words to each category in the perception. In Gottman Connect, couples do this rating online or even on their cell phones.

To get a feeling for the task we are asking people to do, we've included some of these emotion words we sometimes use to help people with the rating dial task. As they watch their video, they rate every moment by clicking on a number from 1 to 10, depending on how they felt in that moment.

To Help People Do the Rating: Emotion Words We Have Used

Negative 1: You felt put down by your partner, hurt, hopeless, dejected, resentful, irate, furious, disgusted, ashamed, or guilty;

Negative 2: You felt unsafe, frustrated, angry, lonely, abandoned, withdrawn, numb, or embarrassed;

Negative 3: You felt fearful, anxious, worried, cranky, grumpy, irritated, sad, or disappointed;

Negative 4: You felt tense, slightly annoyed, emotionally distant, aloof, or slightly sad;

Neutral 5: You felt neither positive nor negative at that moment;

Positive 6: You felt safe, relieved, peaceful;

Positive 7: You felt slightly happy, some real interest, curiosity, affection, or amusement;

Positive 8: You felt really happy, warm, content, secure, or hopeful;

Positive 9: You felt enthusiastic, excited, playful, very interested, grateful, empowered, or energized;

Positive 10: You felt loved, appreciated, cherished, trusting, understood, fascinated, laughing, joyful, or empathetic.

The Couple's "Emotional Bank Account." Using a computer program, we create a kind of Dow Jones–type graph of a conversation by plotting the cumulative sum of their positive-minus-negative perception data. We do this by transforming the 1-to-10 scale into a scale that ranges from −4 to +5, with the old 5 or midpoint of the scale as the new 0. The cumulative sum ("Cumsum") is a measure of what is currently in their *emotional bank account* as they interact. This isn't a very complicated process. In fact, there was once a *Saturday Night Live* skit in which couples' interaction was imagined to be an Olympic sport. Couples got points by the judges for shutting one another out of emotional connection. In that skit a sleepy husband came into the kitchen and poured only himself a cup of coffee. The judges gave that a 6 out of 10 because he hadn't thought that his wife might want a cup of coffee as well, so he was being selfish. When she sat down after pouring herself her own cup, the husband then opened a newspaper that totally blocked her view of him. For shutting her out visually, the judges decided that this was worth a 10, a superb move for destroying connection. As we graph this cumulative sum for *both* conversations, we can decide whether there is what we call "spillover of negativity" from the conflict part of a relationship to the everyday interaction of catching up with one another in the events conversation. Spillover of negativity is a common occurrence in a negative conflict-ridden relationship. In such a relationship negativity pervades even a potentially enjoyable situation like a vacation.

3. Physiological Emotion Dynamics

Synchronized to the video time code we collect data on what is happening in each person's body as they talk to one another. With Gottman Connect, synchronization of the videos for both partners happens even if partners are in different countries and the therapist is in a third country. In a therapist's office we often use wireless pulse oximeters to obtain two indices of physiological activity: heart rate and percent oxygen in the blood. We can also now measure heart rate for any skin tone from a videotape of a couple's interaction. Research by Loring Rowell has indicated that at a heart rate of over 100 beats a minute, or 80 beats per minute if the partner is especially athletic, people begin secreting adrenaline and cortisol. Physiology can also be synchronized between two people. We have called that "physiological linkage." It is generally mediated by negative affects like anger and sadness. As you will recall, we first noted that linkage in a study by Kaplan et al. (1964) in which pairs of roommate nurses interacted while each person's skin conductance (mediated by sweating from the palms of their hands) was linked, but only if the nurses disliked one another. In our research, marital unhappiness mediated the physiological linkage. In subsequent research, Levenson and colleagues have also discovered that positivity like shared humor can also mediate physiological linkage.

For Events and Conflict Conversations: What We Compute for the Couple's Report

Here is what we include in the couple's report after our assessment. The couple's report is less detailed than the therapist's report. For the most part, it includes only relationship-level analyses. The therapist can go over this report with a couple and use it to jointly select the goals of the therapy.

We are going to use this information later when we propose our couples' typology. Right now we'll focus on just one couple's events conversation. But we'll be using the same types of graphs for the conflict discussion too.

1. **The startup positive-to-negative ratio.** A couple entered John's practice—let's call them "the Johnsons"—after the wife learned that her husband had secretly sought out, hired, and slept with a number of sex-worker escorts during the prior 4 years. The couple had been married for 10 years, and had one child, a 7-year-old named Betty. In their RCU questionnaire assessments, just about every score box was colored red (seen as dark gray in the reproductions in this book), indicating a multitude of challenges. The husband's affairs had

shattered trust and commitment, along with every level of the SRH. The Johnsons had been working on their marriage on their own, making some but not very significant progress in healing their relationship from these affairs. Surprisingly, however, when the couple recorded their two 10-minute conversations, John noticed two strengths the couple possessed. First, during each conversation they each took some responsibility for miscommunications they had had in their big fights. Second, in their conflict discussion the wife thanked her husband for having recently increased his involvement as a dad with their child. In turn, he responded very positively to her gratitude. These strengths were reflected in the fact that their startup positive-to-negative ratio exceeded 5 to 1 in both conversations. It was especially surprising that this was also the case in their conflict discussion. However, in both conversations, negativity later crept in, so their overall conversations' positive-to-negative ratio eventually dropped below a healthy 5-to-1 ratio. Because their startup ratio was higher than the typical ratio for disaster couples of 0.8, some strength was revealed in their conversations that the questionnaires had failed to capture. There was reason to have hope.

Events-of-the-Week Conversation

2. **The overall positive-to-negative ratio.** They couldn't quite maintain their positivity. Their rating dial data must have taken a turn for the negative. Still, there was reason to be optimistic. The overall ratio

Conflict Conversation: Overall Positive-To-Negative Ratio

hadn't fallen very much below the startup ratio. This was good news for the Johnsons.

3. **The Dow Jones cumulative sum (Cumsum) graph. Tracking the couple's "emotional bank account" during the conversation.** Precisely when did the interaction go right or wrong? The Johnsons's point graphs showed a downward dip within 3 minutes of the start of each conversation, for both partners. By analyzing the video John could see that the wife's pain about the affair (as indicated by the black, dotted line) understandably turned toward blame, criticism, and contempt, which shut the husband down. Still, his graph stayed reasonably level, and even took a turn upward toward the end, as did the wife's. More reason to hope.

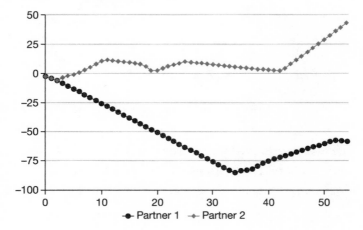

4. **How stuck are they in the negative emotional state, once they enter it?** The number in the dial below indicates how likely it is that they will become negative and stay negative during their events-of-the-week conversation. If the number is less than 10, this indicates that friendship/intimacy is a strength for them. But a number of 10 or more indicates that the couple's conversation has drifted into negative territory and cannot stop being negative. It's as if they have stepped into a quicksand bog of negativity that is impossible to escape, and their attempts at repair are failing. Here's the couple's current Achilles' heel. As they go negative, they enter a quicksand bog. Whatever they do, they still sink deeper and deeper into negativity. This is called a "Markov absorbing state" of negativity. We have pinpointed one of their serious interactional problems. This is bad news for the Johnsons.

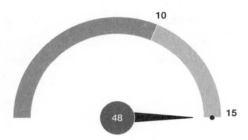

5. **The emotion pie chart.** In what percentage of their conversation were they both positive, both negative, or one negative and the other positive?

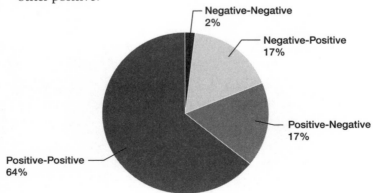

In examining the amount of time they spent in positive or negative rating dial territory, we see a real strength here: During the majority of the time (64% of their interaction), they were in Quadrant 1, the positive–positive quadrant. So, there is again reason for hope for the Johnsons.

In summary, for any couple, like the Johnsons, our therapist's and couple's reports contain RCU scores and whether each of their relationship dimensions is a strength or a challenge. Their assessment also adds diagrams similar to the ones above, depicted separately for each conversation. These diagrams reveal the couple's dynamics, compared to what we would expect to see for a successful and stable relationship versus a troubled and unstable relationship. We can view what happens across time dynamically, like, for example, what happens with the other partner if the first partner goes negative. And then what happens next? Moment by moment, our algorithms can map out during these 10-minute conversations how the partners respond to one another, and whether or not those patterns bode well for the relationship. If the forecast is dire, we can combine our portraits of these dynamics, like the ones above, with our RCU data to generate interventions that will address the couple's negative patterns and hopefully alter them.

CHAPTER 7

The Gottman Connect Assessment Reports

In this chapter we will illustrate the Gottman Connect Assessment reports, which form the basis for talking to the clients about the therapeutic objectives. We'd like to show you what the final assessment reports look like. These reports are generated automatically by the Gottman Connect platform that the therapist uses for tele-couples therapy, or in live sessions with an iPad or computer that is connected to the internet. Note that what we are describing is the clinician's report. The couple's report is simplified and does not include comorbidities, as scores on these could trigger serious consequences, especially those indicating domestic violence or emotional abuse.

By the time of the first session, the couple should have already taken the RCU (Relationship Checkup questionnaires). The Gottman Connect platform will have generated a scoring summary, which we reproduce here for a fictional couple as Figure 7.1. The first block of the scoring summary presents each partner's scores in two columns. A dark gray box is a challenge for that person in the relationship; a light gray box represents a strength.

RCU Scoring Summary

- The first segments of three boxes on the top left of the scoring summary are
  - the Locke–Wallace score of relationship happiness (population mean = 100, standard deviation = 15),

- the global relationship satisfaction score (which controls for conflict avoidance), and
- the Weiss-Cerreto Divorce Proneness Scale (cutoff is 4).
- The next segment below on the left gives scores on the SRH scales:
  - Love Maps
  - Fondness and Admiration
  - Turning Toward or Away
  - Negative Sentiment Override
  - Harsh Startup
  - Accepting Influence
  - Repair Attempts
  - Compromise
  - Gridlock
  - Four Horsemen
  - Flooding
  - Emotional Disengagement and Loneliness
  - Passion and Romance
  - Quality of Sex
  - Frequency of Sex
  - Shared Meaning—Rituals
  - Shared Meaning—Goals
  - Shared Meaning—Roles
  - Shared Meaning—Symbols
  - Trust
  - Commitment
- Individual Areas of Concern:
  - Suicide Potential
  - Depression
  - Anxiety
- On the right-hand side, top, are listed comorbidities:
  - Drug and Alcohol Abuse
  - Drug and Alcohol Frequency Screening
  - Domestic Violence—Situational
  - Domestic Violence—Characterological

- Emotional Abuse—Social Isolation
- Emotional Abuse—Degradation and Humiliation
- Emotional Abuse—Sexual Coercion
- Emotional Abuse—Property Damage
- Three Detour Scales:
  - Chaos and Control
  - Meta-emotion (Emotion Dismissing)
  - Family History (Traumatic History)
- 11 Areas Checklist, specific content areas of conflict:
  - Stress
  - Relatives and Extended Family
  - Jealousy
  - Emotional or Sexual Affairs

	P1	P2
Locks-Wallace	69	78
Global Relationship Satisfaction Inventory	18	24
Weiss-Cerretto	5	2

Sound Relationship House	P1	P2
Love Maps	3	4
Fondness and Admiration System	1	4
Turning Towards or Away	3	4
Negative Sentiment Override	5	3
Harsh Startup	3	5
Accepting Influence	2	2
Repair Attempts	4	1
Compromise	4	2
Gridlock	3	0
Four Horsemen	5	3
Flooding	27	23
Emotional Disengagement and Loneliness	5	2
Passion and Romance	2	3
Quality of Sex	1	1
Frequency of Sex	1	1
Shared Meaning—Rituals	4	3
Shared Meaning—Goals	3	4
Shared Meaning—Roles	4	3
Shared Meaning—Symbols	4	4
Trust	25	16
Commitment	26	22

Areas of Individual Concern	Source	P1	P2
Suicide Potential		0	0
Depression	SCL-90	24	8
Anxiety	SCL-90	7	4

Co-Morbidities	P1	P2
Drug & Alcohol Abuse	2	0
Drug & Alcohol Frequency Screening	3	4
Domestic Violence Situational	0	0
Domestic Violence Characterological	1	0
Emotional Abuse—Social Isolation	21	29
Emotional Abuse—Degradation and Humiliation	26	26
Emotional Abuse—Sexual Coercion	9	8
Emotional Abuse—Property Damage	6	4

Three Detour Scales	P1	P2
Chaos and Control	2	2
Meta-Emotion (Emotion Dismissing)	20	18
Family History (Traumatic History)	9	8

11 Areas Checklist	P1	P2
Stress	1	2
Relatives and Extended Family	5	0
Jealousy	6	7
Emotional or Sexual Affairs	7	7
Basic Values and Goals	0	0
Housework and Childcare	6	1
Financial Issues	4	1
Having Fun Together	5	2
Spirituality, Religion, Ethics	2	0
Children	0	1
Distressing Events	0	0

- Basic Values and Goals
- Housework and Child Care
- Financial Issues
- Having Fun Together
- Spirituality, Religion, Ethics
- Children
- Distressing Events

Appended to this are any written comments the partners provide.

The assessment procedure we recommend our therapists follow in the early sessions is:

1. NARRATIVE. Get their narrative, which is their responses to the question "What brings you to therapy at this time, and what would you like to accomplish?"

2. ORAL HISTORY INTERVIEW. Do an abbreviated OHI starting with the question "Take me back to the very beginning of your relationship. How did you meet and what were your first impressions of one another?" We then ask them to describe the history of their relationship and how it has changed over time, paying special attention to major life transitions.

3. THEIR PRIMARY FAMILIES, AND OTHER RELATIONSHIPS. We ask questions about their families growing up, and the nature of relationships in those families, asking about their relationship histories, parents, siblings, and so on, including the question "Who comforted you as a child when you were upset?"

4. THE TWO CONVERSATIONS. We record a 10-minute events-of-the-week discussion and a 10-minute conflict conversation. Each conversation is preceded by a 1-minute silent baseline period. Following the completion of the two conversations, partners do the video-recall rating dial task while their partner is in the individual interview. They switch roles after the first partner does the rating task.

5. INDIVIDUAL INTERVIEWS. We take turns seeing each person separately for about half an hour, asking about their individual concerns,

their possible primary family traumas, prior relationships, children, and stepchildren, including inquiring about this relationship: especially asking about domestic violence, affairs, and their concerns about the relationship and this therapy. We make it clear that there are no secrets.

6. CLINICIAN CHECKLIST. The clinician then fills out a brief checklist after these interviews, and Gottman Connect generates the reports.

We will now walk you through the therapist's report and then the couple's report. The couple's report differs from the therapist's report in providing only relationship-level summaries, not information that could be attributed to an individual. That is done to minimize blame. The therapist can add their observations to this summary report to guide the couple through the assessment results, and to give them hope. The couple's report can be sent to the couple and the therapist can go through the couple's report in the feedback and goal-setting session.

The Therapist's Report

We will now take a look at the therapist's report for a couple. Our couple (not their real names) is Jade Johnson (Partner 1) and Bill Johnson (Partner 2).

RCU Data: Before Our First Session

We get the RCU data before we even meet this couple. We will start looking at the RCU summary page.

We can see from the first two scales that this is an unhappily married couple. Not a big surprise. But notice that from *her* Locke–Wallace score, we see that she is a lot more unhappy than he is; $(100 - 53)/15.0 = 3.1$ standard deviations below the mean, whereas Bill is only 1.1 standard deviations below the mean. Also, she's a lot more divorce prone, with a score of 10 on the Weiss–Cerreto, whereas Bill's score is zero.

There are a lot of strengths in friendship: Both partners' Love Maps, Fondness and Admiration, and Turning Toward scores have light gray boxes. Their friendship seems to be in good shape. Look down a bit. Romance, Sex Quality, Sex Frequency, Trust, and the four Shared Meaning scales are strengths in this relationship. That's very good. But there is a challenge in Commitment. Now we get some idea that both people are worried about the relationship possibly ending. Perhaps Bill is aware of Jade's plans to leave (her 10 on the Weiss–Cerreto). We need to be aware of that possibility.

However, the trouble really begins with the conflict scales. They both have dark gray boxes for Harsh Startup and for Negative Sentiment Override (the negative perspective). But there's a strength in Accepting Influence. That's good, because each person's Accepting Influence scale is how their partner rated them (the only valid way to do this scale—turns out everyone thinks they accept influence, so their partner's judgment is much more accurate). For Repair Attempts, Compromise, the Four Horsemen, Flooding, and Loneliness, *it is only Jade* who has dark gray boxes, whereas Bill's boxes are light gray. That's not good. Jade is again much more distressed than Bill about conflict, and *only she is lonely*. However, they're both dark gray on thinking that their conflicts are gridlocked.

There are no serious individual issues in Suicide Potential, Depression, or Anxiety. Very good.

Let's look at the comorbidities. There are no signs of drug or alcohol abuse problems or domestic violence, either situational or characterological. Once again that's good news. However, in the Emotional Abuse scales, Bill scores high on Degradation/Humiliation, meaning he feels degraded by Jade, and Jade reports experiencing significant sexual coercion by Bill. We need to ask about this in our individual interviews.

In the Detour scales, they are both high on Chaos, meaning that they both feel out of control. They are matched on both being emotion dismissing. That could be a strength, because they are matched about their feelings about expressing and experiencing emotion. They are both dismissers of their negative emotions. This is not necessarily a problem. Or it could be a serious problem because they *both* need to be able to express their feelings to one another, but may not know how. Jade's loneliness is a key toward understanding what's gone wrong. Does this have to do with the spirituality issue? (See below, as spirituality is named as one of their conflict areas.) Also, we see that Jade has a traumatic family history background, but Bill doesn't. That alerts us to potential triggers that Jade may have that may escalate their conflicts.

What specific areas create conflict? We see that Relatives and Extended Family is an issue for both. However, Jade flags three specific issues we need to find out about: Emotional or Sexual Affairs; Basic Values or Goals; and Spirituality, Religion, and Ethics. We have a lot to ask about in our interviews.

The Two Conversations

In the events-of-the-past-week conversation, we see that their startup positive-to-negative ratio is below the recommended 5-to-1 ratio, but not by very much. A very good sign is that the overall positive-to-negative ratio has meaningfully increased over its startup value, and it is well above the 5-to-1 ratio. When we look at the Emotional Bank Account (Cumsum) graphs, we see that something very positive happened for Jade a few minutes into the events conversation. A little later Bill's Emotional Bank Account (Cumsum) also showed a nearly parallel increase. When we look at the video, Jade talked about going to a church meeting that was very meaningful for her, and she worried that Bill wouldn't understand her new strong sense of connection to this community. She was surprised that he shared her feelings about it, too. He said that he was really impressed with the new female minister. That delightfully surprised Jade, because she knew that Bill had reservations about the minister at first. Another good sign is that in the events conversation neither of them is stuck in a negative state. The pie chart shows that still over 50% of the time they are in the positive–positive Quadrant 1.

We now are ready to focus on how this couple deal with conflict, and interview them about the specific areas of conflict they encountered.

Below you will find the Gottman Connect therapist's report, followed by the couple's report.

The Therapist's Report. This is the first report you will see below. Note that there are many scores and charts that are drawn for each partner separately. This is only for you to see, so that you can fine-tune your interventions with sensitivity to each partner's particular thoughts and feelings about the relationship. Partner 1 refers to Jade, and Partner 2, to Bill.

The Couple's Report. We have attached next the couple's report, which we emailed to Jade and Bill, and went over with them in our teletherapy session. We want you to notice that, for the most part, in the couple's report, we've presented primarily relationship-oriented data, so that neither partner will feel blamed by the findings. There are lots of reasons for hope with this couple.

LOVE LAB ANALYSIS
personalized on Jun 18, 2021, for the therapist of Jade Johnson and Bill Johnson

Contents

Gottman Assessment Scoring Summary

	P1	P2
Locks-Wallace	53	84
Global Relationship Satisfaction Inventory	19	19
Weiss-Cerretto	10	0

Sound Relationship House	P1	P2
Love Maps	4	5
Fondness and Admiration System	3	3
Turning Towards or Away	3	5
Negative Sentiment Override	4	5
Harsh Startup	4	5
Accepting Influence	2	4
Repair Attempts	2	5
Compromise	3	5
Gridlock	4	4
Four Horsemen	4	0
Flooding	23	19
Emotional Disengagement and Loneliness	4	0
Passion and Romance	6	8
Quality of Sex	3	5
Frequency of Sex	5	4
Shared Meaning—Rituals	5	5
Shared Meaning—Goals	5	5
Shared Meaning—Roles	4	4
Shared Meaning—Symbols	4	5
Trust	15	13
Commitment	9	19

Areas of Individual Concern	Source	P1	P2
Suicide Potential		0	0
Depression	SCL-90	0	0
Anxiety	SCL-90	0	0

Co-Morbidities	P1	P2
Drug & Alcohol Abuse	0	0
Drug & Alcohol Frequency Screening	0	0
Domestic Violence Situational	0	0
Domestic Violence Characterological	0	0
Emotional Abuse—Social Isolation	10	17
Emotional Abuse—Degradation and Humiliation	8	24
Emotional Abuse—Sexual Coercion	10	5
Emotional Abuse—Property Damage	4	4

Three Detour Scales	P1	P2
Chaos and Control	4	52
Meta-Emotion (Emotion Dismissing)	16	16
Family History (Traumatic History)	10	0

11 Areas Checklist	P1	P2
Stress	1	0
Relatives and Extended Family	2	6
Jealousy	0	0
Emotional or Sexual Affairs	5	0
Basic Values and Goals	2	0
Housework and Childcare	1	0
Financial Issues	0	0
Having Fun Together	0	0
Spirituality, Religion, Ethics	2	0
Children	0	0
Distressing Events	0	0

Your Couple's Story: A Snapshot
1. Your couple's overall purposes in seeking therapy are to:
   - Evaluate and improve their relationship in order to make a good thing even better.
   - Become more emotionally connected.
   - Improve their sex life. Sexual coercion?
   - Stop escalated quarrels and find calmer and more constructive ways of dealing with conflict.

2. Your couple has described their relationship as follows:
   - Their relationship is unstable and has weakened.
   - One or both partners are not committed to the relationship.
   - They both trust each other.
   - They are currently struggling with serious relationship problems.
3. Your couple has described the history of their relationship as follows:
   - They still have a close friendship.
4. Your couple's friendship could be characterized as follows:
   - Overall, they have good emotional connection and a close friendship.
5. Your couple's conflict management can be described as follows:
   - They are not managing conflict well.
   - There are certain issues on which they get stuck and can't make any progress no matter how hard they try.
   - Conflicts are not extremely stressful for either partner.
   - They are not able to repair conflict if it goes off track.
   - They can rarely reach a compromise.
6. Your couple's sense of purpose and shared values can be described as follows:
   - They have many goals in common.
   - They have many lifestyle preferences in common.
7. Your couple is also coping with the following issues:
   - There are no additional couple issues.
8. Your couple is coping with one or more individual issues:
   - There are no individual issues for either partner.

The Sound Relationship House

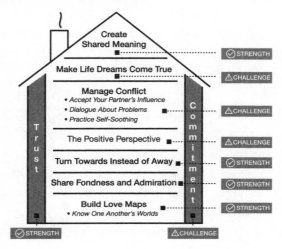

Your Couple's Sound Relationship House

1. BUILD LOVE MAPS

The most basic level of friendship, Love Maps refers to knowing your partner and feeling known by them. It is the road map you create in your mind of your partner's inner world that includes thoughts, feelings, hopes, aspirations, dreams, values, and goals. Love Maps are built by asking open-ended questions and remembering the answers. ⊘ STRENGTH

2. SHARE FONDNESS AND ADMIRATION

This level describes partners' ability to notice and express what they appreciate about each other. To build a culture of respect, partners catch their partner doing something right and convey appreciation, respect, and affection verbally and nonverbally.

Fondness and admiration is built with a positive habit of mind in which you ignore your partner's mistakes and instead notice your partner's positive contributions to the relationship. Both partners need to actively express appreciation, fondness, affection, and respect. ⊘ STRENGTH

3. TURN TOWARD BIDS

When couples were simply "hanging out" together (in the Apartment Lab research study), they often verbally or nonverbally communicated their needs for attention or connection to one another. We call this making a bid for connection.

When a bid for connection has been made, the other partner can either turn toward the bid by responding positively to it, turn away from the bid by ignoring their partner, or turn against the bid by verbally attacking their partner for making the bid. When partners turn toward each other's bids for connection it's like putting money in an emotional bank account that gets built up over time.

There is a hierarchy of bidding, from asking for and getting the partner's attention to asking for and receiving the partner's empathy and emotional support. ⊘STRENGTH

4. POSITIVE OR NEGATIVE PERSPECTIVE (SENTIMENT OVERRIDE)

If the first three levels of the Friendship system are working well, then couples will be in positive sentiment override. Conversely, when the friendship is ailing, couples will be in negative sentiment override. This concept was initially proposed by Weiss (1980).
⚠CHALLENGE

Positive Perspective (Positive Sentiment Override)

Here the positive sentiments or feelings we have about the relation-ship and our partner override negative things that our partner might do. We don't take negativity personally, but merely as evidence that our partner is stressed. We tend to notice negative events but not take them very seriously. We tend to accurately see the positive things our partner is doing and minimize the negative, perhaps even distort-ing toward the positive, and seeing even negative interactions and gestures as neutral.

Negative Perspective (Negative Sentiment Override)
Here the negative sentiments or feelings we have about the relation-
ship and our partner override any positive things our partner might
do that are good. We are hypervigilant for put-downs; we tend not
to notice positive events. We tend to distort positive events and see
them as neutral or sometimes even as negative. That is to say, we tend
to minimize the positives and maximize the negatives in our relation-
ship. We might even rewrite history. This is not something that one
chooses; rather, it is something that happens to us when the relation-
ship hasn't been going well for a long time.

5. MANAGE CONFLICT
Conflict is natural in relationships. Furthermore, it has functional, positive aspects because through our conflicts we learn more
about ourselves and our partners, which can lead to greater intimacy.
The masters of relationships are gentle toward one another, they
start conflict discussions without blame (including preemptive repair,
such as "I know I'm partly to blame here"), they accept influence,
they self-soothe, they repair and de-escalate, they use positive affect
(especially humor and affection) during conflict to de-escalate physiological arousal, and they are able to make compromises.

Longitudinal research indicates that over time, only 31% of
couples' problems are solvable. The rest, or 69%, of couples'
problems are perpetual. They don't get solved over time. Typically,
perpetual problems stem from differences in personality and
lifestyle preferences between partners. The masters of relationship
can dialogue about these perpetual issues, while the disasters of
relationship get "gridlocked" about them, meaning they either have
escalated fights about these issues or avoid talking about them
altogether. Perpetual issues often contain an underlying dream or
existential need for each partner that must be expressed for a couple
to better understand each other's position on the issue. ⚠CHALLENGE

6. MAKE LIFE DREAMS COME TRUE

A crucial aspect of any relationship is to create an atmosphere that encourages each person to talk honestly about their dreams, values, convictions, and aspirations, and to feel that the relationship supports those life dreams. ⚠CHALLENGE

7. CREATE SHARED MEANING

A relationship is about building a life that has a sense of shared purpose and meaning. Couples create meaning together in many ways, including formal and informal rituals of connection. Rituals of connection are ways of spending time together that make the time special and reliably positive. Examples include anything from ways of celebrating holidays to ways of saying goodnight. Successful couples share their individual goals and life missions with each other. They support one another's basic roles in life, and may also share similar values and meanings they give to certain symbols in life. ⊘STRENGTH

8. TRUST

Partners trust one another when each person acts in ways that maximize benefits for their partner, not just for themselves. To build trust, partners are finding out "Will you be there for me?" in lots of different situations. For example, "Will you be there for me if your mother criticizes me?" or "Will you be there for me if I'm sick or depressed?" Couples need to know that their partner will keep them physically, mentally, and emotionally safe. ⊘STRENGTH

9. COMMITMENT

Commitment exists when each partner believes that this relationship is a lifelong journey, for better or for worse. When there's a true sense of commitment, partners are loyal to one another, see each other as their best choice, and cherish each other. There is no one else that they would rather spend their life with. When partners lack commitment, they often make negative comparisons between their current partner and a real or fantasized alternative partner. In these comparisons, their current partner is found lacking. ⚠CHALLENGE

Friendship and Intimacy

 1. LOVE MAPS

Each partner knows the other's inner world and feels known by the other. ⊘ STRENGTH

STRENGTH—YOU BELIEVE YOU KNOW YOUR PARTNER
WELL AND YOU FEEL KNOWN BY YOUR PARTNER. YOU ARE
INTERESTED IN UPDATING YOUR LOVE MAPS
OF EACH OTHER.

2. FONDNESS AND ADMIRATION

Each partner feels admired, appreciated, and respected.
⊘ STRENGTH

STRENGTH—YOU BELIEVE THAT YOUR PARTNER HAS SOME
POSITIVE FEELINGS FOR YOU AND RESPECTS YOU.

3. TURNING TOWARD OR AWAY

Partners are responsive to each other.   ⊘ STRENGTH

STRENGTH—YOU FEEL THAT YOUR PARTNER IS RESPONSIVE
TO YOUR BIDS MOST OF THE TIME.

Trust and Commitment

These are the weight-bearing walls of the SRH.

1. TRUST

Both partners maximize benefits for their partner as well as for themselves. Partners have one another's back and value each other's needs. ⊘ STRENGTH

STRENGTH—YOU BELIEVE THAT YOU CAN TRUST YOUR
PARTNER TO HAVE YOUR BACK AND HAVE YOUR BEST
INTERESTS AT HEART.

2. COMMITMENT
Partners are loyal to each other and see this relationship as their preferred choice for life, instead of looking around for better relationship options. ⚠ CHALLENGE

CHALLENGE—ONE OR BOTH OF YOU QUESTION WHETHER THIS IS THE BEST RELATIONSHIP TO BE IN FOR THE REST OF YOUR LIFE.

Shared Meaning

1. RITUALS OF CONNECTION
Rituals are your daily routines and family traditions. You can count on them—like having dinner together every night, or talking about your day before bedtime, or celebrating a birthday by dining out. ⊘ STRENGTH

2. SUPPORTING ROLES
Roles refer to the various hats that each partner wears—husband/wife, mother/father, son/ daughter, employee, lover, etc., and how supported each partner feels within each of those roles. ⊘ STRENGTH

3. SHARED GOALS
This refers to how similar your goals are for both yourselves and your relationship—like wanting to have children, to travel together, or to save money for the future. ⊘ STRENGTH

4. SHARED SYMBOLS
Symbols refer to your values, beliefs, and philosophy of life—how similarly those are aligned and how supportive each partner is around those symbols. One such symbol might be a home. One partner might want their home to be "Grand Central Station," (meaning, a place open to many other people), while the other partner might want their home to be a "refuge," a place closed to others. ⊘ STRENGTH

Your Couple's Events Conversation Analysis

1. STARTUP POSITIVE-TO-NEGATIVE RATIO

The number you see inside each gauge diagram represents the ratio of positive-to-negative interactions for each partner at the beginning of their events conversation.

The way a conversation begins is very important since the couple hopes to establish emotional connection through their conversation. If a partner's number is less than 5, the conversation has begun negatively for that partner. It is likely that poor conflict management has spilled over into the Friendship–Intimacy system, affecting even non-conflict conversations. Homework needs to focus on rebuilding emotional connection.

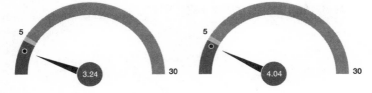

2. OVERALL POSITIVE-TO-NEGATIVE RATIO

(5 to 1 is the Gottman "magic ratio")

The number you see inside each gauge diagram represents the ratio of positive-to-negative interactions for each partner throughout their entire conversation.

The way a conversation continues on is very important since the couple hopes to establish emotional connection through their conversation. If a partner's number is less than 5, the conversation has continued on negatively for that partner. It is likely that poor conflict management has spilled over into the Friendship–Intimacy system, affecting even nonconflict conversations. Homework needs to focus on rebuilding emotional connection.

3. CUMULATIVE SUM (EMOTIONAL BANK ACCOUNT)

We are looking for the following patterns in this graph:

> –*If both lines are steadily going up from left to right, this pattern signals that friendship/intimacy is a strength for this couple.*
>
> –*All other patterns indicate that friendship/intimacy is a challenge for this couple.*
>
> –*If both lines are descending, this indicates that the couple struggles with repairing negative interactions.*
>
> –*If the slopes are going in opposite directions, meaning the line for one partner is going up while the line for the other partner is going down, this pattern could suggest a ZERO-SUM METRIC, which in turn indicates a power struggle between the partners. This pattern is associated with potential betrayals.*

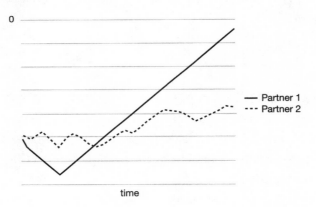

4. HOW STUCK ARE THEY IN THE NEGATIVE EMOTIONAL STATE?

The numbers in each chart indicate how likely it is that each partner will become negative and stay negative while talking with the second partner during their events conversation. If a specific partner's number is less than 10, this indicates that Friendship/Intimacy is a strength for that partner.

But a number of 10 or more indicates that this partner goes negative and cannot stop being negative throughout the couple's conversation. Negativity has probably spilled over from conflict and contaminated that person's Friendship–Intimacy System. It's as if the partner has stepped into a quicksand bog of negativity, which is impossible to escape, and attempts at repair are failing.

5. PARTNERS' PAIRED EMOTIONS PIE CHART

Each section of the pie chart below indicates the amount of time the partners spend in each of four emotional states:

- *–Both partners are simultaneously in a negative emotional state.*
- *–The first partner is in a positive emotional state while the second partner is in a negative emotional state.*
- *–The first partner is in a negative emotional state while the second partner is in a positive emotional state.*
- *–Both partners are simultaneously in a positive emotional state.*

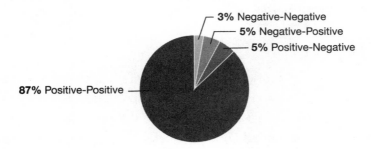

Conflict Management

1. HARSH STARTUP

The way conflict discussions begin sets the tone for the rest of the conversation. If the conversation begins with blaming and critical words, we call this a harsh startup, and the discussion is likely to spiral down into negativity. The typical beginning sounds something like "You always leave your stuff everywhere. You're too lazy to pick anything up." ⚠CHALLENGE

CHALLENGE—YOU STRUGGLE WITH HOW TO EXPRESS YOUR HURTS AND DISAPPOINTMENTS IN THE RELATIONSHIP. THE WAY YOU COMMUNICATE YOUR FEELINGS CAN END UP SABOTAGING YOUR GETTING LISTENED TO.

2. THE FOUR HORSEMEN OF THE APOCALYPSE

The following four behaviors have been shown by research to be very destructive to relationships: ⚠CHALLENGE

- *Criticism—blaming a problem on a personality flaw in your partner*
- *Defensiveness—denying any personal responsibility for a problem by either playing the innocent victim or counterattacking*
- *Contempt—verbally attacking your partner through name-calling, sarcasm, mockery, and put-downs from a place of superiority*
- *Stonewalling—shutting down, not talking, and giving your partner no verbal or nonverbal signs that you are listening*

CHALLENGE—YOU STRUGGLE TO BE CAREFUL AND RESPECTFUL WHEN YOU ATTEMPT TO MANAGE CONFLICT.

3. FLOODING

Sometimes during arguments people's heart rates escalate to the point that they cannot take in their partner's perspective. When this happens, we say that the partner with the elevated heart rate is "flooded." Physiological flooding blocks the partner from hearing what the other person is saying. In fact, no matter what is said, all they can see or hear is attack, and all they can think about is getting away, lashing out, or shutting down.

This state is similar to "fight-flight-or-freeze." Anyone can get to this point. When this happens, it means the relationship does not feel emotionally safe. ⚠CHALLENGE

CHALLENGE—ONE OR BOTH OF YOU TEND TO GET
"FLOODED" OR PHYSIOLOGICALLY OVERWHELMED WHEN
DISCUSSING CONFLICTS. (FLOODING IS NOT AN EMOTIONAL
STATE—IT'S A PHYSIOLOGICAL ONE.)

4. ACCEPTING INFLUENCE

Accepting influence means that each person is willing to take in their partner's perspective as valid, and they look for ways in which their partner's point of view makes sense. Masters of relationship find ways to say "Yes" or "Good point." This doesn't mean that they give up their own position on the issue, but rather that they understand that both perspectives warrant consideration. ⚠ CHALLENGE

STRENGTH—YOU ARE ABLE TO TAKE IN ONE ANOTHER'S
PERSPECTIVE AS VALID.

5. COMPROMISE

Compromise means that each person is willing and able to be flexible in order to solve ongoing problems. Partners seek out common ground. Compromise does not mean giving up one's own position, but rather looking at both positions and working to build a bridge that encompasses a part of both partners' wants and needs. ⚠ CHALLENGE

CHALLENGE—COMPROMISE IS DIFFICULT AND OFTEN FEELS
LIKE YOU'RE GIVING UP *OR GIVING IN.*

6. REPAIR ATTEMPTS

Repair attempts are any means of soothing hurt feelings or fixing a misunderstanding or conflict. They can be a simple "I'm sorry" or "I didn't mean to say it that way." ⚠ CHALLENGE

CHALLENGE—IT IS DIFFICULT TO SAY "I'M SORRY" AND THERE MIGHT BE A TENDENCY TO WANT YOUR PARTNER TO HURT AS BADLY AS YOU DO AFTER A PAINFUL CONVERSATION.

Your Couple's Conflict Conversation Analysis
1. STARTUP POSITIVE-TO-NEGATIVE RATIO
The number you see inside each gauge diagram represents the ratio of positive-to-negative interactions for each partner at the beginning of their conflict conversation.

The way a conflict conversation like this starts is very important since it predicts how the entire conflict conversation will go 96% of the time. If the number is less than 5, it means that conflict management is a challenge for this couple.

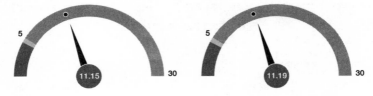

2. OVERALL POSITIVE-TO-NEGATIVE RATIO
(5 to 1 is the Gottman "magic ratio")
The number you see inside each gauge diagram represents the ratio of positive-to-negative interactions for each partner throughout their entire conflict conversation.

A number less than 5 indicates that the conversation continues on negatively for that partner. Overall, the couple's conflict management is dysfunctional. During a conflict conversation, successful couples have five positive interactions for every negative interaction (a 5:1 ratio). The overall way that a conflict conversation is handled is predictive of the future of the entire relationship.

3. CUMULATIVE SUM

We are looking for the following patterns in this graph:

 *—If both lines are steadily going up from left to right, this pattern
 signals that conflict management is a strength for this couple.*

 *—All other patterns indicate that conflict management is a challenge
 for this couple.*

 *—If both lines are descending, this indicates that the couple struggles
 with repairing negative interactions.*

 *—If the slopes are going in opposite directions, meaning the line for
 one partner is going up while the line for the other partner is going
 down, this pattern could suggest a ZERO-SUM METRIC, which in
 turn indicates a power struggle between the partners. This pattern
 is associated with potential betrayals.*

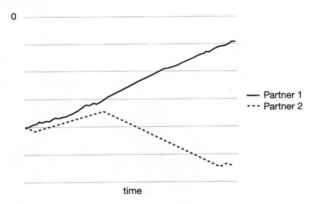

4. HOW STUCK ARE THEY IN THE NEGATIVE EMOTIONAL STATE?

The numbers in each chart indicate how likely it is that each partner
will become negative and stay negative while talking with the second
partner during their conflict conversation. If a specific partner's
number is less than 10, this indicates that conflict management is a
strength for that partner.

But a number of 10 or more indicates that this partner goes
negative and cannot stop being negative throughout the couple's
conversation. It's as if the partner has stepped into a quicksand bog of

negativity, which is impossible to escape, and attempts at repair are failing.

5. PARTNERS' PAIRED EMOTIONS PIE CHART

Each section of the pie chart below indicates the amount of time the partners spend in each of four emotional states:

> –*Both partners are simultaneously in a negative emotional state.*
> –*The first partner is in a positive emotional state while the second partner is in a negative emotional state.*
> –*The first partner is in a negative emotional state while the second partner is in a positive emotional state.*
> –*Both partners are simultaneously in a positive emotional state.*

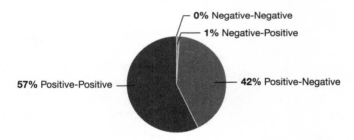

Gottman Treatment Plan

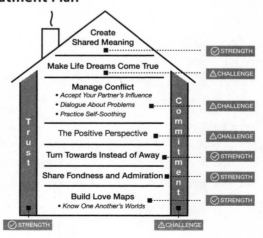

Areas of Strength

Notable History *(abuse, trauma, affairs, family origin, relationship)*

Comorbidities

Presenting Problems

Preliminary Treatment Goals

Notes: Focus on conflict, and the specific conflict areas.

Now the Couple's Report (Review With Them)

Note that Partner 1 is Jade, and Partner 2 is Bill. But in all the charts and diagrams, Gottman Connect algorithms have calculated analyses for the couple combined, rather than for each individual partner. This protects either partner from blame.

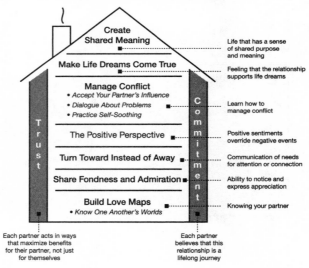

LOVE LAB ANALYSIS
personalized on Jun 18, 2021 for
Jade Johnson and Bill Johnson

Contents

Your Story: A Snapshot

1. Your overall purposes in seeking therapy are to:
   - Evaluate and improve your relationship in order to make a good thing even better.
   - Become more emotionally connected.
   - Stop bad fights and find calmer and more constructive ways of dealing with conflict.
2. The two of you described your relationship as follows:
   - Your relationship is unstable and has weakened.
   - Either one or both of you are not committed to the relationship.
   - You both trust each other.
   - You are currently struggling with serious relationship problems.
3. You have described the history of your relationship as follows:
   - You still have a close friendship.
   - You used to share adventures together, but no longer do.
   - You still try to support each other's individual dreams.
4. Currently, your friendship could be characterized as follows:
   - Overall, you have good emotional connection and a close relationship.
   - One or both of you do not feel that you can count on your partner as a friend.
5. Your conflict management can be described as follows:
   - You are not managing conflict well.
   - There are certain issues on which you get stuck and can't make any progress no matter how hard you try.
   - You are not able to repair conflict if it goes off track.
   - You can rarely reach a compromise.
6. Your sense of purpose and shared values can be described as follows:
   - You have many goals in common.
   - You have many values in common.
   - You have many lifestyle preferences in common.

7. Your relationship is also coping with the following issues:
 – There are no additional couple's issues reported.
8. You are coping with one or more individual issues:
 – There are no individual issues reported.

1. BUILD LOVE MAPS
The most basic level of friendship, Love Maps refer to knowing your partner and feeling known by them. It is the road map you create in your mind of your partner's inner world that includes thoughts, feelings, hopes, aspirations, dreams, values, and goals. Love Maps are built by asking open-ended questions and remembering the answers.

2. SHARE FONDNESS AND ADMIRATION
This level describes partners' ability to notice and express what they appreciate about each other. To build a culture of respect, partners catch their partner doing something right and convey appreciation, respect, and affection verbally and nonverbally.

Fondness and admiration is built with a positive habit of mind in which you ignore your partner's mistakes and instead notice your partner's positive contributions to the relationship. Both partners need to actively express appreciation, fondness, affection, and respect.

3. TURN TOWARD BIDS
When couples were simply "hanging out" together (in the Apartment Lab research study), they often verbally or nonverbally communicated their needs for attention or connection to one another. We call this making a bid for connection.

When a bid for connection has been made, the other partner can either turn toward the bid by responding positively to it, turn away from the bid by ignoring their partner, or turn against the bid by verbally attacking their partner for making the bid. When partners turn toward each other's bids for connection it's like putting money in an emotional bank account that gets built up over time. There is a hierarchy of bidding, from asking for and getting the partner's attention to asking for and receiving the partner's empathy and emotional support.

 ### 4. POSITIVE OR NEGATIVE PERSPECTIVE (SENTIMENT OVERRIDE)

If the first three levels of the Friendship system are working well, then couples will be in positive sentiment override. Conversely, when the friendship is ailing, couples will be in negative sentiment override. This concept was initially proposed by Weiss (1980).

Positive Perspective (Positive Sentiment Override)

Here the positive sentiments or feelings we have about the relationship and our partner override negative things that our partner might do. We don't take negativity personally, but merely as evidence that our partner is stressed. We tend to notice negative events but not take them very seriously. We tend to accurately see the positive things our partner is doing and minimize the negative, perhaps even distorting toward the positive, and seeing even negative interactions and gestures as neutral.

Negative Perspective (Negative Sentiment Override)

Here the negative sentiments or feelings we have about the relationship and our partner override any positive things our partner might do that are good. We are hypervigilant for put-downs; we tend not to notice positive events. We tend to distort positive events and see them as neutral or sometimes even as negative. That is to say, we tend to minimize the positives and maximize the negatives in our relationship. We might even rewrite history. This is not something that one chooses; rather, it is something that happens to us when the relationship hasn't been going well for a long time.

5. MANAGE CONFLICT

Conflict is natural in relationships. Furthermore, it has functional, positive aspects because through our conflicts we learn more about ourselves and our partners, which can lead to greater intimacy. The masters of relationship are gentle toward one another, they start conflict discussions without blame (including preemptive repair, such as "I know I'm partly to blame here"), they accept influence, they self-soothe, they repair and de-escalate, they use positive affect (especially humor and affection) during conflict to de-escalate physiological arousal, and they are able to make compromises.

Longitudinal research indicates that over time, only 31% of couples' problems are solvable. The rest, or 69%, of couples' problems are perpetual. They don't get solved over time. Typically, perpetual problems stem from differences in personality and lifestyle preferences between partners. The masters of relationship can dialogue about these perpetual issues, while the disasters of relationship get "gridlocked" about them, meaning they either have escalated fights about these issues or avoid talking about them altogether. Perpetual issues often contain an underlying dream or existential need for each partner that must be expressed for a couple to better understand each other's position on the issue.

6. MAKE LIFE DREAMS COME TRUE

A crucial aspect of any relationship is to create an atmosphere that encourages each person to talk honestly about their dreams, values, convictions, and aspirations, and to feel that the relationship supports those life dreams.

7. CREATE SHARED MEANING

A relationship is about building a life together, a life that has a sense of shared purpose and meaning. Couples create meaning together in many ways, including creating formal and informal rituals of connection. Rituals of connection are ways of spending time together that make the time special and reliably positive. Examples include anything from ways of celebrating holidays together to ways of saying good-night. Successful couples share their individual goals and life missions with each other. They support one another's basic roles in life, and may also share similar values and meanings they give to certain symbols in life.

8. TRUST

Partners trust one another when each person acts in ways that maximize benefits for their partner, not just for themselves. To build trust, partners are finding out "Will you be there for me?" in lots of different situations. For example, "Will you be there for me if your mother criticizes me?" or "Will you be there for me if I'm sick or depressed?" Couples need to know that their partner will keep them physically, mentally, and emotionally safe.

9. COMMITMENT

Commitment exists when each partner believes that this relationship is a lifelong journey, for better or for worse. When there is a true sense of commitment, partners are loyal to one another, see each other as their best choice, and cherish each other. There is no one else that they would rather spend their life with. When partners lack commitment, they often make negative comparisons between their current partner and a real or fantasized alternative partner with whom they think they'll be happier. In these comparisons, their current partner is found lacking.

Friendship and Intimacy

1. LOVE MAPS

Each partner knows the other's inner world and feels known by the other.

> STRENGTH—YOU BELIEVE YOU KNOW YOUR PARTNER
> WELL AND YOU FEEL KNOWN BY YOUR PARTNER.
> YOU ARE INTERESTED IN UPDATING YOUR LOVE MAPS
> OF EACH OTHER.

2. FONDNESS AND ADMIRATION
Each partner feels admired, appreciated, and respected.

STRENGTH—YOU BELIEVE THAT YOUR PARTNER HAS SOME POSITIVE FEELINGS FOR YOU AND RESPECTS YOU.

 3. TURNING TOWARD OR AWAY
Partners are responsive to each other.

STRENGTH—YOU FEEL THAT YOUR PARTNER IS RESPONSIVE TO YOUR BIDS MOST OF THE TIME.

Trust and Commitment

These are the weight-bearing walls of the SRH.

1. TRUST
Both partners maximize benefits for their partner as well as for themselves. Partners have one another's back and value each other's needs.

STRENGTH—YOU BELIEVE THAT YOU CAN TRUST YOUR PARTNER TO HAVE YOUR BACK AND HAVE YOUR BEST INTERESTS AT HEART.

2. COMMITMENT
Partners are loyal to each other and see this relationship as their preferred choice for life, instead of looking around for better relationship options.

CHALLENGE—ONE OR BOTH OF YOU QUESTION WHETHER THIS IS THE BEST RELATIONSHIP TO BE IN FOR THE REST OF YOUR LIFE.

Shared Meaning

1. RITUALS OF CONNECTION
Rituals are your daily routines and family traditions. You can count on them—like having dinner together every night, or talking about your day before bedtime, or celebrating a birthday by dining out.

2. SUPPORTING ROLES
Roles refer to the various hats that each partner wears—husband/wife, mother/father, son/daughter, employee, lover, and so on, and how supported each partner feels within each of those roles.

3. SHARED GOALS
This refers to how similar your goals are for both yourselves and your relationship—like wanting to have children, to travel together, or to save money for the future.

4. SHARED SYMBOLS
Symbols refer to your values, beliefs, and philosophy of life—how similarly those are aligned and how supportive each partner is around those symbols. One such symbol might be a home. One partner might want their home to be "Grand Central Station," meaning a place open to many other people, while the other partner might want their home to be a "refuge," a place closed to others.

Your Events Conversation Analysis

1. STARTUP POSITIVE-TO-NEGATIVE RATIO
The number you see inside the gauge diagram represents the ratio of positive-to-negative interactions at the beginning of your events conversation.

The way a conversation begins is very important. If the number is less than 5, the conversation has begun negatively. It is likely that poor conflict management has spilled over into the Friendship–Intimacy system, affecting even non-conflict conversations.

2. OVERALL POSITIVE-TO-NEGATIVE RATIO

(5 to 1 is the Gottman "magic ratio")

The number you see inside the gauge diagram represents the ratio of positive-to-negative interactions throughout the entire conversation.

The way a conversation continues on is very important. If a number is less than 5, the conversation has continued on negatively.

3. CUMULATIVE SUM

We are looking for the following patterns in this graph:

- *If both lines are steadily going up from left to right, this pattern signals that friendship/intimacy is a strength for you.*
- *All other patterns indicate that friendship/intimacy is a challenge for you.*
- *If both lines are descending, this indicates that you struggle with repairing negative interactions.*
- *If the slopes are going in opposite directions, meaning the line for one partner is going up while the line for the other partner is going down, this pattern could suggest a ZERO-SUM METRIC, which in turn indicates a power struggle between the partners.*

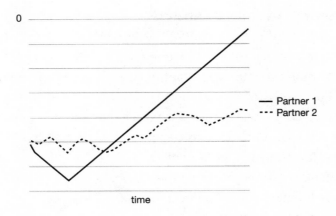

time

4. HOW STUCK ARE YOU IN A NEGATIVE EMOTIONAL STATE?

The number in the chart below indicates how likely it is that you will become negative and stay negative during your events-of-the-week conversation. If the number is less than 10, this indicates that friendship/intimacy is a strength for you. But a number of 10 or more indicates that you become negative and cannot stop being negative throughout the conversation. It's as if you have stepped into a quicksand bog of negativity that is impossible to escape, and attempts at repair are failing.

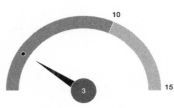

5. PARTNERS' PAIRED EMOTIONS PIE CHART

Each section of the pie chart below indicates the amount of time you spend in each of four emotional states:

- *Both of you are simultaneously in a negative emotional state.*
- *The first partner is in a positive emotional state while the second partner is in a negative emotional state.*
- *The first partner is in a negative emotional state while the second partner is in a positive emotional state.*
- *Both partners are simultaneously in a positive emotional state.*

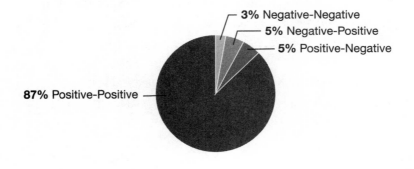

Conflict Management

1. HARSH STARTUP

The way conflict discussions begin sets the tone for the rest of the conversation. If the conversation begins with blaming, critical words, we call this a harsh startup, and the discussion is likely to spiral down into negativity. The typical beginning sounds something like "You always leave your stuff everywhere. You're too lazy to pick anything up."

CHALLENGE—YOU STRUGGLE WITH HOW TO EXPRESS YOUR HURTS AND DISAPPOINTMENTS IN THE RELATIONSHIP. THE WAY YOU COMMUNICATE YOUR FEELINGS CAN END UP SABOTAGING YOUR GETTING LISTENED TO.

2. THE FOUR HORSEMEN OF THE APOCALYPSE

The following four behaviors have been shown by research to be very destructive to relationships:
- *Criticism—blaming a problem on a personality flaw in your partner*
- *Defensiveness—denying any personal responsibility for a problem by either playing the innocent victim or counterattacking*
- *Contempt—verbally attacking your partner through name-calling, sarcasm, mockery, and put-downs from a place of superiority*
- *Stonewalling—shutting down, not talking, and giving your partner no verbal or nonverbal signs that you are listening*

CHALLENGE—YOU STRUGGLE TO BE CAREFUL AND RESPECTFUL WHEN YOU ATTEMPT TO MANAGE CONFLICT.

3. FLOODING

Sometimes during arguments people's heart rates escalate to the point that they cannot take in their partner's perspective. When this happens, we say that the partner with the elevated heart rate is "flooded." Physiological flooding blocks the partner from hearing what the other person is saying. In fact, no matter what is said, all they can see or hear is attack, and all they can think about is getting away, lashing out, or shutting down.

This state is similar to "fight-flight-or-freeze." Anyone can get to this point. When this happens, it means the relationship does not feel emotionally safe.

CHALLENGE—ONE OR BOTH OF YOU TEND TO GET "FLOODED" OR PHYSIOLOGICALLY OVERWHELMED WHEN DISCUSSING CONFLICTS. (FLOODING IS NOT AN EMOTIONAL STATE—IT'S A PHYSIOLOGICAL ONE.)

4. ACCEPTING INFLUENCE

Accepting influence means that each person is willing to take in their partner's perspective as valid, and they look for ways in which their partner's point of view makes sense. Masters of relationship find ways to say "Yes" or "Good point." This doesn't mean that they give up their own position on the issue, but rather that they understand that both perspectives warrant consideration.

STRENGTH—YOU ARE ABLE TO TAKE IN ONE ANOTHER'S PERSPECTIVE AS VALID.

5. COMPROMISE

Compromise means that each person is willing and able to be flexible in order to solve ongoing problems. Partners seek out common ground. Compromise does not mean giving up one's own position, but rather looking at both positions and working to build a bridge that encompasses a part of both partners' wants and needs.

CHALLENGE—COMPROMISE IS DIFFICULT AND OFTEN FEELS LIKE YOU'RE GIVING UP OR GIVING IN.

6. REPAIR ATTEMPTS

Repair attempts are any means of soothing hurt feelings or fixing a misunderstanding or conflict. It can be a simple "I'm sorry" or "I didn't mean to say it that way."

CHALLENGE—IT IS DIFFICULT TO SAY "I'M SORRY" AND THERE MIGHT BE A TENDENCY TO WANT YOUR PARTNER TO HURT AS BADLY AS YOU DO AFTER A PAINFUL CONVERSATION.

Your Conflict Conversation Analysis

1. STARTUP POSITIVE-TO-NEGATIVE RATIO

The number you see inside the gauge diagram represents the ratio of positive-to-negative interactions at the beginning of your conflict conversation. The way a conflict conversation like this starts is very important since it predicts how the entire conflict conversation will go 96% of the time. If the number is less than 5, it means that conflict management is a challenge for you.

2. OVERALL POSITIVE-TO-NEGATIVE RATIO

(5 to 1 is the Gottman "magic ratio")

The number you see inside the gauge diagram represents the ratio of positive-to-negative interactions throughout your entire conflict conversation. A number less than 5 indicates that the conversation continues on negatively for you. During conflict conversations, successful couples have five positive interactions for every negative interaction (a 5:1 ratio). The overall way that a conflict conversation is handled is predictive of the future of the entire relationship.

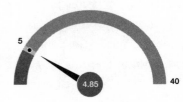

3. CUMULATIVE SUM

We are looking for the following patterns in this graph:
- *If both lines are steadily going up from left to right, this pattern signals that conflict management is a strength for you.*
- *All other patterns indicate that conflict management is a challenge for you.*
- *If both lines are descending, this indicates that you struggle with repairing negative interactions.*
- *If the slopes are going in opposite directions, meaning the line for one partner is going up while the line for the other partner is going down, this pattern could suggest a ZERO-SUM METRIC, which in turn indicates a power struggle between the partners.*

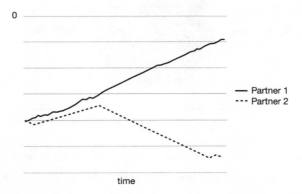

4. HOW STUCK ARE YOU IN A NEGATIVE EMOTIONAL STATE?

The number in the diagram below indicates how likely it is that you will become negative and stay negative during your conflict conversation. If the number is less than 10, this indicates that conflict management is a strength for you. But a number of 10 or more indicates that you become negative and cannot stop being negative throughout the conversation. It's as if you have stepped into a quicksand bog of negativity that is impossible to escape, and attempts at repair are failing.

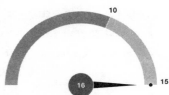

5. PARTNERS' PAIRED EMOTIONS PIE CHART

Each section of the pie chart below indicates the amount of time you spend in each of four emotional states:

- *Both of you are simultaneously in a negative emotional state.*
- *The first partner is in a positive emotional state while the second partner is in a negative emotional state.*
- *The first partner is in a negative emotional state while the second partner is in a positive emotional state.*
- *Both partners are simultaneously in a positive emotional state.*

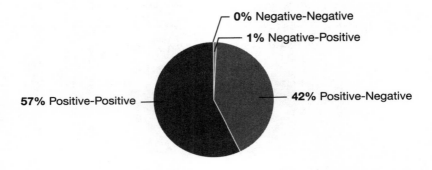

Now that you've learned how Gottman method assessment works, by using Gottman Connect, you can see what particular challenges a couple may face, versus the strengths they already possess. With these in mind, it will be much easier to provide each couple with therapeutic interventions that fit what they need in the moment, along with pertinent history or points of view that may shape your interventions accordingly. The report not only provides you with a road map of where your couple needs to go and how to get there, it also helps you more accurately tune in to the inner worlds of your couple. Also, the insight you gain through their relationship's assessment can facilitate your connecting with each partner more quickly and accurately, so they can experience being witnessed and seen by you early on, thus fostering your therapeutic alliance with them.

CHAPTER 8

An Emotion–Dynamic Typology of Couples We See Every Day

In this chapter we present our best guess at a typology of the kinds of couples we have seen in our lab and in clinical practice over the past 52 years. We focus here on the time-based process and relationship dynamics of each type of couple. These descriptions are supplemented by the questionnaire data provided by the RCU. We introduce the idea of wife–husband "phase space" diagrams for couples.

When John and Bob brought couples back into their labs repeatedly, sometimes following couples for as long as 20 years, they discovered that couples' interactions had about 80% stability over time. This meant we can imagine in a couple's map there were some quadrants that couples would spend more time in than other quadrants. We suggest that you envision a "husband–wife plane" divided into four quadrants: (1) Quadrant 1 is the husband positive–wife positive quadrant where both partners were engaging in positive affects; (2) Quadrant 2 is a husband positive–wife negative quadrant; (3) Quadrant 3 is a husband negative–wife negative quadrant; and (4) Quadrant 4 is a mirror image of Quadrant 2—the wife is positive and the husband is negative (see Figure 8.1).

Summary of Our Typology of Couples

Figure 8.1 and Table 8.1 summarize our typology of all the couples we tend to see either in our lab or in couples therapy. Once again, envision a horizontal x-axis for Partner 1 (arbitrarily called "wife"), and a vertical y-axis for Partner 2 (arbitrarily called "husband"). Both axes range from very positive to very negative. That plane is called the "phase space" plane.

We tend not to see the couples in the positive-positive Quadrant 1 in couples therapy, but we made sure we oversampled these happy relationships in our lab. We are quite aware of the fact that our typology of 14 couple types we see in therapy is a lot, but we think they will fit your clinical experience. We don't count the couples for whom marital therapy is contraindicated, or the couples who inhabit Quadrant 1, but when they are displayed this way in phase space, we hope aspects of their dynamics will become clear, and they are probably very familiar to many clinicians. Our typology is thorough, and fits both our lab and clinical experience.

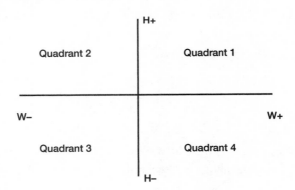

FIGURE 8.1: Wife–Husband Phase Space

As you can see, Table 8.1 has two rows, for couples close to the origin in each quadrant and couples far from the origin. It also has four columns, one for each of the four quadrants of phase space. Quadrant 1, the positive–positive quadrant, we call the "good quadrant," or "heaven." This quadrant is inhabited by the masters, with a positive-to-negative ratio greater than or equal to 5 to 1. There are five couple types in heaven. Quadrant 3, the negative–negative quadrant, we call "hell." It is inhabited by very unhappily married couples. In both quadrants, the interactions of the two partners are symmetric. There are also five couple types in hell. In Quadrants 2 and 4, however, there's asymmetry between partners. There are six couple types in each of these quadrants of phase space.

TABLE 8.1 Our Typology of Couples We See Every Day, Based on Their Conflict–Discussion SPAFF

	QUADRANT 1 THIS IS HEAVEN	QUADRANT 3 THIS IS HELL	QUADRANT 2	QUADRANT 4
	Symmetric, both positive, $N=5$ types Couples we rarely see in therapy, but might see in workshops	Symmetric, both negative, $N=4$ types	Asymmetric (W–, H+), $N=5$ types	Asymmetric (W+, H–), $N=5$ types
NEAR THE ORIGIN	• Validators • Volatiles • Conflict avoiders, non-self-disclosing	• Devitalized	• Matriarchal, can be satisfied, or not; if husband not happy, this couple becomes the wife-abusive type • Failed avoiders • Wife impaired; husband supportive	• Patriarchal, can be satisfied, or not; if wife not happy, this couple becomes the husband-abusive type • Failed avoiders • Husband impaired, wife supportive
FAR FROM THE ORIGIN	• Dreams Within Conflict • Conflict avoiders, self-disclosing	• **Hostile.** Failed validators and volatiles • **Hostile and violent.** And situationally violent • **Hostile-detached.** Mental illness for one or both partners • **Couples therapy contraindicated.** • Husband or wife characterologically violent, an ongoing affair, or an affair with no remorse	• Husband psychologically abusive • Wife affair with remorse or wife in addiction recovery	• Wife psychologically abusive • Husband affair with remorse or husband in addiction recovery

The Details of Our Couple Types

Our First Typology: Validators, Volatiles, and Avoiders

We want to give you some idea of what John originally discovered about three types of master couples, which he called validators, volatiles, and avoiders. In this section we will give you some examples of conflict dialogues that these three types of couples typically have. Later, we also discovered two additional types of couples: hostile and hostile-detached.

Validators. These couples influence one another using both positive and negative affect. They use persuasion, but first, they build an agenda, then engage in discussion and persuasion, and conclude by moving toward compromise. Validators, like all three couple types, do well when their positive-to-negative ratio during conflict equals or exceeds 5 to 1.

Wife (W): We just don't save enough, we live hand to mouth. There's just nothing left over to save at the end of the month.

Husband (H): Why is this a problem?

W: It makes me insecure that we have no cushion, in case something happens.

H: What are you worried about?

W: An emergency. Or our retirement, which is a long way off, I know, or some great travel opportunity. And then we'd have to borrow.

H: How much would make you feel comfortable?

W: Saving maybe 10% to 25% of what we bring home every month.

H: Wow, that's a lot.

W: I know, but I need that.

H: Well, I don't agree. We're young, and I want to live more for the moment, have some fun now, while we can enjoy it. Not save everything.

W: Not save everything, I agree with that, but save some.

H: I disagree with your philosophy. My uncle Ned died with millions in the bank. Everyone was shocked. He lived like a pauper, in a one-room apartment, stingy and mean, with not much of a life at all. I am not going to be like my uncle Ned.

W: No, but we need to compromise here.

H: OK. Let's talk about a percentage. Give me a percentage I can live with.
W: OK, 10%.
H: I can live with 10%.
W: This is going to be a very advantageous discussion.
H: I'm just a really great, wonderful guy.
W: I wouldn't go that far (laughs).
H: (laughs).

Validating couples spend some time exploring each person's point of view, asking questions and getting clarification, before engaging in the processes of persuasion. Their discussions tend to start neutrally and calmly, as if they are first building an agenda. Sometimes they become heated and emotional during the persuasion phase of the discussion, but they are able to then smoothly move into a compromise phase on the heels of this persuasion phase. We've created an amalgam above and below of three fictional couples, just to illustrate this initial typology.

Volatiles. The volatile couples, unlike the validators, spend no time talking about each person's point of view before beginning the processes of persuasion. In other words, persuasion starts right out of the gate. There's no agenda building as we see with validators. There's also very little question asking, and very little listening to one another. All the points of view emerge at once as part of a hot, intense debate, where each person argues tooth and nail for their position. Interestingly, they also seem to relish this engagement. There is lots of fighting but there's also lots of positive affect, especially humor. However, their arguments can sometimes dissolve into endless bickering with no subsequent compromise. If a volatile couple discussed the same topic as the validator couple above, here's how they might sound:

W: We just don't save enough, we live hand to mouth. There's nothing left over to save at the end of the month. That stinks! I hate it!
H: Well, I refuse to live for the future. I want to live for now! You're not going to destroy all my fun in life.
W: Fine! Then when the future comes, you'll just be a pauper.

H: What's wrong with that? I'll be a happy hobo. I don't care. A happy hobo, riding the rails with you. At least I will have lived, not like Uncle Ned who died with millions in the bank. Everyone was shocked. He lived like a pauper, in a one-room apartment, stingy and mean, with no life at all. I am not going to be like my uncle Ned.

W: But Ned was right about some things. He wasn't totally wrong. Saving some money is just smart. What if we have an emergency? What if one of us can't work for a while? What about our retirement, or if some great travel opportunity comes up?

H: Then we'd just have to borrow money for it. We'll borrow from Ned.

W: No, we won't. I don't like borrowing money. And Ned is dead (both laugh). We need to save now, maybe 10% to 25% of what we bring home every month. You will just have to adjust your wild and crazy lifestyle to accommodate my needs here.

H: No way. I am living for this moment, not for some unknown tomorrow.

W: Well, what about what I need?

H: You can save *your* money. I am going to spend my money. But I'm OK spending it on us.

W: That won't work.

H: Well, it won't work to ram something I don't want down my throat.

W: Not down your throat, just down your wallet.

H: (laughs) . . .

Conflict avoiders. Conflict-avoiding couples seem to be the exact opposite of volatile couples. They do engage in the agenda-building part of the discussion, but they avoid any persuasion attempts. Instead, they minimize the issue, emphasize their common bonds, and agree to disagree on the issue. Later in our work we discovered that there were actually two types of avoiders, ones that avoided any discussion of feelings, and another group of avoiders that did talk about feelings, and were very accepting of one another's feelings. Both types of avoiders skipped the persuasion phase of discussion. Here is a dialogue of avoiders who do discuss feelings:

W: I have been wanting to bring something up with you. I think that we just don't save enough, we live hand to mouth. There's just nothing left over to save at the end of the month.

H: Why is this a problem?

W: It makes me insecure that we have no cushion, in case something happens.

H: What are you worried about?

W: An emergency. Or our retirement, which is a long way off, I know, or some great travel opportunity. And then we'd have to borrow.

H: How much savings would make you feel comfortable?

W: Saving maybe 10% to 25% of what we bring home every month.

H: Wow, that's a lot. Tell me why you need that much to be saved.

W: I don't really know, but I need that.

H: For what, for retirement, for travel or vacations, for the kids' education?

W: Some of all of that, I guess. What do you want?

H: Well, I can see your point of view here and I think that I am more emphasizing increasing our income so we can have everything someday.

W: I don't see it that way. I think you save a percentage, no matter how much you earn. That's just smart.

H: Well, honey, I love you and this family. I don't think this is a big deal, really. We are just going to have different points of view on this topic. Let's just agree to disagree. It won't help to argue about this.

W: OK, but this is frustrating.

H: I know, but we're doing all right, aren't we?

W: I agree, we are. We're fine, at the moment.

H: Then fine. Let's drop it. Or table it, or whatever.

W: "Whatever," that's our kids' favorite term.

H: I'm starting to like it, too.

W: Fine, whatever.

The issue never got resolved, but the conversation never got heated. Notice that they are pretty good at airing their side of the issue, as validators do, but then they drop the issue rather than moving on to create a compromise. This may be because they find the persuasion phase so aversive. So once each viewpoint is aired, that's it. No more discussion, please. What hurts conflict-avoiding couples, especially the ones who have less than a 5-to-1 ratio of positive-to-negative affect, is that they can stockpile grievances. If they do, they may end up having mean-spirited arguments with escalating negative affect. These fights don't lead to any constructive resolution of the issues, but instead result in hurt feelings and alienation. We see withdrawal and sullen emotional distance rather than an attack–defend pattern. Withdrawal is their Achilles' heel.

Now let's discuss the types of couples that typically fall into each quadrant. We've organized our quadrants into the symmetric ones (1 and 3), in which both partners are positive, or both are negative; and the asymmetric quadrants, in which one partner is positive while the other is negative (2 and 4).

The First Symmetric Quadrant 1: The "Heavenly" Positive–Positive Quadrant

As a goal, we want our couples in therapy to eventually spend most of their time in Quadrant 1, the most peaceful and positive quadrant of phase space. For the masters of relationship, Quadrant 1 is home sweet home. Still, no relationship is perfect. Couples may temporarily drift into the other three quadrants of phase space, particularly if the couple's "footings" are not particularly stable. This is OK, as long as they know how to return to "heaven" and they mostly reside there.

So, who lives in Quadrant 1? There are five types of couples who make it their home.

Quadrant 1.

We will rarely see these couples in therapy, but we might see them in workshops. One neighborhood in which couples reside lies close to the origin (the 0,0 point at the center of phase space). Couples who fall into this area are mildly positive. Another cluster of couples lies in Quadrant 1, but farther away from the origin point, near its outer boundaries. Their affects are very positive.

The couples who have neighborhoods that are close to the origin for their SPAFF mapping include couples who have low-intensity affects, couples with a lot of neutral affects (which is good during conflict), and couples who have negative affects that are largely offset by their positive affects. These include three types of couples. Our math modeling discovered that these couples have matched influence functions (see our appendix; Gottman et al., *The Mathematics of Marriage*; or Gottman, *Principia Amoris*).

a. *CONFLICT AVOIDERS WHO DO NOT SELF-DISCLOSE.* As we noted, conflict avoiders skirt the persuasion and compromise phases of a typical conflict discussion. They express their points of view on their issue, but then don't proceed further. They conclude their discussion by simply agreeing to disagree. Also, these couples mostly avoid talking about their own emotions. For the most part, they seem quite neutral, and are polite and respectful to one another. They resemble the stereotype of Ma and Pa Kettle, people of few words and not much affect. However, these couples appear to be well matched and happily married. Their relationships contain clearly demarcated areas of life in which one or the other partner has autonomy, and they may have separate spaces in their homes that are the domain of one or the other partner. Because their discussions are minimally positive, their representative points lie close to the origin point, where affects are only mildly expressed.

b. *VOLATILES.* Volatiles are the exact opposite of conflict avoiders. These couples fully discuss an issue and do so passionately. They relish debating each other, and they're less inhibited about expressing negative affect. They tend not to be very good at accepting influence or down-regulating their own negative emotions. In fact, their affects at times may even include belligerence and domineering SPAFF codes. But these couples relish persuasion and, amazingly, they do so *right from the get-go*, with lots of debate, agreement, disagreement, and self-disclosure. Later they will often progress and attempt to problem-solve and reach compromise. While affirming their unity as a couple, it's clear that they love the give-and-take of their debates. And because they feel free to vehemently disagree with one another, they usually earn many negative as well as positive SPAFF codes. They would hate having an accommodating, placid, and agreeable partner, who might seem cold and disinterested in the conversation. These couples tend to have the highest scores on validation, empathy, interest, and shared humor. They also commonly have a positive-to-negative SPAFF ratio that equals or exceeds 5 to 1. Due to their negative codes and positive codes offsetting each other, their phase space points typically lie closer to the origin point in Quadrant 1.

c. *VALIDATORS.* Validators are couples who fully discuss an issue. They engage in persuasion, lots of debate, and both agreement and disagreement, including self-disclosure. In addition, they usually move into problem-solving and compromise. Like other groups of couples, these partners also affirm their unity, and tend to score moderately on validation, empathy, interest, and shared humor. They also excel at accepting influence and at down-regulating negative affect. However, because they feel free to disagree with one another, they tend to still earn many negative SPAFF codes that offset their positive codes. Thus their points typically land near the phase space origin, just like the non-self-disclosing conflict avoiders.

Two Couple Types Who Land In Quadrant 1 but Far From the Origin

There are two additional types of couples whose interactions yield points deep in Quadrant 1. Their conversations tend to be extremely positive, more so than couples whose "neighborhoods" exist close to the origin point.

a. *CONFLICT AVOIDERS WHO DO SELF-DISCLOSE.* These conflict avoiders also skip the persuasion phase of a typical conflict discussion. However, they freely express their feelings about the issue, and respond to their partner's point of view with understanding and acceptance. They often employ positive affect to influence their partner, and just like non-self-disclosing avoiders, they agree to disagree, minimize the importance of their differences, and reaffirm their unity as a couple, rather than problem-solving or creating a compromise for their issue. They especially affirm their acceptance of one another and one another's feelings. The interaction of these couples is quite positive, and the home they make in phase space is considerably away from the origin, well into Quadrant 1. They also have a positive-to-negative SPAFF ratio that equals or exceeds 5 to 1 during conflict.

b. *DREAMS WITHIN CONFLICT COUPLES.* There is another group of couples who have discussions about their perpetual issues that include unearthing and describing the historical and existential cornerstones beneath each of their positions on their issue. These couples are high in marital satisfaction. They may be the highest of all the couples we've observed. They affirm each other's fundamental beliefs and support their partner's wishes, hopes, and dreams regarding the issue. Their interactions are quite positive, which lands them well into Quadrant 1, far away from the origin. However, their neighborhood's distance from the origin depends, as do validating couples' neighborhoods, on how they manage any potential negativity they express before coming to their Dreams Within conflict discussion. Their SPAFF and perception data gathered from their events-of-the-week discussion also place them in Quadrant 1. Even their OHIs tend to be very positive, as they discuss being enriched by their differences and take pride in their common values, beliefs, and overall relationship. And as expected, they have a positive-to-negative SPAFF ratio that exceeds 5 to 1.

The Second Symmetric Quadrant 3: This Is Hell. Negative–Negative Quadrant.

There is only one type of couple who typically has a SPAFF neighborhood near the origin of Quadrant 3. We call them devitalized couples.

Devitalized Couples

These couples epitomize the Dan Wile "fallback position" of withdrawal. They have protected themselves from pain by withdrawing from one another, and, sadly, they have usually also shut down their love and many of the usual pleasures of the heart and mind that happier couples share. They have grown so distant from one another that their relationship feels like cohabiting with a stranger. It naturally follows that both partners tend to feel very lonely. If there is any togetherness at all, it's only found in their comanaging an infinite to-do list. They may function well in a managerial manner, but it does not resemble a love relationship. This couple is low in affection, interest, and curiosity in one another. We are not the first to detect this kind of couple. Cuber and Haroff did so many years ago, in 1965.

The devitalized couple neighborhood is negative–negative, definitely in Quadrant 3, but close to the origin. The conflict and events conversations of these couples appear to be quite dead—very neutral, flat, and affectless. There is not much conflict seen. However, more frequent, subtle negative SPAFF codes of low tension show up, plus low-level irritability, anger, and sadness (often with lots of sighing).

In their perception map, the devitalized couple's neighborhood is also in Quadrant 3, but this time, it typically lies far from the origin, because these couples hold a *very* negative view of their relationship. On the RCU their friendship, sexual intimacy, shared meaning, and loneliness questionnaires all tend to be scored as challenges (dark gray boxes).

Our data show that devitalized couples tend to divorce an average of 16.2 years after the wedding, in contrast to couples who display the Four Horsemen of the Apocalypse and tend to divorce an average of 5.6 years after the wedding. In an old marriage-counseling joke, these are the couples who claim that they were waiting for the kids to die before divorcing. They are the ones you see in restaurants who sit eating in stone-cold silence, saying nothing to one another. Maybe they're on their cell phones. Having spent many years being lonely, by midlife, these devitalized partners are likely to have an affair, or at least dream of one.

They even struggle with their events conversations. Their events SPAFF

maps typically lie close to the origin in Quadrant 3, while their events perception data land them far from the origin and deep into Quadrant 3. To the
therapist they might say that they don't really know *what* to talk about, or it
feels phony to talk with one another this "long" (10 minutes). Often, these
couples haven't had sex in years.

There are three types of couples who have SPAFF coding in Quadrant
3 but far from the origin point.

a. HOSTILE COUPLES (sometimes called the "RICHARDSON ARMS RACE" COUPLES) who are failed validators and volatiles

These couples exemplify the Dan Wile "attack–defend" fallback position.
They have turned their partner not just into a stranger but into an enemy.
They often speak to one another with righteous indignation, or portray
themselves as an innocent victim, rather than simply describing their own
pain and need. Hence, these couples are at war with one another, with peri-
odic skirmishes punctuated by the Four Horsemen. In therapy these couples
may have some tender moments of expressing love and admiration for one
another, but these moments are shattered by renewed indignation in which
each partner proclaims that they have done much more for the relationship than their partner, and they feel unacknowledged and unappreciated.
Sometimes one partner will announce that they have changed but their
partner has not. Many regrettable incidents and fights must be processed
before they can begin to trust one another again and take the first step
toward reconciliation.

Earlier we nicknamed these couples "Richardson arms race" couples.
We'll briefly explain why by introducing a new concept that we will flesh out
further in the next chapter: influence functions. For now, consider that a
person can influence their partner by expressing either positive affect, negative affect, or both. Validators use both to influence their partner. However,
volatile couples tend to use only negative affect for influence; and conflict
avoiders, only neutral and positive affect.

Because volatile and validator couples therefore both have nonzero negative affect influence functions (unlike conflict avoiders), there is always a potential for runaway negative affect. However, the couples erupt only when their positive-to-negative ratio drops far below 5 to 1 during conflict.

This mounting negativity is called a Richardson arms race. It is named for the man who mathematically modeled the escalation of arms buildups that preceded World War I. Richardson actually modeled all violent conflicts. His book was self-published, distributed mostly to his friends, and rapidly went out of print, but Anatol Rapoport personally paid for its revival. As you may know, Rapoport worked for international peace and against war. Richardson showed that violence is actually not that difficult to understand and model mathematically. It's cooperation that is the most complex.

These couples are very difficult for most couples therapists to deal with. In fact therapists often find themselves yelling above the couple to even be heard, when the couples' interactions escalate right in the office. Richardson arms race couples have a neighborhood in Quadrant 3 far from the origin. They can be both validator and volatile couples for whom the conflict positive-to-negative ratio has dropped far below 5 to 1. Their influence functions, in the past, may have made them effective validators or volatiles. But now, their attempts to use positive affect for influence will fall flat. If there's any way to influence the opposite partner, it's only through escalated negative affect.

These couples are now stuck in a negative cycle. It's as if they're stepping into quicksand. It's much easier for them to sink down into negative affect than to climb back up and out of it. We call that state a Markov absorbing state of negativity. And as with quicksand, the more they try to wriggle out of this state, the more stuck they get. One or the other partner will ruin a good conversation startup or what seems like a healthy repair attempt. And many repairs are actually damaged repairs, like backward compliments that combine a compliment with criticism. In other words, these couples have runaway attack–defend interaction, with stampeding Four Horsemen of the Apocalypse: contempt, criticism, defensiveness, and stonewalling.

In the most extreme cases, the Markov absorbing state spills over into the events conversation. In his book *Topics in Mathematical Modeling*, K. K. Tung mathematically models these couples using differential equations. His work reveals why the conflict-avoider marriages are potentially the most stable marriages of all types, despite the fact that most therapists and researchers think validator marriages are the best kind. Yet the graphic shape of the influence functions in validator couples shows that they are a higher-risk marriage, because they can slide down into the Richardson arms race if their positive-to-negative ratio declines. Then they flip from Quadrant 1 to Quadrant 3. Still, when validator and volatile couples work well (during conflict, greater than the 5-to-1 positive-to-negative ratio), they are very satisfying and intimate relationships. And along with potential benefits, avoider relationships carry their own risks. There's no perfect type of relationship out there.

b. *THE HOSTILE-DETACHED COUPLE: SEVERE MENTAL ILLNESS OF ONE OR BOTH PARTNERS*

How can there be a type of couple that is worse for a therapist to deal with than the hostile couple type we just described? The answer is the hostile-detached couple. These couples are not only stuck in the attack–defend position, they are also stuck in the withdrawal fallback position. The withdrawal makes their relationships look drained of life and love. The partners are both enemies and distant strangers. But if they poke the withdrawn partner with a little negativity, they can expect a ferocious attack in return. There is absolutely no forgiveness here, and grudges are nursed and maintained. They also actively show one another that they don't care for one another, and are unwilling to meet their partner's needs. They are only out for themselves. This is a zero-sum game relationship, where one person's winning happiness is a threat because it means that the other person has lost. Their arguments are the classic standoff, the game of chicken. Every issue is a potential power struggle. Neither partner feels loved or respected.

The neighborhood for these couples lies far from the origin in Quadrant 3. In the worst of these relationships, one or both partners have a severe mental illness. Examples include a partner diagnosed with borderline personality disorder who is mated with someone who fits the passive–aggressive narcissist personality type. Either one or both can be hostile and withdrawn. These couples are also stuck in a negative cycle, the Markov absorbing state of negativity. Moreover, their negativity also tends to darken their events conversation. They will definitely *not* show up in the Quadrant 1 events conversation for either SPAFF or perception maps. They are also likely to have a neighborhood in Quadrant 3 for their physiological data map. (See the appendix for more information about these couples.)

c. *THE HOSTILE AND VIOLENT COUPLE: SITUATIONALLY VIOLENT COUPLES*

These couples not only strike out verbally with the Four Horsemen during conflicts, they also strike out physically. These are called "situationally violent couples." Their domestic violence is mostly symmetric, meaning both partners become violent. There isn't a clear perpetrator and victim. Their violence is also fairly low level. It doesn't cause serious injury, and doesn't include threats with a knife or a gun. It may consist of a slap, a shove, or an object thrown that isn't dangerous. After one of these violent episodes, these partners tend to feel very guilty and ashamed of their violence. Both also take responsibility for the violence, and they avoid externalizing blame. They do not feel that verbal attacks justify physical retaliation. Their violence often results from physiological or psychological flooding, and a lack of skill in both conflict resolution and sustaining close friendship and intimacy. This type of domestic violence is effectively treatable with couples therapy (see Chapter 18). These couples also tend to reside in Quadrant 3 for both events conversations and conflicts. They contrast with the characterologically violent batterer couple, for which couples therapy is contraindicated.

d. *COUPLES THERAPY CONTRAINDICATED:*
   THE CHARACTEROLOGICALLY VIOLENT COUPLE,
   AND COUPLES WITH UNTREATED ADDICTIONS, AN
   ONGOING AFFAIR, OR AN AFFAIR WITH NO REMORSE

These are the couples for whom couples therapy is contraindicated. We choose not to see these people in couples therapy, in part because these couples are extremely hard if not impossible to treat with our current known methods. In the case of characterological domestic violence, we believe that engaging in couples therapy at all can result in colluding with the batterer, because couples therapy typically examines the roles of both partners in creating their relationship problems. Thus, along with the batterer, the victim is held responsible for the violence, too. But this form of domestic violence has a clear perpetrator and victim. It is not the victim's fault or the relationship's fault; it is the perpetrator's fault. Thus, doing couples therapy here is immoral. The violence is not at all a couples issue. Couples in which extreme characterological violence exists fall into two subtypes: the hostile "pit bull" borderline batterer, and the hostile-detached antisocial "cobra" batterer (see Jacobson & Gottman's *When Men Batter Women*). Couples therapy may also be contraindicated when a partner suffering from addiction adamantly refuses treatment. As long as the "third party," the toxic substance, is alive in the relationship, it will be very difficult to conduct treatment. In addition, a couple troubled by an ongoing affair, or a past affair or other form of past betrayal where there's little to no remorse, will be nearly impossible to treat as well. These cases will have interactions characterized by intense negative affect on the part of both partners, which places them firmly in attack–defend mode. Their Quadrant 3 neighborhoods land them most distantly from the origin in Quadrant 3. (See the appendix for more information about these couples.)

The Asymmetric Quadrant 2: Husband Positive–Wife Negative Quadrant

Couple Neighborhoods in SPAFF Quadrant 2. All the couples who show up in the husband negative–wife positive quadrant have a low positive-to-negative ratio in their conflict interactions. In the conflict discussion we can differentiate two types of couple neighborhoods that are close to the origin in Quadrant 2.

Asymmetry Is an Extra Challenge for the Therapist. There is an inherent asymmetry in these relationships. At times therapists are in danger of liking one partner while disliking the other. Here Dan Wile interventions are a great aid for the therapist, and also assist in minimizing countertransference. Wile's book *After the Fight* rightfully suggests that the therapist do doubling with the partner the therapist dislikes the most.

Neighborhoods of Couples Close to the Origin in Quadrant 2

a. *THE MATRIARCHAL MARRIAGE.* A consistent finding in the relationship literature is that wives are much more unhappy in their relationships than husbands. However, a common type of marriage we find in the United States is one in which the wife expresses negative affect by complaining, which can resemble bickering, whining, sadness, nagging, and anger. Yet the husband responds positively by accepting her influence. These marriages can be quite happy. But if he resents her negativity, these marriages can be unhappy and meld into the wife-abusive marriage (see below).

b. *THE FAILED AVOIDER COUPLE.* In failed avoider couples, the wife has become more confronting, which elicits a great deal of resentment from the avoidant husband. Typically, the confrontive wife has become very lonely, while the avoidant husband withdraws and stays neutral or positive. For one reason or another, the wife has changed from her past avoidant style. She wants more connection than the typical conflict avoider marriage can offer. Both partners become unhappy with this new failed arrangement, and both partners can also get physiologically aroused during conflicts. Their events conversations may also follow this same failed avoidance pattern.

c. *THE WIFE-IMPAIRED, HUSBAND-SUPPORTIVE COUPLE.* There is a kind of relationship that has been consistently described in the literature in which the wife is impaired or disabled, clinically depressed or anxious, but she is happily married, because her partner is so positive and supportive. Marriages where the wife has dementia with a caretaker husband have been recently studied in the Levenson lab. These marriages are asymmetric, but they can work. However, eventually the caretaker may become very stressed, as he is responsible for caretaking while she suffers. In these cases we can code his affect as negative because this caretaking role is exhausting and can take its toll on him. As a result he may become less positive, while she remains very positive. This is especially true where one partner suffers from dementia, but this relationship shift depends on the nature of her dementia, and the location of the lesions in her brain.

Neighborhoods of Couples Far From the Origin in Quadrant 2

a. *THE HUSBAND PSYCHOLOGICALLY ABUSIVE MARRIAGE.* In our laboratory, relationships land far from the origin in Quadrant 2 when the husband is psychologically abusive, highly domineering, very critical, and disapproving of his wife, while the wife is fearful, compliant, and "positive" only in her acquiescence (she shows only low-level validation). In our Emotional Abuse Questionnaire (EAQ) there are four scales of emotional abuse: (1) social isolation of the victim; (2) degradation and humiliation of the victim; (3) sexual coercion of the victim, and (4) threats by the abuser, including verbal threats or actual damage done to property, pets, or children. These are very tricky relationships to work with, and they require the therapist to become very active in confronting the abuser, while at the same time empathizing with the abuser and keeping his trust, while simultaneously supporting the victim. These neighborhoods are populated by couples who are characterized by the wife's high loneliness, both partners rating negative–negative in their perceptions, and the wife's physiological arousal.

b. *COUPLES HAVING A WIFE'S AFFAIR, OR PAST AFFAIR WITH REMORSE, OR THE WIFE IN ADDICTION RECOVERY.* When one partner is in addiction recovery there is a lot we can do in couples therapy. (See our Couples Addiction Recovery workshop, designed by Dr. Robert Navarra.) When a wife has had an emotional or sexual affair and has remorse for it, and the couple wants to decide what to do or actually wants to move forward in repairing the marriage, we can generally provide help. These couples can be tough to work with because every level of the SRH has usually been shattered. The hurt partner also often suffers from PTSD caused by the affair. While many other couples therapies say that it is first necessary to control the hurt partner's storm of negative affects, we do not agree. A neighborhood far from the origin of Quadrant 2 initially characterizes an affair couple who are working on rebuilding the marriage. The hurt partner needs to express their pain without attack and without the Four Horsemen, while the betraying partner listens and then expresses her remorse. Doing Dan Wile interventions for both partners can be very helpful here. (See Chapter 17 for a description of our atone–attune–attach therapy for treating affair couples. See also Glass and Staeheli's excellent 2007 book, *Not "Just Friends,"* for further insights on how to treat affair couples.)

The Asymmetric Quadrant 4: Husband Negative–Wife Positive Quadrant

Couple Neighborhoods in SPAFF Quadrant 4. All the couples who make a home in the wife positive–husband negative quadrant have a low positive-to-negative ratio in their interaction. In the conflict discussion we can differentiate three types of neighborhoods.

Neighborhoods Close to the Origin of Quadrant 4

a. *THE PATRIARCHAL MARRIAGE.* In our laboratory this neighborhood characterizes relationships in which the husband is domineering, bickering, and somewhat critical and disapproving of his wife. The husband can also be nice, but only to some degree, unless his authority is threatened. In response to his negative affect, the wife tends to be agreeable and compliant and to respond positively or even apologetically. In many cultures on the planet, particularly in Africa, Asia, and South America, and in parts of the United States as well, these kinds of male-domineering patriarchal marriages are traditional and, to varying degrees, culturally accepted. They can even be quite happy. But if the wife feels dominated, oppressed, and trapped, she will not be happy. If the woman tries unsuccessfully to rebel, or quietly suffers degradation, these marriages can be a nightmare for the woman. In that case, these relationships meld into the husband-abusive relationship. To more closely discern the nature of the relationship, we need to also examine the couple's quadrant position in the perception map, and their questionnaires and physiology.

b. *THE FAILED AVOIDER COUPLE.* In failed avoider couples, the *husband* has become more confronting and negative. This elicits a great deal of resentment from the avoidant wife, who tries to avoid conflict and remain positive. Typically, the avoider withdraws and becomes more distant, which leaves the confronting partner very lonely. Both partners grow unhappy with this failed arrangement, and both partners can eventually become physiologically aroused. Their events conversations follow this same failed pattern. The 1980 movie *Ordinary People*, directed by Robert Redford and starring Mary Tyler Moore, Donald Sutherland, and Judd Hirsch, beautifully depicts this type of marriage, in which the husband and son become closer after the oldest son (Mom's favorite child) has drowned in an accident. The remaining son and the husband want to talk about the tragedy and establish a different kind of self-disclosing avoidant or non-avoidant family, but they keep failing with Mom, who wants to stay non-self-disclosing-avoidant. This film illustrates one liability of the non-self-disclosing-avoidant relationship: its inability to deal with grief or life tragedies. For this reason, the non-self-disclosing-avoidant marriage has a brittle (rather than resilient) quality.

c. *THE HUSBAND-DISABLED, WIFE-SUPPORTIVE COUPLE.* This is a kind of relationship that has been consistently described in the literature, in which the husband is disabled, or clinically depressed or anxious, but he is reasonably happily married, because his wife is so positive and highly supportive. These marriages are asymmetric, but they can work well. She is the caretaker, and he is the sufferer. We can, however, eventually pick up the negativity in her affect, because caretaking takes a toll on her.

Neighborhoods Far From the Origin in Quadrant 4

a. *THE WIFE PSYCHOLOGICALLY ABUSIVE MARRIAGE.* In our laboratory these neighborhoods tend to describe relationships in which *the wife* is abusive, highly dominant, very critical, and disapproving of her husband, and the husband is compliant and positive only in his acquiescence. In our EAQ, there are four scales of emotional abuse: (1) social isolation of the victim; (2) degradation and humiliation of the victim; (3) sexual coercion of the victim; and (4) threats by the abuser, including either threatened or actual damage done to property, pets, or children. These are very tricky relationships to work with, and they require the therapist to become very active in confronting the abuser, while at the same time empathizing with the abuser and keeping her trust, while supporting the victim. This neighborhood contains couples who are characterized by high loneliness and physiological arousal of the husband while, in perception, they land in the negative–negative field.

b. *THE HUSBAND AFFAIR WITH REMORSE COUPLE (OR HUSBAND IN ADDICTION RECOVERY).* When one partner is in addiction recovery there is a lot therapists can do to help the couple. (See our Couples Addiction Recovery workshop designed by Robert Navarra.) When the husband has had an emotional or sexual affair, feels remorse for it, and the couple wants to either decide what to do or repair the marriage, we can often help this couple. They are tough to work with because every level of the SRH has usually been shattered, and the hurt partner is usually suffering from PTSD from the affair. While many other therapies believe that it is first necessary to control the storm of negative affects the hurt partner feels, we do not agree. We need to help the hurt partner express their negative emotions without using the Four Horsemen, while the betraying partner listens and expresses remorse. Only after the completion of this phase should there be attempts to repair the marriage itself. (See Chapter 17 for a description of our atone–attune–attach therapy.)

All of the above typologies of relationships can help determine the strengths and challenges that couples face in therapy. By attending to these, we can decide in general what therapeutic interventions may or may not be useful and, through our work together, hopefully move our couples into Quadrant 1, the positive–positive quadrant.

CHAPTER 9

Understanding Our Typology: Patterns of Social Influence and the Relationship Builder

In this chapter we talk about how people influence one another, and we review our older mathematical modeling. In this chapter we also describe the Relationship Builder for outlining the interventions now available on Gottman Connect.

First, We Ask, How Do Partners Influence One Another?

To understand how to treat all the couples in our typology of couples, we need to be able to describe how partners influence one another. To do that we need to use mathematics. The great thing about math is that it's the only area of human knowledge where, if you prove something using logic and reasoning, it is irrefutably true forever. There's no room for debate or contrary opinions. Well, it turns out that there's mathematical proof that if you stir a mug of coffee, there is always one particle of coffee that is exactly in the same position it started in. It's called the Brouwer fixed point theorem. Isn't that an amazing result? It's even more amazing that this fact is provable mathematically.

What's the math of coffee got to do with treating relationships? The answer is that, under some very general conditions, when people interact and influence one another, there always exists at least one fixed point in their interaction. That fixed point can be one or several points, or it can also be a patterned orbit in their interaction. It's even the case that the orbit can have a beautiful fractal geometry. These fixed points or orbits are called "attractors" if they are stable, and "repellers" if they are unstable. They are called "strange attractors" if they have a fractal geometry. In our chapter on a couples typology we've been calling these fixed points the "neighborhoods" in a positive-to-negative two-partner phase space that describes how couples interact a lot of the time and what that looks like in husband–wife phase space. We've used these fixed points to classify the kinds of couples, based on their interaction in this phase space plane.

For the past 30 years it's been John's obsession to describe these fields and their fixed points, orbits, and flows in the love relationships that he's observed in the Levenson–Gottman Love Lab. In fact, over 20 years ago, the esteemed mathematician James Murray, his students, and John published a book titled *The Mathematics of Marriage* (2002) that described the geometric fields that resulted from our very simple mathematical equations. Our mathematical modeling began with the work of James Murray and his students, and continued with Vladimir Brayman and Rafael Lisitsa. When John's mathematician colleagues said they required an understanding of his couples' influence functions, his initial reaction was total horror. How the heck *did* people influence one another? What theory could be called upon? He didn't have a clue.

The answers came very slowly, over a long 15-year period. Here is a little summary of what our research adventure taught us. We needed to clarify the importance of **nine parameters** to write down our equations.

1. *TRUST.* Trust and commitment form what we call the weight-bearing walls of our SRH theory. We used a branch of mathematics called game theory to talk about the two pillars of a lifelong love relationship: trust and commitment. Game theory was first developed in economics by John von Neumann and Oskar Morgenstern in 1949. Ten

years later it was brought into psychology by three social psychologists: Harold Kelley, John Thibaut, and Anatol Rapoport. Their ideas were amplified by the pioneering research of Caryl Rusbult, whose work fostered a precise analysis of commitment. Rusbult's research is the only work that can actually prospectively predict sexual infidelity in heterosexual couples. So John used game theory to precisely define and validate a trust metric and a betrayal metric using couples' SPAFF coding paired with their perception data; these ideas were proposed in John's book *The Science of Trust*, and in John and Nan Silver's book *What Makes Love Last?* The idea was that:

With high *trust*, people act so as to maximize their partner's benefits, as well as their own; therefore, they act so as to maximize the sum of their video-recall ratings.

That high-trust idea implies that you can count on the fact that your partner "has your back," because your partner is always thinking about what's best for you, not just what's best for themself. This implies that high-trust couples will try to find what is called a "Nash equilibrium" in their interactions. The Nash equilibrium is defined as that point where neither partner can do any better by shifting their behavior. It's the best that both people can do. People who build trust work to find that sweet spot.

2. *COMMITMENT.* Rusbult discovered that commitment means the following:

With high commitment, people cherish their relationship, nurturing gratitude for what they *do* have with this partner, rather than thinking of what is missing and growing resentful for what they *don't* have. High-commitment partners are more likely to give voice to their complaints with their partner, so the relationship can be strengthened. These couples also amplify their partner's positive qualities and minimize their partner's negative qualities. And they put a wide fence around other potential relationships, evaluating these alternative pairings as negative compared to what they already have. In this way, cherishing their partner grows over time, as does their commitment. In contrast, low-commitment partners amplify their partner's negative qualities, and minimize their partner's positive qualities, thereby trashing their partner, eroding their commitment, and building toward betrayal. These couples think thoughts like "I can do better than my current relationship." Thoughts like these bring a third person into the center of the primary relationship and build toward betrayal.

- Rusbult measured this process and called it the "comparison level for alternative relationships." Betrayal is the opposite of loyalty, and loyalty is a component of commitment. Our **betrayal metric** was based on the rating dial data, computed as positive-minus-negative points, and then cumulated over time. A high betrayal metric resembled a zero-sum game. In a zero-sum game, these cumulated graphs, added over partners, were nearly constant. We simply computed the correlation between partners' cumulated sums. If the correlation was negative, that pattern in game theory was a zero-sum, or betrayal metric, pattern. The pattern indexed how "betrayal prone" a specific relationship was. In sum, we learned from our mathematical modeling that the absence of commitment can be assessed reliably by a competitive win–lose pattern during conflicts, whereas commitment can be assessed reliably by a collaborative win–win pattern during conflict. As you can see, trust and commitment are not at all the same thing. We need both for a sound (happy and stable) relationship.

3. *STARTUP*. We realized that we needed a *startup constant* that represented what each partner "brought to the table" at the very start of any interaction. Part of that "STARTUP" originates in the past history of the relationship, and part stems from the sum-total temperament of each partner. Startup might also vary from day to day, or even hour to hour, if one day a partner is particularly grumpy, or hasn't had a good night's sleep, or has been particularly unhappy. Stress might also be a factor in the startup constant. Robert Levenson wrote a paper called "The Remains of the Day" that reported the results of a study of the marriages of policemen and their wives measured periodically over a month's time. Sure enough, stresses that the cop had experienced during the day often "spilled over" into the couple

interaction. So external stress spillover, and its management, is also a contributor to startup. In subsequent research, a skill called "dyadic coping with stress," pioneered by Swiss researcher Guy Bodenmann, revealed that a couple can have a specific kind of stress-reducing conversation that minimizes stress spillover.

4. *EMOTIONAL INERTIA.* As we continued our mathematical work, we also realized that we had to take into account how people influence *themselves.* Each person may do that very differently. Normally a person's current behavior influences their immediate future behavior. Some people are quick to change, quick to react, and quick to forget. Others are slower to react—for example, slower to anger and disappoint, but they may also hold grudges. We call that self-influence "emotional inertia." It's a term borrowed from physics. A Mack truck has more inertia than a feather. It takes much more force to get the truck started in motion or, once moving, to stop, compared to a feather. If you imagine one partner trying to influence the other partner, high emotional inertia means it will take much more push from the influencer to move them in a direction you want them to go. Intuitively, however, it seemed that having no emotional inertia might be a bad thing as well. The research literature, in particular, supported the idea that women who were too agreeable had currently happy husbands, but in the long run the relationship satisfaction of these couples actually declined. That's because agreement was often just compliance, and not a very satisfying compliance in the long run. Lowell Krokoff and John first reported this finding in the 1980s, but it has been replicated many times since. So maybe there is an optimum emotional inertia for each partner in a particular relationship. Have too little inertia, and you can get pushed around. Have too much inertia, and you can't accept any influence from the person you love.

5. *THE TRIUMPH OF NEGATIVE OVER POSITIVE AFFECT.* John recognized that a replicable effect in his lab, as well as in all the couples research literature that included observational methods, was this: Negative affect had a greater ability to predict the current relationship unhappiness, or even the eventual demise of a relationship,

than positive affect had to predict the current happiness and eventual happy continuance of a relationship. This is a very general phenomenon. John called this the "triumph of negative-over-positive affect." It's a large effect. Negative affect delivered by our partner tends to stop us. Positive affect received from our partner tends to just accelerate or magnify whatever we were already doing. There are more negative emotion words in all languages we know of than there are positive emotion words. The two seminal books that the great emotion researcher Silvan Tomkins wrote were *The Positive Affects* and *The Negative Affects*. The second book was much fatter than the first. This is a gross effect, but it can be represented mathematically in how we think of social influence in love relationships. Because we do couples therapy, we also need to change how unhappy couples exhibit social influence.

6. *FLOODING.* A very early discovery that came from the Levenson–Gottman laboratory was that couples who were physiologically aroused during their discussions—that is, those who had faster heart rates, faster blood velocity, more sweat from the psychologically responsive eccrine glands of their hand (the signal used in polygraph lie detection), had faster and more shallow respiration, and jiggled around more in their chairs—had marriages that became more unhappy over time. That effect held true regardless of their initial relationship satisfaction. We called this combination of physical signs diffuse physiological arousal, or *flooding*, following a suggestion made by Paul Ekman. The research literature on stress and cardiovascular reactivity added much more information. When people become flooded, they aren't very good listeners. They tend to repeat themselves, often louder and louder. They think that they will be more persuasive if they do so. They are worse at being creative problem solvers, and worse at processing incoming new information. They become more stubborn, they attack and defend more, or they withdraw and shut down. Also, they go into fight-flight-or-freeze, and become more aggressive or defensive. As listeners, they stonewall more, especially if they are male. As speakers they tend to repeat their own position.

But instead of expressing their own feelings, they take adversarial or withdrawn fallback positions. They use you-statements instead of I-statements. They attack their partner's character and tend to use words like "You always" or "You never." These findings point to the great importance of physiological self-soothing. It also points out the importance of building a variable called "vagal tone." Vagal tone assesses the functioning of the largest nerve in our body, the 10th cranial nerve, which is responsible for restoring calm in the body and for allowing us to respond positively to emotional connection (see Porges, 2015). Flooding is also contagious. It has been measured as physiological linkage, mediated by negative affect. Recently, physiological linkage has also been discovered by Levenson and Fredrickson in moments of shared positive affect (particularly humor), and in that case it is calming rather than flooding.

7. *REPAIR.* Miscommunication in relationships is actually a very common event. Even in mother–infant interaction, studied with observational methods, John's friend Edward Tronick discovered that moms and 3-month-old babies are miscoordinated 70% of the time. Tronick found that the moms who notice this miscoordination and repair it are more likely to later have securely attached babies when the babies are 1 year old. When we started studying how couples repair their negativity, we found that once a conversation's cumulative sum, our version of the Dow Jones affect average of a conversation, turns negative, only 4% of the time are people able, on their own, to turn it around. Over most couple conflict discussions, negative affect increases the longer the conversation goes on. In therapy it became one of our goals to improve the chances that repair would be effective. Janice Driver and Amber Tabares developed a repair coding system to study how people actually repair in our newlywed sample. They found that some repairs were far more effective than others. Briefly, anything that would work in a business meeting was doomed as a repair in a love relationship. Among newlyweds, cognitive repairs like "Let's examine our alternatives," or "Let's look at this situation rationally," were doomed to fail. They just escalated negative affect. Also, the

earlier the repair attempt was made in the descent into negativity, the more effective it was. The early repairs didn't have to be as big as the later repairs to be effective in reducing negative affect overall. The repair had to be an emotionally based repair, and it had to be humble. Self-disclosures, summarizing the partner, and emphasizing that "we're OK" were effective repairs. "Failed repairs" in which a backward compliment was given made things much worse, sending the couple deeper into Quadrant 3. Successful repair attempts could really make a difference, and could propel a couple from the negative–negative Quadrant 3 to any other quadrant in the map.

8. *CARRYING CAPACITY FOR THE PARTNER'S NEGATIVE AFFECT.* Another effect came to light in our research. John called it a person's "carrying capacity for negative affect of the partner." If you imagine a person carrying a bucket into which their partner is pouring brackish water, the amount of water that can be poured in and carried before water splashes everywhere is the equivalent of someone's carrying capacity for negative affect. With high carrying capacity there might be a one- or two-beat time delay before that person responds negatively to their partner's expressed negative affect. And given their high carrying capacity, the "bucket carrier" will probably voice their own affect more gently. With low negative carrying capacity, a person who hears a bit of resentment might hyper-react with rage.

The negative affect carrying capacity of a person turned out to be easily measured with a 59-item questionnaire John designed. The amazing finding about the carrying capacity variable was that it correlated significantly with just about everything we measured in the lab, including SPAFF coding during conflict, Buehlman Oral History coding, and other questionnaires of relationship satisfaction. It seemed that if one had to boil down all of our results to one finding, we could do it with the variable of negative affect carrying capacity. If someone had low negative affect carrying capacity, they could be admonished to breathe deeply first, then replace their rage with words like these: "My love, when you're upset, the world stops, and

I listen." This conveys the following message: "I don't respond negatively. I don't judge you. I want to listen to understand." Motivated by that finding, my (John's) graduate student Dan Yoshimoto designed a great doctoral dissertation. He designed an interview asking each partner, individually, how they and their partner responded to negative emotions. The emotions Dan picked were sadness and anger, and he asked about it, depending on whether the negativity was about the relationship, or not. What Dan discovered was that he could predict the emergence of the Four Horsemen during the conflict conversation very strongly by whether people felt they could talk to their partner calmly about their anger or sadness and receive an empathetic response, instead of the partner minimizing or dismissing those negative affects. A pattern emerged. The conflict escalated to the extent that a person reported being dismissed emotionally by the partner during non-conflict attempts to connect emotionally.

9. *TURNING TOWARD, AWAY, AND AGAINST.* In our apartment lab Julie and John studied 130 newlywed couples, starting a few months after the wedding, and following them as they became parents. This was our first lab where couples had no instructions whatsoever. They also went through the standard Levenson–Gottman lab, having 15-minute events-of-the-day and conflict conversations, with physiology synchronized to the video time code. In the lab they wore Holter monitors that collected their electrocardiograms. We also evaluated stress hormones in their urine, and took blood to measure their immune functioning. The most important thing we did was to have three cameras in the lab that could follow the couple using our split-screen technology. Camera operators in the control room learned that quite often one partner would try to engage the other in what we called "a bid for connection." Our staff team quickly swung another camera to record the other partner's response to the bid. Janice Driver coded these responses to bids as either "turning toward," "turning away," or "turning against." Turning toward was any acknowledgment of the bid; even a grunt would do. Turning away was no response at all. Turning against was an irritable response like "Would you be

quiet? I am trying to read." As we already noted, after 6 years, 17 couples had divorced. Jani discovered that these divorced couples 6 years earlier had turned toward their partner's bids an average of 33% of the time, whereas the couples who were still married 6 years later had turned toward their partner's bids an average of 86% of the time. Furthermore, Jani discovered that higher turning toward was correlated with more shared humor and affection during conflict, both of which reduce physiological arousal. Couples who stayed married 6 years later had more shared humor and affection during their conflict conversation. Humor and affection during conflict were powerful forces for good. Here was a potential intervention: Could we increase humor and affection by increasing turning toward? If it worked, it would be a powerful intervention because bids usually happened when people were calm, during frequent, everyday events.

Therapy Goals Derived From Our Nine Parameters

For any particular conversation a couple has, we can think of parameters that describe their social influence processes quite precisely, and pinpoint what we need to change in therapy. Our parameters give us eight precise goals for our therapy.

1. *WE NEED TO SOFTEN THEIR STARTUPS, AND ELIMINATE THE FOUR HORSEMEN OF THE APOCALYPSE.*

    We teach couples to use a startup that has three components: (a) I feel (some emotion); (b) about what (not about who), and (c) here's what I need, a positive need (not "here's what I don't need"). We developed the Gottman–Rapoport Conflict Blueprint to help with startups and the partner's response to the softened startup. The four behaviors we called the Four Horsemen of the Apocalypse included criticism, defensiveness, contempt, and stonewalling. Contempt expresses criticism with an air of superiority, disrespect, or insult. Stonewalling is the absence of the usual listener-tracking cues like eye contact, head nodding, brief vocalizations, and facial movement. The "antidotes" for these relationship poisons are, respectively, softened startup, taking responsibility for even a part of the problem, expressing needs, and self-soothing. We are trying to yank a couple out of Quadrant 3.

2. *WE NEED TO INCREASE TRUST THROUGH INCREASING "ATTUNEMENT."*

Attunement is like instruments in an orchestra tuning to one another, resonating together. Dan Yoshimoto's thesis discovered that our trust metric is increased by a special kind of listening. It's listening not for a rebuttal, but to understand the partner's emotions by putting oneself in the partner's shoes, asking open-ended questions to improve understanding at a deep level, and then expressing empathy.

3. *WE NEED TO REDUCE EMOTIONAL INERTIA BY INCREAS-ING THE ACCEPTING OF INFLUENCE.*

A strange paradox exists in relationships. It is this. One cannot be powerful in a relationship unless one accepts influence. That fact at first appears paradoxical. However, we discovered it in John and Neil Jacobson's 9-year longitudinal study of physically violent couples. The couples where there was a male perpetrator and a female victim—which we called "characterologically violent"—had conflict conversations in which the male rejected every attempt of the partner to influence the conversation. They reminded John of baseball players practicing their batting with automatic pitching machines. Everything their partners threw at them got batted back with a big NO. The insight was that if one has a partner who always says NO, then one learns to go around them to get anything done and decided, rather than talking with them. So, the partner who always says NO eventually becomes entirely powerless. (That insight is also the basis of the Japanese martial art of aikido, a handy metaphor.)

4. *WE NEED TO INCREASE POSITIVE AFFECT DURING CON-FLICT, AND IN GENERAL.*

Build friendship, love maps, and fondness and admiration. Hold meetings to work with the Expressing Needs Card Deck. Build emotional connection. Use blueprints that emphasize a habit of mind in which people scan their social environment and look for what their partner is doing right, rather than what they're doing wrong. Increase gratitude for what is there rather than resentment for what is missing. We owe this insight to a brilliant study by Robinson and Price (1980). Also, we work on turning toward in all the positive affect systems, following Panksepp's analysis of the emotional command system in the brains of all mammals. They include (a) exploration and adventure; (b) attachment security, trust, commitment, and emotional connection and bonding; (c) play, fun, and humor/amusement/delight; and (d) lust, passion, and sexual connection.

5. *WE NEED TO BUILD PHYSIOLOGICAL CALM AND INCREASE VAGAL TONE.*

The ability to wait two beats before responding results from increased vagal tone. We need to help couples reduce their reactivity.

6. *WE NEED TO INCREASE THE POWER OF REPAIR.*

Our Repair Checklist helps supply brief repairs one can make during a conversation when it's sliding downhill to get it back on track again. The Aftermath of a Fight or Regrettable Incident exercise helps couples to truly put behind them bad fights or regrettable incidents they've had that still fester inside. The state-of-the-union meeting may combine some of the above processes, but primarily it's a great way for the couple to check in with each other on how the relationship is doing. Repair may also be the way out of the Markov absorbing state of negativity, and spillover of negative affect into non-conflict interactions.

7. *WE NEED TO INCREASE CARRYING CAPACITY FOR NEGATIVE AFFECT.*

Emotional check-ins and stress-reducing conversations can help with this. Deepening emotional connection and attunement will aid in building trust.

8. *WE NEED TO BUILD AWARENESS OF TURNING TOWARD BIDS FOR EMOTIONAL CONNECTION.*

Not only during emotion-based conversations but also during

everyday requests for help, companionship, or other particular needing to be met.

Now, how do we accomplish all this in couples therapy?

The Relationship Builder:
A Guide to All Our Interventions

*We now describe the Relationship Builder of Gottman Connect.
The Relationship Builder is a software platform that presents 34
"modules," each describing a different intervention. The modules
include videos and text that provide the rationale for a particular
intervention, the instructions, the materials that are needed to
perform each intervention, and two additional videos: how to do
an intervention correctly, and how to sabotage the intervention.
We add this latter video to each module to demonstrate that any
intervention can be sabotaged, and also to add some humor to
the module.*

Modules of the Relationship Builder
Here is the list of the modules of our first release of the Relationship Builder:

1. **The Sound Relationship House Theory.** This module describes for
   your client couple the SRH theory and gives them a language they
   can use for understanding part of your therapy.
2. **What Predicts the Future of the Relationship?** This module
   describes for your client couple the basic research that John and Bob
   conducted that predicts the future of relationships.
3. **Replace the Four Horsemen With Their Antidotes.** This module
   explains to your client couple what the Four Horsemen of the Apocalypse are, and also explains their antidotes.
4. **Use Softened Startup.** This module explains to your client couple
   what gentle startup is, which is talking about one's feelings, about a
   specific situation, and expressing a positive need.
5. **List of Perpetual Problems.** This list helps couples identify

potential problems they have repeatedly, due to personality differences between them.

6. **The Gottman–Rapoport Conflict Blueprint.** This module explains
   to your client couple how to deal with current conflicts. It replaces
   active listening.

7. **Dreams Within Conflict.** This module explains to your client couple
   how to deal with gridlocked issues that have an existential "hidden
   agenda" behind one or both positions on the issue.

8. **Compromise.** This module explains to your client couple our "bagel
   method" of compromise, using two circles to represent core needs one
   cannot compromise on, and areas of greater flexibility.

9. **Physiological Flooding.** This module explains to your client couple
   what physiological and psychological flooding is about and how it
   affects the escalation of conflicts.

10. **Taking Effective Breaks.** This module explains to your client couple
    how to take effective breaks so that conflict is less likely to escalate.

11. **Guided Relaxation.** This module explains to your client couple how
    to self-soothe during a break. Self-soothing can accompany mindful
    meditation and the use of HeartMath's emWave2 biofeedback device,
    which help build high vagal tone.

12. **Aftermath of a Fight or Regrettable Incident.** This module explains
    to your client couple how to process a past regrettable incident or bad
    fight as a tool for healing past emotional injuries. (This intervention
    is shown in five separate segments.)

13. **Repair.** This module explains to your client couple what repair is all
    about, why it is needed, and how to use the Repair Checklist to keep
    fights from escalating.

14. **The State-of-the-Union Meeting.** This module explains to your cli-
    ent couple what this 1-hour meeting is all about for talking to one
    another about how the relationship went that week, and how to cre-
    ate small connections.

15. **The Magic 6 Hours a Week.** This module explains to your client
    couple how to create immediate improvements in their relationship
    by just changing what they do for 6 hours a week.

16. **Build Love Maps.** This module explains to your client couple what love maps are, and how to build them.

17. **Ask Open-Ended Questions (for Dates).** This module explains to your client couple how to build their love maps on dates by asking open-ended questions.

18. **Share Fondness and Admiration.** This module explains to your client couple how to build affection and respect in their relationship and how to create a habit of mind where they are scanning their social environment for positive events, rather than a habit of mind that scans the social environment for one's partner's mistakes.

19. **Identifying Your Truth.** This module explains to your client couple how to read the signals of their own bodies so that they will know which feelings are true for them and which are not. It is a potential prelude to teaching Eugene Gendlin's focusing, for people who don't seem to be able to articulate what they are feeling. This module can be used effectively with the Feelings Card Deck.

20. **Turning Toward, Responding to Bids, Sliding Door Moments.** This module builds awareness for your client couple about what bids and turning toward, turning away, and turning against are and their roles in building an emotional bank account in a relationship. It also builds gratitude for the partner having turned toward them in the past.

21. **Expressing Needs.** This module builds awareness for your client couple about what their needs (synonym for "wishes," "desires," "wants," "hopes," "preferences") are. Using the Expressing Needs Card Deck, this module helps you work with your client couple to set up an expressing needs meeting as a regular weekly ritual, one that works in coordination with the state-of-the-union meeting.

22. **How to Be a Great Listener.** This module builds awareness for your client couple about what reflective listening is all about, and specifically how to listen to anger, sadness, and fear. This kind of listening is essential for attunement conversations.

23. **The Stress-Reducing Conversation.** This module builds awareness for your client couple about what the stress-reducing conversation is all about, and how powerful it is in avoiding relapse.

24. **Build Rituals of Connection.** This module builds awareness for your client couple about how to build traditions in their relationship that create times of meaningful emotional connection for both formal and informal rituals. The rituals of connection are our answer about how to make sure that therapeutic changes last.

25. **Improving a Couple's Sex Life. What Is Sex?** This module builds awareness for your client couple about what "sex" can be in a couple's life, and how to adopt the motto that "everything positive you do in a relationship is foreplay."

26. **Improving a Couple's Sex Life. The 13 Habits for a Great Sex Life.** This module builds awareness for your client couple about what actually, surprisingly, discriminates couples worldwide who say they have a great sex life from those who say that they have an awful sex life.

27. **Improving a Couple's Sex Life. Building an Erotic Love Map of Your Partner.** This module helps build for your client couple a real erotic love map of their partner's sexuality. It builds awareness through 100 questions to ask a woman and 100 questions to ask a man about their feelings and ideas about various aspects of sex.

28. **Improving a Couple's Sex Life. Initiating and Refusing Sex.** This module builds a ritual of connection for your client couple about how to initiate lovemaking, and how to respond to "no."

29. **Improving a Couple's Sex Life. Exploring Sensuality.** This module builds sensual responses for your client couple about what steps on their sexual "brake" and what steps on their sexual "accelerator."

30. **Improving a Couple's Sex Life. The Salsa Card Decks.** This fun module builds sexual activities for your client couple at three levels of "hotness."

31. **Shared Goals Exercise.** This module builds creating shared goals for your client couple.

32. **Building Trust Through Attunement.** This module builds for your client couple the critical skills of attunement, which is one way of creating greater trust.

33. **Understanding Your Emotions.** This module builds awareness for

your client couple about what they feel about the experience and expression of the emotions.

34. **Building Commitment.** This module builds awareness for your client couple about what commitment is, and how to build loyalty and commitment in their relationship.

How to Use the Relationship Builder Videos and Materials

The Relationship Builder's videos and materials on Gottman Connect can be used in your office. You can watch the videos of a module together with your clients, answer their questions, and apply the module directly to the couple's current issue. The videos are brief, and need not take up a great deal of time in your session with the couple. They are only there to serve as an aid to your work.

Very soon we will also have created an app that couples can have on their cell phones so that they can access the Relationship Builder at home for two purposes: one for homework you assign them, and another for any crises that may have emerged since the last session. For these crises, the app for couples will eventually have a Gottman Assistant, which can guide the couple to the appropriate module, and help them troubleshoot any difficulties they run into. The Gottman Assistant will hopefully be helpful to them if they encounter a crisis in between sessions, and can help them solve in the moment.

CHAPTER 10

Fixing Active Listening: The Gottman–Rapoport Conflict Blueprint and Making Repairs Mid-Conversation

In this chapter we introduce the Gottman-Rapoport Conflict Blueprint, which is our fix for the problems with active listening. We call our kind of listening "reflective listening." Then we discuss how couples can make repairs to get a conversation back on track. Finally we offer tools to help listeners learn how to express empathy.

The Gottman–Rapoport Conflict Blueprint

This is a "blueprint" that comes from the brilliant work of Anatol Rapoport. Rapoport's major book was *Fights, Games, and Debates*. He worked primarily in the area of international relations using two-person game theory. His basic idea was that people postpone persuasion and problem-solving until:

Each person can state their partner's position to their partner's satisfaction.

This means that **understanding must precede persuasion**, advice, debate, and problem-solving. To accomplish this, partners take turns as speaker and listener. One person speaks while the other simply listens. It's OK for the listener to ask questions, but not for the sake of rebuttal, only for clarification.

The blueprint has two parts. The first part we call reflective listening and validation.

Reflective Listening and Validation

Listener's Role

Here the listener acts in a very special way, listening with love, compassion, and empathy, trying to step into the partner's shoes and feel the partner's entire position. To facilitate this process and to curtail reactivity, we ask the listener to take notes. The listener temporarily puts their own position on the back burner, and tries to get in touch with the speaker's pain. This listening is not in order to rebut the partner's position but to compassionately understand it by getting into the speaker's head and temporarily seeing the world from within the speaker's perspective. This is like doing a "Vulcan mind meld," which the character Mr. Spock excelled at in the old *Star Trek* TV show.

The listener uses a clipboard and yellow pad to take extensive notes when listening. The more defensive the listener feels, the more the listener should slow down the speaker so the listener can jot it all down. After the speaker has concluded their statement and answered any questions the listener may have, the listener reflects back what they heard by summarizing the speaker's position, and validating it. Let us explain what validation means. It does not mean the listener has to agree with the speaker. The listener is entitled to their own point of view, which can be expressed when the listener becomes the speaker. Validation simply means communicating that there is some part of what the speaker has said that makes sense to the listener. For example, the listener might complete a sentence like "I get why, from your point of view, you would have these feelings and needs, because . . . " In summary, the listener is communicating, "OK, I get it . . . " Empathy is communicated by sincerity and a real attempt at understanding, as much as the listener can do. The therapist will probably have to help. If either of your clients gets stuck, consider doing a Dan Wile, doubling for either the speaker or the listener. Remember, don't be a perfectionist. We're going for "good-enough" listening. This differs from the old Guerney (1991) active listening model in asking the listener to summarize the speaker's entire position on the issue, not just the speaker's last few lines.

Speaker's Role

In this blueprint there are also responsibilities for the speaker. This is also where active listening and reflective listening diverge. In active listening, typically, the speaker is free to use criticism, defensiveness, and even contempt when voicing their position. In reflective listening, the speaker can describe their position only by describing themselves—their feelings, thoughts, and needs—and not their partner's traits. In other words, the speaker cannot be in attack or defend mode, for no one can be expected to validate an attack, unless they are the Dalai Lama, and he isn't married. Instead, the speaker's task is to express how they feel about a specific situation, and then express their positive need regarding the situation. A positive need is a way of stating what you DO want, rather than what you DON'T want. It paints a picture of how the listener can shine for the speaker regarding this particular situation. The therapist may have to help out with wording here. And if you get stuck, consider doing a Dan Wile: doubling for the speaker. Remember, again, don't be a perfectionist. We're going for "good-enough" speaking in self-disclosure mode.

Here is the speaker's recipe. There are three parts:

I FEEL. Tell your clients: Do not describe the partner, describe yourself, how you are feeling. Try not to use you-statements, which describe your partner's motivations, thoughts, or behaviors. Instead use I-statements. What are you feeling? The original idea in I-statements was to complete a sentence like "When you do X, in situation Y, I feel Z." In our blueprint we omit the "When you do X," and stick with only "I feel." That change is designed to minimize the listener's defensiveness.

ABOUT WHAT? Tell your clients: Stay specific. Don't go global, describing patterns of behavior. What's the specific situation you are concerned about? Otherwise, it becomes criticism ("You always . . . " or "You never . . . " are criticisms because they are global, like traits).

I NEED. A need here describes what the speaker does want, not what the speaker does not want. Here the word "need" is synonymous with "preference," "desire," "wish," or "want." This is hard to do. So, help the speaker dip into their past memories of what did not go right, then ask the speaker to flip that on its head in order to ask what would work instead. If a client has trouble with this, the therapist can use the magic wand question: "If you could wave a magic wand to make the world exactly how you'd like it to be regarding this situation, what would it be like? What would be different? How would you know that the world had changed?"

The best positive need is a specific doable recipe for how the speaker's partner can be successful with them right now. For example, a vague positive need is "I need you to make me feel happy." A better positive need would be "I need you to turn off your cell phone and just talk to me during dinner." This is a speaker's precise recipe for how the listener can shine for the speaker. This "gentle startup" differs from the old active listening admonition for speakers, which was to use the formula "When you do X, I feel Y." We dislike that old formula because describing the listener will inevitably lead to the listener's defensiveness. Our formula differs from the old active listening formula in two ways. First, it summarizes the entire speaker's point of view, not just a fragment. Second, the speaker describes only the self, not the partner.

Also, a positive need (a want, a desire, a wish, a preference) requires no rationalization or justification. These positive needs usually come up when, on some level, the speaker doesn't feel entitled to have their need met. No such entitlement is required, especially since justification can sound like a veiled attack, which creates defensiveness. For example, if I say, "I'd like a baguette with dinner from Rose's Bakery," that's a clear need. But if I say, "I'd like a baguette with dinner from Rose's Bakery because, since you're always on a diet, I haven't been able to have that," those words will probably sound like an attack. If your client tries to justify their need, you can simply remind them that they're entitled to it.

Compromise

The second part of the Gottman–Rapoport Blueprint is compromise. In this exercise, ask your partners to each individually draw a bagel (or doughnut) on their yellow pad. It will look like a large circle with a smaller circle inside it. Then ask each partner to write down the core aspects of their position in their inner circle. Core aspects may include a core need, value, or dream.

This core need is the part of each partner's position that they can absolutely not compromise on, for if they did, it would feel like giving up the bones of their body. The idea behind this inner circle is that compromises fail when, just for the sake of peace, people give up what they really need. Resentment inevitably results from that much surrender. Next, in the outer circle each partner writes out what they can be more flexible about in their position. These flexible aspects tend to be more of the details in a potential compromise, such as when something will be done, how often it will be done, how much something might cost, a destination, how long something will last, and so forth. After each partner's writing is complete, the partners share what they've written in each circle. Then they explain why those inner-circle aspects are so primary to them. After reading aloud their writing, the partners can finally entertain suggestions for a compromise that could satisfy both people's core needs through compromising on what's more flexible. Couples can ease their way into potential compromises by discussing what goals they have in common, and in what flexible areas there may be overlap. Our experience is that creating a compromise is usually 5% of the process, while the other 95% takes place first: reaching mutual understanding. As a visual aid, it helps to photocopy the following page and hand it out to the couple.

GOTTMAN–RAPOPORT CONFLICT BLUEPRINT

STEP 1: LISTENING AND VALIDATION.

PRINCIPLE: Postpone persuasion until each person can state their partner's position to *their partner's satisfaction*.
Take in information and energy, instead of practicing defensive listening. Be in "What's this?" mode, not "What the hell is this?" mode. SLOW THINGS DOWN. Take turns as:

Speaker's Responsibility:

- No blaming, no "you-statements."
- **I FEEL:** Your feelings using "I-statements."
- **ABOUT WHAT:** A specific situation. Describe in neutral terms. Avoid the trap, "I feel that YOU ... "
- **I NEED:** State your **POSITIVE NEED.** Within every negative affect there is a longing, a wish. Within that longing there is a recipe for the partner.
- ***Listener's Responsibility: (spells ATTUNE)***
- **Awareness:** Postpone your own agenda and just LISTEN, take in information.
- **Turn toward: REFLECT BACK, SUMMARIZE PARTNER. Repeat speaker's feelings and needs and perspective (the story):** Understand partner's enduring vulnerabilities.
- **Tolerance:** You agree that there are two valid realities, both right.
- **Understanding:** Try to **understand**, not change. OK to ask questions.
- **Nondefensive listening:** Don't react. Wait. **Tune in to your partner's pain:** It's not facts, it's perception that matters. There is no immaculate perception.
- **Empathy: VALIDATE.** Respectfully validate speaker, "It makes sense to me that you would feel that way and have these needs, because ... "

FLOODED?
STOP IMMEDIATELY!
TAKE A BREAK, HALF HOUR.
APPOINTMENT TO RETURN,
SELF-SOOTHE, DON'T RUMINATE.

It is important to reduce threat and increase safety. Become allies, not adversaries. **Take responsibility for even a part of the problem.**

HARD TO COMPROMISE?

When compromise seems like a deal-breaker, **there are hidden agendas**. THERE ARE UNADDRESSED DREAMS WITHIN EACH PERSON'S POSITION IN THE CONFLICT.

Listener Asks:

1. What beliefs, ethics, and values do you have that relate to your position on this issue?
2. Is there some story behind this that relates to your history or childhood in some way?
3. What are all your feelings on this issue?
4. Tell me why this is so important to you.
5. What would be your ideal dream here?
6. Is there a deeper purpose or goal in this for you?

STEP 2: COMPROMISE and PROBLEM-SOLVING. ACCEPT INFLUENCE.

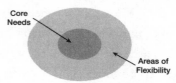

Core Needs

Areas of Flexibility

Explain why they are core to you. Give-and-take. What is your common ground? Shared goals? Propose solutions. Experiment with a temporary compromise. Reevaluate later.

"STATE-OF-THE-UNION MEETING" 1 HOUR A WEEK

1. What's gone right this week?
2. FIVE appreciations each.
3. What has gone right in the relationship this week?
4. Deal with any current conflict or aftermath if a regrettable incident has happened.
5. "What can I do next week to make you feel loved?"

The Bagel Method of Compromise. Below is a helpful handout to give to couples when they are ready to work on compromise. Once each partner has filled out the two circles of the bagel, the inner circle containing their core needs, or what they cannot compromise on, and the outer circle, the areas of flexibility in their position, they explain what they wrote down in each circle, then discuss their answers to the questions provided in the handout below.

The Art of Compromise

Yield to Win: Compromise with me like I am someone you love.

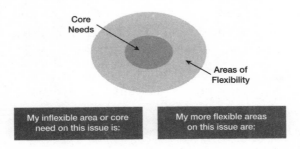

My inflexible area or core need on this issue is:

My more flexible areas on this issue are:

Getting to "Yes"
Discuss these questions with your partner:

For issues where a Dream Within Conflict exercise has not been used:
- Help me understand why your inflexible area is so important to you.
- What are your core feelings, beliefs, or values about this issue?

For all compromise issues:
- Help me understand your flexible areas.
- What do we agree about?
- What are our common goals?
- How might these goals be accomplished?
- How can we reach a temporary compromise?
- What feelings do we have in common?
- How can I help to meet your core needs?

Our compromise that honors both our needs and dreams is:

The Process of Repair

About 15 years ago, a social worker named Nancy Dreyfus came to John's lab. She had written a flip book titled *Talk to Me Like I'm Someone You Love: Relationship Repair in a Flash.* It was published finally in 2013. The idea Nancy had is that often during a conflict conversation that is going south, we wish we knew what to say to make things better, but these thoughts do not occur to us in the middle of the usual conflict discussion. So Nancy wrote a book where you could just flip through it and find a great thing to say that would repair things. An example was "I'm starting to get defensive. Could you say that to me in a gentler manner?" What a great idea! Rather than going defensive, a person says that they're feeling defensive, and then asks for easier phrasing to hear. Who would think to say that when they're getting upset?

Nancy's idea was also great because miscommunication is actually quite likely in a relationship; after all, there are two brains here instead of one. In fact, as we noted, John's friend Edward Tronick studied mother–infant communication during parent–infant play when the babies were 3 months old, and he found that moms and babies were miscoordinated a whopping 70% of the time. The baby was actually thinking, "Huh?" and the mom was thinking, "What?" during these moments. But some moms noticed that the baby wasn't getting the face-to-face play, and they made repairs. When the babies were 1 year old, those moms who had made repairs early on had securely attached babies, and this could be measured. The moms who didn't repair had babies that turned out to be insecurely attached. Tronick developed a whole theory about the importance of repair, because he suggested that two people fixing the interaction together are actually creating a new sense of meaning right on the spot. That's some great thinking.

Of course, we responded to Nancy's ideas by studying how real couples actually make repairs. The project was undertaken by a team of John's graduate students: Janice Driver and Amber Tabares. They created a repair coding system. They discovered that repair attempts are most effective when they are done early, before the interaction gets too negative. Early repairs can be smaller than later repairs, when the interaction has gone not only off the rails but over the cliff. They also discovered that many people did "damaged repairs," which are repair attempts they sabotage by adding a criticism, sarcasm, or veiled insult. One of the worst repairs was "Calm down." The humorist Dave Barry writes dialogue where he tells his wife to calm down, and her response is always in capitals, "DON'T TELL ME TO CALM DOWN!!!"

Driver and Tabares also found that any repair that would work in a business meeting will fail in a love relationship. These business repairs tend to be cognitive and rational, like "Let's consider all our options and pick the best one," or "Let's try to be rational." The only repairs that worked were emotion-based repairs, usually self-disclosing, or asking questions about the other's emotions, or summarizing both people's emotions. Another repair that was very effective was what they called a "We're OK" repair, meaning that even if there was a conflict, overall their relationship was OK. We've prepared a Repair Checklist that couples have found helpful to have with them when they have a conflict discussion. Of course, for a repair to be effective the partner must take it in as a legitimate and humble attempt to make things better. To paraphrase Shakespeare, "The quality of repair is not strained. It drops as the gentle rain from heaven upon the place beneath. It is twice blest. It blesses him that gives and him that takes."

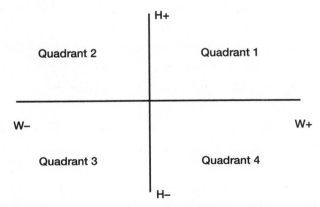

Become a Great Listener

We want to talk about this very special kind of listening. We recommend that your clients periodically take their partner's "emotional temperature." Here's what we mean by that. Every now and then, one partner will ask the other these two questions:

> "HOW ARE YOU DOING, BABY?
> WHAT'S ON YOUR HEART AND MIND?"

Partners won't be asking these two questions when they're in a hurry and are just trying to be polite. They'll reserve these questions for times when they really want to know the answers. How often is "periodically"? They might start out by asking them once a week.

OK, so what does one partner do when their partner answers? First, to become a good listener, each person needs to get out of their own head. They need to set aside their own agenda. Great listening isn't about being *interesting*, it's about being *interested*, so becoming genuinely interested in is key. They need to tune in to their partner's world, and become like a tourist in the landscape of their partner's mind. When people are tourists they are full of questions, like "Who built that church? How old is it? Where is the market?" Couples need to listen especially for any negative emotions like stress, tension, sadness, fear, anger, or disgust . . . and listen to their partner's pain. Even if they don't agree with the situational details. That's not important. Hearing the emotions is what's most important. Partners need to see their partner's world from their perspective, not their own, and ask more questions to understand the feelings even better. This takes thought.

Here's the basic principle: Attune, don't dismiss. That means it's the partner's job as a listener to TUNE IN to their partner and avoid minimizing their feelings.

Now here is a big mistake people make as listeners that is helpful to point out. When partners listen they should be sure to take absolutely *no responsibility* for their partner's feelings. Their job is not to make their partner feel better, nor is it to solve their partner's problems. A partner should NOT try to cheer up the other partner. Their goal is only to understand. And, it turns out, that's enough.

Partners should not ask "why" questions. Partners should try to avoid all "why" questions, like "Why did you do that?" or "Why didn't you do that?" or "Why can't you just relax and chill out?" "Why" questions are almost always criticisms. They are things teachers do when they confront their students. Partners shouldn't be "teachery." Instead, they might ask "what" questions, like "What did you experience?"

Partner listens to the answers, then reflects back what they've heard. You may want your partner to summarize what they heard in order to make sure they got it. They can complete the following sentence: "So what I'm hearing is that you are feeling . . . " and then validates. For example, partners can say, "It makes sense to me that you feel this way." Validation doesn't mean they agree, it only means that they understand. You might share this idea with them:

> THERE IS A MYSTERY, A WISH, WITHIN EACH
> EMOTION, AND WITHIN EACH NEGATIVE EMOTION
> THERE IS A LONGING. TRY TO FIND AND UNDERSTAND
> THAT LONGING.

How to listen to sadness. In sadness often something is lost or missing from the person who is sad. Suggest that the speaker try to find out what's lost or missing. A common pitfall of listening to a partner's feelings is to try to change them. We hear sadness, for example, and our response is to try to cheer up our partner, or make them laugh. Your couples should avoid doing this. Instead, they can try to understand what the sadness or the tears are about. They might say, "Talk to me, baby. I want to hear more about how you feel, so I can understand it."

How to listen to anger. A common pitfall of listening to a partner's anger is taking it personally and becoming defensive. Most angry feelings are composed of one or more of the following: (1) a goal, (2) something that is blocking that goal, or (3) an injustice or unfairness. It can also arise from the unavailability of someone whom one partner needs to be close to (like the other partner). The listener should try to learn: What's the goal? What's frustrating or getting in the way of reaching the goal? Partners might ask each other questions like *"What are your concerns?"* That one is one of our personal favorites. Partners should also avoid trying to make the anger go away. If they hear anger directed at themselves, for example, they may try to immediately apologize. But they shouldn't rush into an apology before they fully understand the nature of the anger. They also should avoid changing the subject or getting defensive, or getting angry back.

How to listen to fear. Everyone needs to develop a strong intuitive sense of when their world isn't safe for them. Something is making a fearful person's world feel unsafe. What is it? A common pitfall of listening to fear is to try to minimize it for the purpose of being reassuring. Instead partners can ask, What are your concerns? What has happened recently that has made you feel unsafe? What do you need to feel safe? What can I do to be helpful to you?" If the fear is about the other partner, the listener needs to start by taking some responsibility for even a small part of the problem, and avoid becoming defensive or counterattacking. For example, if one partner says, "I get scared when you yell at me," the other shouldn't say, "I wouldn't have to yell if you just obeyed me!" Instead, they might say, "Yes, I'm sorry. I know I can get pretty loud sometimes. I will try to watch that behavior." Here's a list of dos and don'ts for your couples:

Listening DOs and DON'Ts
   DON'T
   Don't minimize your partner's concerns or feelings.
   Avoid judgment.
   Don't cheer your partner up.
   Avoid giving advice.

Don't be critical.
Don't be defensive.
No put-downs or superiority at all.

DO

Ask open-ended questions (not questions that have just a yes or no
  answer). These questions open the heart.
Accept, don't judge.
Breathe. Breathe again. Self-soothe.
Make exploratory statements that help you understand (like "Tell me
  the story of that").
Communicate respect.
Communicate understanding and empathy.
Listen as "witnessing."

A big part of listening is witnessing. That means when one partner listens, it
helps the other partner to not feel so alone. As we've noted, a powerful way
to witness and to *"be there"* for the other partner is to repeat back in their
own words what they've heard their partner saying, and communicate validation. That means one might say something like:

> "I HEAR THAT YOU'RE SAYING . . .
> [FILL IN THE BLANK WITH YOUR OWN WORDS] . . .
> AND IT MAKES TOTAL SENSE TO ME WHY YOU
> WOULD FEEL THAT WAY, BECAUSE . . .
> [FILL IN THE BLANK WITH YOUR OWN WORDS]"

For example, one partner might witness their partner's sadness by saying
something like "I hear you saying that it gets worse at night, and that you
really miss the times we used to go out for Chinese food and a movie. I totally
understand that. I miss those times too. I get it." They shouldn't jump in and
offer a suggestion, problem-solving, or advice.

Or, another example: One might witness their partner's anger by saying
something like "I hear you saying that my sister can be hostile and mean. I

have seen that in her myself at times. I totally understand why she made you mad last week. She has gotten my goat many times in the past."

Partners also need to listen to HOW their partner is saying things, not just to WHAT they are saying. For example, people sometimes speak in METAPHORS, sort of like poetry. They may say things like "This apartment is becoming my prison," or "In my life I feel like the train has left and I'm still standing on the platform." Partners can try to tune in to those ways of talking and, in turn, use them as they reflect back what they hear to convey understanding. What can a listener say? See the *italics below.*

"This apartment is becoming my prison." *"Wow, sounds like you really feel trapped. Is that right? Am I getting it?"*

"In my life I feel like the train has left and I'm still standing on the platform." *"So you feel like the world is passing you by, and your own life is at a standstill. Is that right? That must be a crappy feeling to have."*

What follows is our "Attune Guide for Great Listening." It's a helpful tool for teaching your couples how to ask questions or make statements that can deepen their understanding of each other, followed by words they can use to express empathy. The word "attune" is short for awareness, turn toward, tolerance, understanding, nondefensive listening, empathy.

Anyone can become a good speaker and a good listener: It just takes practice using the right tools.

The ones we've provided are what our successful research couples commonly use. We give them to you to share with your couples because they work!

Case Example

Here's a bit of their OHI:

Therapist (T): So, tell me how the two of you met, and what were your first impressions of one another?

Wife (W): We met in a café in Venice. Just by chance.

Husband (H): We were both on a big European adventure.

The Attune Guide for Great Listening
Questions You Can Ask Your Partner as You Listen

Questions	More Questions
1. What are you feeling?	22. Is there anything you've learned from this? Who is going to be most affected here? How will they be affected? Why?
2. What else are you feeling?	
3. What are your primary needs here?	
4. What do you really wish for?	
5. How did this all evolve?	23. Does this remind you of anything else in your personal history?
6. Who are the main characters in these feelings you're talking about?	24. What meaning does this have for you to bring this up now?
7. What would you really like to say here, and to whom?	25. How does this affect your identity, your idea of yourself?
8. What are the feelings here you are afraid to even think about?	26. How does this situation touch you?
9. Do you have any mixed feelings here? What are they?	27. How does this situation change you?
10. What are your choices as you see them?	28. How have you changed or how are you changing now, and how has that affected this situation?
11. What are the positive and negative aspects of each of your choices?	29. How did this all begin, what was the very start?
12. Do you think this has affected our relationship (or another relationship)? If so, how?	30. What's your major reaction or complaint here?
	31. Who do you think is most at fault here?
13. Is there some way you wish you could have done things differently? How so?	32. How do you think things would be resolved in the next 5 years?
14. What are your obligations (or duties) here?	33. How do you WISH things would be resolved in the next 5 years?
15. Do you have a choice to make?	34. Pretend that you had only 6 more months to live. What would be most important to you then?
16. What would you really like to ask of me?	
17. What do your values tell you about all this?	35. What are your goals here?
18. Think of someone you really admire. What would they do and how would they view this situation?	36. How are you thinking about how all of this fits into your life as a whole?
	37. What, if anything, makes you angry here?
19. Do these feelings and needs have any spiritual, moral, ethical, or religious meaning for you?	38. What are the "shoulds" here? (What should you take responsibility for?)
20. Is there anyone or anything you disapprove of here?	39. What is your biggest "turnoff" here?
21. Is there anything or anyone you admire here?	40. Are there parts of yourself that are in conflict?

Exploratory Statements to Explore a Partner's Feelings and Needs as You Listen

Samples below:

Exploratory Statements	More Exploratory Statements
1. Tell me the story of that. 2. I want to know everything you're feeling. 3. Talk to me, I am listening. 4. Nothing is more important to me right now than listening to you. 5. We have lots of time to talk. 6. Tell me your major priorities here. 7. Tell me what you need right now. 8. Tell me what you think your choices are. 9. It's OK not to know what to do here, but what's your guess? 10. I think you're being very clear. Go on. 11. Tell me all of your feelings here.	12. Help me understand your feelings a little better here. Say more. 13. I think that you have already thought of some solutions. Tell me what they are. 14. Help me understand this situation from your point of view. What are the most important points for you? 15. Tell me what you're most concerned about. 16. Tell me more about how you are seeing this situation. 17. Talk about what the decision is that you think you have to make. 18. If you could change the attitudes of one of the key people in this situation, talk about what you would do.

W: Separately. Yeah. But once I saw him, I just knew, that's the man I'm going to marry.

T: What were you thinking?

W: He's handsome. I could see he was kind in the way he treated the servers in the café, and there was just something about him.

T: Your first impressions?

H: My first impressions were all about her eyes and her laughter. You know there are some people who laugh and it grates on you, like a kind of bark? And some people who laugh and it's forced, phony? But her laughter was like a stream bubbling over rocks, just happy and joyful, it makes me laugh too.

T: So what happened next?

Express Empathy and Understanding as You Listen

Samples below:

Empathic Statements	More Empathic Statements
1. You're making total sense.	24. That must have annoyed you.
2. I understand how you feel.	25. That would make me mad too.
3. You must feel so hopeless.	26. That sounds infuriating.
4. I just feel such despair in you when you talk about this.	27. That sounds very frustrating.
5. You're in a tough spot here.	28. That is very scary.
6. I can feel the pain you feel.	29. Well, I agree with most of what you're saying.
7. The world needs to stop when you're in this much pain.	30. I would have also been disappointed by that.
8. I wish you didn't have to go through that.	31. That would have hurt my feelings also.
9. I'm on your side here.	32. That would make me sad too.
10. I wish I could have been with you in that moment.	33. POOR BABY!!!
11. Oh, wow, that sounds terrible.	34. Wow! That must have hurt.
12. You must feel so helpless.	35. I understand what you are feeling.
13. That hurts me to hear that.	36. You are making a lot of sense to me.
14. I support your position here.	37. OK, I think I get it. So what you are feeling is . . .
15. I totally agree with you.	38. Let me try to paraphrase and summarize what you're saying. You're saying . . .
16. You are feeling so trapped!	39. I would have trouble coping with that.
17. That sounds like you felt really disgusted!	40. What I admire most about what you're doing is . . .
18. No wonder you're upset.	41. That would make me feel insecure.
19. I'd feel the same way you do in your situation.	42. That sounds a little frightening.
20. I think you're right.	43. Tell me what you see as your choices here.
21. I see. Let me summarize: What you're thinking here is . . .	
22. You are in a lot of pain here. I can feel it.	
23. It would be great to be free of this.	

H: She suggested we travel together, finish the rest of our tour of Italy together.

T: And?

H: I thought it was a great idea.

W: Yeah, we're great together on vacation. But when we got home . . . and right away we moved in together . . .

H: We each had some baggage. Me from my first marriage.

W: And me from my abusive mother.

T: So, what happened next?

W: A lot of fighting happened.

H: A lot.

T: And how did you wind up getting married after all that fighting?

H: I didn't propose, she did.

W: Not exactly, we decided to take another trip—

H: To Italy again. And she came up with her ultimatum.

W: Yes, either we get married or we break up. But there we were on a gondola in Venice again, and—

H: I proposed. I didn't want that gondola ride to ever end.

W: So we got married.

T: And the fighting?

H: It started up again.

W: So here we are.

Pre-Intervention Conversation (during assessment)

H: I can't believe you. How could you do this to me? I think it was pretty sudden today, the way you told me, like an 8.9-force earthquake. That was also really unfair. You're trying to control me. Why must you always try to control me?

W: You're so selfish that I couldn't think of a better way to tell you.

H: Just for the camera let me say that I just sit down in my chair, and I feel this lump, and I pull it out, and it's a pair of baby socks. I'm just confused, nonplussed. What the hell? Baby socks?

W: What did you think it meant?

H: I had no idea. I looked at you and I said, "What the hell?" And then you tell me that you're PREGNANT? What an effing shock. I then tell you

I want to leave you right then and there. Jane, how could you do this to me? No "LET'S TALK ABOUT HAVING KIDS, WHAT DO YOU THINK, Todd?" No, it's a done deal.

W: So, now you know, so now what's your reaction? Try not being such a jerk. This means a lot to me.

H: I'm a jerk? How do you figure that? So, you want to talk about that now?

W: Yes, I do. Why not? We'll find out if we have a chance through this process. Let's see if we have a chance of making it together.

H: Did you get a test? We were doing birth control. How the hell did this even happen?

W: I am sure. We are pregnant. And I'm as surprised as you are, Todd.

H: So what are WE gonna do about it? Get an abortion? What about you going to medical school?

W: I am gonna have this baby, that's what we're gonna do about it. And I'll also go to med school. Face it, you're going to be a father. That's a fact. I did not plan this, Todd. It's time for us to become a family, Todd. We wouldn't even be married if I didn't insist.

H: Think about the timing, Jane. The financial timing.

W: I know that I love you. And I know that you love me. This is the only way we were ever going to become a family. You were a reluctant groom. Now you'll be a reluctant father.

H: I'm not happy about this.

W: We are having this kid. Start getting happy about it.

H: Maybe.

Gottman–Rapoport Conversation

W: So, let's do that one over. How do you want to begin? Let's try this blueprint.

T: Ask her about her position.

H: OK, I want to ask you what's important to you about being pregnant. What goes in your inner circle when we get to compromise?

W: You know that I have always wanted a family, because I never had one growing up. I want to do this right. Now I want to be a mom with you, and to try to be a loving mom. Before I met you I wasn't sure I could be a good mom. I don't have a real role model, not in my abusive mother, or in my absent father. I want to be part of a really loving family.

T: Don't react. Try reflecting back what you heard and validating.

H: OK, so to summarize, you want a family, you always have wanted one, but you weren't sure until you met me. You're not sure you can do it right, but you think we can, right?

W: Yeah, even if we have no role models.

H: Right, I get that. Well, it makes sense to me that you'd want to have a baby with me. It feels right to me that you would want a chance to do this right, not like your parents, who totally screwed this up.

T: Did he get it?

W: Yes he did, that's my position.

H: Yeah, that makes a lot of sense. Can you say more about that, so I can understand what you won't compromise on?

T: Good question, Todd.

W: You know how abusive my mother was. She always saw me as competition for my father's love, and she always made sure she came out the winner. I want to tell myself a completely different story, that I can help create a loving family. I think I can, with your help. But I'm completely in terror about it. I'm sad that I did this without talking to you about it, I feel very guilty. That was not fair to you at all.

T: Ask her what her positive need is.

H: What's the positive need here?

W: That you would be enthusiastic about having this baby together, but I can't control that, can I? I want to continue my studies in medical school, and that will take a lot of sacrifice on your part. You'd have to be a very active dad.

H: Wait a minute, I . . .

T: Todd, summarize first.

H: OK, I understand that you need me to be accepting of it, and much more, you need my support if you're going to get through med school as a parent. That's a big ask.

T: Did he get it?

W: Yes, he did.

T: Jane, ask him what his position is.

W: What's in *your* inner circle?

H: A happy family to me means that both people get what they want, and I want us to have a great relationship that's romantic, independent of being parents. It also means that we stop fighting and use these tools instead. My parents were totally devoted to their kids, and never had that romance. I also believe that we should still travel and have a sense of adventure in our own lives. That's my ask. I tried once to create a family, in my first marriage. But, as you know, we had big infertility problems. And then, when we found the perfect doctor to treat us, and, after many tests, he finally said, "Don't worry. I'll have you guys pregnant this year," I was elated, but Dorothy was suddenly real quiet. So, turned out that she had changed her mind. She didn't want children after all. And because I loved her, I tried to get my mind off ever becoming a dad. But I couldn't do it. I just couldn't do it. So, we went into therapy, and we broke up. It was a very painful breakup, because I think we still loved one another. And then, years later, I met you. And I couldn't decide about marriage again, but then you made it an ultimatum. I get that, I'm not accusing you of anything here. So, we got married, and I get that you thought, "Well, he was a reluctant groom, he'll be a reluctant father too," and so you unilaterally went off the pill. I get why you did that, it makes sense. But it didn't give me time to think it over and get back onto the Daddy train of thought. So, I'm worried. Are we going to lose our own passion, our own romance, our sense of adventure—because we both love to travel, especially in Italy—what's it going to cost? And I don't want to bring a kid into all our fighting. That's got to end.

W: Whew! That's a lot.

T: Jane, summarize and validate.

W: OK, so to summarize your point of view, you wanted kids in your prior relationship, but you're still a little shell-shocked by the breakup. Since we met you feel differently, but you need our fighting to come to an end, right? Did I get it?

H: Pretty much.

T: Add the validation.

W: Well, that makes a lot of sense to me. I'm the one who got us to this therapist, so I also want our fighting to stop.

H: Thank you.

W: What's in your inner circle?

H: I do want to be a dad. I really want that with you. You'll be a great mom,
I'm sure of it, just like I'm sure you'll be a great doctor. So, I want that.
But then I'm really scared. What's this going to do to my life? My dad and
mom gave up everything to become parents, their dreams about career,
and probably their own relationship intimacy as well. They were a great
team, but I wouldn't say that they stayed in love at all. So I'm scared too.
And your med school and residency will require a lot of child care time
from me. What about my career? How can we manage all this? I don't
know if I can do it.

W: He's being so negative!

T: Just try summarizing and validating.

W: OK. So, you're adding to your own point of view. You don't want to wind
up like your parents. You want romance and adventure in your life as
well. That makes a lot of sense to me.

T: Good job.

H: Yeah, you got it.

T: How is this feeling?

W: I think we can make it work.

H: I think we can too. I want to know what you are flexible about.

W: We can get lots of help, like a nanny share. So we can travel even with a
baby, or young kid. I'm flexible about all the details, the how of what we
do. What are you flexible about?

H: I can limit the romantic getaways to about two a year, with one big adventure a year. If you can get away enough. I'm still upset that we didn't plan
this, that it's so sudden.

W: I agree with you. Ideally we would have waited. It is sudden.

H: We have to figure out how to make this work financially.

W: You're worried about what it's going to cost. I get that.

H: Yeah.

W: I understand that. I'm worried about that too. But we do have your savings and my trust fund money.

H: Yeah, but I don't want to touch that.

W: I get that, but we may have to.

H: Can we really manage romance and adventure with parenting and med school? That sounds impossible.

W: I get that you're worried if all this is really practical, right?

H: Exactly. Adventure may be tough in med school. And especially in residency.

W: You're worried that adventure and romance may die in med school, right?

H: Yes.

W: I get that, I really do. I know that it's really asking a lot of you. But I know of several med schools that have that kind of flexibility for med students who are parents.

H: That'd be great. I am willing to be a great partner and father.

W: That's great to hear you say. And I promise to work on these blueprints so we stop fighting.

H: I appreciate that. I will too.

W: I think we can start an overall compromise here.

H: That's a real relief!

W: It's kind of surprising.

H: I know.

T: So, let's get to work and forge a first compromise. One we can revisit over time.

CHAPTER 11

Meta-Emotion Mismatches, Distrust, and Attunement

In this chapter we describe our theory of meta-emotion. Every relationship needs to define its own emotion culture. Mismatches in meta-emotion are probably one of the most common problems in couples therapy.

We've discussed that flooding escalates conflicts. Are there any other factors that contribute to harsh conflicts? The answer is a desperate kind of loneliness between partners, in which they cannot ever seem to connect emotionally. The problem is usually—but not always—a meta-emotion mismatch. "Meta-emotion" refers to our feelings about the emotions. It includes the history of our experiences with each emotion, and our philosophy about whether or not to express particular emotions. We discovered that this one variable, a match or a mismatch in meta-emotion between partners, predicted stability or divorce, respectively, with 80% accuracy over a 6-year period for a sample of couples with young children. In this chapter we will explore the role of meta-emotion in couples' relationships and how it relates to trust or distrust through a process we call "attunement."

Introducing the Concept of Meta-Emotion

When the two of us started working together, we first ran a parents' group. We began the group by asking people to talk about their own emotion culture growing up. This was akin to conducting a meta-emotion interview with the group. We asked questions like "What's been your experience in your life with anger? With sadness? Growing up, could you tell when your father was angry? How about when your mother was angry? What effect did this have on you? What has been your own relationship with anger? How did your parents show you that they loved you?" We also asked, "Was your family physically affectionate, or uncomfortable with affection? How did your parents show you that they were proud of you?" and "Who comforted you when you were upset as a child?" Personal experiences of pride and other positive emotions (play, fun, adventure) were also explored. These questions and more grew out of John's earlier research with meta-emotion, which he conducted with his former student, professor Lynn Katz. These questions always led to lively group discussions.

What made the meta-emotion interview special? We were attempting to learn how people feel about the emotions, and what they believe about expressing and experiencing each one. The word "meta" in front of another word makes that word reflective. For example, meta-cognition is how we think about our thinking, and meta-communication is how we communicate about our communication. Meta-emotion is how we feel about feelings. Here's what's interesting about meta-emotion: Even across families within the same culture, how people feel about feelings is extremely varied, which means that two partners may easily have very different meta-emotions.

On the other hand, scientists have discovered that people all over the planet, at least some of the time, experience and display at least seven basic emotions in pretty much the same way. These universal emotions are generally believed to include anger, sadness, disgust, contempt, fear, interest, and happiness. Carroll Izard's research with children and Paul Ekman's cross-cultural and U.S. research established these facts to our satisfaction. For example, people often show essentially the same spontaneous facial expression when they feel sad. When sad, the inner corners of their eyebrows move up and together, forming a brow that looks like an upside-down V. That expression in the brow is called "Darwin's grief muscle," because Charles Darwin was the first to describe it in his 1872 book, *The Expression of the Emotions in Man and Animals*. When people feel angry, their brows tend to come down and together, forming a vertical furrow between their eyebrows; their upper lip may also tighten so the lip color isn't visible, or their lips may be pressed together. That's not the only way people express anger, but those expressions on the face are usually an index of at least feeling some anger. When people are surprised, their entire brow may go up, their mouth may drop open, their upper eyelids may raise, and their eyes may widen. When people are afraid, their brow may become nearly horizontal, the whites of their eyes may show, and their lips may become tightly stretched horizontally. If they feel disgusted, their nose may wrinkle or their upper lip may become raised. If they feel contempt, the left corner of their lip may be pulled to the side by the lateral muscle called the buccinator (pronounced "buxinator"), thereby creating a dimple; this contempt look may be accompanied by an eye roll and/or a scoffing exhalation of air.

This research doesn't mean that people *always* show identical facial expressions when feeling a particular emotion. There are obviously many ways of expressing any one particular feeling. Moreover, different cultures may impose constraints on particular displays of emotion, depending on the setting. If you're British, keep a stiff upper lip in public, or so the stereotype goes, but that's not necessary if you're Italian. People also can easily mask what they show on their face. Keep in mind, these days there is controversy regarding whether or not emotion expressions in the face are universal. However, our take on this field is that there are reliable expressions of emotion that can be tapped by John's highly reliable SPAFF coding system. The acronym "SPAFF" stands for "specific emotions." SPAFF is based, in part, on Ekman's facial theory of universality, but it integrates the emotional content of words, paralinguistic features (like stress), and vocal cues (like pitch and pitch excursions). All these cues are evaluated in the context of dyadic interaction. Why is that important? Because, for example, if the husband is angry and his wife is subsequently also angry, she may be angry at him, or angry with him at something he is angry with; in that case her angry facial expression is actually empathy. Therefore, the dyadic context changes what emotions mean. SPAFF takes all that, and culture, into account. Recently, amazingly, we have used machine learning to automate SPAFF coding, and soon it will be incorporated into our automated clinician's report, together with the use of specific video playback as a therapeutic tool.

There is even some evidence that people across the planet have the same autonomic physiological responses to each emotion. This "autonomic specificity hypothesis," created by Robert Levenson and Paul Ekman, is still controversial, even though it's been replicated in two studies, and one cross-cultural study of a preliterate culture in Sumatra. For example, Levenson and Ekman discovered that heart rate increases in fear and anger, but decreases with disgust, plus the hands become hot with anger, and cold with fear.

The meta-emotion interview turned out to be a powerful tool for insight into both a couple's relationship and the individuals within it. The interview revealed that, across individuals, there is huge variation in feelings about particular emotions, histories with these emotions and their expression, and various internal experiences of emotion. Extreme differences between relationship partners in these factors result in what we call "meta-emotion mismatches." Many of the couples in our studies who had escalated quarrels turned out to have meta-emotion mismatches. Meta-emotion was also a useful tool in studying parenting. In the latter study, our data uncovered the fact that there are basically two types of people: "emotion-exploring" people, and "emotion-dismissing" people. We are simplifying a bit here, because people can be one way with a specific emotion but another way with a different emotion, so the results of the meta-emotion interview can be very complex. In general, some people were very positive about their own, their partner's, and their children's negative emotions. They acted like "emotion explorers" with their partners, and as "emotion coaches" with their children. Emotion coaches view their own, their partner's, and their children's expression of negative emotions as an opportunity for teaching or for intimate connection. They noticed less intense negative emotions in themselves, in their lovers, and in their children. Overall, they went through five steps during talking about an emotional event. We called these five steps "emotion exploring."

Other people were much more uncomfortable with the negative emotions and tried to minimize the role of these emotions in their lives. We called these people "emotion dismissers."

What John's former student Dan Yoshimoto discovered using the meta-emotion interview was that there was a strong relationship between an emotion-dismissing approach to a partner's everyday negative emotions and the presence of the Four Horsemen of the Apocalypse (criticism, defensiveness, contempt, and stonewalling) during conflict discussions. This finding implied that everyday emotional connection (versus the lack of it) sets the stage for constructive conflict conversations. It was as if, in good love relationships, people had an ironclad motto:

WHEN YOU'RE UPSET, THE WORLD STOPS, AND I LISTEN.

John also discovered that when relationship partners were both emotion explorers, they tended to "attune" to one another's negative and positive emotions every now and then, and their emotionally connected **attunement** to one another was correlated with a high trust metric. Therefore, the meta-emotion idea turned out to be very helpful in understanding relationships and the escalation of conflict, and in understanding loneliness within a relationship, the biggest precursor of affairs. Furthermore, the meta-emotion idea also extended into parenting relationships.

Let us give you a few examples. There was one woman John interviewed who described the deathbed scene she had with her dad. She had held his hand and said to him, "Dad, you have never told me that you love me. It would mean so much to me if you said it now." Her father said, "If you don't know by now, you never will." And just after saying that, he died. She left his death room furious with him, unable to mourn his death. We asked her what the effect of this experience was on her. She said it made her determined to not let a day pass without telling her children that she loved them. John interviewed another woman, who said that at a young age, she and her sisters made a pact to always convert their sadness into anger, because they saw their mom, who was bullied by their father, become deeply sad, and then depressed. This woman had made the decision to convert her sadness into anger when she was 8 years old. She may have thought that feeling sadness would inevitably lead to being depressed—a condition she wanted to avoid. From that time on, she said that she was never sad; she was angry instead. How had this decision affected her? She replied that now, she was acting as a crusader in the community for various social causes, and she was also strongly advocating for their dyslexic son at school. But when John asked, "What do you do when Sam [her 4-year-old son] is sad?" she said, "I go for a run." She couldn't deal with her son's sadness and so, literally, she ran away from it. In this family, Dad was the one who talked to Sam when he was sad. They had resolved the problem of their mismatch by making sure someone was there—in this case, Dad—to support Sam when he was sad.

Speaking of sadness, we were saddened when we asked people, "How did your parents show you that they were proud of you?" and saw many people break down and weep in response. Many said that their parents never came to even one of their games, or plays, or recitals. When we asked them, "What are the implications of this for your own family?" people usually had a lot to say about how important they felt it was to express pride in their children. However, there was a lot of cultural variation in the expression of pride, too. Therapists we trained in Norway said that Norwegian culture has a strange relationship with the emotion of pride. The culture follows the unwritten "Yanta law." That "law" stems from a novel about a fictional town where no one could be better than anyone else in the town in any way, because that constituted arrogance. So, any person who was talented in any way had to agree to a handicap. A fast runner, for example, had to wear a ball and chain. In Norway if you had a 4-year-old daughter who played the violin very well, you would *never* have your neighbors over to hear her play. That would be seen as very rude, as if you wanted to show off how your children were more talented than your neighbors' children, for example. In our own study on meta-emotions, one man said, "When someone gets angry with me it's like they are relieving themselves in my face." But another man said, "Anger is like clearing your throat, natural, just get it out and go on." These two fathers had very different emotional experiences when their children became angry with them. As you can see, there is tremendous variability in people's meta-emotions, how they feel about feelings.

We also observed people who tried to get their partners or their children to change their emotions. They wanted others to transform what they viewed as *negative, toxic emotions* into *positive, constructive emotions*. They used many techniques, like distraction, or admonishing their partner or child to just "roll with the punches" and do away with how they felt. They believed that an individual could make a conscious, rational choice about what emotions to feel. Thus, they expressed impatience when their partner or child was "choosing" to feel a negative emotion. We called this attitude toward negative emotions "emotion dismissing," which also included disapproving of negative emotions. These people valued optimism and a positive attitude in their engagements with other people and with the world in general.

Here's what **emotion-dismissing** people were like:

- They didn't notice lower-intensity emotions in themselves, in their partners, or in their children. In one interview we asked two parents about how they react to their own and to their daughter's sadness. They both said they were hardly ever sad; "We just cut that off when it happens, we don't give in to it." What about when Jessica is sad? we asked. The mom asked the dad, "Has Jessica ever been sad?" He said he didn't think so, except maybe one time when she went to visit Grandma alone and she was 4 years old. "When she boarded the airplane alone, she looked a little sad," he said. But all children actually have a wide range of emotions in just a few short hours. A crayon may break, and the child becomes immediately sad and angry. These parents didn't notice much of their own negative emotions and Jessica's more subtle emotions.
- They viewed negative affects as if they were toxins. These people wanted to protect their partner and their child from being poisoned by negative emotions (i.e., having any of them). They preferred a cheerful partner and a cheerful child. That attitude served to protect them from these toxins.
- They believed that the longer their partner or their child stayed in a negative emotional state, the more toxic its effect would be.
- They were impatient with the negativity of others. In relationships they had a lot of trouble with their partner's anger and sadness. In parenting,

they said that they sometimes reprimanded a child for being angry, even if there was no misbehavior.

- They strongly believed in accentuating the positive in life. This resembles the "power of positive thinking" philosophy espoused by Norman Vincent Peale. It is a very American view. The idea is "You can have any emotion you want, but if you choose to have a negative one, it's your own fault that you feel bad." They think, just pick a positive emotion to have. Then you will have a much happier life. So, they will distract, tickle, and cheer up a child to create that positive emotion. And with their partner they will take responsibility for their partner's negative emotion, as if it's a problem for them to solve. They're trying to alleviate suffering. Their strategy for accomplishing this is to suppress the negativity, to minimize or banish it, and replace it with a positive emotion.
- They see introspection or internally examining one's emotions to determine what one is feeling as a waste of time, or even dangerous, inviting mental illness.
- They usually have no detailed vocabulary for the emotions. If they were asked by their partner, "What are you feeling?" they might just reply, "I'm fine," no matter what they feel. If pressed for more information, they would tend to get frustrated with many of the questions.

Here's an example of an emotion-dismissing attitude between lovers. One emotion-dismissing husband said, "When my wife comes down for breakfast, I look at her face. If she's got a stormy look, I leave. I've had it up to here with her negativity." An emotion-dismissing wife said, "He will come to me with his sadness, whining about his job, and I just tell him to suck it up. I don't want a third child. I want a strong husband." Emotion dismissing sometimes was also emotion disapproving—that is, it could include a moral judgment that the negative emotion was somehow a bad thing. Or a weak thing.

In a study of parenting, John interviewed one particular father. When asked about his daughter's sadness, the man said, "When she is sad, I tend to her needs. I say, What do you need? Do you need to eat something, go outside, watch TV?' I tend to her needs." The dad distracted his daughter when she was sad, mostly by offers of food. In the future this child might confuse being sad with being hungry. Here's another emotion-dismissing example: A father said, "Say my kid has a problem with other kids. Let's say someone took something of his. I say, 'Don't worry about it. He didn't mean it. He will bring it back. Don't dwell on it. Take it lightly. Roll with the punches and get on with life.'" This father's message was "Don't dwell on negativity. Get over it. Minimize its importance." In contrast, another father, who represented more of an emotion-exploring philosophy, for that same peer situation said, "If a kid were to be mean to my son, I would try to understand what he's feeling and why. Some kid may have hit him or made fun of him. I stop everything then, my heart just goes out to him and I feel like a father here and I empathize."

The **emotion-exploring** (or coaching) philosophy was quite different from the emotion-dismissing philosophy. John interviewed one emotion-exploring couple in our lab. She was actually a professional cheerleader, and he was a quarterback for a professional football team. She told John that the reason she liked her husband was that she once came across a smiley-face calendar from her youth when she was unpacking and moving in with her husband. It reminded her that when she was a little girl, if she was cheerful that day, her parents would put a smiley sticker on the calendar. If she got 20 smiley faces a month, she got to buy a toy. She hated that calendar. She said, "What I like about my husband is that I can be in a crabby mood, and he still wants to be with me. I don't have to be cheerful."

To summarize, here is what we discovered about **emotion-exploring** people:

- They noticed lower-intensity emotions in themselves, in their partners, and in their children. The partner and their children didn't have to escalate the intensity of the emotion to get noticed.
- They saw these emotional moments as an opportunity for intimacy and connection or, with their children, an opportunity for teaching.
- They saw these negative emotions as a healthy part of life, or of normal development. They saw being sad, or angry, or afraid as important information.

- They were not impatient with a partner's or a child's negative affect.
- They didn't take responsibility for changing a partner's or a child's negative emotion. Instead, they saw their job as only trying to understand the negative emotion.
- They communicated understanding of the emotions, and didn't get defensive.
- They helped a partner or a child explore and verbally label all emotions they were feeling. With a child, what does having words do? They are important. With the right words, the child can process the emotions usually associated with withdrawal (fear, sadness, disgust) very differently. It becomes a bilateral frontal lobe processing. Withdrawal emotions are still experienced, but they are tinged with optimism, control, a sense that it's possible to cope.
- They empathized with the partner's or child's negative emotions. With a child, they even empathized with negative emotions behind misbehavior. For example, they might say, "I understand your brother made you angry. He makes me mad too sometimes." They do this even if they do not approve of the child's misbehavior. In that way they communicate the value "All feelings and wishes are acceptable."
- To a child's misbehavior, they communicated their family's values, and they set limits. In that way they communicated to their children the value "While all feelings and wishes are acceptable, not all behavior is acceptable." We had parents who did everything else in exploring but this step of setting limits, and when we followed their children they turned out to be aggressive. These emotion-exploring parents were clear and consistent in setting limits to convey their values.
- With their partners, they avoided problem-solving unless their partner asked for it. With their children, they problem-solved when there was negative affect without any misbehavior. They were not impatient with this step either. For example, they got suggestions for solutions from the child first.
- With children, they believed that emotional communication is a two-way street. That means that when they were emotional about the child's misbehavior, they let the child know what they were feeling, but not in a pejorative or insulting manner. They said that was probably the strongest

form of discipline, that the child is suddenly disconnected from the parent, less close, more "out."

It was interesting to us that emotion-dismissing and emotion-exploring people also had different metaphors about negative emotions. Dismissing people saw anger as like an explosion, like losing control, or as aggression. Emotion-exploring people saw anger as a natural reaction to a blocked goal. They suggested understanding the frustration, the goal, and what was blocking it. The emotion-dismissing people saw sadness as wallowing in self-pity, as inaction, passivity, akin to mental illness, and they had metaphors of sadness as death. Emotion-exploring people saw sadness as something important that was missing in one's life. They said that they slowed down to discover what was missing. Emotion-dismissing people tended to see fear as cowardice, inaction, as being a wimp. Emotion-exploring people said that fear was telling you that your world was unsafe. They said that when they felt afraid they tried to find out how to make their world safer. About negative emotions in general, emotion-dismissing people said feeling the negativity leads nowhere, that one should "roll with the punches," "get over it," and "move on." They viewed examining negative emotions as akin to pouring gasoline on an open fire, as very dangerous or explosive. In contrast, emotion-exploring people said that exploring a negative emotion wasn't dangerous or scary. They said that it gave a person direction in life. It was described as like a person's "GPS" in life. Emotion-dismissing people thought of being positive emotionally as a rational choice, and they viewed "dwelling" on negative emotions as harmful and pessimistic. They thought it simply invited chaos.

Other things were different about these two types of emotion philosophy. In particular, these philosophies were very different in the way they taught their children something new. An honors student of John's named Vanessa Kahen-Johnson (now a psychology professor) discovered this. We will discuss emotion-exploring or coaching parents versus emotion-dismissing parents with their children in order to fully spell out the nuanced differences between emotion-dismissing and emotion-exploring partners. Emotion-dismissing parents taught their child in the following ways:

- They gave lots of information in an excited manner at first.
- They were very involved with the child's mistakes.
- They saw themselves as offering "constructive criticism."
- The child increased the number of mistakes as the parents pointed out errors. This is a common effect during the early stages of skill acquisition.
- As the child made more mistakes, the parents escalated their criticism to insults, to using trait labels such as "You are being careless," "You are spacey." They sometimes talked to each other about the child in the child's presence, as in, "He is so impulsive. That's his problem."
- As the child made more mistakes, the parents sometimes took over, becoming intrusive.

In a book adult sons wrote about their fathers, a professional writer named Christopher Hallowell said that when he was age 6 his dad said, "Son, I'm gonna teach you how to make a box. If you can make a box, you can do anything in the wood shop." Chris's first box was a little shaky, but it had a lid. His dad examined it and said, "Chris, this is a wobbly box. If you can't even make a box, you can't do anything in the wood shop." Chris, at age 35, still has that box on his nightstand. He still sees his dad's face in the lid, saying, "Chris you'll never amount to anything." Small teaching moments can have huge implications for kids, because children tend to believe their parents, even about themselves.

In our lab not all children of emotion-dismissing parents did poorly on the task their parents taught them. Some children with parents dismissing of their negative emotions during learning the task got angry with their parents and did well on the lab task. It seemed as if they did well to spite their parents. So, the parents got a good performance out of their kid, but at the expense of trust. The dissertation (2006) of Eun Young Nahm, a professor and a former graduate student of John's, compared parenting in Korean American and Euro-American two-parent families with a 6-year-old child. The Korean American parents were primarily emotion dismissing or disapproving, using shame-based tactics to encourage their children during a tower-building task, while the Euro-American parents were primarily emotion exploring, using praise-based tactics to encourage their children during a tower-building task. The Korean American children did significantly better on the task than the Euro-American children. However, the level of depression in the Korean American children was significantly higher than in the Euro-American children. Higher achievement may come at an emotional cost for emotion-dismissing parents.

Vanessa Kahen-Johnson (1998) also discovered that emotion-coaching parents taught their children in a dramatically different way than emotion-dismissing parents. Emotion-exploring parents followed a particular pattern:

- These parents gave little information to the child, just enough for the child to get started.
- They were not involved with the child's mistakes; they ignored them.
- They waited for the child to do something right.
- Then they came in and offered specific praise, and then added a little bit more information. They seemed to believe that the best teaching offers a new tool, just within reach. One emotion-coaching parent said, "Then learning feels just like remembering."
- The child attributed the learning to their own discovery.
- The child's performance also went up and up in learning a new task.

It's important to point out that we found when we measured parental warmth that emotion-dismissing parents were not less warm than emotion-coaching parents. In our coding we found that warmth was statistically independent of emotion coaching or dismissing. For example, an emotion-dismissing parent can very warmly say, "What's wrong, sweetheart? Put a smile on your face. There, that's Daddy's little girl. Isn't that better now?" It is not cruel to be emotion dismissing. Parents really mean well when they do it.

In fact, we are not claiming that emotion dismissing is "bad" parenting. It is an action orientation and problem-solving orientation to issues. Both exploring and dismissing attitudes are important in parenting, but we discovered that they need to happen in the right sequence. For example, our daughter was once afraid of learning mathematics, and she discussed her fears with John. John empathized with her fears and she felt a lot better.

However, after all that understanding, she actually did need to learn the math. Problem-solving and an action orientation are both absolutely necessary in life and in parenting. However, as Haim Ginott once said, advice is always more effective when *words of understanding precede words of advice*. First a child needs to feel that they are not alone. Children and adults need to feel understood and supported. Then we are more likely to be able to turn toward action.

In our initial study, as we followed the 3 to 4-year-old children, there were consequences of these two types of emotion philosophy. We discovered that children who were emotion coached at age 4 turned out to be very different at age 8 and at age 15 compared to the children of emotion-dismissing parents. Here is a summary of the results for children who had been emotion-coached at ages 3 to 4:

- Coached children had higher reading and math scores at age 8, even controlling statistically for IQ differences at age 4.
- This effect was mediated through the attentional system. Coached children have better abilities with focusing attention, sustaining attention, and shifting attention.
- Coached children had greater self-soothing ability even when upset during a parent–child interaction.
- Coached children delayed gratification better and they had better impulse control.
- Parents didn't have to down-regulate negativity as much.
- Coached children didn't whine very much.
- Coached children had fewer behavior problems of all kinds (e.g., aggression and depression).
- Coached children had better relations with other children.
- Coached children had fewer infectious illnesses.
- Coached children, as they entered middle childhood and later, adolescence, maintained their appropriate "social moxie."
- The emotion-exploring approach of parents buffered children from almost all the negative effects of an ailing marriage, separation, or divorce (except for their children's sadness). The negative effects that dissolved

were (1) acting out with aggression, (2) falling grades in school, and (3) poor relations with other children.

- Lynn Katz, Carole Hooven, and John reported in our book *Meta-Emotion* that coached children as they develop seem to have more emotional intelligence.

Summary of Emotion Coaching With Children

With children, there were five steps that crystallized in emotion exploring, and there are now materials that teach these skills to parents. These five steps are not difficult to teach parents. They are:

1. Notice the negative emotion before it escalates.
2. See it as an opportunity for teaching or intimacy.
3. Validate or empathize with the emotion, even if it occurs alongside misbehavior.
4. Help the child to name all the emotions the child is feeling.
5. Set limits on misbehavior, or problem-solve if there is no misbehavior.

By the way, dads mattered a lot. Our research showed that dads made a great deal of difference both for sons and for daughters. Fathers who emotion-coached their children were better dads, and better husbands. Their children felt closer to them, and moms appreciated them more. With their wives during conflict, emotion-exploring dads were not contemptuous; they were respectful. They also knew their wives well, and communicated a lot of affection and admiration for them in our OHI, so their OHT was quite positive. For the dads we studied, marriage and parenting arose and grew out of the same secure foundation.

To read more about this meta-emotion study, see John's book with Joan DeClaire, *Raising an Emotionally Intelligent Child*, and John's book with Lynn Katz and Carole Hooven called *Meta-emotion*. Emotion coaching has been tried and tested in three randomized clinical trials with kids conducted by Sophie Havighurst, in Melbourne. She has demonstrated the very large effects on children—across the life span—that emotion exploring has in creating effective parenting. Emotion coaching also works in South Korea and the UK. Two hundred thousand teachers in South Korea have been trained in emotion exploring by Christina Choi. In the UK, emotion coaching has been found effective in research by Janet Rose.

With a Partner, There Were Also Five Steps of Emotion Exploring

1. Be aware that the spouse is having a negative emotion.
2. Know that all emotions are an opportunity for intimacy to be attended to, not dismissed.
3. Respond nondefensively and listen to the partner's emotions—they are important to understand. (Motto: "When you're upset, the world stops and I listen.")
4. Assist yourself and the partner to understand their emotional experiences by asking open-ended questions about their thoughts and emotional experiences.
5. Deeply empathize, support, and comfort the partner (and, only if asked, problem-solve) regarding the situation that led to the emotions.

One Cultural Basis of Meta-Emotion Mismatch

In Chapter 1 we reviewed the research of Wilkinson and Pickett about the effects of income inequality. One effect of income inequality is that a partner may experience the world of work and their employer or manager as very competitive, emotion dismissing, dictatorial, narcissistic, and even psychopathic. If a person brings back home that work-centered emotion-dismissing philosophy, it can seriously erode trust and create greater emotional distance between the partners. In the UCLA Sloan Center study of 30 dual-career couples in Los Angeles, the researchers discovered that their couples' lives had devolved into a long to-do list. Their relationships were on the road to becoming managerial marriages, and at risk for becoming devitalized marriages.

A Case of Meta-Emotion Mismatch

Jan and Ron came in to see John for couples therapy. They were in their early 40s, and they had three children: Jack, a boy aged 10; Molly, a girl aged 7, and James, a 1-year-old. Ron was a successful entrepreneur and CEO of his small computer company in Seattle, and Jan had been an experienced emergency department nurse, but was currently a homemaker.

John began with an assessment. They had already taken the Relationship Checkup questionnaires on the Gottman Connect software platform before their first session. What became immediately clear from their RCU questionnaires was that there was a huge asymmetry in this marriage. Jan was very unhappily married, but Ron appeared to be quite happy. The Locke–Wallace Marital Adjustment Test was 105 for Ron, but was 34 for Jan. Since the population average for this scale is 100 and the standard deviation is 15, Ron scored close to the mean, as he was fairly happy, but Jan scored 4.4 standard deviations below the mean (100 − 34 = 66 divided by 15 = 4.4). But they had one interesting exception: They both scored green on sexual frequency and quality. Then again, Jan scored dark gray for romance, whereas Ron scored light gray. Yet another challenge.

Friendship again showed a huge asymmetry. Jan was very lonely, and for love maps, fondness/admiration, and turning toward, she scored dark gray, whereas in these areas Ron scored only light gray. In shared meaning we once again saw a big asymmetry. Jan thought that they weren't doing well on building rituals of connection, sharing goals, supporting one another's roles, or agreeing on major symbols (like "What is a home?" and "What is love?"). But Ron thought they were doing fine on all of these measures.

It also turned out that this couple had a big mismatch on meta-emotions. Jan scored as emotion exploring while Ron was emotion dismissing. This was also reflected in their two conversations. And while there had been no affairs, there were big issues for Jan in feeling lonely, handling stress, and relating to in-laws. Jan also scored above cutoffs for depression on the SCL-90 scale, and she believed that Ron's alcohol consumption had worsened their fights. In the area of conflict management, Jan and Ron at least agreed on the fact that they were struggling. They both scored dark gray on many conflict scales. They agreed that their conflicts started harshly, they often got flooded, they typically failed at making repairs or compromising, and they were gridlocked on a number of issues, like handling housework, child care, in-laws, and relatives.

We always use the first session of therapy to complete our assessment in several steps, beginning with the couple narrating why they're seeking therapy. We listen, summarize, and validate their concerns, then reflect back what we're hearing about their goals. We opened up this couple's first session by asking, "What brings you here at this time, and what would you like to accomplish in this therapy?" Both Jan and Ron wanted to work on the marriage and improve communication. Ron wanted more sex and less fighting, and so did Jan. But Jan said that for her the marriage was in crisis. She was lonely, she had been for a long time, and she didn't want that kind of marriage anymore. She saw this therapy as make-or-break for their relationship. This greatly surprised Ron. He had had no idea that his wife was that desperate. He thought all they needed was a "tune-up." We reflected back how differently they viewed the relationship at this point.

Then John moved on to the couple's OHI. It began with the statement "Let's switch gears here. Take us back to the very beginning of your relationship. How did you meet, and what were your very first impressions of one another?" John noticed that their facial expressions shifted from serious and grim to smiling. Here is a tidbit of their conversation, just to give you a flavor of the case. (This conversation, and the others we present, have been highly edited to protect confidentiality.)

Jan: We met when we were 13 years old on a church camping trip. Ron was so inventive.

Ron: Yeah, the two of us didn't bring a tent. So we built a Native American wickiup, using branches, wood strips, and leaves. I'd read about it.

Jan: It was so cozy. And I built a reflecting fire wall. It poured that night. Pouring rain.

Ron: But we stayed dry and warm. All the other kids got soaked.

Jan: (laughs). And we had our first cuddle together. We were still so innocent.

Ron: We learned about sex by trial and error after getting married.

Jan: I didn't have an orgasm until 2 years later. I didn't even know what that was.

Ron: Our parents never talked about sex.

Jan: That was totally taboo.

Ron: Later I went on an evangelical mission and grew up a little, learned how to take a lot of rejection.

Jan: You also learned you could be a leader on that mission.

Ron: Yeah, I learned that a team is best when you're talking to strangers about religion. Easier to deal with rejection.

Jan: Ron came back a totally different person. Self-confident.

Ron: Yes, confident for the first time in my life. Very useful in business.

Jan: Then we went to the same college, Ron was a year ahead of me. But we didn't date one another. We dated lots of other people.

Ron: Yeah, we'd get together occasionally and talk about our dates. Laugh about them, mostly.

Jan: And we traveled together some of the time.

Ron: In groups mostly.

Jan: We always had lots of fun together, but not as girlfriend and boyfriend.

Therapist: What changed that?

Jan: I was a junior and Ron was a senior. During a big storm, Ron knocked on my parents' door. He'd had a dream. Once again in our lives it was pouring rain.

Ron: Yeah, God appeared to me in that dream and told me to marry Jan. No kidding. So, I knocked on her door and told her about it and I said we had to get married. She said OK. Then I asked her dad for her hand.

Therapist: Is religion still important in your lives?

Jan: Very much so, but we haven't talked about it in a long time, so I'm not sure how Ron feels.

Ron: We do need to talk about it. I have some doubts these days I haven't talked to you about.

Jan: So do I. I haven't told you.

Ron: You do?

Jan: Yes, I do. But I think Gottman wants to hear more about the proposal. It was very formal. And really cute. He'd already asked me, and I'd said yes. But then he went to ask for "my hand" to my parents.

Ron: And her dad said no. No way.

Jan: My dad said I was too young. He was a former marine sergeant. Very protective. Very authoritarian. In my teenage years I hated that. He always said, it's "my way or the highway." After this my dad and I stopped being as close. But Ron stood up to him.

Ron: I told him we were meant to be together, that I'd protect her and take care of her. But he still said no. So, we dated for 2 more years, and then he finally agreed.

Jan: Once you started your business, and when it was successful, then he agreed. He respected that.

Ron: I found I had a talent for investing other people's money.

Jan: And for building a great work environment.

Ron: I'm good at creating a positive work world. Full of optimism. And positive energy.

Jan: And getting people to trust you with their life savings.

Ron: The business grew really fast, and that won her dad over.

Therapist: So, all that fun and adventure together, the proposal, and then you start the business. When it looks like it's going to be successful, her dad finally agrees. What was the wedding like?

Jan: It was a total nightmare. His mom totally took over all the planning of the wedding. We were just sidelined. Never consulted about a thing! Before we knew it, she'd mailed out the invitations, invited 100 people, hired the hall, set a date, got the band, decided on all the food, and picked my wedding dress.

Ron: She turned into a bridal demon.

Jan: There was just no stopping her. She was a freight train going downhill at 1,000 miles an hour.

Ron: And that's still a big problem. Our "in-law" problem. And I had to learn to stand up to her too.

Jan: It created a lot of damage between us. His mom still tells me how to parent.

Ron: You have to learn to ignore her. I do. Just don't think about it. That's what I do.

Jan: I can't ignore her when she comes to our house and just takes over. She actually rewashes my dishes!

Ron: Just don't pay her any attention. That's always my solution. I keep telling you that!

Jan: As you can see this is still one of our issues. But the honeymoon was all us and only us! And we had a ball on that trip.

Ron: It was so romantic. And really fun.

Jan: It was a great trip. We went to Turkey. Saw the whirling dervishes. We loved the music and more.

Ron: The food! Was so exciting and delicious. The huge towers in Cappadocia, full of caves and then worn down by erosion over centuries. Like giant penises with carved caves in them all the way down, due to erosion. We took a helicopter ride over the countryside. Amazing.

Jan: The music, the rugs, the pottery, the food. Remember that great restaurant in that stone cave?

Ron: Yeah, I do. They played really great music. The whirling dervishes! The Sufi wisdom. All those cultures coming together over centuries. The Trojan War. Amazing!

Jan: The early Christians escaping Roman persecution. And Rumi's poetry. The Sufis.

Ron: The early Muslims creating a new religion.

Jan: And the caves and underground cities the people built to hide from the invading armies.

Ron: Living underground for a year until the armies left on their own. Unbelievable. We loved that trip.

Therapist: So, all that fun, romance, and adventure, what became of that?

Ron: We came back from Turkey pregnant.

Jan: Romance is a very distant memory.

Ron: I don't agree. We still vacation together.

Jan: Yes, but we vacation now with the kids. And it's my job to manage them. It's not much fun for me, Ron.

Ron: What about our Italy trip?

Jan: He's talking about our latest trip where we got child care. He arranged all that. Those Italians really love kids. God bless them. That was a great trip. Especially Venice.

Ron: We got to see the Murano glass, without kids.

Jan: Weren't those chandeliers amazing?

Ron: Beautiful. I want one.

Jan: Me too. But our trouble started when you buried yourself at work, and the kids became my job.

Ron: Three babies later and here we are. Sad. Now we need professional help.

Jan: I feel so lonely. I don't think you know who I am anymore.

Ron: I disagree. I know who you are. I've always known who you are.

Jan: Then why do you think I'm lonely and you're not?

Ron: I really have no idea, Jan. I know you blame me. It's always my fault. I can never do enough to please you.

Jan: Ron, you don't get it. I have been the one all these years to try to bring us closer, and none of it has worked. Now I've given up trying. Maybe you haven't noticed, but I have given up. I'm exhausted.

Ron: I'm here. Do I get any credit for that?

Jan: Yes, I do appreciate that. He set this whole thing up. I really do appreciate that you're here. But I need a lot more from you if this marriage is going to work. Do you understand that this marriage is in a state of crisis?

Ron: I do. Yes. I did arrange it all, and I booked this hotel room so we could do the marathon therapy. I arranged for travel and food.

Jan: Ron, you need to do a lot more than that. You need to really work here because I've really pulled away. I expect a lot more. Years of being dismissed by you. Years!

Ron: (turns to therapist) Help!

Therapist: Let's see if I can summarize what I'm hearing. Your relationship goes way, way back to childhood, and you were great friends in the beginning, enjoying fun, play, and adventure. You have a lot of religious beliefs in common still.

Jan: Maybe. I really don't know anymore. I really don't. He doesn't get it.

Therapist: OK, you still need to have that conversation. But your relationship started changing when you became parents.

Ron: That's true, but, we do really love our kids.

Jan: Yes, of course we do. But there's a lot to talk about with the children too. And we never have that talk.

Ron: I'm a great dad. I have no problems when it comes to the kids.

Jan: Yes, you are a great dad, when you're there. But you're mostly not there, Ron. I want you there more. I want you to show up more often for your kids. And listen to them better.

Ron: Yeah, well, I really do need help with Jack. We're in a power struggle these days.

Jan: He needs his dad a lot more now. In a different way. It's not just about playing catch. It's about listening to his feelings, understanding his struggles.

Ron: (to therapist) I'm gonna need some guidance there.

With a few closing comments, the OHI is completed. Then the two video-taped conversations are introduced.

Therapist: I want to shift gears now and have you guys do two conversations. One is an events-of-the-week conversation, just catching up on how your week went, and the other is a conflict conversation in which you'll discuss an issue you haven't yet solved. Both are 10 minutes long, following 1 minute of silence at the very beginning of each conversation. The tones you hear will tell you when to start talking, and when to stop each conversation. I will be silent during these conversations, taking notes. After you're done recording these conversations, we'll shift gears again. One of you will stay in this room, and I'll do an individual interview with you, while the other partner will go into a separate room with their own computer, to work with what we call the rating dial. Here's how that process works: To do the rating dial, you'll first log on to Gottman Connect with your email address, and you'll see what looks like a ruler at the bottom of the screen, numbered from 1 to 10. After you click on Start, you'll see a replay of each of your videotaped conversations. By using your mouse or pad as you watch, we'd like you to move a cursor along the 10-point scale and click on the number that represents whether the conversation felt good to you at that moment or not so good. The numbers range from 1 = *very negative* to 10 = *very positive*, with 5 as *neutral*. It's important to keep moving the cursor to click on different ratings moment by moment as you watch the tapes, so the numbers accurately reflect your feelings.

Don't keep the dial in one position or it will invalidate all the data. And remember, the ratings will accurately represent how you felt DURING each of the two conversations, not how you feel now as you watch them. When you've finished rating both tapes, you can knock on my office door. We'll let you know if it's time to switch roles yet. When it's time, you'll switch places. The first partner will exit the room and work on the rating dial using their own computer, with the other partner now being individually interviewed. In this way, you will both get to be individually interviewed, and both will complete the rating dial task. Any questions? Now let's talk about a good topic for the conflict conversation.

Here are some excerpts of their two conversations:

Events-of-the-Week Conversation

Ron: So how was your week?

Jan: Really busy. I'm on that church board placing kids in foster homes, and in that book club. This week we're discussing racism in America. I'm having a real reawakening of what it means to be a white woman in America. Blows my mind. And I want to talk to you about faith, and women's role.

Ron: Yeah, so, umm, great to hear that. We should talk about that sometime. My week was also busy. Very weird too.

Jan: What was your week like?

Ron: First we had the Gold Cup weekend for the shareholders, celebrating the founding of my company. That took a lot of arranging. Stressful. There was a lot of alcohol too. But people mostly behaved themselves and they had a really good time. Great music at night, dancing, and the final night we had karaoke. There was one woman who was really an amazing singer. After those 3 days I was so exhausted.

Jan: What was a highlight and what was a lowlight of those 3 days?

Ron: Well, the absolute highlight was the unexpected award I got from the shareholders. It was really moving. They gave me a gold cup, with a great inscription.

Jan: You've helped a lot of people who never thought they had enough to get through retirement. A lot of grateful people out there because of you.

Ron: Yeah, I know, and they had one couple there that spoke and they brought me almost to tears. I don't know how they found that couple, but I did remember them.

Jan: Sweet. You deserve that award. And the lowlight?

Ron: There was a woman who I think was coming on to me. She just about stalked me. And she's also an important client. And, get this, she's married, with kids. Can you imagine? She's beautiful too.

Jan: Oh, crap. What did you do? How did you handle that?

Ron: Not very well, I'm afraid. I was very abrupt. I just said, "No, I'm very married. I don't do that. Just stop." Maybe I said it a bit too loud. She acted pretty hurt. I think she was drunk.

Jan: What happened then?

Ron: Next day she pretended like it had never happened. At least I didn't lose her business. She made that clear. So, I also pretended it'd never happened too.

Jan: That's a relief.

Ron: Yeah.

Jan: I really appreciate you telling me about incidents like that. They make me feel much more secure.

Ron: I hope so. People are so weird. I don't want to have an affair.

Jan: Then don't have one. But again I do appreciate it if you tell me about incidents like that, rather than if you don't. It increases my trust of you.

Ron: So, I'm doing some things right?

Jan: Yeah, you are. But I need a lot more. Now ask me about my week.

Ron: I already did.

Jan: No, you didn't. I just asked you about your week.

Ron: Oh. Really?

Jan: Really.

That was the essence of their events-of-the-week conversation. The rest of the conversation continued the same way, with Ron briefly asking Jan about her week, but mostly him talking about his work. The important dramatic thing to notice is that Ron never asked Jan open-ended questions about her week. He was content with her brief summary, and then happy to have the conversation focus on his week. Also, it is meaningful that in Ron's rating he rated the conversation as quite positive all the way through, but Jan rated it as negative all of the way through. Yet, during the conversation, when she called attention to the fact that Ron hadn't asked her much to explore her week, he was surprised. So, the emotional bank account (the cumulative sum) of their rating dials shows them going in different directions.

In the events-of-the-week conversation, here are their data. Their startup positive-to-negative ratio was very close to the ideal 5.0, but their overall positive-to-negative ratio had fallen considerably. So we see that the data flag a potential problem here.

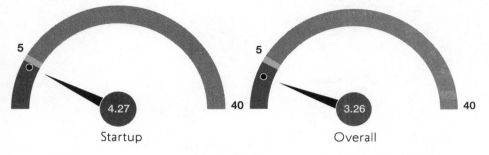

Startup   Overall

So, John then took a look at their emotional bank account curves to examine where things might have taken a nosedive. Right from the start!

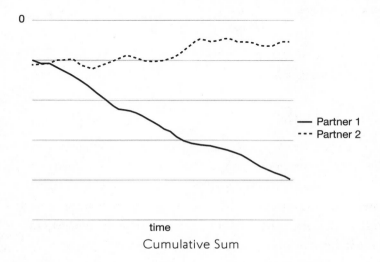

time
Cumulative Sum

These data showed a huge asymmetry between Jan (Partner 1), whose curve took a nosedive from the beginning, and Ron, whose emotional bank account kept increasing from the beginning. Just how clueless was Ron? Very. These asymmetrical curves are characteristic of a zero-sum game, which can be evidence either of a betrayal, or of win–lose, no-compromise standoffs during conflict. To decide which is the case, we examine their questionnaire data and the conflict conversation.

But first, let's take a look at how much they are stuck in negativity when it occurred during the events conversation. And what was their percentage time in a negative–positive state in the events conversation?

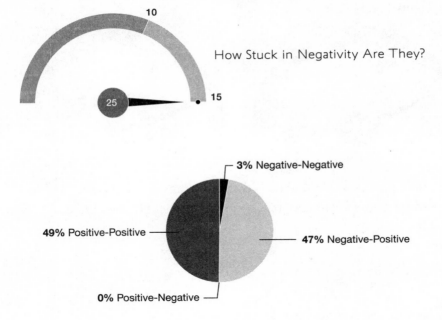

Pie Chart

They are clearly very stuck in negativity once they enter that state, even in the events conversation. They spent 47% of their time with one partner negative and the other partner positive. That's serious for an events conversation, and it shows evidence of the spillover of negativity from conflict. These are all signs that the marriage is in a state of crisis. So, now let's take a look at their conflict conversation.

The Conflict Conversation

Jan and Ron chose to discuss family/work balance as their conflict topic. Here are some excerpts of that conversation:

Jan: So, admit it, there *is* no balance. None at all. It's all work in your life. No time for family.

Ron: You're exaggerating. This is ridiculous. I spend lots of time with you and the kids.

Jan: No, I'm not exaggerating, Ron. Take your obsession with the phone. During dinner, all evening, every night.

Ron: Jan, you don't ever understand that I have to deal with about 150 emails a day, and the texts are about emergencies that require my attention then and there. I have no choice. You like the money I earn, I know that.

Jan: Ron, you can keep the money. I just want you. Just turn the phone off for 2 hours every night, that's all I'm asking. And be there. Just like you're there at work. You are amazingly present at work.

Ron: Well, people actually like me at work. At home I'm not so sure. And Jan, you like nice things, admit it. Why don't you see that I *can't* just ignore the phone at night? And even if I could, you know that it wouldn't be enough for you. I'd still get criticized for not doing enough, not "being there." Whatever that means. "Being there" is such an Oprah Winfrey phrase.

Jan: You know damn well what it means. Don't act like you don't. You listen to people at work just fine. Why can't you do it at home?

Ron: Because people actually *like* me at work, Jan, that's why. They appreciate their jobs. They appreciate me. You're the only one in my life who criticizes me, and nags me.

Jan: That's not true. I do appreciate what you do at work and for this family. And I wouldn't nag if you'd put away your socks, clean up the kitchen, just help out when you see something that needs doing. And turn off the phone. Please?

Ron: Why do you get so worked up about socks on the floor? Every little thing is a big deal to you. I'm not perfect. Just accept it. It's easier to just pick up my socks than nag me to get me to do it. That introduces such negativity at home. That doesn't happen at work.

Jan: I'm not asking for perfection. Yes, it's small. But it's like lowering the toilet seat. Picking up your socks is about respecting me. I'm picking stuff up all day from three kids, and it's an endless task. Listening to me is about loving me. I want to feel loved. I want to feel that I matter.

Ron: I tell you all the time that you matter.

Jan: You say it, but you don't show it.

Ron: I actually don't have a clue about how to please you. And that's a fact.

Jan: Sure, you do. Be affectionate, ask me questions, pay me compliments, be romantic, make love to me. Make me feel like I matter. Help out at home so I don't feel like a slave.

Ron: I do all that, Jan, and it's still not enough for you. I just need you to be more positive and less negative. There's always something that's bothering you. I never come home to a peaceful house, to a grateful wife. You have everything, but you appreciate nothing.

Jan: I don't have *you*. Not really. I miss you.

Ron: I just don't get that. How can you miss me when I'm home every night?

Jan: What was great in Venice was that for a short time it was just you and me. Like our past adventures. I had your attention then. That was the magic I'm missing.

Ron: But that's a fantasy, it's not everyday life. We can't go to Italy every night.

Jan: Somehow, some of that magic has to become a part of our everyday life.

Ron: I'm at a loss. I know how to solve problems at work. At home I'm totally lost.

Jan: I know you are. Let me show you how. Turn off the phone. Pay attention to me and to Jack.

Ron: This is a standoff, Jan. There's no way I can win at home!

Jan: Just give in, let *me* win, and throw that phone away for 2 hours every night, and pretend we're in Venice.

Ron: I know that won't be enough for you. I'll always let you down.

Jan: You're here. Maybe they can help.

Ron: Let's hope so. Because I can't see my way out of this. It's always raining complaints at home.

Jan: Then get a darn umbrella.

Ron: I wish I knew where to get one.
Both: (laugh).

And so it continued. In the conflict conversation both their startup and overall positive-to-negative ratios were dangerously low.

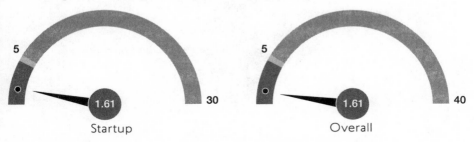

Startup   Overall

Let's take a look at how stuck they are in negativity during conflict. Wow! Extremely stuck.

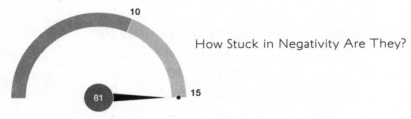

How Stuck in Negativity Are They?

Their startup and overall positive-to-negative ratios were dangerously low, and they got stuck in negativity during conflict, so let's now take a look at the emotional bank account data. As we can see from the figure, the conflict conversation was a disaster for both of them. Both curves take a nosedive

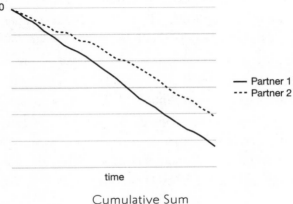

— Partner 1
--- Partner 2

time

Cumulative Sum

from the start and never repair. In the pie chart they spent 70% of their time in a negative–negative quadrant, and the rest of the time (30%) in a negative–positive quadrant.

Pie Chart

Both rating dials were in the negative ranges most of the time, so the cumulative sum of the rating dials just drifted downward, like the Dow Jones average during a bear market. Jan is right. This marriage is in a crisis.

Individual Interviews and Their Families Growing Up

Despite the fact that both Jan and Ron grew up in a similar religious Christian community in a small Midwestern town, their families were actually quite different emotionally. Both Jan and Ron had three siblings and were the second-born child. They joked about that compatibility. Ron's family was seemingly strict, but his blue-collar parents were so busy trying to make money that the family was actually laissez-faire. Both of Ron's parents worked hard, but there was never enough money. So, Ron had enormous freedom as a kid, and the siblings were very distant. No one ever talked much about emotions, or showed much affection. When John asked him who comforted him as a kid he said, "Me." Ron was clearly avoidantly attached. To him relationships didn't seem much like a source of comfort. When he was a teenager, Ron started working after school as a stock boy in the local grocery store, contributing to the family income. Later on in life he would buy a new home for his aging parents, who moved to be near the grandkids. On the other hand, Jan's family was run like an army barracks. Her father's word was law, but she and her mom had a loving relationship. Jan was very close with her three siblings, and the home was affectionate and emotionally close. When she was a teenager, she began to resist, and she challenged her father's authority, and then it was war at home for her. Going to college was her final declaration of independence from her father. By then, she and her dad were so alienated that her dad refused to pay her tuition. So she found a way to pay for college herself, in part thanks to a generous and loving grandmother, her mom's mom. In answer to the question of who comforted her as a kid, Jan said, "My mom for sure, and my grandmother. I was her favorite." Jan was securely attached as a child. It was an emotion-exploring family culture. After she married Ron, Jan and her father made up and he turned out to be a loving grandfather.

The big news of the individual interviews came from Jan, who said that she was a lot closer to leaving the marriage and getting a separation than she had indicated on her questionnaires. For her this therapy was her last-ditch effort. She wasn't confident that Ron saw how alienated she'd become, that she had quit trying, or how lonely she was. Her Weiss–Cerreto scale assessing thoughts about divorce and separation was 7 (the cutoff is 4), while Ron's was 1, so John did have some inkling that she'd been thinking a lot about separation.

The Report

After John filled out a brief clinician checklist, a couple's report was automatically generated, which became the basis for the feedback session with the couple, setting therapeutic goals. John went over their strength of sexual quality and frequency. Both of them smiled about that strength. Then John talked about the asymmetry in their questionnaires. The bottom line was that Jan didn't feel romanced by Ron, she also didn't feel that Ron was turning toward her, and she didn't feel very respected by Ron. So the friendship clearly needed work. Also, she was very lonely, and both of them indicated that conflict was a real challenge.

John then zeroed in on the meta-emotion mismatch. He explained his research on meta-emotion, and said that in the United States there were two meta-emotion languages, one for work (which was usually emotion dismissing), and another that worked for home (which respected the negative as well as the positive emotions). The problem with the marriage was that Ron had to learn to be "bilingual" with meta-emotion. They also needed some work on their friendship. At work in the United States, it wasn't OK to show one's emotions very much. It was necessary to be polite, optimistic, and cheerful. Negative emotions were supposed to be suppressed. Ron was comfortable with that. But at home the opposite was true. Negative emotions were a potential source of connection. They needed to be expressed. Ron had a lot of trouble with the emotion-exploring motto. John explained that negative emotions only escalated when they didn't get listened to, unless a person was triggered. He explained that behind every negative emotion there is a longing, and that within that longing there is a recipe for success. He had them read the Gottman Institute booklet *How to Be a Great Listener*. They talked about triggers and about physiological arousal, flooding, and taking breaks when flooded. This was starting to make more sense to Ron.

Then they began working on the Gottman–Rapoport Conflict Blueprint. We've described this blueprint in Chapter 10, so here we simply provide a brief review of its components. This conflict blueprint came from the work of a brilliant thinker working on international peace. His seminal 1960/1974 book was titled *Fights, Games, and Debates*. It is a way of fixing what is wrong about active listening. Rapoport's basic principle is to:

POSTPONE PERSUASION UNTIL EACH PERSON
CAN STATE THEIR PARTNER'S POSITION TO THE
PARTNER'S SATISFACTION.

In our version of Rapoport's principle, partners take turns as speaker and listener, and there are specific roles for *both* the listener and the speaker. Both partners get a pen and a yellow pad. Both partners are told that perception is all we have in any discussion, and that there is no immaculate perception. We know that all perception is flawed, and that we remember with biases toward ourselves, and that every time we access a memory and store it back in our brains we add a little more bias. So, it's a waste of time arguing for what "the facts are." There are no facts, only distorted perceptions. But these perceptions are what really matter.

- **The listener** takes notes on what the speaker is saying, and must reflect back, to the speaker's satisfaction, with added validation, what has been said. The reflection must include both the content and the emotions of the speaker. This "reflective listening" needs to be nondefensive, nonjudgmental, and compassionate. This isn't easy, because we are asking listeners to postpone their own agenda, not argue for the validity of their own point of view, and listen with empathy, the only goal being compassionate understanding of the speaker's point of view.

- **The speaker** also has constraints. There can be no blaming, no attack, no defensiveness. We ask speakers to avoid, as much as possible, describing their partner, and to avoid using you-statements, talking instead with I-statements that describe the speaker's feelings, about what specific issue, and the speaker's positive needs (or wants, wishes, preferences, or desires). A positive need is what the speaker does want, not what the speaker doesn't want. The positive need should come as close as possible to a recipe for the listener to be successful and "shine" for the speaker.

The Gottman–Rapoport Conflict Blueprint is ordinarily quite powerful. For Ron and Jan, it was a breakthrough. Jan wanted Ron to go first. Each partner was given a yellow pad and pen for note-taking. Here are some excerpts:

Ron: I want our home to be a place of peace. That's it. I'm done.

Jan: You want to come home and have no arguing, no fighting. You want to be appreciated. I can work on that. You want to be supported. Am I right?

Ron: Yes, you are. You got it. Thank you. That's it.

Jan: What does that support look like?

Ron: Neutral is good enough. And maybe a little appreciation. Show up for me.

Jan: I can try to show up for you more. But it sounds like you want that I don't get emotional about anything. Is that what you want?

Ron: Exactly.

Therapist: Jan, can you add some words of validation now? Does any of that make sense to you?

Jan: Sure, I get why you want that, Ron. I want that, too. It all makes sense.

Ron: Thank you.

Therapist: Did she get it?

Ron: Yeah, she did.

Therapist: Are you ready for her to be the speaker?

Ron: Yes, I am.

Jan: (leaning forward, looking very angry) Are you kidding me? I support you so much! I am always listening to your problems at work. My tank is empty, Ron. My support is just not reciprocated.

Therapist: Jan, try talking just about what you do need, not what you don't like or resent.

Jan: It's a respect thing. Call me *before* you schedule something. And at home I want more of you. I married you for you. Not for financial success, and whatever it means. Yes, I'm happy you're successful. But *be there* at home for me and also for our kids. Do this listening he's talking about. Reflecting back. It's about quality, not quantity. Just being home does not imply that you are present. You're great at work at making people feel loved. Don't plan a big extravaganza birthday party for me. Just be there for me at night. Every night.

Ron: Can you be more specific?

Jan: You want a list?

Ron: I'd die for a list. Because I am lost. Totally lost. I'm there every night, and you say I'm not there. What does "being there" look like?

Jan: It's about the small day-to-day things. Ask me about my day. Ask me questions about it, show interest in what I'm saying. Be excited when I get excited, be sad when I'm sad. Ask me questions. Like the booklet says. Try to learn more about the everyday things that are my whole life with our children. They are not about world-class finances, they're small things, but earth-shatteringly important to me and to our kids.

Ron: I do understand where you're coming from. I admit that I come home tired and not present. It's true. I'm not purposeful about being home. In fact, I'm still on my phone taking care of work matters. You said it's quality, not quantity. So I need to know when enough is enough. Small things count, you say. I need to make you feel special and loved. So, what's enough? What's "quality" to you?

Jan: Your attention and genuine interest is all I need. That's it. That's love to me.

Ron: I can do that. You want to know that when I'm home, I'm really home, at last, not with half my mind at work. My paying attention to you and being genuinely engaged is what you want. I can work on that. Is that really all you've been asking me for?

Jan: Yes, a thousand times, yes. Yes. Yes. Yes. And, Ron, pick up after yourself. When you don't, it conveys a lack of respect for my time. How do you ever expect the kids to pick up after themselves if they see that their dad doesn't do it?

Ron: That's a good point there. So, picking up is "respect"? To you? Really? Really?

Jan: Like lowering the toilet seat is.

Ron: That one I've mastered.

Jan: Yes, you have. Finally. Thank you. I need you also to see more good than bad in me, to appreciate what I do, instead of approaching me as if I'm going to dump on you. Approach me as somebody who loves you and misses you all day. Not as a complaint rainstorm.

Ron: Here we go again. Oh, boy!

Therapist: Jan, try to stick with just your positive needs, OK? And Ron, try to reflect back now.

Ron: OK, I'll try. You feel that I'm not showing up. Making plans without consulting you, not picking up and helping around the house, not listening to you with real interest. You need me to work on showing up for you.

Jan: Is that OK with you? Is that too much?

Ron: Yeah, it is OK. It's not too much. No wonder you're lonely. Also, I need to express appreciation. I've been wanting appreciation, and not giving it. I get that much.

Jan: That's it exactly. You heard me, finally.

Ron: This isn't so hard.

Therapist: I'm glad you feel that way.

Ron: Somehow writing down what she's been saying all along made it seem more reasonable, and more important to me.

Jan: Yeah, it felt the same way to me to see you writing down my words.
Ron: It kept me calm too.

That was it. A new beginning for both of them, a way to bridge the meta-emotion mismatch. That day they stayed up all night talking and listening, going over what the "magic" was in Italy, and long ago in Turkey.

Ron and Jan had a total of 15 hours of teletherapy with John, all done in 3 days, our "marathon" couples therapy format (5 hours per day on 3 consecutive days). In their next session they began with an emotion check-in, and Ron said he felt great, optimistic. Jan said that Ron had opened up a safe space where she could talk without him withdrawing and becoming defensive. Ron said he asked Jan to be patient with him, and she agreed. Ron said that he'd leave therapy with a big weight on his shoulders because the biggest commodity to him is time, and this was going to require his time and attention. When Jan frowned at that, he quickly added, "But you're worth it to me," and she smiled.

In therapy John next worked on creating "rituals of connection." Rituals are regularly scheduled events where you can count on emotional connection. They decided to have a daily emotion check-in with the phone off for an hour with Jan, and an hour of listening with Ron learning emotion coaching with the kids. In further sessions of therapy they created their own rituals of connection. They also followed our typical suggested rituals: (1) a weekly "Express Your Needs" exercise using the Express Your Needs Card Deck (part of a free app available in the Apple App store by typing in "Gottman Card Decks"); (2) a weekly "state-of-the-union" meeting. The state-of-the-union meeting begins by talking about what has gone right in the relationship this week, giving one another five appreciations each, and then using the Gottman–Rapoport Conflict Blueprint to exchange views on any issue that has arisen that week; and (3) a weekly romantic date, starting with our *Eight Dates* book. They added quarterly romantic trips without the children, the first one a trip back to Turkey for two weeks. Even with meta-emotion mismatches, couples can strengthen their relationships, given tools to help them learn the language of emotion expression, nondefensive listening, and empathy.

CHAPTER 12

Not All Conflicts Are the Same: Perpetual Conflicts and the Dreams Within Conflict Intervention

In this chapter we talk about our discovery that not all conflicts are the same. Some conflicted issues are bigger; they are potential deal-breakers. Behind these "gridlocked" conflicts are historical and existential underpinnings of each person's position on their issue. Unearthing these can help pave the way toward compromise. Our Dreams Within Conflict Blueprint is the tool we use.

Here's a personal story about the two of us. After we'd been married for about 6 years, we had a fundamental conflict in our marriage. Our fights became so bad and so escalated that we sought out a couples therapist for help. This stressful period occurred long before we started our work together to generate our theory and therapy interventions. Here was our issue: We lived in Seattle, but we also loved vacationing on Orcas Island three hours north of us. Every August, we would rent a cabin on the water and canoe together. At two in the morning one year, our 6-month-old daughter crawled for the first time, and we were both awake to see it. The next year we stayed longer there, and had a magical time. Orcas was so restful and fun.

After several years of renting cabins, Julie proposed that we buy a small cabin of our own on Orcas Island. John was extremely opposed to this idea. Fighting ensued that grew more heated by the week. Eventually we got that we couldn't solve this issue on our own. So, away we went to a therapist. The therapist loved asking John about his research. Julie sat quietly and just listened. The therapist seemed to like John better than Julie, so John thought she was a great therapist. Julie wasn't so sure. Then one day the therapist said to John: "John, you do *not* have to compromise with her. You can lay down your own boundaries and stick by them. Julie will just have to adapt to them. That's individuation, that's how relationships are supposed to work." John was horrified by what she said. After we returned home, John turned to Julie and asked, "Do I sound like her?" Julie replied, "Well, sometimes, yes." To his enormous credit, John said that actually, he didn't want a marriage like that. He wanted a marriage with consensus.

So, that night, we fired our therapist, and tried talking to each other very differently. We looked deeper, listened better, and asked each other more meaningful questions about owning an Orcas Island little home. We shared our dreams (Julie) and nightmares (John). Julie told John an important childhood story. She had grown up in Portland, Oregon, near Macleay Park, the largest wild municipal forest in the country. Beginning around age 7, she spent as much time there as she could, even sneaking out of her house sometimes to sleep there overnight, returning before sunrise the next day. Her parents never noticed her absence. One tree there became Julie's "mother tree," who spoke to Julie and comforted her when her family became too harsh or neglectful. Other trees felt to her like father and grandmother trees. They imparted their wisdom to Julie. She also loved the little bit of what she knew about Salish tribal beliefs; all of nature was honored so deeply. And so wild nature became her fountain of beauty, truth, and strength. Her desire to own an island cabin emanated from her dream to care for and honor a small piece of sacred island land.

John then shared his own story. His Jewish parents were born and raised in Vienna. In late 1938, they just barely escaped the Nazi roundup of Jews meant to herd them into concentration camps. This followed the terrible night called Kristallnacht, when the Nazis destroyed and set fire to every Jewish business and synagogue they could find. His parents' rapid escape meant leaving behind all their property and belongings. They prepared only by changing into their best suit of clothes and stuffing into their pockets a package of sugar and a package of salt. That was it. From this experience, John's father believed that owning property was just asking for trouble, because as a Jew, you never knew when you might have to flee again from persecution. John's father also inculcated in John the belief that, as a Jew, he must always be prepared to flee, meaning he shouldn't acquire things, which he'd have to leave behind anyway. His father said, "The only thing you'll be able to take with you is your mind, and your education."

John went on to explain a second point. As a former New Yorker, "nature" to him meant going by subway to Central Park, spreading out a blanket, having a nice picnic, and returning home, being careful to wipe the "nature" off before coming into the apartment.

Wow, what a difference in perspectives! Once we understood our very different beliefs and personal histories, we softened. Reaching a temporary compromise was no longer such a challenge. After a little more conversation, we decided that we would buy a small cabin and try it out for 2 years. If John still felt the same way after 2 years, that is, uncomfortable with owning a cabin—we'd sell it and go back to renting a place when visiting the island. In exchange, Julie agreed to keep kosher, which meant following a strict Jewish format of which foods were eaten and when, and preparing, rearranging, and using all the kitchen utensils according to kosher laws. This was a big, complicated change that John wanted. So how did our experiment turn out? After just one summer, John fell in love with our having our own small home on Orcas. The cabin we bought was in a community with a shared beach. When there, we often canoed with our daughter to a wonderful restaurant on the sea, and John wrote papers happily up in the cabin loft, surrounded by nature and its blissful quiet.

We wondered, meanwhile, whether other couples suffered through multiple fights like ours. So as usual, we returned to the lab to study it. By bringing the same couples back to the lab every few years, we made a startling discovery: Only 31% of couples' conflicts ever got solved. A full 69% of couples' conflicts never at all reached a resolution. We called these "perpetual" conflicts, ones that never faded away. They seemed to arise from either differences in personality or lifestyle preferences between the partners that never went away.

We discovered over the years that every relationship has these perpetual conflicts. At this point we've studied perpetual conflicts across the life span in relationships between parents and children, siblings (including identical twins), and friends. All have been observed to have perpetual problems. So maybe "conflict resolution" isn't the right goal for couples' conflicts. We concluded that conflict "management" makes more sense as a therapeutic goal than conflict "resolution."

What do we mean here? Sometimes, particularly for unhappily married couples, these perpetual problems become gridlocked. Unhappy couples don't come close to compromise or partial problem-solving. Their conversations instead are grim, escalated, or bitter. Looking at our SPAFF codes, we saw that there was little positive affect when these unhappy couples discussed their gridlocked issue. Instead, over time, their positions on their issues became even more polarized, and led to vilifying their partner. Sometimes their gridlocked negativity boiled over into everything else like acid, burning away any positive affect they may have once shared. In studying 950 SPAFF codings, transcripts, and videos of our research couples' gridlocked conflicts, we discovered a key to unlock them: There was always a hidden wish, an unexpressed core need, or a dream that dwelled deep inside each person's position. But instead of discussing these dreams or goals directly, couples skimmed the surface, arguing only about the issue's superficial details. For example, a couple might talk and fight about the logistics of an issue, but not the *meaning* of each partner's position on it. The meanings were the hidden agendas within the gridlocked conflict. Drawing on the importance of meanings as central to gridlocked issues, we decided to integrate an existential approach into couples' discussions of perpetual issues. In fact, we saw that the masters of relationship were already doing this. Viktor Frankl, a psychiatrist who wrote extensively about the human search for meaning, was the perfect theoretician to draw from. We had both loved and respected Frankl's ideas in graduate school, and they had never diminished in value. Here was a very practical application of Frankl's broader thinking.

Julie saw a couple whose perpetual issue seemed simple to solve but, in fact, had become intensely gridlocked. Shari wanted her husband, Michael, to gift her with a little present now and then, spontaneously, with no holiday tied to it. But the couple had filed for bankruptcy several years earlier. Thinking of this, Michael stomped his foot and said, "Nope, no extra spending." Shari didn't give up. She insisted it didn't have to cost much—just something small she could cherish. Their fights over this issue escalated into screaming matches and went nowhere. There was lots of anger and many tears. They both ended up repeating themselves over and over again, insisting they were right—a sure sign of flooding. Clearly this model of conversation was a disaster. They needed a massive change. I presented them with the Dreams Within Conflict (DWC) intervention, explained it, gave examples, then sat back and hoped for the best.

The DWC is a series of six questions each partner asks the other. It slows down the conversation, and prevents escalations. When one partner (the listener) reads aloud the questions, the other partner (the speaker) answers them, while the first partner simply listens. The listener may not rebut their partner's answers or raise their own point of view. Instead, the listener simply asks, listens, and does their best to absorb their partner's answers. After the first partner finishes asking the questions and listening to the answers, the partners reverse roles, with the same questions now being addressed to the second partner. Here are the questions:

1. Do you have any core beliefs, ethics, or guidelines that are part of your position on this issue?
2. Is there a story behind this for you, or does this relate to your childhood or background history in some way?
3. Tell me why this is so important to you.
4. What feelings do you have about this issue?
5. What would be your ideal dream here?
6. Is there a deeper purpose or goal in this for you?

As you can see, these questions dive deep beneath the surface. The speaker must reflect and think with heart and mind in order to answer them.

When Shari and Michael worked on the DWC, much emerged. Shari answered first. She believed that small gifts meant love. They were a way for Michael to convey that she was his treasure, that he appreciated who she was, that he wanted to express how much he loved her. Small gifts also meant that he knew what she'd like because he knew her so well. Simple enough to understand. Now, for her answer to background history? It was a story full of heartache. Shari's parents had both been drug addicts: One had been jailed; the other ran away. Shari was left to be raised by her grandmother, aunt, and uncle. At the time, her aunt and uncle's kids lived in their home, too. During Christmas and birthdays, the other children would receive a myriad of wonderful gifts—bicycles, games, fancy clothes, fun toys, and so forth. "Their gifts would stretch from one end of the room to the other," Shari said. "Meanwhile, I would receive a package of socks. Or maybe nothing. I was less than an afterthought." Over the years, all of these adults had either physically abused Shari, sexually molested and raped her, or both. To Shari, the socks meant she was worthless, not worth even a glimmer of thought about who she was or what she might like. So why were these gifts that she wanted now so important to her? "Because they are a material representation of your love for me," she said. "Words aren't enough sometimes." Her feelings matched what you'd expect from such negligence and abuse: despair, hopelessness, sadness, and self-doubt. Tears fell as she noted these. Her ideal dream was nothing grand. Just a little thing now and then—perhaps a new notebook for writing, or a scarf, T-shirt, book, or music. As for an underlying purpose? Just to know that Michael cared, deeply, and wanted her to feel loved, worthy, and happy. That was it.

Michael's story was altogether different. He noted that gifts could be falsely given—a way to manipulate him into trusting the giver, when trust should not have been proffered. His childhood and background explained what underlay this belief. His parents were educators and community leaders. Wonderful outside the home, but mean-spirited and cruel behind the curtains. Dad hit and at times battered him. Mom blamed him for everything his brothers did as well as his own missteps. Only his godmother treated him kindly. She was his fourth-grade teacher and really took a shine to him, recognizing how brilliant and talented he was. For holidays and birthdays, Michael thought he'd gone to heaven. She showered him with special gifts she knew he'd adore. Still, the streets were calling. Michael joined a gang and began selling drugs at 12 and soon worked his way up the chain, making more money than he knew what to do with by the time he was 18. Of course, he was collecting guns along with his thousands. Around this time, Shari entered the scene. They fell in love and made a lifelong commitment to each other. During this time, his "friends" often approached him for loans, which turned out to be free handouts. They would also turn against him in a heartbeat if the chance came up for them to advance their own standing. Michael quickly learned to distrust them all. Everyone was out for a buck, and since he had some, they were out for him. He was shot several times, once seriously enough that it took a 12-hour surgery to save his life. But this time, while on the operating table, he had what he called a religious vision. As he regained consciousness later, with Shari by his side, he vowed to quit the drug world and to now serve the community with compassion rather than decimating it with crime. That meant no more large lump sums coming in. Their money disappeared quickly, after which their cars were repossessed, their house had to be sold, and they had to move into a small apartment with their three kids. Michael wanted to save every dime he made from his community work so they could preserve some kind of security for their family. He also noted that eventually his godmother deserted him, too, like all the rest. No more gifts. So why should he trust that gifts meant love? No way. To Michael, they were just another form of manipulation. Even gifts from Shari? Yes, even those. I noted, "If you're blocking yourself from fully receiving Shari's gifts, that means you're also blocking out the love she's trying to give you." You can see how gifts meant entirely different things to this couple—no wonder they were gridlocked.

Working with the DWC, both partners could envision the rocky shoals of each other's inner worlds. They also got why a seemingly trivial subject had taken on such heavy significance, and why this issue was a perpetual one. The streets had saturated Michael with suspicions of being manipulated by gifts. Shari's home had curdled her heart with loveless negligence and abuse. The couple understood their differences through a new lens. Their positions softened with awareness. Only now were they ready to work on a compromise.

As we continued studying conflict management at the lab, we expected that the masters of relationship would handle perpetual problems very differently from the disasters of relationship. The master couples' conversations were spiced with self-deprecating humor and affection. The partners also communicated acceptance of each other's unique personalities, dreams, and core needs. They asked questions similar to our DWC questions to learn what their partner's position meant to them, and only then did they work on building temporary compromises. Temporary, because they understood that the basic conflict would always sit between them. After all, it was their perpetual problem.

Here's an example of a master couple's conversation. This couple—in their 40s—had very different personalities. She was an extrovert, and he was an introvert. He was attracted by her vivacious personality and knew that without her he would probably not have much of a social life. She appreciated his steadiness, his calmness, his loyalty, and his thoughtfulness. She trusted him and could count on him. But then, when they married, she noticed that he tended to withdraw when he was stressed and upset. At these times, she tried to draw him out, which was quite difficult. He said he was just not a "feelings kind of guy." In their conflict discussion she started with these topics: finances and expressing feelings. The following is an edited version of their actual conversation:

Chandra: I really appreciate you taking me on that long drive yesterday.
Jamal: You are very welcome.
Chandra: That was very thoughtful. It was a beautiful drive (pause). But you got so quiet. What was on your mind?
Jamal: I didn't want to worry you.
Chandra: About what? What worry?
Jamal: The insurance. This month I don't think I can afford to pay the health insurance, ours or the kids'. And then we're going to be losing something so vital that we put into it. You've got preexisting conditions,

your diabetes, and I have high blood pressure. I've racked my brain, but I can't figure out a way to come up with that payment this month.

Chandra: Well, I'm glad you didn't talk about that on the drive. It would have ruined the whole atmosphere. But, see, that's my whole point. When these things come out, you've got to talk to me, tell me your feelings. Don't go quiet.

Jamal: I didn't want to burden you.

Chandra: Yeah, you're Mister-Don't-Burden-Anyone. That's you. I get it, you're a quiet man. Don't like to probe your feelings.

Jamal: You know that about me. But *everyone* knows what you feel and think at all times. You're so out there. I can't match that.

Chandra: You know I have a big loud mouth. Blah-blah-blah, that's me. I'm not asking you to be me. I'm perfectly OK with you being you. But it's no burden on me, baby, to hear what's making you stressed. You've just got to tell me. Because I can help. I always have some money put away to help others in the church, but we got to help ourselves first, right? You got to talk to me.

Jamal: That's what I say. You're easy to talk to. I've got to remember that about you.

Chandra: (laughs) You just got to tell me. How much is it we owe?

Jamal: (he tells her the amount)

Chandra: Well, that's a lot, but I think I can handle that OK this month. I'll just pay it.

Jamal: I really appreciate that.

Chandra: But baby, you got to promise me you'll talk to me when you get worried or whatever, OK? That's my whole point. You get so quiet. And I know you are thoughtful and considerate. I love that about you. But just don't go dark.

Jamal: I'll try. How come you've got extra money I don't know about? We have different ideas about money, we always have had. I'm not a saver. Where do you get all this money from?

Chandra: Don't you worry about it, Mr. Don't-Burden-Anyone. (Both laugh) You just leave that with me. I manage fine, right? Don't I?

Jamal: Yes, you do. I give you that. But I want that money you're stashing.

Chandra: . . . and I help out those in need as well. But you ain't getting my money. No way. You know I always think that way. Heaven is looking down at us and at how we spend our money to help those less fortunate.

Jamal: Yes, I do know you think that. OK, I'll try to talk to you more when I'm stressed.

Chandra: That's all I ask. Talk about all of your feelings (said humorously).

Jamal: *Feelings, ugh!* (disgust facial expression) (Both laugh)

There was a kind of implicit acceptance and appreciation of one another in that conversation. That acceptance is what Andrew Christensen at UCLA believes to be the center of his acceptance-based behavioral couples therapy. But we add to that the idea that there also needs to be acceptance of the existential dreams of each partner within the conflict. This couple's perpetual problem was the difference in how they each handled stress. One talked about it; the other clammed up. And you can understand how this difference could indeed feed into a perpetual problem for them.

For disaster relationships, these gridlocked conflicts can become deal-breakers and sever a couple's connection to one another. Disaster couples will have the same conversation on one of these issues over and over again, but without interest, humor, validation, or affection. There will be no listening to one another, no curiosity about what lies beneath the other's position, no voiced acceptance of each other. That's why we created the DWC (other than for ourselves, to solve our own seemingly intractable problem): to help couples like these learn the same skills master couples use in order to have calm and fruitful dialogues rather than screaming matches.

These questions are so powerful in helping couples make break-throughs on gridlocks that in our couples' workshops, 87% of people made significant progress toward a better understanding of why they were gridlocked and were able to craft a temporary compromise. Julie's innovation was to add these DWC questions to the Gottman–Rapoport Conflict Blueprint.

Sometimes what seem like very small issues from outside a relationship have this existential gridlock. Here's an example of a couple who came into our lab, gridlocked about what to do with discarded dirty clothes. This task, seemingly so trivial, had them tied up in knots. Here is a slightly edited transcript of their responses to the DWC questions:

Jim: OK, Question 1. Do you have any core beliefs, ethics, or values that are a part of your position on this issue?

Charise: Yes, I do. You leave your clothes on the floor, and I have moved the laundry hamper into the living room, but you still don't use it. You throw your clothes all over the living room floor. The living room is a shared space, so we have to keep it neat. In your den you can do what you want. Also, it's not just the woman's role to clean up. It's not fair, unless we do it together—equally. I believe that.

Jim: OK, Question 2. Is there a story behind this for you, or does this relate to your background or childhood history in some way?

Charise: Yeah, you know when my dad left, I was 10, and my mom started drinking heavily and I'd come home from school and she was passed out on the sofa, the house was a mess, and no food to eat, and I had to take care of my three sisters because I was the oldest.

Jim: I don't drink.

Charise: I know you don't, and I appreciate that. But when I walk in the door these days and see the clothes all over the place, I am right back there. I think I can even smell the alcohol, even though I know there isn't any.

Jim: I did not know that.

Charise: But it's true.

Jim: Well, that sucks. Tell me why this is so important to you.

Charise: I made a vow to myself as a little girl that someday I'd grow up and have my own house and it would be neat and tidy and not chaotic, and it wouldn't be all me having all the responsibility to keep it clean. I'd have a Prince Charming to help me out.

Jim: That's me.

Charise: Yeah, that's you.

Jim: What feelings do you have about this issue?

Charise: You know that I'm angry, but I'm also sad. This stupid thing is driving me away from you, and I hate that.

Jim: Here's a good one. What would be your ideal dream here?

Charise: It doesn't have to be neat all the time. Just before dinner, if we cleaned up the living room and dining room, that'd be ideal.

Jim: Is there a deeper purpose or goal in this for you?

Charise: To be closer to you. The arguing is driving a wedge between us.

Jim: I'd like that too.

Charise: Good.

Now Charise asked Jim the same questions.

Charise: Do you have any core beliefs, ethics, or values that are a part of your position on this issue?

Jim: Yeah, I think a home should be comfortable, and for me that means it should be a little messy. It shouldn't look like a museum, with a guard keeping it neat.

Charise: Oh boy! We're in trouble. (They both laugh) Is there a story behind this for you, or does this relate to your background or childhood history in some way?

Jim: Well, yeah, there is. You saw my parents' house, or I should say my mom's house.

Charise: She was a little nuts.

Jim: Yeah. She has all the furniture encased in plastic, and even then you couldn't sit on it. And plastic runners on the rugs you had to walk on. And she was always 409-ing the plastic. So when I went away to school, I lived with a bunch of guys and we didn't even have drapes, and the dishes piled up in the sink. I loved it. Once she came to visit me, and about had a heart attack. I don't want to live like that now, but it was fun to have no rules. So I rebel against rules.

Charise: Tell me why this is so important to you.

Jim: I've given that some thought. Why am I so stubborn? I think it's because I hate my job now.

Charise: You do?

Jim: Yes, I do. I have to dress a certain way, talk to customers a certain way. So when I get home, I take off my suit and tie and stomp on it a little.

Charise: I noticed those footprints. (More laughter)

Jim: And I get my sweats on and I read the obituaries, hoping to find one of my supervisors in there. But I rebel against you, and I know that isn't fair.

Charise: What feelings do you have about this issue?

Jim: Mostly small-minded fuming frustration.

Charise: What would be your ideal dream here?

Jim: For our home to be a nag-free zone. You know one of those red circles with the word "nag" in it and a red line through it.

Charise: I'd like that too. I hate to nag you.

Jim: Now we're getting somewhere.

Charise: Is there a deeper purpose or goal in this for you?

Jim: Yeah, it's to be closer to you, to be your Prince Charming, and have lots more sex and lots less fighting.

Charise: I agree with those goals!

Understanding the underlying dreams, values, beliefs, meanings, and histories of a partner's position on an issue is usually about 95% of the struggle. The art of arriving at compromise is just 5% of the job of finding temporary solutions to gridlocked conflicts on perpetual issues.

Accepting Influence

When couples are wrestling with a gridlocked conflict, we also always talk to them about the "skill" of accepting influence. We explain that in a relationship, one cannot be powerful unless one can accept influence. This principle sounds paradoxical at first. But here's an extreme example: In our studies of couples with severe domestic violence, we encountered men who would absolutely not accept a drop of influence from their wives. Whenever their wives said or requested anything (in most of these couples, the men were the violent ones), they immediately responded with "No!" It turns out that if your only answer is "No!" you're like someone who hears a doorbell but always ignores it. If you never open the door, you never get to hear about your partner's wishes, needs, and dreams. Instead, you keep your door locked up tight. Eventually your partner will stop ringing the bell. Instead, they'll treat you like an obstacle that blocks them from fulfilling those needs and wishes. And what does one do when one encounters an obstacle? One goes around it. Think of what happens when you're driving and encounter a truck double-parked in front of you. What do you do? Carefully, cautiously, you drive around the obstacle, and then keep going. But if you happen to be that obstacle, you've essentially made yourself powerless to influence or problem-solve together with your partner, because you've blocked out a connection with them. They've already driven around you, and are down the road, headed elsewhere.

CONCLUSION: THE ONLY WAY ONE CAN BE POWERFUL IN A RELATIONSHIP IS TO ACCEPT SOME INFLUENCE.

This principle is also the basis of the Japanese martial art of aikido. Aikido has no attack moves. One merely moves in the same direction as the opponent while staying balanced oneself. The goal is for no one to get hurt. That was the basis for aikido's widespread use in conflict resolution. Accepting influence is also easy. It doesn't require much. All a person has to do is focus on the common ground between themselves and their partner, try to be cooperative, and say things like:

- Good point.
- I can see what you're saying.
- You're making total sense.
- I can do that.
- I get why this is so important to you.
- Explain to me what you need.
- I agree with this part of your position, but not with that part.
- Help me understand your point of view.
- How can I help you accomplish your goals here?
- Interesting. Say more.

And so on.

Compromise

In our studies we've seen that for compromise to work in gridlocked conflicts, partners may think they have to "sell themselves out," give up what is most precious to them, just for the sake of making peace. But as you've seen, for one or both people there may be a core need, value, or dream hidden deep within their position that may live in the heart of what each partner believes about themselves. These core elements may feel essential to who they are. Giving them up in order to compromise may feel like losing one's core identity, leaving nothing but air for an identity. Our research couples have shown us that couples get gridlocked for good reason. It's not because they are selfish, narcissistic, or neurotic, or have some other psychopathology. It's because every person is a meaning maker. All our lives are based on the fundamentals of our identity: our histories, values, dreams, and needs. Without understanding each person's foundational core as it relates to their issue, and working to preserve at least that for each partner, building a compromise becomes impossible.

With this insight in mind, we again used our bagel method of compromise. This exercise is a follow-up to DWC work. In session, we give each person a pad of paper, and we ask them to draw two big concentric circles on their pad. We ask each person to write down in the inner circle their core needs, wishes, or dreams regarding the issue they're discussing—in other words, what they cannot compromise on. Next, they write in the outer circle the aspects of their position on which they can compromise, what they're more flexible about. These tend to be the nitty-gritty details of their position, like when something will happen, where it will happen, who will do what, how much can be spent, how long something will last, and so forth. Once they've finished their writing, they read to each other what is in each of their circles. Sometimes when they are only tackling a solvable problem, the DWC may be omitted. But in that case, they should take a few minutes to explain to each other why their core items are so important to them. Now, they discuss together their answers to a set of questions, with the hope that doing so will help them to reach at least a temporary compromise. Here are the questions they should address:

1. What feelings do we have in common?
2. What core goals or dreams do we have in common?
3. How might these goals be accomplished?
4. Help me understand your flexible areas.
5. What flexible areas do we have in common?
6. How can I help you meet your core needs?
7. What temporary compromise can we reach on this problem?

Answering these seven questions usually results in a very creative temporary compromise on a solvable problem but especially on those gnarly gridlocked conflicts. Julie once worked with an older couple who had totally
opposing ideas on what to do next year, when they both retired. They'd
agreed so far on wanting to sell their house. But from there on, they hit
a wall. Sam dreamed of buying a sailboat and sailing around the world,
even if it took years. Now listen to his wife's dream. Mary Ann's family
had owned a "century farm," a place where every generation in her family
had at least partially lived since 1895. Her dream was to take her place in
this long line of ancestors, and go live on the farm. In this way she'd be
honoring the legacy of her family. And where was this farm? Iowa. Julie
thought, "Hmm, how do you sail around the world from Iowa?" Julie led
the couple through the DWC questions. Then she introduced the bagel
method of compromise. As expected, Sam put "sailing" in his center circle; Mary Ann put "live on the farm." But their compromise answer lay in
their flexible areas. Sam and Mary Ann both wrote, "whose dream goes
first," "how much we spend," "how long a trip or residency lasts," and so
forth. When they co-answered the compromise questions, they discovered
they had so much more flexibility to work with than they expected. In only
20 minutes they succeeded in creating a compromise that honored each
of their dreams. They would sell their house, then buy a sturdy sailboat,
and take off, sailing for 1 year and traveling as far as they could in that
amount of time. At the end of their journey they'd return to the United
States near their old home, put their boat up in dry dock, and go live on
the farm, also for a year. After 2 years, they'd review their dreams for their
next adventure.

We need to also be realistic here. For some couples, a compromise might just not be possible. One person's dream might be the other person's nightmare. Examples might include whether to live in one country or another, or whether to have a child or not—big issues where there's no halfway solution. If a couple encounters a deal-breaker issue like that, the couple may have to break up, but at least they will know why they had to break up. That realization may be very helpful in selecting partners for their next relationships. But for most couples, compromise is reachable, especially if couples first understand the underpinnings and dreams tucked away inside their issues. It's not as hard as we think.

CHAPTER 13

Healing Old Emotional Wounds: The Aftermath of a Fight or Regrettable Incident

In this chapter we present a blueprint for healing past emotional wounds in the relationship. In our analysis we talk about healing comorbidities that accompany relationship distress, and the "triggers" that may exacerbate them.

Is there anything else that escalates conflicts? Yes, absolutely. Couples often arrive in our offices with a legacy of emotional hurts and traumas they carry from their past. These can easily be activated in an intimate relationship. Past wounds may arise during those times when one partner wasn't there for the other, especially at significant times when that partner was very much needed. Or couples' conflicts may blow sky high with destructive fighting that itself creates cracks in the relationship. Other regrettable incidents may also sour the sweetness in the relationship and leave behind a bitter taste, one that lingers far beyond the time of the incident. Given these wounds that can show up from the past or be new from the present, how can we help our clients to recover? We need a way to shepherd our clients into healing through helping them process their past explosive fights or regrettable incidents. Susan Johnson also discovered that many of her couples who failed in emotion-focused couples therapy had an unprocessed emotional wound, which she referred to as an "attachment injury."

What is an unprocessed emotional wound and how is one supposed to process it? Many people believe that the past is gone; it's immutable, so why worry about it? We can't change the past, right? Instead, we should simply forgive and forget and just move on, putting the past behind us. However, the brilliant writer William Faulkner knew better. In his 1951 book *Requiem for a Nun*, he said, "The past is never dead. In fact, it isn't even past." Faulkner wisely understood that the past often dwells to this day in our bodies as emotional memories. The past doesn't disappear. For this reason, we can actually revisit a past regrettable incident and process it. Not solve the conflict at its center, mind you. We have other conflict blueprints for that. But instead, we can understand better how our communication slipped sideways: what we each remember saying and hearing, what actions we took and how they were interpreted, and what we experienced internally throughout the incident. We can actually heal these past emotional wounds, or attachment injuries. This is our third conflict blueprint.

So far we have presented you with two conflict-management tools: the Gottman–Rapoport Blueprint, to help your couples solve current problems, and the DWC Blueprint. That second blueprint helps break through gridlocks on perpetual problems, replacing the logjams with calm and constructive dialogue. Now we get to our third conflict blueprint, the Aftermath of a Fight or Regrettable Incident Blueprint, for processing past emotional injuries.

The Aftermath exercise should be attempted only when both people are calm. Rarely can it follow on the heels of the fight or bad incident itself. Some time needs to have elapsed—20 to 30 minutes may be enough if both partners can calm themselves in that amount of time. More likely, it's at least several hours or a day or two later. Both partners need to have a bit of emotional distance from the incident. They should feel as if they're sitting in the upper balcony of a theater, and they've just watched Act 1 of a play (which stars the two of them). Now it's intermission, and they're going to discuss and analyze what happened between the "actors" (them) down on the stage.

Another assumption for doing this exercise is that there is no such thing as an absolute truth when it comes to couples. Both partners will have their own point of view about what happened, and sometimes these may be night and day apart. Both perspectives must be considered valid. Here's an example of this concept: You ask both partners to draw a picture of the same green plant in your office. But one partner is sitting by the door, while the other is sitting next to the opposite wall. Although there's only one plant being drawn, the two pictures will look very different. The same holds true for describing fights, conversations, and regrettable incidents. Each person will have their own point of view about what they experienced with their own eyes and ears. They don't share the same eyes and ears, nor do they have the same brain to digest what they're experiencing. Thus, two points of view will emerge—and both are right.

The couple begins this exercise by choosing a past regrettable incident or fight to discuss. The incident may have happened yesterday, or 20 years ago. It doesn't matter. Important, though, is that at least one partner remembers it fairly well, and still aches from it. This blueprint has five steps. We'll introduce you to these.

Step 1. Feelings

In Step 1, each person takes a turn reading aloud any of the words on the list below that fit what they felt during the incident. *They do not explain why they had those feelings; that will come later.* They can read as many feeling names aloud as they want to, but should limit them to only those on this list. When one has read all the words that fit for them, the other partner should then take a turn and do the same. When listening, they also cannot comment on their partner's selection of feelings. They should simply listen while their partner is speaking.

Here is the list of feelings:

I FELT	I FELT	I FELT	I FELT	I FELT
Defensive	Not listened to	My feelings got hurt	Totally flooded	Angry
Sad	Disgusted	Unloved	Misunder-stood	Criticized
You didn't like me	Not cared about	Worried	Afraid	Tense
I was right and you were wrong	Both of us were partly right	Out of control	Over-whelmed with emotion	Morally justified
Frustrated	Righteously indignant	Unfairly picked on	Unappreci-ated	Stupid
Taken for granted	Like leaving	Like staying and working this out	Not calm	Stubborn
Powerless	I had no influence	I wanted to win this one	My opinions didn't matter	There was a lot of give-and-take
I had no feel-ings at all	Insulted	Lonely	Alienated	Ashamed
Guilty	Culpable	Abandoned	Disloyal	Exhausted
Remorseful	Shocked	Tired	Belittled	Put down

Step 2. Subjective Realities

In Step 2 we tell people that there are always two sets of perceptions in any regrettable incident, and that there is no "immaculate perception." We give credit to Dan Siegel for that term. In fact, all our perceptions are flawed. Modern neuroscience has discovered that when we store a memory in our brain, we store it with a tinge of favorable bias toward ourselves, and every time we recall it again, and store it again, we add some more favorable bias. So, perception and memory are always flawed. For those reasons, we conclude that perception is everything. It's all we ever have. It makes no sense to argue about what *really happened*. If it's a part of one's perception, it really happened, for that person.

To begin Step 2, one person will be the speaker and the other, the listener. The listener should have a pad of paper and pen or pencil to jot down notes for what the speaker is saying. The speaker narrates the story of what happened during the regrettable incident from the beginning to the end of the story. The speaker must avoid blame and criticism, and stay, as much as possible, in self-disclosure mode. The speaker, like a reporter, talks about what he or she experienced. The speaker stays away from describing or analyzing the partner, avoiding, as much as possible, you-statements, and instead trying to focus on I-statements. Here is where the speaker can explain the feelings they had during the incident. The story should be limited to only what happened during the pocket of time of this regrettable incident. There may have been other times a similar pattern emerged in the couple's communication. But this is NOT the time to bring up those other incidents. If necessary, each past incident can be processed separately using this tool. So a story may sound like this: "I heard you say you were going shopping. So I thought you'd be in a good mood tonight. But I saw on your face an angry look . . ." Note how the speaker is using phrases like "I heard you say," "I saw this look on your face," "I imagined you were thinking," and so forth.

Following the speaker sharing their story, the listener, who has been taking notes, summarizes back to the speaker what they heard them say. It's a special kind of listening they've done, where the listener suspends judgment, doesn't formulate a rebuttal, but takes notes so that they can reflect back what was heard, and add words of validation. Then the listener checks with the speaker to see if they got the essential story right. After their summary, the listener needs to try hard to step into their partner's shoes in order to empathize with them and to say, "I get it. I can see how you felt that way. That makes sense to me." These are words of validation. In other words, the listener needs to add something akin to these words. Keep in mind, validation doesn't mean agreement. The listener may have had a totally different point of view on what happened. Nonetheless the listener needs to give those words of validation out of empathy for the partner. Then the two partners reverse roles. Now it's time for the first speaker to instead listen, take notes, summarize, and validate their partner's story. Then the couple can move on to Step 3.

Step 3: Triggers

Triggers are feelings that first began in memorable and often traumatic or painful events. These feelings are left over from another, earlier relationship or from childhood. Old feelings like these create enduring vulnerabilities. Triggers may have been activated in this regrettable incident, and escalated the intensity of the interaction in an unfortunate way.

These triggers, or (to use Tom Bradbury's term) "enduring vulnerabilities," create "crazy buttons" that make us especially vulnerable to escalated feelings of threat, even if the current situation is very different from the earlier experiences that spawned them. Triggers are like scar tissue that we carry inside. Scar tissue is more brittle than our normal, elastic tissue. If pushed, those scars can easily break open and rise to the surface. They intensify our emotions, recruit a host of other negative emotions and memories, and make us go "ballistic." Notice that not all regrettable incidents contain triggers. If there are no triggers in a regrettable incident, the couple skips this step of the Aftermath Blueprint.

In this step, if there were triggers, each partner takes a turn to reflect on the feelings they had in order to identify any triggers that may have surfaced during the regrettable incident. If they are aware that their triggers played a part in the regrettable incident, they tell the partner about their trigger feelings and a story about how that feeling may have occurred in their lives long before this relationship ever began. Note that our definition of triggers implies that triggers cannot happen in THIS relationship. If there are events that were painful or injurious during THIS relationship, then they are considered as separate regrettable incidents that can be processed at another time if needed.

The feelings that are listed below typify trigger feelings. Each partner can look at this list and pick a trigger that may fit them, but they shouldn't limit themselves to this list. The list is here to simply provide a few examples for each partner to consider. Actual trigger incidents can be very complicated and very personal.

- Feeling harshly judged
- Feeling humiliated or belittled

- Feeling excluded
- Feeling criticized
- Feeling ashamed
- Feeling intensely lonely
- Feeling powerless
- Feeling frightened
- Feeling attacked
- Feeling controlled
- Feeling trapped
- Feeling abandoned
- Feeling out of control
- Feeling disrespected

In a relationship, once we know our partner's triggers or enduring vulnerabilities, we can try to avoid them, and be more compassionate if they do get triggered.

After sharing these trigger stories, we move on to Step 4.

Step 4. Taking Responsibility and Apologizing

Apology comes much later in the Aftermath Blueprint, because a quick apology is less meaningful since it occurs before we know what to truly apologize for. Our earlier steps help couples to fully understand the hurt that has been caused by the regrettable incident and what it meant to our partner. Only after gaining understanding does it truly make sense to apologize.

Each person goes through all the parts of Step 4. First, we get people into an admitting mode by having them read aloud any of the 20 statements that were true for them during the time of this incident. These phrases describe their state of mind that "set them up" for their part in this regrettable incident. Since it's fairly easy to admit to any of these states of mind, this step gets people into a mode of admitting at least some responsibility for the regrettable incident and it prepares each person to then move on to describe what they specifically regret doing or not doing, in order to finally give a sincere and very specific apology. After they apologize, the listening partner says whether or not they accept the first partner's apology. If they don't accept the apology, the other person can ask what their partner needs to hear in order to accept the apology. The first partner can then also apologize for that part initially left out. After this, the other partner takes a turn doing all the parts of Step 4.

What set me up? At that time:

I'd been stressed and irritable	I hadn't asked for what I needed	I'd been overly sensitive	I had a chip on my shoulder
I'd been really stressed	I'd been depressed	I'd been very anxious	I'd taken you for granted
I hadn't made time for good things between us	I hadn't wanted to take care of anyone	I hadn't been a good listener	I'd been overly preoccupied
I'd been experiencing a lot of failure	I needed to be alone	I was running on empty	I hadn't had much confidence in myself
I'd been feeling a bit like a martyr	I hadn't been very affectionate	I'd been very lonely	I felt a real sense of alienation from others

After describing their state of mind at the time, they move on to say what they specifically regret doing or not doing during the regrettable incident. The more specific these regrets are, the better. Next the speaker apologizes for these regrets. They can begin with the phrase below:

"I WANT TO APOLOGIZE TO YOU FOR ..."

Some typical things that people apologize for are overreacting, being defensive, not listening, being demeaning or attacking, not being respectful, being impulsive, being unreasonable, being stubborn, being insulting, and so on. These are just general examples. A good, heartfelt apology needs to be specific.

After apologizing the speaker asks their partner:

"DO YOU ACCEPT MY APOLOGY?"

If the answer is yes, the couple moves on to Step 5. If the answer is no, the speaker asks:

"WHAT ELSE DO YOU NEED ME TO APOLOGIZE FOR?"

Then the speaker apologizes for what their partner added. And now move on to Step 5.

Step 5. Constructive Plans

Each person now takes a turn stating one thing they could do differently next time, and one thing their partner could do differently next time to avoid this kind of regrettable incident happening again. They need not agree on a specific plan, but hopefully, each partner will do what was suggested.

Now the therapist can ask them how they feel after this intervention. Hopefully, better.

With this last step, they have completed the processing of their selected regrettable incident or bad fight. What we've observed is that couples will, of course, still remember the incident, but their attitude will dramatically change with their newly learned understanding of why this incident occurred. They'll also know more about their partner's internal world, especially given that they've listened to the triggers their partner may have described, which will hopefully create more compassion for their partner. And we hope they will also succeed in preventing an incident like this from reoccurring in the future.

Case Example

Let us give you an example of how this process actually sounds.

Jill had had a bad fight with her partner, Suzanne. Suzanne had decided to stop by her friend's house after work, but hadn't informed Jill she'd be doing so. Suzanne had stayed quite late, having a few drinks throughout the evening. Jill sat waiting for her through dinner and through watching TV, and waited in bed late at night for her partner to arrive home. Jill was furious with Suzanne, saying to her, "You're so thoughtless, I can't believe you!" Suzanne responded by saying, "Why are you making such a big deal out of it? Just knock it off!" And they were off and running . . .

Let's listen to their Aftermath of a Regrettable Incident. We'll just relay what the couple said, step by step, following the instructions described above.

Step 1: Feelings

Suzanne started: "I felt attacked, sad, unloved, flooded, alienated, angry, and tired."

Jill responded with her own feelings: "I felt alone, alienated, worried, afraid, tense, angry, impatient, and sad."

Step 2: Subjective Realities

Next each partner explained her own reality without blame or criticism. The listener summarized her position afterward and said a bit of validation.

Jill started this time: "I had made a great dinner—all your favorites: rice, beans, chicken, salad, and even chocolate cupcakes. As there was no call, only silence from you, I began to really worry. I thought maybe you'd had a terrible car accident or something. I called every hospital in the city. No Suzanne. I had no idea what had happened to you. Maybe you were injured, alone on a dark street, what? It didn't occur to me that you might have gone to Jackie's house. I watched TV to take my mind off you not being there. Three episodes! Then I began to really freak out. I think I had a panic attack. It lasted maybe 20 minutes—I couldn't breathe, felt faint, it felt like the sky was caving in on me. Finally I took some melatonin and tried to go to sleep. When you came home, I smelled alcohol on your breath. I remember saying I was furious. 'The least you could do is call me to let me know where you were. That didn't happen. 'How could you,' I remember saying. I was so upset, panicked, really. 'Where were you? Who were you with?' I added. Then I saw an angry look on your face. I remember you walking out of the room. I followed you. I think my voice got louder. I heard you say something like, 'What's the big deal? You're making a big thing out of nothing. Stop yelling at me!' I was so upset I realized I better leave the room, or I'd say something worse. I left and didn't sleep most of the night. You slept in the living room."

Suzanne had taken notes, so she was able to summarize quite accurately what Jill had said. She then added, "You know? I can see why you would have been so upset, especially worried that I'd gotten into an accident or something. And why you got more angry as our talk went on. That makes sense to me."

Jill thanked her. Then it was Suzanne's turn to do Step 2.

Suzanne started. "I had had a terrible day at work. I was in such a bad mood. I had promised to drop in at Jackie's but I guess I forgot to tell you about it. I went there because I didn't want to dump a load on you about my boss. She knows him soooo well because she's worked there even longer than I have. And she knows what an asshole he is. So we talked about him and then got into talking about her dad's dying. I felt really sorry for her. We opened a bottle of wine and ended up drinking the whole thing. Then I got worried about being on the road with the drinks I had, so I thought I better wait till some of it had left my system. I didn't realize how late it was getting. I was so engrossed in Jackie talking about her dad that I guess I just forgot to call, forgot I should reach out to you, maybe even invite you over to support Jackie, too. Finally I didn't feel the drink anymore, and drove home. When I got there I knew you'd be mad. So I guess I armed myself. I remember you saying that I was selfish, mean, thoughtless. I couldn't get a word in edgewise. So I left the kitchen and went into the living room. You followed me, I think. I just wanted to be alone. I was really tired. I think your words continued, only louder. I began to feel flooded. Then I remember saying, 'You're making such a big deal out of nothing. So what if I came in late? Don't I always come home straight after work? The least you could do is cut me some slack and just relax about it.' Then you left the room and we went to bed. I figured I should stay away from you, so I slept in the living room. I slept OK."

Jill followed this narrative by summarizing Suzanne's story. Then she added, "I can totally understand how you got caught up in Jackie's grieving over her dad. And your losing track of time. I also understand that it was hard for you to hear how angry I was, especially as I started shouting. That all makes sense to me."

The couple then moved on to Step 3, Triggers.

Step 3: Triggers

Jill started: "I've got plenty of triggers here. You remember, my ex had three affairs. And after every single one, she'd apologize, cry, say she'd never do it again, and then she'd do it again. Every time she did I was absolutely devastated. My therapist told me I'd gotten PTSD from these experiences. And that's what got triggered. I had these images of YOU being with someone else, you cheating on me, and I couldn't stop them from coming. I even imagined you having sex with someone. Maybe you'd gone to a bar and picked up someone, like my ex used to do. My fear of being betrayed got so big that I finally had this panic attack where it felt like the whole world was crashing in. It was horrible. I think you came home shortly after that. Your responses even reminded me of my ex's a little: 'No big deal.' So I think all the anger and panic I felt was really about her and not you, although I was still upset by no phone call or anything. My ex never took responsibility for anything she did. It was so agonizing. And it's still so easy to get triggered into imagining you're just like her, even though you're not at all like her."

Suzanne nodded, and said, "Wow, I never thought of that, since I would never in a million years betray you. But I get how there's so much damage from what your ex did to you that it would be easy to slip right back into those fears and feelings again. Ugh!"

It was Suzanne's turn to do Step 3 now: "Well, I think I got triggered too, but really differently. When I heard Jackie talking about her dad, his dying in that awful accident and her being so grief-stricken, I remember how when my dad died, nobody helped me through it at all. No one asked me how I was doing, how I was feeling. Nobody gave me a hug and just sat with me while I cried. I hated the thought of Jackie going through that, too, and imagined she was feeling like I was feeling. So I really wanted to be there for her in a way that no one had been there for me. That's why I stayed so long. During our fight, I got triggered again. Your anger reminded me of how my mom would yell at me if I came home 20 minutes late from school. She was so OCD! I always felt controlled by her, and hated her yelling at me. I'd get really scared that she'd hit me or something. So I just went defensive, felt angry because I thought that you were trying to control me like she did, and punishing me for being late like she did. It was pretty awful. I got flooded and left. So two triggers there."

Jill said, "Oh, right. That totally makes sense—you and your dad and nobody there for you, and your crazy OCD mom controlling every step you took, or trying to. I get it."

On to Step 4.

Step 4: Taking Responsibility

Suzanne began. She said, "I've been tired, I've needed time alone, I've been running on empty, I haven't made time for good things between us, I've felt like a martyr. I think that's it.

"I regret not calling you immediately when I knew I was going to Jackie's, and causing you so much worry and even panic. I feel really terrible about that. I apologize for that. And I also regret forgetting about your ex and the PTSD her affairs caused. I was just thinking about myself, and then about Jackie, but not about you and your feelings. I also regret coming home so late, and drinking so that when I finally did come home I couldn't respond well to your feelings.

"I'm really sorry about those, too. I was such a terrible listener! Do you accept my apology?"

Jill responded, "Yes, I think I can."

Suzanne: "Are you sure?"

Jill: "It would be nice if you could apologize for getting defensive when I tried to share my feelings."

Suzanne: "You're right. I apologize for that, too."

Jill: "OK."

Now it was Jill's turn. She said, "I've needed time alone, too, I haven't made time for good things between us, I think that's it.

"I regret not separating you out from my ex. You're so much more trustworthy! I knew that you wouldn't cheat on me, but I let you have it anyway. I regret yelling at you, and not calming down first before telling you what I felt. I regret taking all my rage at my ex and laying it on you.

"I'm really sorry I did that, and I'm sorry I didn't trust you and think better about who you really are—a loving partner with maybe a good reason to have not come home till late, though I'm so glad you hadn't been in an accident. Do you accept my apology?"

Suzanne: "Yeah, I do."

On to the last step, Step 5.

Step 5: Constructive Plans

Suzanne said, "One thing you could do is to know that I'm not your ex, and try to give me the benefit of the doubt, even if I make a crappy mistake like I did of not reaching out to tell you my plans. And one thing I could do is CALL YOU if I'm going to be late! I don't think I'll ever forget that one again."

Jill said, "Likewise, it would have all been different if you'd called, so please call me, let me know what's happening! And one thing I could do differently is write you a note for when you come home so you'll find it easily, maybe spelling out my feelings but not with criticism, and then watch three more episodes till you come home!"

Suzanne said, "Sounds great."

That's what an Aftermath of a Regrettable Incident sounds like. Fortunately, this couple did a great job at it, and thus they were able to safely relegate this incident to the past without still feeling injured by it.

CHAPTER 14

Building Friendship and Intimacy

In this chapter we talk about what friendship is and how to build and sustain it. We introduce the seven Panksepp emotional command systems that we share with all mammals, and our need for emotional connection in all of them as the basis for building friendship and intimacy. Next, we discuss specific tools for building friendship and sexual intimacy. Then we discuss how to heal failed bids for emotional connection, plus a tool for processing a positive event.

In a "dismantling study," separate components of therapy and their interactions are evaluated. So far, there have been only two dismantling studies done in the couples therapy literature. Neil Jacobson (1984) conducted one study and our lab did the other. So far, the data suggest that we cannot achieve lasting change by focusing on either just friendship/intimacy or just conflict management. We need to do both. Let's examine this finding.

We need both components, especially for therapy effects to last. However, the *order* in which we do this work seems to be immaterial. Usually, most therapists begin couples therapy with conflict issues, because that is often what couples first bring to us. Or a couple might want to discuss the problem of the day.

However, a great many fights and regrettable incidents turn out to actually be the result of failed bids for emotional connection. That means that the regrettable incident does not have a specific topic, or a specific issue behind it. It results from the couple's momentary inability to connect with one another, and an inability to "solve the moment." Often their conflict issue, they will claim, is "how we communicate." Sometimes this issue results from feelings of rejection or loneliness from failed attempts to connect emotionally, romantically, and/or sexually. The general complaint is that one's partner was not "there for them." Therefore many issues that are presented as conflict issues are actually issues in friendship and intimacy.

In fact, in our lab and our clinical experience, most couples, most of the time, seem to fight about absolutely nothing. For many couples their presenting "issues" seem to arise out of thin air. In hundreds of research interviews about conflict at home, we also found that couples do not necessarily argue about "issues." There may be no topic to the argument. The conflict, as in the following example, appears to be about the interaction itself. This couple have made popcorn and are settling down to watch TV . . .

Wife (W): Stop channel surfing. Just leave it. I might just want to see this show.
Husband (H): (*holding the remote*) OK, sure. Just let me just see what else is on.
W: No. I might want to watch this show.
H: In a minute. There could be a great film on.
W: Leave it.
H: Fine!
W: That's the problem! The way you just said "Fine!" Why did you say that? We were having a perfectly good time until you said that.
H: I said "Fine" because you have to have it *your* way, so you're going to have it your way, anyway. So, what the hell, fine!
W: Fine! I don't even want to watch anything with you now.
H: Fine (husband leaves the room).

On the surface, this fight is about nothing. There is no topic or issue. However, a deeper look suggests that there are hidden agendas based on accepting or refusing influence regarding different preferences (or personality needs). In a similar way, momentary "conflicts" can arise from different ideas about punctuality, affection, power, money, fairness, or even about emotion itself.

The above dialogue exemplifies a difference in preferences, but it also reveals each partner refusing to turn toward the other's request or bid for connection. We call this event a "failed bid for connection."

We need a system for understanding these failed bids. The remarkable work of the late researcher Jaak Panksepp provides us with one. It is important to understand the intricacies of how partners turn toward each other's bids for emotional connection. We have augmented our theory about turning toward with knowledge provided by Panksepp's superb guides to the unexplored worlds of positive and negative affect in all mammals. These are presented in his masterpiece books, *Affective Neuroscience* (Panksepp, 1998), and *The Archaeology of Mind* (Panksepp & Biven, 2012). In an intellectual tour de force, Panksepp documented seven studied affect systems that have distinct behavioral and neurophysiological patterns shared by all mammals. In Gottman and DeClaire's (2001) book, *The Relationship Cure*, we modified Panksepp's systems slightly, simplified their names, and called them "our emotional command systems." Our emotional command systems are fairly close to Panksepp's, with just a few of our own modifications. We won't go into the neuroanatomy of these systems here, but we will mention the neurotransmitters related to them.

Here are our emotional command systems:

1. *The Sentry*, with the primary affect of fear and the state of being vigilant for danger, and its opposite, the feelings of security and safety. The primary neurotransmitter of this system is norepinephrine, and the primary hormone is epinephrine (also called adrenaline). The sensing of vigilance for danger for all mammals starts with the nose, because so much sensing resides there for determining safety. Panksepp had a running $100 bet for any student who could condition any mammal to approach its food with its butt. He never lost that bet. The mammals would approach food only with their head and nose in order to sniff out the safety or danger in eating a given food.

2. *The Nest Builder*, with the feelings involved in bonding: security, affection, love, connection, and attachment, along with the opposite emotions of separation: distress/panic, grief, sadness, depression,

and loss. The primary operative hormones of this system are oxytocin and vasopressin. Unlike Panksepp's theory, we include grief and separation panic in this emotional command system, because we think that our grief is proportional to our prior attachment—that is, we grieve loss and separation to the extent to which we were previously attached to someone or something. (That assertion of ours is as yet untested.)

These first two systems are the ones most central to the very important workings of emotionally focused couples therapy, developed by our dear friend Susan Johnson. However, there are an additional five emotional command systems needing inclusion. All seven emotional command systems are central to building friendship and intimacy in our couples therapy.

1. *The Explorer*, or the *seeking system*, with primary affects of curiosity and joy in learning, exploration, and adventure, the sense that something wonderful is about to happen, or, in a more limited view, the anticipation or the expectation of reward. The primary hormones and neurotransmitters of this system are glutamate, norepinephrine, and especially dopamine. Olds and Milner (1954) called this system the "pleasure center," but Panksepp demonstrated convincingly that it is actually the seeking system that is activated. Animals will work to stimulate this center above all other drives. This is a very powerful system; it does not satiate like other drives. It is especially powerful in our species.

2. *The Commander-in-Chief*, with its primary affects of anger, hostility, rage, and dominance; its sense of being in control, having high status, and feeling competent and confident; plus its opposite feelings of submission and helplessness. The primary hormones of this system are testosterone and epinephrine.

3. *The Sensualist*, with affects involved in experiencing sexual desire, sensuality, erotic sexuality, physical novelty, and lust. The primary hormones of this system are testosterone, oxytocin, and estrogen.

4. *The Jester*, with affects related to experiencing play, fun, humor,

amusement, mockery, laughter, joy, and a sense of the absurd. The neurotransmitter of this system is dopamine.

5. *The Energy Czar*, which is involved in managing bodily needs for energy, food, warmth, shelter, and so on. This system is primarily regulated by the hypothalamus. This system was added by us; Panksepp did not recognize this system.

Panksepp found that these seven emotional command systems are fundamentally the "primary emotion colors" of affect for all mammals. Sometimes, however, couples therapists base their work on different beliefs about what are primary and what are secondary affects. For example, many therapists believe that anger and hostility are actually not primary emotions; they are just the skin on top of fear. Panksepp and many other researchers, however, have shown that this idea is wrong. Anger is a primary "approach emotion," very different from the "withdrawal emotions" of fear, sadness, and disgust. Davidson and Begley (2012a) have provided us with information about the separate frontal electroencephalogram (EEG) asymmetries and physiologies of approach and withdrawal emotions: fear, disgust, and sadness are primarily activated in the right hemisphere, while interest, amusement, curiosity, and anger are primarily activated in the left hemisphere. This finding has been replicated by Davidson, so we can be quite confident that this system can be a primary affect system. Often this system is activated in us humans by a sense of injustice or unfairness.

The seven emotional command systems can operate individually, but are often recruited in the service of one another. For example, the Explorer may be recruited in the service of finding a sexual partner. Or the Sentry and Nest Builder may be employed along with the Commander-in-Chief to create a potentially ferocious protector of the young. A good example of these three in combination is a mother bear; in protecting her cubs, she will often take on a predator three times her weight.

Turning Toward/Away/Against

We believe that these seven emotional command systems form the affective underpinnings for turning toward/away/against in all relationships. Whether in pure forms or blends, these systems color a relationship's interactions with a very rich mixture of affects.

Feelings of loneliness and rejection sometimes result from failures to connect (turning away or against) in all four of the positive affect systems: (1) the Jester—seeking play, humor, silliness, and fun; (2) the Nest Builder—searching for comfort, security, and closeness; (3) the Explorer—seeking adventure, novelty, and new learning; and (4) the Sensualist—searching for enhanced sensuality, sexual connection, and erotic fulfillment. Once we start thinking of escalated negative emotions that result from failed bids in these emotional command systems, we can see that building emotional connection and intimacy by turning toward in all positive affect emotional command systems is not just about enhancing a couple's sex life but also about giving them access to the other positive affect systems.

In extreme cases, conflicts or blocks to intimacy can result from failed bids. Challenges can also emerge in the following systems: (5) the Commander-in-Chief, as when standoffs in dominance and power struggles exist beneath presenting conflicts; (6) the Sentry, when there has been violence or psychological abuse that leads the victim to not feel safe with the perpetrator; or (7) the Energy Czar, when the environmental demands on a couple exceed their own energy, and the relationship becomes stress-ridden.

Because these areas of a relationship are so connected with one another, our work on friendship and intimacy and work on conflict management are often done in tandem. We always begin a session with whatever a couple presents to us that day. Our weekly sessions are always at least 75 minutes in length. We also conduct marathon therapy if a couple requests it. This format consists of 3 consecutive days of 5–6 hours of therapy a day. We begin each session or therapy day with an "emotion check-in" by asking a question like "What's on your heart and mind right now?" Using the couple's interactions and Dan Wile's doubling method for "solving the moment," we then call on the specific blueprint that can maximize progress for that particular session. We also pay special attention to blockages in friendship and intimacy, and choose the emotional command systems on which to focus.

Tools for Directly Building Friendship

On smartphone app stores, therapists can find "Gottman Card Decks," a collection of 14 card decks that are free of charge. It's useful to download these, and have your clients do so also on their phones. Below, some examples from some of these decks are presented as lists.

1. Build Love Maps

Our free app contains two love map exercises. We especially love working with our Open-Ended Questions Card Deck. Each partner reviews this app's list of questions, then picks three to five questions on the app to ask their partner. Then they take turns asking their partner one of their selected questions, listening to the answer, then answering the same question themselves. Then it's the other partner's turn to select a question they have picked, ask it aloud, listen to their partner's response, and in turn answer it for themselves. These questions are great for dates and romantic trips. We originated this exercise early in our marriage when we went on weekly dates that needed to cost next to nothing. There is a beautiful hotel in Seattle that has a grand stone fireplace in the lobby, with luxurious couches resting in front of it. We'd enter the hotel, commandeer a couch, and pretend we were guests. We'd order one drink, sip it throughout the date, and ask each other these types of questions. John always brought a yellow pad and took notes on Julie's answers. Julie had to be careful with how she answered the questions; after all, her reply might get used in a book someday. These dates were wonderful and helped us to stay deeply connected despite leading very busy lives. Now we use them during a honeymoon we take every year (with the exception of the COVID years).

The goal of this exercise is to jump-start the process of clients eventually generating their own open-ended questions to ask one another. The card decks or lists of questions render this whole process more doable and fun. This process was also the backbone of our book *Eight Dates: Essential Conversations for a Lifetime of Love* (2018). We are trying to spark the partners' curiosity about each other. This exercise is usually a lot of fun, and it builds closeness.

Examples of Open-Ended Questions

What do you want your life to be like in, say, 3 years?

How do you see your work changing in the future?

How do you feel about our physical home? Any architectural changes you'd like to make?

How would you compare yourself as a mother (father) to your own mother (father)?

What kind of person do you think our child(ren) will become? Any fears? Any hopes?

Is our child like anyone in your family? Who?

How do you feel about your family right now? Have these feelings changed lately?

How do you feel about work now?

How are you feeling now about being a mother (father)?

What do you find exciting in life right now?

What are your biggest worries about the future?

How do you think we could have more fun in our life?

Who are your best allies and close friends right now? How have they or you changed?

Have any of your friends drifted away or become a bit weird?

Who in your life is most stressful to you? Why?

What do you need right now in a friend?

What things are missing in your life?

How have you changed in the last year?

Have your goals in life changed recently?

What are some of your life dreams now?

What goals do you have for our family?

What goals do you have just for yourself right now?

What is one way you would like to change?

What legacy do you want our family to take from your family? From your culture?

What are some unfulfilled things in your life?

What would you change about our finances right now?

Where would you like to travel?

What adventures would you like to have before you die?

Has your outlook on life changed in the past 2 years?

2. Build Fondness and Admiration

We suggest that you use an exercise with your clients called the Positive Adjective Checklist. It is composed of a list of flattering traits. In the exercise you ask each partner to choose three to five adjectives that describe their partner and to give an example of a time when they displayed that trait. This can be a great exercise for building fondness and admiration in a couple.

However, we need to tell you about Amber Tabares's doctoral dissertation. John's lab did a study where 100 couples had two 15-minute conflict conversations. Following the first conversation, couples were randomly assigned to one of four conditions. One condition used the Positive Adjective Checklist, and another condition used the Areas of Concern Checklist. That list contained only unflattering adjectives like "stingy," "selfish," "mean," and so on. There were the same instructions for the latter list: Choose three adjectives that are concerns you have about your partner, and give an example of a time when they displayed that trait. There were also two control groups. In one control group, which was designed to simulate a *real break*, couples just read magazines for the same amount of time as allowed for the exercises, without talking to one another. In a second, *damaged break* condition to simulate rumination, they first did the rating dial task based on the first conversation *before* reading the magazines and not talking to one another. Then all the couples continued their conflict discussion (called Conflict Conversation 2) for a second span of 15 minutes.

John predicted that the couples in the positive adjective condition would become more positive in Conflict Conversation 2, that the areas-of-concern group would become more negative in Conversation 2, and that there would be change in only the *real break* control group. John was right about the control groups. Both reading-magazine control groups lowered the people's heart rates, especially for the men. But only the control group that did not do the rating dial (the no-ruminations group) became more positive in Conversation 2. Once again, however, John was wrong about the two adjective groups (he is wrong 60% of the time with his hypotheses). There were no changes at all for the two adjective groups. How disappointing!

One of John's graduate students, Dan Yoshimoto, fortunately said that he had looked at a bunch of the videos of couples doing the adjective tasks. He said that many couples did not follow the instructions. For example, a wife with the positive adjectives group said to her husband, "I looked over this list and I don't think you have any positive qualities, so instead I picked three I'd like you to work on." Or some people said, "I'm very disappointed with the adjectives you picked. Why didn't you pick . . . ?" Similarly, in the areas-of-concern list, one husband sweetly said, "I don't have any of these concerns about you." And the wife responded with, "I know I'm not perfect, so tell me if you have a concern," and then they had a great conversation.

So it became Amber's job to code *how* people used the two adjective lists. When they used either list in a gentle or positive manner, Conversation 2 got a lot more positive. When they used either of them in a hostile manner, Conversation 2 got a lot more negative. Then Amber came up with another question. Could she predict how a couple would use the exercises from Conversation 1? The answer was absolutely yes. If they had the Four Horsemen in Conversation 1, they used either adjective checklist with hostility. If Conversation 1 was more positive, they used either adjective checklist with affection. So the findings were (1) to become more positive after a break, take the break without ruminations; and (2) any exercise can be sabotaged.

Here is the Positive Adjective Checklist:

Loving	Funny	Committed	Witty
Sensitive	Considerate	Involved	Relaxed
Brave	Affectionate	Expressive	Beautiful
Intelligent	Organized	Active	Handsome
Thoughtful	Resourceful	Careful	Silly
Generous	Athletic	Reserved	Calm
Loyal	Cheerful	Adventurous	Lively
Truthful	Coordinated	Receptive	Strong

Energetic	Graceful	Reliable	Assertive
Sexy	Gracious	Dependable	Protective
Decisive	Playful	Nurturing	Sweet
Warm	Creative	Caring	Tender
Imaginative	Virile	Gentle	Powerful
Fun	Exciting	Kind	Flexible
Attractive	Thrifty	Shy	Practical
Supportive	Vulnerable	Genuine	Lusty
Understanding	Empathetic	Irresistible	Makes me feel safe

3. Build Turning Toward

3a. Turning Toward During Everyday Events Checklist. Here you are try-ing to build in your clients a heightened awareness of how their partner makes bids for connection, and how they'd like the other partner to respond. Consider all these ways of turning toward to be what are commonly called "love languages." As you can see, there are many. This suggests that there are actually an infinite number of love languages in a relationship.

> *Instructions for your clients:*
>
> *From the list below, select areas in your life for which you would like to thank your partner for having turned toward you in the past. Pick three to five items, and give an example for each. Turning toward you means that you wanted greater connection with them, emotionally, and they responded in a satisfying way. Then discuss your choices with your partner and clearly express your gratitude.*
>
> *"I appreciate you having turned toward me in the past in the following way:" Pick three.*

1. Reunion at the end of the day and talk about how the day went.
2. Staying in touch with kin—for example, calling parents (mom, dad, grandmas) or siblings and in-laws.
3. Shopping for groceries.

4. Cooking dinner, baking together.
5. Shopping together for presents for a friend (e.g., friend's wedding) together.
6. Family going out to breakfast on Saturday or Sunday.
7. Reading the morning paper together.
8. Planning a dinner party together.
9. Having a dinner party.
10. Calling your spouse during the workday.
11. Thinking about your spouse during the workday.
12. Going out on a date with your spouse (no kids).
13. An overnight with spouse at a romantic place.
14. Morning breakfast together during workweek.
15. Going to a church, mosque, or synagogue together.
16. Yard work together.
17. Physical workouts together.
18. Weekend outings (e.g., picnics, drives) together.
19. Time together with kids—bedtimes, baths, homework, together.
20. Traveling together (plane, bus, train, car).
21. Long drives together.
22. Renting a video and watching it together.
23. Ordering dinner in or takeout together.
24. Watching TV together.
25. Double-dating with another couple or friends.
26. Watching sports events on TV together.
27. Doing a favorite activity together (e.g., bowling, going to the zoo or an amusement park, bicycling, hiking, horseback riding, camping, canoeing, sailing, boating, water-skiing, swimming).
28. Building a fire at home. Sitting in front of the fire and talking or reading together.
29. Listening to music together.
30. Going to a concert together.
31. Going dancing together.
32. Going to a night club or jazz club together.
33. Going to the theater together.

34. Going out to eat together.
35. Going to a kid's birthday party together.
36. Taking a kid to lessons together.
37. Going to aid's sporting event together.
38. Going to a kid's performance (recital, play, etc.) together.
39. Writing letters or cards together.
40. Going to a community event (e.g., church auction) together.
41. Going to a party together.
42. Driving to or from work together and just talking.
43. Planning vacations together.
44. Taking vacations together.
45. Making plans, dreaming together.
46. Walking the dog together.
47. Reading out loud together.
48. Playing a board game or card game together.
49. Hobbies (e.g., painting, sculpting, making music together).
50. Talking while drinking (alcohol, coffee or tea) together.
51. Going out to your favorite bar or haunt together.
52. Time to just talk together without interruptions.
53. A regular time when you know you can have your spouse really listen to you.
54. Playing together.
55. Philosophizing together.
56. Gossiping (talking about other people) together.
57. Phone calls together catching up with people you know.
58. Visiting a sick friend together.
59. Doing other things to help out other people together.
60. Time to just talk and cuddle.
61. Time to caress romantically.
62. Time to make love.
63. Time for some real affection between you.
64. Talking over the events of the day.

3b. Turning Toward by Ritualized Daily Emotion Check-Ins. Have your clients pick a time for a regular daily emotional connection in which they ask one another, "What's on your heart and mind right now?" But also tell them to postpone asking this question if either of them is in a hurry, and to save it for another time that day.

3c. Turning Toward by the "Expressing Needs Weekly Meeting." Have your clients use the Expressing Needs Card Deck in our free phone app. They can also just use the list below.

This is a weekly exercise for your clients that creates a ritual of connection for them. Each partner selects three needs, either from the list on the app or from the list below. Then they take turns, presenting one of their needs to their partner. Since the items on the list are somewhat general, encourage them to make each need they've chosen more personal and specific relative to their relationship. The responding partner may first ask questions about the speaker's need, as long as the questions help the respondent to better understand that need. Then the respondent should reply to their partner's need. They might say: (1) "Yes, I agree to meet that need this week"; or (2) "No, I can't meet that need right now, and here's why . . . "; or (3) "I will try to meet that need this week." They can also personalize their reply beyond these options. If the respondent agrees to meet a need this week, have them write that need down as a self-reminder. Then it's time to trade roles, with the other partner taking a turn to describe one of the needs they've chosen and hear the reply. In this way, they should proceed until they've worked with each need they selected. If they are holding weekly 1-hour state-of-the-union meetings at home, they might want to review their experiences of getting their needs met, and any additional details they might like to add to improve their experience.

Express Your Needs
I need you to initiate sex.
I need to cuddle more.
I need to know when you find me irresistible.
I want to talk more about our kids.

I need you to ask me about my hopes and aspirations.

I need to have a real conversation with you.

I need to talk to you about my day every day this week.

I need our reunions at the end of the day to be warm and affectionate.

I need you to be more affectionate with me, to touch me more.

I need you to ask me about what's going on at my work.

I need you to put down the paper or mute the TV when I want to talk.

I need a foot rub.

I need you to put down your phone when I want to talk.

I need you to show interest in me.

I need you to come up with some fun activities we can do together.

I need a back rub or a massage.

I need for you to offer to do a household chore so I can get some relief.

I need you to tell me I look nice.

I need you to speak calmly to me when you are upset.

I need you to answer me when I call your name.

I need to be able to tell you about my sadness without you getting upset.

I need a romantic drive or getaway.

I need phones and computers off at dinner.

I need appreciations for the hard work I've been doing.

I need you to listen and not try to give advice.

I need to go out to dinner and a movie.

I need to hear more compliments from you.

I need to hear that you find me attractive inside and out.

I need to take a long bath together.

I need you to cook a meal or order food in one night a week.

I need to see my friends with you.

I need for us to have an adventure together.

I need you to text me often that you're thinking of me.

I need you to "sext" me sometimes.

I need a kiss good-night every night.

I need to tell you about my stresses and for you to be interested.

I want to talk about how I'm changing.

I need us to visit my family.

I need you to tell me every day that you love me.

I need you to take my side when your family (or mine) criticizes me.

I need to cuddle nonsexually before we go to sleep.

I need for you to do more housework.

I need to get dressed up and go out with you.

I need to go to a music or dance concert.

I need you to surprise me more with gifts.

I need us to have a closer relationship with my family.

I need to travel with you.

I need you to visit my family alone.

I need to have a dinner party with some of our friends.

I want to go dancing.

I want you to tell me that you love only me.

I need to know that you feel proud of me.

When I feel angry, I need you to listen to me and empathize.

I need for us to have a savings plan.

I need to have more respect from you.

I need to know that you think I'm sexy.

When I feel depressed, I need you to listen to me and
    empathize with me.

I need you to tell me what you want for our future.

I need to hear that you are still my best friend.

I need you to ask me more questions.

I need for us to travel more.

I need for us to have a better balance between work and family.

I need you to plan a romantic evening together.

I need to have a weekly date.

I need you to get a checkup and go to the doctor.

I need some regular time alone for myself.

I need your support with my weight-loss process.

I need you to talk about how I have changed.

I need for us to do a romantic overnight in a B&B.

I need your help getting into better physical shape.

I need you to hear my anger without you getting upset or defensive.

I need some quiet time alone when I first come home.

I need to buy some new clothes.

3d. Turning Toward by Expressing Appreciations. Within a session, try having your clients do this exercise. Have them pick five things for which they'd like to express appreciation and then take turns doing so. This list can also be used in the weekly state-of-the-union meeting.

Express Your Appreciations

Thanks for doing the dishes.

Thanks for making dinner. It was delicious.

Thanks for cleaning up the kitchen.

Thanks for doing the laundry.

Thanks for supporting me when I talked about my stresses.

Thanks for taking care of the kids.

Thanks for being such a great dad. [Give example]

Thanks for being such a great mom. [Give example]

I really appreciated your giving me a hug.

Thanks for listening to how my day went.

I really appreciated your being so affectionate lately. [Give example]

I really enjoyed the conversation at dinner.

Taking a walk together was really nice.

Thanks for being understanding when I talked about that rude person I met.

I enjoyed making love to you.

I want to thank you for the card and the great words on it.

Thanks for bringing me flowers.

That gift was terrific.

You look great in that.

Thanks for spending time with me.

Thank you for caring about what I need.

That is a fantastic color on you.

Thanks for spending time with me. [Give example of what you did]

Thanks for making me feel like I come first in your life.

I am really proud of you. [Give example]

I have so much respect for you. [Give example]

It matters to me a lot when you are so great with the kids.
[Give example]

The way you treat my family means a lot to me. [Give example]

Thanks for putting on music that I love.

Thanks for putting up with [fill in the blank with an obnoxious person's name].

Thank you for desiring me.

Thanks for calling my mother.

Thank you for just being there when I felt sad.

Thanks for all the driving you are doing.

You taste delicious.

Thank you for listening to me.

Thanks for calling the plumber (electrician, handyman, carpenter, gardener, etc.).

Thank you for taking me out to dinner. That was great.

Thanks for taking a bath with me.

Thank you for comforting me.

I had fun at the party. Thank you for being with me.

Thank you for being empathetic with me.

Thanks for taking the kids to the pediatrician.

Thanks for lighting candles.

Thank you for being gentle with me.

Thank you for being on my side.

Thank you for inviting our friends over.

Thank you for laughter.

Thank you for telling me what you need.

You are a great kisser.

Thanks for spending time with the kids.

Thanks for saving money for us.

It was fun playing cards. Thank you.

Thank you for last weekend.

Thank you for holding me.

I loved the picnic we had.

Thanks for taking care of me when I was sick.

Thanks for giving me some time to myself.

I really appreciate that drive we took.

Thanks for taking over the chores. [Give example]

I really appreciate how great you look tonight as we get ready for bed.

I can hardly take my hands off you.

Thank you for greeting me so warmly when I come home.

Thanks for making our home so beautiful.

Thanks for making coffee for me.

Thank you for telling me how you feel.

You smell so good.

Thank you for loving me.

Thanks for spending time with my family.

I love touching you here. [Give more detail]

I appreciate what a loyal partner you are.

Thanks for sticking up for me when I got criticized. [Give example]

Thanks for the way you handled that teacher conference.

Those pastries were delicious. Thanks for getting them.

Thanks for calling the doctor when I needed an appointment.

Thanks for the way you are paying the bills.

3e. Turning Toward in Play, Fun, and Adventure. These are exercises you can do with your clients.

From the list below have your clients select together three items they will commit to doing every week for the next month.

Fun and Play Suggestions

1. Play a board game together.
2. Take a drive this weekend.
3. Go to a new place we have never been and explore.
4. Buy something together for our home.
5. Plan a picnic.
6. Go to the shopping mall together.

7. Rent a video and make popcorn.
8. Plan a meal together and invite friends over.
9. Cook something totally new together.
10. Play catch.
11. Learn a new language together.
12. Go bicycling.
13. Row a boat or canoe or kayak together.
14. Take a long walk in a new city.
15. Go out to dinner in a totally new restaurant.
16. Go to a bookstore.
17. See an old movie we both love.
18. Go dancing.
19. Go to a concert.
20. Buy music we both like and listen to it over a glass of wine.
21. Work out together.
22. Go to a party.
23. Go to a mall and follow a couple, pretending to be them.
24. Have a party in our home with old friends.
25. Play music together.
26. Take sailing lessons together.
27. Go to an art gallery.
28. Pretend we are spies.
29. Go to a museum.
30. Go to a theme park or amusement park.
31. Go swimming together.
32. Jog together.
33. Go to a pet store.
34. Go see a very old friend.
35. Color and draw together.
36. Go to a coffee house and secretly sketch caricatures of people. Discuss with each other.
37. Play Frisbee.
38. Learn to tango together.
39. Learn to do Israeli folk dancing.

40. Learn Tai Chi and do it together every day.
41. Plan a dinner party with friends and invite new people too.
42. Do a major film retrospective of an actor or director we love.
43. Plan and make a short animated film together, doing all the drawings.
44. Go on a canoe or kayak camping trip.
45. Learn to cook a totally new cuisine together.
46. Finger paint together.
47. Watch the sunset.
48. Buy a telescope and learn two new constellations.
49. Learn a new card game.
50. Buy a microscope and watch slides of microorganisms.
51. Watch the sunrise.
52. Go on a scavenger hunt.
53. Go get ice cream.
54. Grill something new.
55. Create a joint bucket list.
56. Go to a zoo.
57. Stay in a new hotel just for one night.
58. Arrange old photos into albums.
59. Organize a beach or nature cleanup.
60. Go to a farmers' market.
61. Bake an apple pie.
62. Go to a museum of old instruments.
63. Pick blueberries.
64. Volunteer at a homeless shelter.
65. Invite over neighbors you don't know very well.
66. Go fishing.
67. Go to a beach for the day.
68. Go to an arboretum.
69. Go to the library.
70. Learn archery together.
71. Visit antique stores.
72. Go backpacking.
73. Put together a jigsaw puzzle.

74. Watch for shooting stars.
75. Take a class together in French cooking.
76. Take a new online class.
77. Learn to play a new musical instrument.
78. Go bowling.
79. See an opera.
80. Go to a garage sale.
81. Plan a new diet to do together.
82. Visit a local nursing home and get to know one person there.
83. Plan a garden.
84. Plan two adventures to do together this month.
85. Explore local history.
86. Make a plan to get into great physical shape together.
87. Go car camping.
88. Go to a pottery workshop.
89. Visit an oriental carpet store together.
90. Pick a brand-new church, mosque, shrine, or synagogue to visit.
91. Take an art class.
92. Play basketball.
93. Learn to sing harmony together.
94. Plan the perfect lemon tart and bake it together.
95. Go to the gym and work out together.
96. Learn how to cook Chinese cuisine.
97. Go to a natural history museum.
98. Pick someone you admire and read a biography of that person together.

From the list below, have your clients pick one adventure they'd like to do, and will commit to doing sometime in the next 6 months.

Adventures
1. Pick a country you want to visit and plan a trip there.
2. Learn a new language together and then visit a country where they speak that language.

3. Pick something new to learn together.

4. Get a kit and learn to launch a rocket together.

5. Do your honeymoon over again.

6. Learn to play two new instruments, and then play together.

7. Learn climbing rock walls together.

8. Pick a mountain to both climb together.

9. Go skydiving together.

10. Learn to draw caricatures together and then go to your favorite coffee- or teahouse and do caricatures of the people you see around you.

11. Learn how to raise bees.

12. Learn to fly a plane together.

13. Learn to sail together.

14. Take up gardening orchids together.

15. Go to a butterfly museum.

16. Learn to watercolor together.

17. Get in great aerobic shape together.

18. Get a massage together.

19. Pick a fancy hotel for an overnight.

20. Learn how to cook a new kind of cuisine together.

21. Ride a roller coaster together.

22. Pick a play and read it together, playing the roles.

23. Pick a book of poetry to read out loud to one another.

24. Learn to do a brand-new sport together (baseball, hockey, basketball, soccer, tennis, golf).

25. Visit a planetarium together.

26. Plan a vacation together that is based purely on going to concerts or hearing great music around the world.

27. Join a really weird club, one you would never have thought of joining.

28. Pick two new skills to learn together.

29. Learn to ballroom dance together.

30. Take a cruise up the west coast of Norway together.

31. Rent an all-terrain vehicle and go on an adventure with it together.

32. Learn how to do-it-yourself for something brand-new to both of you.
33. Go bird-watching together.
34. Go see an opera together.
35. Go paragliding together.
36. Visit the Taj Mahal.
37. Tour a new city on a Segway or scooter together.
38. Go hunting with a bow and arrow or a camera together.
39. Get *1,000 Places to See Before You Die* and plan to visit one new place a year together.
40. Go to the Irish island of Inisheer and attend a bodhrán (Irish drum) workshop together.
41. Make a movie together.
42. Go bungee jumping together.
43. Go backpacking together.
44. Learn the tango together.
45. Go snorkeling in the Great Barrier Reef in Australia.
46. Learn aikido together.
47. Learn some ballet or modern dance together.
48. Get two For Dummies books and learn how to do them.
49. Go on a safari together to Botswana.
50. Write a song together.
51. Take a two-day canoe or kayak trip down a river together. If you don't know how, go to a river canoe or kayak school.
52. Go mountain biking together.
53. Buy a telescope and learn how to use it to see Jupiter's moons together.
54. Plan a sailing trip to the Greek islands.
55. Go to Alaska and kayak among the glaciers together.
56. Learn to hang glide together.
57. Try out for a play. Learn how to act together.
58. Try out for a chorus. If you can't sing, learn how. Get the book *Singing for Dummies.*
59. Go to the Galápagos on a ship together.
60. Go waterboarding together.

61. Take a snowmobile trip together.
62. Learn to use a microscope together.
63. Visit the Grand Canyon and take a mule ride down it together.
64. Go to Antarctica together.
65. Take two of the Great Courses together.
66. Learn to surf together.
67. Take a trip to Yosemite together.
68. Go zip-lining together.

A Tool for Building Emotional Connection in the Positive Affect Systems: The Aftermath of a Failed Bid, and the Aftermath of a Successful Bid

Now that we've described lots of ways to help your couples to build emotional connection, it's time to look at methods to process when those ways either fail or succeed. What follows are two tools, one designed to process failed bids for connection, and the other, to savor how a couple's bid succeeded.

The first tool we offer here is how to process failed bids for connection. This tool is akin to our blueprint for processing a bad fight or regrettable incident. Failed bids can refer to a failure to connect in any of the positive emotional command systems. Guide your clients as they follow these steps. You can enhance the power of this experience by doing Dan Wiles, if you like.

The Aftermath of a Failed Bid

The tool we offer here will help you to process failed bids for connection.

Step 1: Talk about what you were each feeling.

From the list below, take turns picking out any of the feelings you had during the failed bid for connection and reading them aloud. You can select as many items to read as you want. Do NOT say why you had the feeling, and don't comment on your partner's choice of feelings. Think of your partner as the expert on what they felt, just as you are the expert on what you felt.

WHAT DID YOU FEEL?	MORE FEELINGS	MORE FEELINGS
1. I felt defensive.	18. I felt that both of us were partly right.	32. I was overwhelmed with emotion.
2. I felt not listened to.	19. I was out of control.	33. I was not calm.
3. My feelings got hurt.	20. I was frustrated.	34. I was stubborn.
4. I was totally flooded.	21. I was righteously indignant.	35. I felt powerless.
5. I was angry.	22. I was morally justified.	36. I had no influence.
6. I was sad.	23. I got unfairly picked on.	37. I wanted to win this one.
7. I felt unloved.	24. I felt unappreciated.	38. I felt that my opinions didn't even matter.
8. I was misunderstood.	25. I felt disliked.	39. There was a lot of give-and-take.
9. I was criticized.	26. I felt unattractive.	40. I had no feelings at all.
10. I took a complaint personally.	27. I felt stupid.	41. I had no idea what I was feeling.
11. I felt like you didn't even like me.	28. I felt morally outraged.	42. I felt lonely.
12. I felt not cared about.	29. I felt taken for granted.	43. I felt alienated.
13. I felt worried.	30. I felt like leaving.	44. I felt rejected.
14. I felt afraid.	31. I felt like staying and talking this through.	45. I felt abandoned.
15. I felt unsafe.		
16. I felt tense.		
17. I was right and you were wrong.		

Step 2: Subjective realities.

The couple takes turns as speaker and listener.

The Speaker's Role. As the speaker, stay out of blaming or criticizing your partner, and only describe what you experienced. You will be talking about yourself: what you saw, what you experienced, what you heard, what you felt, what you imagined, and so on. Try using I-statements, describing what you felt and when you felt it, what you thought, and what you might have needed. Do not describe your partner. Do not analyze your partner. Instead of saying, "You said . . . ," say, "I heard you say." Instead of saying, "You thought . . . ," say, "I imagined that you thought." Describe the situation neutrally. Talk about what you would have liked in this situation instead of what happened. What was the response from your partner that you needed?

Below there are some examples of needs you might have had in this failed attempt to connect. You don't have to pick anything from this list. These are just here as examples for you, to spark your own thoughts. By the way, a "need" is the same as a desire, a want, a wish, or a preference. And needs require no justification. Trying to justify a need usually leads to entering into the attack mode, meaning sliding into blame and criticism and triggering your partner's defensiveness. You're entitled to have needs, and there is no such thing as being "too needy."

I NEEDED	MORE NEEDS
1. I needed you to just listen to me.	17. I needed you to put down the paper or mute the TV when I want to talk.
2. I needed you to hold me.	18. I needed a foot rub.
3. I needed for you to offer to help me.	18. I needed a foot rub.
4. I needed to feel understood.	19. I needed a back rub or massage.
5. I needed to be validated by you.	20. I needed for you to offer to do a household chore so I can get some relief.
6. I needed you to initiate sex.	20. I needed for you to offer to do a household chore so I can get some relief.
7. I needed to cuddle more.	21. I needed you to tell me I look nice.
8. I needed to know when you find me irresistible.	22. I needed you to answer me when I call your name.
9. I wanted to talk more about our kids.	23. I needed a romantic drive or getaway.
10. I needed you to ask me about my hopes and aspirations.	24. I needed to go out to dinner and a movie.
11. I needed to have a conversation with you.	25. I needed to take a long bath together.
12. I needed to talk to you about my day.	26. I needed you to cook a meal or order food in one night a week.
13. I needed our reunions to be warm and affectionate.	27. I needed to see my friends.
14. I needed you to be more affectionate with me, to touch me more.	28. I needed for us to have an adventure together.
15. I needed you to look happy when you first see me at the end of the day.	29. I needed some time alone for myself.
16. I needed you to ask me about my work.	30. I needed . . . (you supply the need).

The Listener's Role. There are always two realities, two perceptions in each failed bid for connection. Remember, as Dan Siegel said, there is no "immaculate perception." Do not argue for your own perceptions. Instead, try to understand your partner's perceptions. When you are listening, take notes. The more defensive you feel, the more you need to slow your partner down to write down everything being said. Listen not to rebut what the speaker is saying, but to empathize with the speaker. Try to get inside your partner's skin and listen with compassion. When the speaker is done, summarize and reflect back what you heard, both the feelings and needs expressed. Then add some words of validation. Validation doesn't mean that you agree with the speaker. You still have your own subjective reality. Validation means that some of what your partner has said makes sense, from your partner's point of view. Words of validation might be "I get it. Your point of view makes sense to me. I can see why you felt hurt (or sad, angry, etc.)."

Now trade roles with whoever listened first, now getting to share their point of view as the speaker while the alternate partner does the listening, summarizing, and validating.

Step 3: Triggers.
There are NOT always triggers in every incident of a failed bid. **Triggers** are enduring vulnerabilities that might have gotten activated in this failed bid for connection. Triggers refer to events that have happened in your past, before this relationship ever began. Those experiences linger inside us, and when the "right buttons" are pushed, they surface again, bringing up all the discomfort of the earliest times they happened. That's what you'll describe to your partner in this step. You'll be taking turns with this step, as you have with the other steps. If you're aware that this type of failed bid has happened many times before in *this relationship*, set aside the other incidents so you can process them separately at another time. Only one incident should be processed at a time. Triggers usually have a story that goes with them of the earliest time before this relationship that a similar distressing event happened. After you've described the feelings that got triggered for you, tell that story to your partner. If it's hard to remember the earlier event, you can try to replay the "videotape" of your life in your mind. Stop at an incident you

remember from your childhood or earlier past in which you got triggered in the same way or had similar feelings to those of this incident. Tell the story of that earlier experience, how it happened, and what you felt.

Try to understand why these are triggers for you, and help build your partner's awareness of them. Here is a list of common triggers. You don't need to select anything from this list. We're providing it for you in case you need examples to spark specific triggers that you may have.

WHAT TRIGGERED ME	MORE	MORE
1. I felt excluded. 2. I felt powerless. 3. I felt not listened to. 4. I couldn't ask for what I needed. 5. I felt scolded. 6. I felt judged. 7. I felt blamed. 8. I felt disrespected. 9. I felt no affection at all. 10. I felt unsafe.	11. I felt uncared for. 12. I felt lonely. 13. You weren't there for me when I was vulnerable and needed you. 14. I couldn't just talk about my feelings without you going ballistic. 15. Once again I was the bad guy and you were innocent. 16. I was not getting taken care of very well.	17. This felt so unfair to me. 18. I had trouble with your anger or yelling. 19. I had trouble with your sadness or despair. 20. I felt trapped. 21. I felt you had no passion for me. 22. I couldn't ask for what I needed. 23. I felt unloved. 24. I felt controlled. 25. I felt manipulated.

LISTENER: Try to listen to your partner's story with empathy, putting yourself in your partner's shoes. If you like, you can also summarize back to your partner what you heard them say.

Now trade roles.

Step 4: Accept responsibility—What role did you play in this failure to connect?

In this step, select items off the list in Part A: "What Set Me Up," that were true for you at the time this incident took place. Read them aloud. You can name as many as you like.

PART A. What set me up—my state of mind at the time was:

WHAT SET ME UP	MORE	MORE
1. I'd been very stressed and irritable lately.	8. I'd been more typically turning away.	16. I'd been feeling a bit like a martyr.
2. I'd not expressed much appreciation toward you lately.	9. I'd been getting easily upset.	17. I'd needed to be alone.
3. I'd taken you for granted.	10. I'd been depressed lately.	18. I'd not wanted to take care of anybody.
4. I'd been overly sensitive lately.	11. I had a chip on my shoulder lately.	19. I'd been very preoccupied.
5. I'd been overly critical lately.	12. I'd not been very affectionate.	20. I'd been very stressed lately.
6. I'd not shared very much of my inner world.	13. I'd not made time for good things between us.	21. I hadn't felt very much confidence in myself.
7. I'd not been emotionally available.	14. I'd not been a very good listener lately.	22. I'd been running on empty.
	15. I'd not asked for what I needed.	

PART B. What specifically was your own contribution to this failure to connect? What do you regret doing or not doing? First describe what you regret, and then apologize for it, making your apology as clear as possible.

Below are some examples for you, but use your own words and refer specifically to your own actions. Then refer to these in your apology. After describing your contribution to this failed-bid incident, you can apologize by completing the following sentence: "I wish to apologize for . . . "

Examples:

1. Disrespecting you	9. Hurting you
2. Turning away from you	10. Leaving you so alone
3. Overreacting	11. Violating your trust
4. Saying something I regret	12. Lying to you
5. Insulting you	13. Not listening
6. Being rejecting	14. Being stubborn
7. Abandoning you	15. Being insensitive
8. Being cold	

Step 5: Figure out how to make it better next time.

Take turns answering the questions listed below.

    a. What is one way that *your partner* can make it better next time this kind of incident happens?

    b. What's one way that *you* can make it better next time? That completes this exercise.

Here is another exercise that can help clients to understand and celebrate a bid for connection going well. It can help your clients to process a success in communication, and figure out how to make that happen more often. It is also loosely based on the Aftermath of a Regrettable Incident exercise.

This exercise was developed by Robert Navarra to highlight and process a positive event, incident, or interaction for one or both partners. The event could be anything that one or both partners did that created positive feelings. "Processing" it means that they will talk about the incident with the goal of providing their partner with a better understanding of their feelings and perceptions. It should be a conversation describing what happened, how they each felt, and how it met their needs.

Aftermath of a Positive Event
(author of this tool: Dr. Robert Navarra)

Before You Begin. Keep in mind that the goal is creating greater understanding of *what is working* in the relationship. Assume that *each* partner's reality has validity, and what is important to one partner may not be as important to the other. Perception is everything. Don't focus on how it could have been, or on how it has been in the past. The key is to emphasize what is working now, rather than what was not working in the past.

Step 1—Feelings: Share how you felt. Each partner will take a turn. When it's your turn, read any of the words aloud from the list below that match how you felt during this incident. You can name as many as you want. Do not say why you felt that way. That will happen in the next step. Also, avoid commenting on your partner's feelings.

I felt . . .

1. Understood
2. Confident
3. Reliable
4. Close
5. Amazed
6. Free
7. Sympathetic
8. Interested
9. Satisfied
10. Receptive
11. Accepting
12. Kind
13. Important
14. Considerate
15. Affectionate
16. Sensitive
17. Tender
18. Devoted
19. Attracted
20. Warm
21. Passionate
22. Loved
23. Comforted
24. Joyful
25. Fortunate
26. Delighted
27. Thankful
28. Festive
29. Cheerful
30. Elated
31. Grateful
32. Inspired

33. Fascinated
34. Curious
35. Playful
36. Energetic
37. Courageous
38. Optimistic
39. Liberated
40. Brave
41. Wonderful
42. Excited
43. Enthusiastic
44. Hopeful
45. Thrilled
46. Reinforced
47. Encouraged
48. Pleased
49. Secure
50. Calm
51. Peaceful
52. Content
53. Relaxed
54. Strong

Step 2—Realities: Describe your "reality." Take turns. Summarize and validate your partner's reality.

Subjective Reality and Validation

a. *Speaker.* Describing yourself, take turns recounting your perceptions, your own reality of what happened to make this a positive event. Focusing on behavior, describe events as they occurred and your feelings at the time. Avoid referring to past events, "the way this happened before." Talk about what you received from your partner. Describe your perceptions like a reporter, giving an objective minute-by-minute description.

b. **Listener.** Stepping into your partner's world, summarize and then validate your partner's experience by saying something like "It makes sense to me how you saw this and what your perceptions and needs were. I get it," or "I can see why this was important to you." Validation doesn't mean you agree, but rather that you understand your partner's experience of the incident.

c. Do both partners feel understood? If yes, move on. If no, ask, "What do I need to know to understand your perspective better?" After summarizing and validating, ask your partner, "Did I get it?" and "Is there anything else?"

Step 3—Meaning: Share what experiences, memories, or stories you have that relate to making this a positive event. What makes this event important for you, what meaning does it have?

As you replay the videotape of your memory, stop at a point where you had a similar set of feelings in the past, before this relationship ever began. Now tell the story of that past moment to your partner, so your partner can understand why this event was meaningful for you.

Share your stories—it will help your partner to understand you. As you think about your early history or childhood, is there a story you remember that relates to why this event brought back those memories? Your partner needs to know you, so that they can be more sensitive to you.

Here are some examples. Try to make your meanings more specific—these are here only to spark your own thoughts. Say how you felt and why it's important, and if there is a theme in your history for any of the feelings you felt.

1. I felt listened to.
2. I felt accepted.
3. I felt included.
4. I felt affirmed.
5. I felt calm.
6. I felt proud.
7. I felt I belonged.

8. I felt appreciated.
9. I felt respected.
10. I felt empowered.
11. I felt in control.
12. I felt . . . (other)

Summarizing and Validation

First, summarize what your partner shared with you. Then tell your partner what part of their story and feelings makes sense to you. After summarizing and validating ask your partner, "Did I get it?" and "Is there anything else?"

Step 4—Responsibility: Acknowledge your own role in contributing to what worked. Each partner affirms what they think they did right that made this a positive event.

   a. **What contributed to the positive feelings?**

Share what may have changed in your perspective to foster the awareness of positive feelings. Take turns reading aloud the items that were true for you from the following list.
   What helped?

1. I've been less stressed and irritable lately.
2. I feel more appreciation toward you.
3. I am more aware of what you do for me.
4. I've felt less sensitive lately.
5. I've been less critical lately.
6. I've felt more comfortable sharing some of my inner world.
7. I've felt more emotionally available.
8. I've been turning toward more.
9. I'm not so easily upset.
10. I've been less depressed lately.
11. I've had less of a chip on my shoulder lately.
12. I've been feeling more affectionate.
13. I've made more time for good things between us.
14. I've been a better listener lately.

15. I've asked for what I needed.
16. I've been feeling more positive.
17. I've felt more engaged.
18. I've been better at self-care.
19. I've felt more present.
20. I've felt more confident in myself.
21. I've felt more energy.

   a. **Specifically, what do you feel was your positive contribution to this event? Don't be modest!**
   b. **What do you wish to express appreciation for?**

Thank your partner for what you feel they contributed to this event. Below are some examples, but try to make your statement more specific.

Thank you for:

1. Listening
2. Being sensitive
3. Your help
4. Talking/sharing
5. Being positive
6. Responding
7. Caring
8. Being gentle
9. Other

Step 5—Constructive Plans: Together, plan one way that each of you can maintain what was positive, what worked.

   a. **Share one thing you can do to create a positive event like this next time (focus on what you can do, not on what you won't do).**
   b. **Then, while it's still your turn, share one thing you would like from your partner to create a positive event like this next time.**

Both partners now make agreements about what they are comfortable with in order to continue this positivity moving forward.

The Art and Science of Lovemaking

Next, we'll talk about another way for couples to turn toward one another: romance and sex.

Women and Fear. But before we dive into discussing lovemaking, let's talk about women and fear. Because of our evolutionary history as a species, women have always been the main protectors of our children. Anthropologists tell us that women have typically bonded with one another to take care of all the clan's children as they hunted small game and gathered food for the tribe. They also looked out for one another and kept one another safe. Because of this focus on maintaining safety, women have always had a special relationship with the emotion of fear. Today women are still easier than men to fear-condition, and slower to extinguish to a new conditioned fear stimulus.

Another reason for women's particular sensitivity to fear is that the world is actually much less safe for women and has been for millennia. In the United States, one out of four girls reports being sexually molested or assaulted by the age of 18, and these numbers include only those who report it. The actual percentage of girls who've been molested is probably much higher when nonreporting victims are included.

Over the centuries, women have been raped during wars and during peacetime in every country on the planet. And most of the time, they have been either blamed or punished for being the victim of rape. In some places, women may even be stoned to death if they're married and someone else rapes them. Until only very recently, rape has also been legal within the confines of marriage and, in some places, still is. In other words, with history like this, even women who've not experienced assault or molestation feel more fear than most of the men around them. It's as if they're born with fear in their bones. And the fear doesn't disappear with maturity. Because of these facts, it is no surprise that a major trait that dating women are looking for is a partner who is trustworthy. It is very important to women that the relationship be a safe haven for them, emotionally and physically.

As a result, *women tend to have more prerequisites for sex than men do.* It's no surprise that gay men have the most sex of any couples, heterosexual couples have the next-most sex, and lesbian couples the least.

All of this is explained by the "dual process model" of sexual desire. This model was developed by Erick Janssen and John Bancroft at the Kinsey Institute. The theory is that we humans have a sexual "brake" and a sexual "accelerator." The two systems are independent of one another. Some people have a more sensitive brake, some have a more sensitive accelerator. The brake says NO to sexuality, and the accelerator says YES. (See also Emily Nagoski's superb book *Come as You Are*.) For clients to really know their partner they have to get to know what things activate their partner's brake and what things activate their accelerator. Also couples need to realize that the things that activate the brake and accelerator will vary from day to day. So communication is very important.

Women's **brakes** tend to become engaged when

- there are important undone items on their to-do list, they don't feel emotionally connected to their partner, and/or
- the situation is not clearly erotic.

The brake is activated when women are stressed, or worried, or if they don't feel safe. When the interaction is safe, affectionate, loving, and explicitly erotic, the brake tends to get released. Only then can the accelerator of desire become engaged. For many women touch leads to desire, whereas for many men desire leads to touch. It's very important for each of them to know what kinds of events engage or release their own and their partner's brakes, and also what kinds of events engage their own and their partner's accelerators.

Seven Things That Can Enhance Your Clients' Love Life

Think of everything as sex

Maybe he is washing the dishes and she comes up behind him, puts her arms around him, and says, "*You know, you look so great right now, it makes me want to take your clothes off.*" That can be sex. Or two men get up in the morning together. As they are getting dressed, one says, "*Wow, that's a great color for you; it really compliments your eyes,"* and he gives his partner a kiss. That also is sex. Or they are a lesbian couple and maybe she comes up to her partner and tells her how hot she looks working out. That is also sex. It *is* sex because it's *connecting emotionally and erotically,* and that's what bonds two people together, not just a particular physical act like oral sex or intercourse. If your clients can look at sex in this way, then the transition from talking to an actual sex act doesn't seem that far removed. One behavior is just a natural extension of the other, because they're really touching one another's hearts when they ask their partner what they need. So, during the day they may send one another texts or emails that say, "Thinking of you," or "Missing you," or "I love you." That is also sex. This suggestion emerged from Shere Hite's (1987) book on female sexuality. Her subjects said that they didn't want their partners to focus so much on orgasm, as if it were a goalpost to be reached in a football game. Masters and Johnson's definition of sex as having to progress through four stages, like a conducted musical performance, mostly makes everyone anxious. Also, Hite's data revealed that only 30% of women would have qualified as subjects in Masters and Johnson's research because their subjects had to have orgasms through intercourse. Only about 30% of women do. And those women tend to use sexual positions that involve clitoral stimulation, like the woman being on top.

Steering the definition of what sex is, away from "the standard model," also helps reframe the sexual "dysfunctions" that Masters and Johnson wrote about. Say, for instance, that a couple is making out, and he gets excited and comes "prematurely." Well, nice for him! He's had a good time and there's nothing wrong with that. It's not a dysfunction or a failure in any way. Of course, the partner may raise the question, "So what about me?" But even if the male's penis has softened after his orgasm, his hands and tongue are workable for loving his partner and meeting their needs. It's nothing to be ashamed about. He just needs to know what his partner likes and needs, and the basis for knowing is being able to talk openly about sex. This reframe takes a lot of the so-called dysfunctions out of the medical arena, unless there is physical pain involved.

The largest study ever done about sex is the study reported in the book *The Normal Bar.* Witte et al. asked one question: What is different about people who say they have a great sex life from people who say they have an awful sex life? They studied 70,000 people in 24 countries. Are there differences? Are these differences the same across countries? The answers they discovered were highly surprising. We thought that they would find that people who have a great sex life would be doing things differently in the bedroom, like having more creativity or novelty, or having more anal or oral sex, or trying bondage, discipline, sadism, and masochism (BDSM) sex. But no. Here are their results. In the list below, we have blended their findings with those of two other studies, one done by the late Bernie Zilbergeld and the other a study we did on the transition to parenthood. Both studies asked the same question.

The Baker's Dozen Habits of People Who Have a Great Sex Life Everywhere on Our Planet

1. They say "I love you" every day, and mean it.
2. They kiss one another passionately for no reason at all.
3. They give one another surprise romantic gifts and compliments.
4. They know what turns their partners on and off erotically.
5. They are physically affectionate, even in public.
6. They keep playing and having fun together.
7. They cuddle. Often.
8. They make sex a priority, not the last item of a long to-do list.
9. They stay good friends.
10. They can talk comfortably about their sex life.
11. They have weekly romantic dates.
12. They take romantic vacations.
13. They are mindful about turning toward.

What is amazing about this list is that none of it takes place in the bedroom. These findings reveal that intimacy and romance are not very complicated. Great sex seems to be about affection, love, and emotional connection. Cuddling also appears important—that's good for us, as we have a special couch at home designated as "our cuddle couch." Of the non-cuddlers, only 4% said that they had a great sex life. We know of sex therapists who have counseled their couples to not cuddle, suggesting that cuddling would destroy the "mystery" that heightens erotic feelings. But 70,000 people can't be wrong. After all, cuddling is literally staying in touch.

Couple these results with those of the Sloan study (Campos et al., 2013). These colleagues at UCLA studied a group of dual-career young couples in Los Angeles. They placed video equipment in the couples' homes and simply filmed what went on there. They discovered that partners spent less than 10% of an evening in the same room! An investigator on the project, the scientist Thomas Bradbury, told John that the average amount of time that these couples talked to one another in direct conversation was 35 minutes a week, and most of that talk was about errands, like who would do what when. The lives of these young couples had devolved into an endless to-do list. Their marriages had become managerial partnerships, but their emotional and intimate relationships were getting ignored. If these data are representative, is it any wonder that so many marriages die of sheer neglect?

We are also aware of the fact that many popular books advise couples how to have great sex, but their advice is not research based, and is often wrong. Many parts of our bodies are very complex. The heart is enormously complex. It took William Harvey a lifetime to understand how it beats. The kidneys are extremely complex, and the brain is extraordinarily complex. However, the penis and the clitoris are not very complex. They like being caressed, licked, and sucked. So these physically based sex-advice books miss the boat. Technique isn't so important. What matters most in sex is safety, vulnerability, emotional connection, and love.

1. Suggest to your clients that they adopt the following motto:
Everything positive you do in a relationship is foreplay.

2. Help your clients to create love maps of each other's sexual world.
As the old song goes, "To know, know, know her is to love, love, love her." We couldn't agree more. We have seen so many couples who are trying to

improve their sex lives, and yet they really don't know much about one another sexually, because they haven't had conversations about their unique sensual and sexual preferences. In some cases they might claim to have had these conversations, but one of them has forgotten what the partner said. In therapy we give them a pen and a yellow pad, and say, "Take notes this time and study them." (And humorously:) "It's going to be on the test!" There's another song relevant here: "Getting to know you, getting to know all about you . . . " So this is really an old idea, but with new questions. In the app and the appendix material to this book you will find about 100 questions your clients can ask a woman about her erotic world, and about 100 questions your clients can ask a man about his erotic world.

3. Remember, clients need to know what activates their partner's sexual brakes and what activates their partner's sexual accelerator.

One of the card decks of our free app contains items that help clients answer these questions. Clients can also ask questions that they're simply curious about.

4. Clients need to be comfortable talking to each other about their sex life.

Studies show that conversing comfortably about sex is *strongly* related to sexual satisfaction. And not just contentment with sex, but with the whole relationship in general. Fifty percent of couples who talk with one another openly about sex are satisfied sexually, and also report being satisfied in general with their relationship. On the other hand, only 9% of couples who don't comfortably talk about sex say that they are satisfied sexually, as well as satisfied with their relationship. That's a difference of 41%! These results are not statistically weak; they are dramatically significant. A couple's happiness is strongly correlated with how frequently they talk about sex and how smoothly their conversations flow. Help couples to get started with this process by having them share what they have really enjoyed sensually and sexually with their partner. That will be a little less threatening.

5. Help your clients to create rituals for initiating and refusing sex.

Communication about sex is often fuzzy or murky because people want to save face and avoid outright rejection. However, research indicates that when couples make clear bids for affection and sex, they are highly likely to be accepted with "Yes" (approximately 85% of the time), especially if they are personal (I desire *you*) rather than impersonal (*I'm* horny). This exercise can help clients to decide on how each partner prefers to make known their sexual desires, and how each partner wishes to have sex initiated. It can also help clients to create a method for refusing sex that will feel gentle and respectful and not hurtful. Clients need to be fully aware of the following guidelines:

> IF A PARTNER SAYS NO TO SEX, GRACIOUSLY ACCEPT THEIR REFUSAL RATHER THAN GETTING ANGRY OR PUNISHING THEM.

Studies have shown that the more angry a partner becomes in the face of sex being refused, the less sex that couple will have. And conversely, the more accepting someone is of their partner's refusal, the more sex they will typically have (Buss, 1989).

Thus, suggest to your clients that they not sulk, not act rejected, not whine. The best way to respond to no is to say something like "I appreciate knowing that you're not in the mood." The sex therapist Lonnie Barbach suggested using a 9-point scale for how amorous a partner feels in that moment. The number 1 means "I'm definitely not feeling amorous"; 5 means "I'm convincible. Let's try making out and see where it goes"; and 9 means "I am definitely feeling amorous right now." Get your clients to adopt the following principle:

> "NO" TO SEX DOES NOT HAVE TO END CONNECTION.

Suggest to your clients that they say something like "Thank you for telling me that you're not in the mood for sex. Is there something you'd like to do together instead? Would you like to take a walk? Would you like to cuddle? Do you want to make some popcorn and watch a movie together?"

6. Non-demand pleasuring was one of Masters and Johnson's best ideas.

It's an evening where a couple removes any expectation of intercourse or orgasm, and partners take turns touching, caressing, or massaging the other while the other partner receives the touch for at least 15 minutes. There are no instructions here, except that the person being touched focuses on savoring the pleasure, taking it in, and communicating to the partner what feels good and what they would like. The touch can be slow, or not, playful, or not. The receiver can have their eyes closed, or not. If the couple isn't feeling close, the touch might be simply a hand or foot massage. If the couple feels more comfortable with each other, non-demand pleasuring can be done in the nude. And it's fine to experiment with various sensual stimuli. If the receiver prefers it, a partner can use oils in this exercise, light candles, have music on, or incorporate different textured materials into the touch. It's entirely up to the couple. The touch can be only sensual, or also erotic, depending on the couple's preferences. Suggest to your clients that before switching turns as giver and receiver, they try holding one another to enjoy feeling close and warm. Kissing is also OK. The important thing for the partners is to stay in touch, literally, and to take it in by *savoring* the pleasure they're giving and receiving. If your clients don't follow the instructions to not have sex and they end up having an orgasm or two, they've still had a successful exercise.

7. Talking during sex enhances intimate trust.

Our app suggests things you can say during sex. This list includes I'm all yours; I love touching you; I could kiss you like this for hours; I would choose you again and again; I want to caress your cock; I want to lick you here forever; I love it when you put your hand there; this part of you is so masculine, it turns me on; This part of you is so feminine, it turns me on; I love the way the light is hitting your shoulder; hmm, I love this curve, I want to kiss it; nothing is sweeter than you; and so on. Of course, partners can also say whatever they like as long as their words feel loving and not hurtful. This talking can be expanded to role-playing and fantasy before sex and during sex. After all, imagination is the sexiest part of us.

8. Salsa cards contain suggestions for fun and sexy things to do together.

The Salsa Card Decks are part of our free app. Each card contains a suggestion for couples to try that can spice up their romantic and sexual life. There are three different Salsa decks, with varying numbers of chili peppers designating which of the three decks it is. The first Salsa Card Deck we call "mild" (indicated by one pepper); the second, "medium" (indicated by two peppers); and the third, "hot" (shown with three peppers). The "mild" deck is best used by couples who are not in a place to have an erotic relationship at the moment, but who do want more romance and emotional connection. The "medium" deck is for couples who are comfortable with more conventional erotic activity—for example, intercourse in the missionary position or with a female on top. The "hot" deck is for couples who prefer more experiment, role-play, and fantasy in their sexual life. Have your clients choose which deck they want to work with. And if they choose different decks from one another, have them work with the more mild choice of deck, as no one should feel pressured to do things out of a "hotter" deck that they are uncomfortable doing. Then have each partner choose a suggestion or two from the deck they've chosen. They will share their suggestion choice with their partner. If the partner likes the suggestion, they should talk about how they can integrate that suggestion into their sensual or sexual time together. Where will it happen? When will it happen? Who will initiate it? How frequently will it be done? How long will it last? How will it draw to a close? Your partners are essentially agreeing on an enhancement to their passionate life, and designing it as a ritual of connection. However, if both partners dislike the other partner's suggestion, ask the couple to return to the deck and each pick a new suggestion to share with their partner. This last step may need to be done multiple times until they land on something that they'd both like to integrate into their relationship. Hopefully, this exercise will help to make your clients' sex life more romantic, affectionate, and creative. Here is a list of some of the suggestions drawn from all three lists:

Lovemaking Suggestions
  Talk to each other about your favorite places to be kissed on your body.
  Talk to each other about your favorite places to kiss your
    partner's body.
  Go on a romantic date, just the two of you.
  Go for a romantic overnight, just the two of you.
  At the end of the day greet each other warmly and have a kiss that
    lasts at least 6 seconds.
  When parting, learn one interesting thing that your partner will do
    today and part with a kiss that lasts at least 6 seconds.
  Catch your partner doing something right and convey your apprecia-
    tion or admiration.
  Make it possible for your partner to take an afternoon or a day off to
    do whatever they want or need to do.
  Buy a surprise present for your partner.
  Hug, kiss, touch, caress your partner in the way YOU would like to
    receive affection. If you both do this for a week, notice how your
    partner expresses affection and then do to your partner what your
    partner has done to you. Be gentle.
    – Talk about how and where you most like to be touched for receiv-
      ing non-erotic affection.
    – Unplug the phone for an evening and just talk to one another.
      Try to be a good listener. Remember, understanding must
      precede advice.
    – Plan an evening to have sex with one another. Think about your
      choices for clothing, music, soft lights, and make sure there is
      enough time. Unplug the phone.
  Buy some body oil and plan to give your partner a nice, long massage.
  Buy some sexy lingerie and model it, or get your partner to model it.
  Rent an X-rated video and watch it together.
  Send your partner a love letter or poem.

Buy your partner your favorite perfume or cologne.

Buy your partner their favorite perfume or cologne.

Read an erotic book out loud together.

Buy your partner their favorite romantic music.

Make a secret reservation at a romantic retreat and plan the overnight as a total surprise. Make all the arrangements (babysitting, etc.).

Schedule a session of phone sex with your partner the next time you are out of town.

Make love early in the morning, while the children are still asleep.

Next time you take a shower together, soap each other's bodies.

Call in late to work one morning after the kids are off to school and have an erotic hour alone together.

Have a quickie.

Decide to have sex in a totally new place.

Take turns initiating sex.

Think of what parts of your partner's body you'd like to lick and then write your partner a sexy note about it.

Masturbate to orgasm thinking of your partner and then write your partner a note about your fantasy.

Think of some dirty, naughty, sneaky sex and then write your partner about it.

Talk to your partner during sex.

The countertop in the kitchen is a great place for oral sex. Try it.

Take turns being the dominant person or the love slave.

Play a game of strip poker.

Act out a fantasy of your choice. Dress the parts. Here are some examples:

- Two strangers on an airplane
- Boss and employee
- Professor and student
- Massage parlor worker and customer
- CIA agent trying to turn a Russian spy

Make bets. The winner gets exactly what they want from the partner.

Use whipped-cream spray or chocolate sauce before kissing and licking
   your favorite body parts of your partner.

Have sex even when you're not in the mood in exchange for a slow
   evening of romance of your choosing.

Help your partner masturbate to orgasm.

Have a pillow fight.

It's very erotic to notice, on your own, what housework needs doing,
   and then to do it. On a regular basis.

Have a naked mud fight.

If your partner expresses a clear need, respond positively and
   not begrudgingly.

Try to notice when your partner needs your attention.

Be mindful of when your partner needs to talk, and then be a fabulous
   listener. Ask questions.

Be aware of when your partner needs emotional support. And then be
   an empathetic listener.

Rent a comedy film and watch it together naked.

Talk about what you liked best the last time you made love.

During foreplay, take your partner's hand in yours and show your partner what feels good, and when your partner does that kind of touch
   for you next time, make sounds of pleasure.

Take your time touching one another, with the rule that there will be
   no intercourse tonight, only pleasuring one another.

Don't talk about what you don't want in sex, just talk about what
   you do want.

Describe your partner's favorite body part to them.

Sit at the back of a movie theater and make out as if you were
   teenagers again.

Think of a sexy nickname for your partner.

Give each other a foot massage.

Take turns and kiss or stroke each other's backs.

Pretend you live in another century. Dress up in costume, go out to
   dinner, then make love.

Gently kiss and suck each other's genitals at the same time.
Describe what you love about your partner's face to them.
Light candles next to the bed at night.
Try a new sexual position and talk about how you liked it.
Dress up and salsa dance together at home.
Turn down the lights at home and slow dance together.
Take dancing lessons together.
Pretend you're different animals, like two panthers, and make love.
Kiss the back of your partner's neck.
Sit facing one another and stroke each other's faces.
Sit facing one another and stroke each other's arms.
Brush and stroke each other's hair.

Conclusion

We hope you'll integrate some of these methods into your couples work. As we've noted, it is just as important to help your couple build friendship and intimacy as it is to provide them with methods for better conflict management. And hopefully they'll enjoy these exercises too.

CHAPTER 15

The Devitalized Couple

In this chapter we talk about a type of couple that occupies Quadrant 3, and divorces three times later than the couples troubled by the Four Horsemen of the Apocalypse. This is the devitalized couple.

We've noted that one group of couples, whom John and his colleague Robert Levenson longitudinally followed, divorced an average of 5.6 years after the wedding. These were couples that commonly used the Four Horsemen during their conversations. Another group of "high-risk" couples John and Robert followed, divorced later, an average of 16.2 years after the wedding. When initially videotaped, this group of "devitalized" marriages lacked escalated negative affect punctuated by the Four Horsemen. Instead, underlying sadness, anger, tension, and flattened energy dulled their interactions. Here is an example of one of their typical conflict conversations:

Devitalized Dialogue

Wife: In all the years we've been married, seems to me that you don't know very much about me at all (distressed tone, angry, whining).
Husband: (avoiding eye contact, long pause, then in a neutral voice tone) Yeah, I'd say that's pretty much true about the both of us.

In that interaction, the importance of the husband's response can be seen by imagining an alternative response of a more actively engaged, non-devitalized husband:

Imaginary Husband: Oh no, that's a terrible way to feel. No wonder you're upset. Let's talk about that and put an end to your feeling that I don't know you. I want to know you. It's very important to me.

If you attend carefully to the wife's complaint, you can see that she is actually making a bid for connection, albeit one colored with mild negative affect. For the husband it is an opportunity for connection. What makes this example so dramatic is that instead of responding with alarm, concern, or empathy, the husband responds from inside a cloud of sadness. You can almost hear him sighing in resignation. His words and tone tell her that turning toward her complaint currently exceeds his carrying capacity for hearing her negative affect. Her complaint seems burdensome to someone already buried by too much complaint; he's just not up to "solving the moment" with some empathy and problem-solving. He'd rather simply complain in return.

We aren't the first to describe these couples. Cuber and Haroff (1965) did so decades ago. In these devitalized couples, partners often lead parallel lives while cohabiting in the same house. They rarely speak to one another unless they have to in order to make necessary tactical arrangements. They rarely do things together. They don't have long, satisfying conversations. It is important to note that many dual-career couples are actually at risk for this kind of devitalization. You may recall the Sloan Center, UCLA study we mentioned earlier. Tom Bradbury et al. found that partners in these managerial marriages spent only 10% of their home time in the same room and conversed together, on average, only 35 minutes a week. For the rest of their time at home, moms either interacted with their children or did chores (the notorious "second shift" [Hochschild & Machung, 2003]), while dads either worked or played games on their computers or phones. These marriages strikingly lacked intimacy and romance.

In the international study we recently conducted of over 40,000 couples about to begin couples therapy, 80% of the heterosexual couples said that "fun had come to die" in their relationship, 83% said that romance and passion had disappeared, 55% said that the quality of sex was an issue, and 60.5% said that turning away from bids for emotional connection was characteristic of their relationship. These figures were similar for gay, transgendered, and lesbian couples. Clearly, many couples are like unmoored boats, drifting onto sandbars of disconnection and getting stuck there.

In our lab we could predict the nature of a couple's conflict discussion by analyzing their emotional behavior during their events-of-the-day conversation. It turned out that it wasn't negative affect during this conversation that was important in predicting bad things during conflict. It was the *absence of interest*. This lack of reciprocated interest was also a lack of reciprocated, or mirrored, excitement. These couples were going out of their way to communicate what Erving Goffman used to call "away behaviors" (1959). Away behaviors communicate "I am not here; I am not interested in anything you have to say; I do not share your enthusiasm or excitement or interest in anything you care about; I feel no affection for the things in life that you feel affection for." These communications are often made nonverbally while the partner is speaking. The listener may act very involved in something else like a pen or some other prop, or gaze intently at nothing, even the ceiling.

People in devitalized relationships have shut down. It is our clinical experience that they haven't just shut down their romance, although Michele Weiner-Davis's *The Sex-Starved Marriage* (2003) probably is, in part, describing the devitalized couple. They have shut down emotional connection and being there for one another. They have shut down sharing sensuality, fun and play, desire and sexuality, novelty, adventure, and learning together. They have shut down many of the mammalian affect systems described by Panksepp, which we renamed: (1) the Sensualist, which is about experiencing sensuality and sex; (2) the Nest Builder, which is about creating attachment, friendship, care, and safety; (3) the Explorer, which is about pursuing excitement, adventure, and learning; and (4) the Jester, which is about enjoying novelty, play, fun, laughter, and silliness.

We suspect that this total shutdown in the positive affect systems is why there have been only relatively weak effects of sex therapy for low-desire couples (Hall & Binik, 2020). Low desire is the most common reason that women seek sex therapy. They say, "I've lost my libido," or "It takes a long time for me to get sexually excited," or "I would be content if we never had sex again" (Agronin, 2014). These responses described 40.6% of women ages

16–44 in a British national survey. Low desire increased with age, and was particularly prominent in postmenopausal women. However, in Dutch studies it turned out that these women also lamented the loss of touch that once kindled their desire for sex. This is a very important research finding. Perhaps much more needed to be fired up than just the mechanics of sex. Basson (2002) wrote that 85% of women who reported high levels of sexual libido occasionally started a sexual encounter with no desire, but a little later, experienced *responsive* desire after intimate touch and caressing. In close relationships, sexual libido often accompanies emotional and physical intimacy, but perhaps, for the devitalized couple, treating low desire also requires opening up these other positive affect systems so the couple can enjoy all the delights a relationship can offer.

We begin our clinical work with the devitalized couple by a slow opening of the couple to one another. We begin by building friendship. We work first on talking and building curiosity in one another, and helping them to ask open-ended questions. Then slowly work toward increasing their vulnerability during self-disclosure, and discussing deeper topics. This often leads to conflicts they've buried but now feel more ready to address. Tools for managing conflict are introduced, followed by unearthing gridlocked conflict issues they may have closeted from each other and themselves. As these are worked on, dreams surface. Sex may be one of these issues, although not always. Harvesting these issues yields greater intimacy and, in turn, may lead to creating a very different marriage, in which a new sense of meaning and purpose is their final reward for hard work done.

Let's take an example. Julie worked with what we'd call a classic devitalized couple. They came in after 17 years of marriage. Jacob (both names changed to ensure confidentiality) worked for a think tank. Susan worked at home, parenting their three kids and running their domestic life. They lived in an 8,000-square-foot house, big enough for one to be working in one wing after work hours, while the other managed the lives of their kids plus her volunteer duties elsewhere in the house. He often left for work at 6 a.m. to get a workout in before landing for his 12 hours in the office. She rose with the kids an hour later, fed them, got them out the door, then did the meal planning, grocery shopping, directing of the housecleaners, and on Wednesdays and Fridays, dispensing food-bank produce. Both their lives were incredibly busy.

Their presenting problem? "We haven't had sex for 8 years, since we conceived our last son." (They had an older and younger son with a daughter in between.) She said, "I don't mind." He said, "I kinda do."

In assessing their questionnaires, it was clear that they were quite unhappy. Both their Locke–Wallace scores hovered in the high 50s. (This questionnaire measures marital satisfaction, with a midpoint of 100 and a standard deviation of 15.) All their friendship and intimacy questionnaires registered as challenges. But their conflict-management scores showed up as strengths. This was a case, however, where those scores were strengths because the couple AVOIDED all conflicts, and thus lacked displays of the Four Horsemen, gridlock, and other indicators of poor conflict engagement. Most striking was their Love Maps score. Both partners noted little to no knowledge of each other, with neither feeling known by the other. That was, as they say in poker, a "tell." The emotional distance between these partners was as broad as the Atlantic. And as cold.

As they described in their Oral History Interview, Jacob and Susan had met in a bicycle riding club after both completed graduate school. Both had busy careers in business. They had fallen in love, and married quickly. They were terrific companions, especially when it came to international travel. They loved it—the more exotic, the better. Together they'd weathered tropical monsoons, desert hikes, storm-ridden sailing trips, and hordes of mosquitoes. Jacob had wanted to prolong this lifestyle—hard work and harder play—for the entirety of their marriage. But Susan wanted children. After many lengthy discussions, as Susan put it, "I won," and they had their first son a year later. Susan was then 34. Two other kids followed, quickly. Like many dads of the day, Jacob thought his duty as a father meant being an even better provider. He began to work more and more hours, 6 to 7 days a week. Soon his contributions at work were noted, and he soared upward in the organizational ranks. But with grander titles came more responsibility. Work swamped him. He started traveling extensively, alone. Still, he enjoyed it immensely. If he had any weekend time free, he devoted it to house projects—cleaning gutters, repairing shutters, planting shrubs.

Meanwhile Susan appreciated his hard work—at least for a while. She'd grown up working class, and loved the security and luxuries Jacob's work provided. Mothering had been a lifelong dream for her. And now she got to do it with no worries about money. Plus, volunteer work compensated nicely for the occasional boredom she experienced, especially during the years when the kids were all under 7.

But now the kids were 15, 13, and 12. They each had their activities after school, and often didn't arrive home until 6 or 7:00 themselves, just like their dad. Susan grew more lonely. She wondered, "I don't know what happened to us. We used to have so much fun. Now I'm lucky if I go to bed and he's still awake. We never spend time together. I eat with the kids. Leave him dinner in the microwave. He gets home later. I go help the kids with homework and then check my email. I stay up late afterward watching shows. He doesn't like any of them. I finally go to bed around midnight."

Jacob piped in, "Yeah, I hate watching TV. And I don't have time for it anyway. I might catch a moment to say good-night to the kids. Then it's finishing up the day's work and to bed early so I can get up at 5 to start again the next day. Not much of a marriage."

And here was the amazing fact: This couple had not had one date, one conversation, even a pleasant chat, for at least 5 years that they could remember. If anything, it was ships passing: "Hi." In reply, "Hi." Period. Not even a review of checklists. That's how ironclad their roles were. Her role: duties inside the house and kids. His role: projects outside the house and job.

So, our first task? Help them to have a conversation for at least 10 minutes when he returned home from work. They planned it as a ritual of connection. Ten minutes felt awkwardly long for a couple whose exchanges totaled maybe a minute a day. Julie needed to coach them on HOW to have this conversation. They should start by asking each other questions about their day, then listen, and at least maintain eye contact and nod their heads in response. Susan was a far better conversationalist than Jacob. Julie gave him our pamphlet *A Guide to Great Listening* for ideas of how to respond with questions, statements, and empathy if called for. The first week they succeeded in 5 out of 7 nights conversing . . . for just 10 minutes. It felt a little phony at first, but grew less stilted as the nights progressed. Susan began to ask Jacob in more detail about his work: his projects, his likes and dislikes of colleagues, his meetings. She began to grasp how stressful work was for him, but how stimulating, too. He learned more about the kids—their school activities, friendships, worries, and triumphs. Also, her volunteer duties at the food bank. He felt a tinge of pride in her. The kids were doing beautifully, despite hardly ever seeing their dad. And her volunteerism represented values he believed in. These conversations slowly lengthened to 20 minutes, then finally topped out at 30. It was time for a date.

Jacob and Susan used to love fine foods. In session they made a list of restaurants to try—a different one every week. But they feared looking like one of those couples in cafés who sit across from one another, silently staring into space and saying nothing. Julie introduced them to both the Love Maps Card Deck and the Open-Ended Questions Deck. They returned from these dates stunned at how little they knew about each other. And how eager they were to find out more. Susan gleefully learned that Jacob wanted to build furniture out of the trees they'd felled when building their house. They needed some! Jacob discovered Susan's yearning to take the kids to Africa. She wanted to pop their fantasy bubble that the rest of the world lived like they did. How else could they become conscious contributors and not just greedy takers? Jacob was gently reminded that Susan's life purpose was to take her privilege and spin it into the gold of kindness and hard work. How about digging wells and crafting an irrigation system for a village starved for water? They could all participate, learn, and form bonds that could last a lifetime. Jacob liked the idea! A surprise for them both.

After several months of rediscovery, conflicts began to bubble up. Susan wanted more weekend time with Jacob, especially in activities with the kids. All three were on swim teams and had meets most Saturdays. Couldn't he come watch? No, he needed to get his house projects done.

Susan: Phooey on the house projects. Don't you want your kids to know you care? And you're proud of them, even if they don't win?

Jacob: I do care. They know that.

Susan: I don't think they do. How would they? You're constantly gone, just an absentee father they hardly ever see.

Therapist: Jacob, how are you feeling hearing that?

Jacob: Crappy. I'd love this conversation to be over.

Therapist: Susan, you may be sabotaging getting listened to, here. You're starting to focus on what you don't want, rather than what you do want. And that sounds like criticism. (Jacob nods his head.) Why don't you try it again, and focus on what your positive need is this time.

Susan: OK . . . I'd love it if you came to at least a few of the kids' swim meets, and I bet they would, too.

Therapist: Any feelings you want to add to that request?

Susan: I'm not sure . . . (long pause).

Therapist: How about if I jump in and help out a little? (She introduces a Dan Wile intervention.) I'd like to try to be your voice, Susan. That means I will pull my stool up next to you, and speak to Jacob as if I were you. But you, of course, are the expert here. You know best what you're feeling. So if I get it wrong, I'd like you to interrupt me and correct what I'm saying, because I want to make sure I'm getting it right. Does this sound OK? (Susan nods her assent.)

Therapist: (Now speaking directly to Jacob as if she were Susan) Jacob, the bottom line is I'm lonely. I love going to those meets. Most of the parents are there, and I've even made some new friends since we see each other every week in the stands. But mostly they both come—dads, too, or both moms. I'm always the one alone. It makes me sad. Sad, not only cuz I'm alone, but because the kids look up at the stands, and all they see is me, not you. They haven't said this, but I imagine they're hoping that one day they'll see you there. And you'll be yelling and cheering for them. And if they win, what a great moment for them if you're there to see it. (Drawing from history Susan had shared earlier) It reminds me of Dad having left us when I was so little, and then remarrying someone else and loving her kids but somehow not us. It's really painful. Our kids? They miss you, too—a lot, just like I do. You may not know it, but they adore you, Jacob. They look up to you and really want you to know them. They're growing up fast, Jacob. Pretty soon they'll be leaving home and gone. And then what? They love you, and they want to know that you love them, too. And that takes time given to them. What I want most is for you and me to be close, and for you to be closer to the kids, too. They'll enrich your life, Jacob. I'm sure of it. (Then, turning to Susan) Did I get that right?

Susan: There's a little more.

Therapist: OK, good. Why don't you try adding that in, and any rewording you might like to do of what I've just said.

Susan: I'm also angry, Jacob. Or maybe just embarrassed and ashamed, because I'm one of the only ones sitting alone up there. It's as if I'm a single mom, just like my mom. But I'm not. And then I imagine others see me and think, "They must have a pretty bad marriage if he never shows up with her." Ugh. That may not be truly what they're thinking, but still, it's my fantasy. And the angrier I get, the more distant I get. And I don't want that. I want us to be a family that is close, that comforts each other if something goes bad, and cheers together if things go well.

Therapist: Jacob, can you try first summarizing what you heard Susan say and add in what I said as well?

Jacob: You're sad, and, I guess, angry that I never go with you to the kids' swim meets. You feel embarrassed, too, that you're always sitting alone. You think the kids may be missing me, too. You want me to go with you to some of these meets. And you want us to be a closer-knit family. Is that about right?

Susan: Pretty much. Don't forget the "lonely" part.

Jacob: Well, it all makes sense to me. I get why you feel lonely, and sad, and ticked off. I guess I would, too, if I were you.

Therapist: Jacob, can you hear the love in what she's saying? If she didn't love you, she wouldn't care whether you were there or not, except maybe for the kids' sake, and not for her sake. But that's not what she's saying. She wants you by her side—no one else. She wants your companionship, your being by her side to experience everything about those meets—the kids' efforts and sometimes, even, the kids' wins. Susan, would you say that your wishes are coming from a place of love?

Susan: It feels scary to say that but yes, there's love in there. Why else would I want you with me?

Jacob: Huh, I didn't really think of that. I just figured you were mad at me.

So I was scared to go. I figured you might use the time to put me down or tell me what else I'm doing wrong.

Susan: Well, speaking of wrong, that's definitely wrong! No, if you were there I'd love it! We'd be together—parents together, cheering our kids on. It would be so fun. What's more important than that? It would be wonderful.

Jacob: That's a different story. But what about the house projects?

Susan: I don't care about the house projects. I care about you and I being close, and the kids knowing you love them, too. That's what really matters.

Jacob: Just shows what a lousy mind reader I am. Let me look at my calendar, and I'll pick some Saturdays where I can come.

Therapist and Susan together: Yay!

From there, the couple began to do even more together, both with the kids and by themselves. It was a slow-building process. They worked on creating meaningful moments they could weave into their daily existence. We call these rituals of connection, times together when they knew what was going to happen, because they'd co-designed moments like these and had committed to doing them regularly. Their closeness grew. They worked on expressing more fondness and admiration for each other. And after learning how to raise their needs in a healthier way, they vented those, too, paying careful attention to turning toward as much as they could, rather than turning away. During one weekend away from home, Susan decided to initiate sex. And joyfully, their sparks were rekindled. It was awkward at first, too. But not for long.

CHAPTER 16

Making Individual Dreams Come True and Building the Shared Meaning System

This chapter talks about how to help couples explore their individual life dreams and make their shared meaning system intentional.

Our attention to the shared meaning system recognizes that when we enter into a lifelong committed relationship, we will be building a new life together with our partner, a life that ideally can be lived with intention, meaning, and purpose. In many cases, we will raise children together, we'll create our own family culture, and we'll form a new social network or community. Together or individually, we may choose to identify with a neighborhood, religious center, political movement, artists' group, or sports team, any group based on a central purpose or geographic location. We may call a nation home, or hope to in the future, but ultimately we are all citizens of the world. How, as therapists, we can help the couples we see to choose a meaningful life journey for themselves is the theme of this chapter.

One powerful way to encourage our couples to create a life of meaning and purpose is to introduce the question "Who are you as a couple?" and plant the seed of their answering that question with intention rather than leaving it all up to chance.

Let's talk about several exercises we can help our couples to do in this very important domain of a relationship. We will talk about this as a four-step process.

- *Step 1.* Make Individual Life Dreams Come True
- *Step 2.* Create Rituals of Connection
- *Step 3.* Create Shared Goals and Support Individual Goals
- *Step 4.* Support the Roles We Play

Step 1. Make Individual Life Dreams Come True

There is a story about Alfred Nobel, the originator of the Nobel Prizes. In 1888 Alfred's brother, Ludvig, died while visiting Cannes, and a French newspaper erroneously reported the death in an obituary for Alfred rather than for Ludvig. In other words, they got wrong which brother had died. The obituary condemned Alfred for his invention of dynamite. It said, "Le marchand de la mort est mort" ("The merchant of death is dead"). It went on to say, "Dr. Alfred Nobel, who became rich by finding more ways to kill more people faster than ever before, died yesterday." Imagine getting to read your own obituary! We can imagine that Alfred was stunned and deeply saddened by what he read and concerned about how he would be remembered after he actually did die. This incident is said to have brought about his decision to create a much more positive legacy to leave behind. He dedicated the money he made from the explosives he patented to funding Nobel Prizes, including the Nobel for peace.

In this exercise ask your couple to individually review the following questions, pick two to answer, and jot down some notes regarding their answers. Then have them share their answers with each other. The listening partner can ask questions about the other's answers, but only for clarification and understanding, not as a challenge to the answer. They should treat this conversation like a brainstorming discussion, in which no one spills sour milk on the other's ideas. This exercise can be done in your office or at home. The questions from which each partner selects two to work on are the following:

1. Over the course of your lifetime, what are you hoping to accomplish?
2. What are your own current life dreams?
3. Do you have a mission for your life? If so, what is it?
4. How do you want to be remembered when you are gone?

Then have them share their answers with each other. Finally, each partner should ask the other person the following question:

• How can our relationship support your dreams?

Step 2. Create Rituals of Connection

The ritual of connection is a method for turning toward one another that is reliable and can be counted on. Both partners create it, so it has meaning and is pleasing for both. Each one knows what to expect, and what their roles will be during the ritual. Nothing is left to chance. It may be a simple ritual, such as how the couple greets each other at the end of the day, or a more significant ritual, such as how birthdays and holidays are celebrated. A valuable book that explores this topic is William Doherty's (1999) book, *The Intentional Family*. It's also important to select a ritual of connection that has personal meaning for both partners. There are *formal* rituals of connection and *informal* rituals of connection. You cannot have too many of them.

Formal rituals involve events that happen repeatedly every week, month, or year, like Thanksgiving, Ramadan, Hanukkah, Christmas, Lent, Easter, New Year's Eve, birthdays, anniversaries, confirmations, bar and bat mitzvahs, Father's Day, Mother's Day, family meetings, Valentine's Day, weddings, the Sabbath, the regular worship cycle for the couple's religion, and funerals, for example. For each of these formal events the couple can design their own ritual for celebrating or honoring the event, one that has personal meaning for them. In that way the yearly holiday cycle will contain repeated events that have deep personal meaning for both partners. In our own life we have redefined the meanings of Thanksgiving, Passover, the Jewish High Holidays, and our birthdays and anniversaries to have special meanings the two of us believe in. It's been joyful to do that together over time, and then look forward to this very personal event in our yearly calendar every year for the past 37 years.

The informal rituals involve events that can be designed to have personal meaning as well. For example, leave-taking at the beginning of the day and reunions at the end of a day. Here are some of our personal rituals of connection: breakfast for the two of us is a ritual where John arrives in the kitchen first, empties the dishwasher, gets the breakfast food out, and makes coffee. He knows just how Julie likes her coffee. Then he makes his own breakfast. Julie first walks and feeds their dog, then puts away dishes in the dish drain, makes her breakfast, and cleans up the dishes and kitchen after breakfast. While eating and sitting together, they start with an emotion check-in over coffee, asking one another, "What's on your heart and mind today, and what's on your calendar for today?" Then John reads the *New York Times* and Julie usually reads *The Week, Discovery* magazine, or an architecture magazine. They exchange information if they come across something interesting. Dinner is another one of their favorite rituals of connection. John usually makes dinner, and after dinner they clean up the dishes, move to the den, get on their big blue "cuddle" couch, and watch British people getting murdered on TV (John's favorite). They also cuddle. An international study on sex found that of all the non-cuddlers in the world, only 4% of them said they had a great sex life. We take that finding very seriously.

Other favorites for us are romantic overnight road trips, usually to a romantic small hotel where we hike, kayak, visit art galleries, and savor good food. And we also take a two-week "annual honeymoon" trip in the summertime. When our daughter was 8, she went to "away camp" for the first time. We decided we should take ourselves to camp, too. For 22 years, before the COVID-19 pandemic, we traveled to the same Canadian B&B with our kayak and rented the same room. And when Canada reopened its border, we started up this ritual again. Along with favorite activities during our honeymoon, we ask each other three questions: (1) What was difficult for you about last year? (2) What did you love about last year? and (3) What do you want next year to be like? We also take along the Open-Ended Questions Card Deck and share our answers to all of its questions. We really use the time to think through the year and then we actually make the changes we decide on. This is our one big vacation per year. It's always been romantic and magical.

Here are some other events that can become rituals of connection for a couple.

1. Leave-taking at the beginning of the day
2. Reunions at the end of the day
3. Mealtimes
4. Family meetings with the kids
5. Eating out
6. Weekly romantic dates
7. After-meal (or after-kid-bedtime) catch-up conversations on your day
8. Stress-reducing conversations
9. Evening cuddle time
10. Bedtimes and saying good-night
11. Morning rituals
12. Dates and getaways
13. When one of you is sick
14. Celebrating a triumph
15. Grieving a setback
16. Rituals for entertaining friends
17. Cooking together
18. Learning something new together
19. Rituals for keeping in touch with family, kin, or old friends
20. Vacations
21. Initiating lovemaking, and saying no
22. Talking about your sex life
23. What should a weekend be? Rituals for weekends
24. Rituals for fun and play
25. Rituals for exercise
26. Rituals for adventure

To work with this exercise in therapy, each partner picks out a card from the Rituals of Connection Card Deck. Then, between the two choices, they pick one on which to focus. Again, if they each disagree with the other's choice, it's time to pick two more cards and see if one suits both partners, since no one should be forced to do something they don't want to do. After just one is chosen to work on, the couple discuss that ritual by discussing together their answers to the following questions (they can write down their answers if that's helpful):

1. What is meaningful to you about this ritual?
2. Who should initiate it, and how will initiation be done?
3. What will happen during the ritual? Who will do what?
4. How long will the ritual last?
5. If money is spent for it, how much?
6. How will the ritual end?
7. How often will this ritual occur?
8. Putting it all together, describe your unique ritual.

Make sure the couple can commit to practicing their ritual as they planned. If one partner can't commit, it may be that they actually didn't like something about the ritual's design. See if they can identify what felt uncomfortable for them, and have the couple review their answers to that detail until the ritual is redesigned to suit both of them.

Step 3. Create Shared Goals and Support Individual Goals

The selection of personal goals and goals for the relationship can be something the therapist guides the couple to also make intentional. Have them ask one another the open-ended questions that follow. This exercise can be spread over several sessions.

1. What would you like our lives to be like in 5 years, and how would that be meaningful for you?
2. What in your life feels incomplete, and why?
3. What adventures would you like to have over the next 5 years?
4. What would you like our family to have accomplished in the next 5 years?

5. If you could change one thing about the way we live now, what would it be, and how would that change make a difference for you?
6. As you look over your own individual life, what goals do you have for yourself in the future?
7. What is your vision for our family?
8. What is your personal vision for yourself?
9. What challenges do you foresee for yourself in the immediate future?
10. How would you change our home, and if our home is changed, how do you see that improving our life?
11. What financial goals do you have for yourself and for us?
12. What educational, training, job, or career goals do you have for yourself?
13. How would you like your personal spiritual life to change?
14. How would you like the spiritual life of our family to change?

Step 4. Support the Roles We Play

This is a potentially powerful way of creating or enhancing shared meaning. Have the couple list all the roles they play in life: (1) husband, wife, or partner; (2) son or daughter; (3) father, mother, or caretaker; (4) sibling; (5) homemaker; (6) career, job, or professional role; (7) friend; and (8) community (or communities) member, or leader.

For at least two of these roles, have each person share what help they need from their partner in order to feel supported in all the roles they play. Use a speaker–listener format of the Gottman–Rapoport Blueprint for these conversations. (Each partner describes help they may need in a positive way rather than criticizing or blaming their partner for past lack of support. While listening, the other partner jots down notes, then summarizes what they heard the speaker say, and concludes with a few words of validation.)

The discussions described above often yield a rich harvest of shared meaning and deep connection. Both partners should be encouraged to be as open as they can with their answers. No criticisms should be allowed. Ideas about purpose and meaning, rituals of connection, goals, and roles often emanate from heartfelt core needs and beliefs. They are fragile, and may have been quashed by others in one's past. Individuals may have even been taught that they have no right to satisfy their dreams or that they're not competent enough to fulfill their goals. So, these exercises offer the opportunity for the couple to do some healing of past negative experiences, which in the long run can make a big difference for the relationship. Here's an example from Julie's practice:

A middle-aged white woman came into therapy. She presented as profoundly depressed. Despite having a loving husband and two middle school-aged twins, she felt suicidal and said that she had nothing to live for. She also lacked the energy to do any of her usual activities: cooking, housework, volunteer work, chauffeuring the kids, helping them with homework, and so on. We'll call this client Mattie. Julie referred Mattie to a psychiatrist for an evaluation to consider medication. Antidepressants and a mood stabilizer were prescribed. For the first 6 months, Julie saw Mattie twice a week, with suicide-prevention contracts in place to keep her safe.

In reviewing Mattie's history, most striking was her clear memory of being sexually abused by her father from age 9 to 11. He worked as a psychiatrist, but was also alcoholic. It was during his binges that the incest occurred. Mattie had never forgotten these experiences. She still suffered from PTSD concerning them, and had for many years. When she described the events in session, her body erupted with sensations matching what would be expected during such experiences. Julie worked with Mattie individually for a year, and eventually also placed her in a group therapy facilitated by Julie for incest survivors, which had been ongoing for 6 years. Together the two components of her therapy helped counter her feelings that she was worthless, stupid, and dirty, that she was to blame for the incest, that she harbored evil darkness within her, and that no one wanted her alive. (In the interest of brevity, Julie won't go into full detail of Mattie's treatment in that first year.)

Eventually Mattie's depression subsided, and her PTSD symptoms surfaced much less frequently. Mattie expressed her wish to now work on her marriage, which had obviously been stunted by her PTSD and depression for many years. Mattie refused to see any other therapist, and her husband was fine with Julie's conducting the therapy. And so, the work began.

Mattie's husband, Joe, was a municipal administrator of a child-welfare department. He had had a relatively normal childhood, and loved Mattie deeply. For the last year, he had taken on all of Mattie's tasks, and was now running pretty ragged with fatigue. The work started with a couple's assessment, then my learning more about him. Friendship building and conflict-management work followed along with identifying both his and Mattie's needs for the relationship. Mattie worked on a more energized approach to fulfilling Joe's needs (with the exception of sex, which came much later), and Mattie also spoke more of needs she had only recently realized she had. One of these was returning to college. She had graduated from a state university, but only just barely, given that she drank her way through all four years of it. She said she'd really learned nothing. Now she was curious: Would there be some field that would kindle curiosity and a passion for learning? Fortunately, Joe was all for it. They worked on establishing routines that would enable Mattie to take classes, two a quarter, as a returning student.

This was a perfect time to work with the "creating shared meaning" interventions. They began with the Life Dreams exercise. Mattie spoke of the love she'd had for school in her early elementary school years, and how she'd read every book their little library had to offer. But her drinking began in high school and only worsened during college. Thus, she felt that she'd lost most of the parts of her education that could have been most meaningful for her. Marriage swiftly followed graduation, plus the two kids, which fortunately led to her shedding her drinking habit. But over time her depression set in, her energy drained away, and a gray malaise settled over her life. Now, finally, she said her energy had returned and she wondered, was she maybe smarter than her college GPA of 2.0 suggested? (Julie knew she was. So did Joe.) By going to school she could find out. This was the one individual dream she held close. She also hoped to discover a potential career path for herself now that the kids were getting older and in a few years would be leaving for college themselves. In the Life Dreams exercise, Mattie responded to the request for Joe to support her dream by voicing her desire to have Joe do a little more of the chauffeuring and cooking, though not nearly as much as earlier. Joe agreed to do so, as long as pizza was a frequent choice! Mattie laughed and said, "Sure." Joe's dream was to have Mattie accompany him to some work events, where he often stood out as the only man alone without his wife. He wanted to present himself to the administration as a "family" man with a strong and stable relationship, especially since his job involved bolstering the welfare of troubled families. He believed that the image of personal family success might help him garner a promotion. Mattie agreed to go to two events a year of Joe's choosing. More than that might feel overwhelming, given her hopefully impending schoolwork.

We next worked on rituals of connection. They chose dinnertimes as their discussion topic. Currently everybody ate at separate times. The twins, who were now in high school, went into their own rooms and immersed themselves in video games while eating. Mattie ate earlier, before the kids got home from extracurricular activities, and Joe ate alone after returning from work. Joe described his wish that dinners together be a time to download from the day, to put the difficult day's events to bed, and to celebrate the day's triumphs. Mattie nodded, and she said that would be lovely, and would give them both a chance to keep up with the internal worlds of their kids as much as they were willing to share—their friendships, classroom and sports activities, and crushes and romances. They agreed to sit down together with the kids to announce this change, and to ask the kids, too, about what ideas they had to make dinners more family-like. They wanted their dinners to include each person detailing the "highs and lows" of their day, and noting anything they'd learned that was either puzzling or exceptionally interesting. More freewheeling conversations could proceed from there. The only exceptions to eating together would be work commitments or the kids' sports or social activities coinciding with dinnertime. Weekends could also be a little looser, since the kids had friends they might want to see, and Mattie and Joe occasionally might want to go out on a date or with friends. Mattie and Joe also thought the kids might want to eat quickly and not linger long. So, it was OK if they were excused a little early, but only after participating in the dinnertime check-in, provided their check-ins were not rushed and rudimentary.

In the next session, the couple cheerfully announced that they'd met with the kids, who agreed to the dinnertime ritual as long as they didn't have to listen to lengthy, lingering conversations after the check-in. And one twin insisted the family dog would get to have a turn, too. That translated into the kids getting to feed him scraps under the table once a week, a practice now curtailed. And one of the parents taking over the dog's nightly walk after dinner. OK. Those kids were good negotiators. The first week practicing their ritual went well, with one exception, where one of the kids insisted their dog get to sit at the table, too. Uh, no. He left the dinner a little too early that night. The next night was better.

Joe and Mattie continued with that ritual, reporting back that they learned a lot about the lives of their kids that had remained underground. Like one having a crush on "an older woman" (she was 16, the twin was 14). This was salaciously reported by one twin about the other. The other was fuming, but admitted it was so. The twin with the crush later got back at the other twin by gleefully reporting that the first one had been called out for detention, a fact his parents didn't know. So much for keeping secrets. Meanwhile Joe did get the promotion he wanted, and Mattie absolutely loved school, especially her science courses.

Finally, the couple tackled the exercise on shared and individual goals, coupled with discussions of the life purpose each partner claimed as their own. Mattie's goal was to finish college, as she had stated earlier, and to embark on a vocational path for herself. She wanted to accomplish this goal not only for herself but also for her husband and kids. Once traveling down her path, she imagined she could add to the family's income and financial stability, and contribute to the world whatever strengths she could offer, which at this point remained unknown. She could also role model for the kids that anything was possible, at any time, and that women were capable of both raising kids and having a career. Her life purpose? To finally become a contributing member of society, giving back to the world as she'd been provided for, for so many years—especially by her husband, whose love and willing support had literally kept her alive during her darkest days.

Joe had already accomplished many of the goals he'd set for himself, including moving up in his agency, having enough influence there to make more of a difference to the families it served, and raising their kids to be decent, moral, and caring individuals who, someday, would meaningfully contribute to their own communities. His future goal was to get Mattie through school, as far as she wanted to go, and to keep channels open with the kids in order to support their successful launch into adulthood. And what did he want his legacy to be? The kids eventually establishing careers that they could be passionate about, and finding mates with whom they could build beautiful families of their own. With maybe a few grandchildren thrown into the mix.

And the goals of the relationship for them both were to resume a fulfilling sex life, in time, cherish whatever time they had on this earth together and with the kids, and to imbue their lives with much more fun and adventure than they'd previously had. As they'd had none for decades, that would be an easy one. Seeing the wildlife of Africa would be at the top of their list, maybe traveling there sometime in the next two years. A wonderful dream!

As it turned out, after several years, Mattie finished all her classes to win another college degree, this time in geology. In one class she even earned the highest score the professor had ever seen on a very difficult test he'd given every year since first teaching. This professor insisted Mattie apply to graduate school. She did so, in urban planning, combined with geology. Soon after graduating with a master's degree, she got a terrific job in her chosen field with the city.

Despite Mattie's terrible, traumatic past, she and Joe successfully resurrected an all but dead relationship, and concluded their work by filling their hearts with meaningful dreams they had lived and accomplished, with more to come. They were well on their way to creating the legacies they longed to provide for their children and community.

CHAPTER 17

Rebuild Trust and Commitment: Treating Affair Couples

This chapter talks about how to treat the greatest violation of trust in a relationship: an affair.

There are many ways of destroying trust. The biggest destroyers include affairs, domestic violence, other betrayals and attachment injuries, and addictions. In this chapter we will explore the world of affairs: why they happen and how to treat them.

Treating Affairs

What do we really know about helping couples who are trying to save their marriage after an emotional and/or sexual affair? Very little, as it turns out. There have been over a dozen books written with couples therapy programs for how to help couples recover from an affair. None of these books were based on scientific studies of the ways couples build versus erode trust, or how they maintain loyalty versus create betrayal. We figured we had to first understand these basic processes before designing and evaluating a therapy for treating affair couples who want to rescue their relationships.

Fortunately, there were clues provided by prior research and insightful clinical writing. First, Gigy and Kelly, in the California Divorce Mediation

Project, reported that affairs were based less on finding a sexual partner than on solving the problem of loneliness. They claimed that divorce often follows a couple drifting apart emotionally. We know a lot about loneliness from epidemiological research. James House published a landmark article in the prestigious journal *Science* documenting the fact that everywhere on the planet, loners, lonely people, die young, much sooner than people with friends, good social support, or a spouse. The late John Cacioppo, who was one of John's teachers about psychophysiology, studied loneliness in his lab, and he discovered that lonely people are very unhappy, and far more negative when meeting a stranger than non-lonely people. Cacioppo discovered that lonely people are also stressed and chronically physiologically aroused, which suppresses their immune system. There has got to be no greater and more devastating loneliness than loneliness while in a relationship. We conclude that loneliness is probably the greatest cause not only of divorce but also of affairs.

The late Shirley Glass's 2004 landmark clinical book on affairs, titled *Not "Just Friends,"* also suggested that extramarital affairs result from the reversal of "walls" and "windows" in a relationship. In a healthy relationship, Glass stated, committed partners open a window between them that allows for continuous transparent communication. A functional couple also encircle their relationship with a strong wall that protects the relationship from outside intrusive forces, like an affair. In contrast, when one partner opens their window to an outside individual that creates intimacy between those two, while erecting a wall that blocks off transparent communication with their original partner, that's the setup for an affair. Walls and windows have become reversed, Glass suggested. She also observed that marriages with an affair have invariably avoided conflict, meaning the partners haven't raised their discontents *with* each other. Initially, they're doing this to avoid bad fights. But conflict avoidance means none of the relationship problems or unmet needs are addressed, let alone solved. Eventually, a partner may grow so lonely and disgruntled that they zero in on an interested stranger, who is quite happy to listen to their marital complaints. It may be a barista, a colleague, or a bus commuter like them; it can be anyone. The unhappy partner's loneliness may be relieved by conversations with this stranger, while the two are drawing closer over time. Eventually, their simple conversations turn into more, and here comes the affair.

Glass was also the first person to maintain that the betrayed partner will suffer a PTSD reaction once they discover their partner's betrayal. This is very important to understand. Here's why. Many of the therapies for treating affair couples include efforts to control or down-regulate the hurt partner's anger, humiliation, fear, and despair to prevent the betrayer's running away from the therapy and, ultimately, the relationship. We believe that this approach risks dismissing or minimizing the strong emotions a hurt partner will naturally feel and want their partner to "get." The hurt partner wants their pain to be met with deep remorse. But that can't happen if the pain isn't honestly expressed. Glass suggested that the hurt partner's emotional state is only natural, given the PTSD embedded inside them now.

Interestingly, very few affairs become actual long-term relationships; only 3% to 11%. Also, marriage to the affair partner doesn't guarantee happiness; 75% of them divorce. Their major issue? Ironically, that issue is trust.

So, since trust is so important, let's first see if we can understand what creates trust. First, trust involves a molecule, what Paul Zak called the "moral" molecule. You'll see why it's called that in a moment. The molecule is oxytocin. Oxytocin has been called the "cuddle hormone," because we mammals secrete oxytocin when we hug for more than 20 seconds, when we kiss for more than 6 seconds, or when we cuddle. We also secrete oxytocin after an orgasm. Women secrete oxytocin when they deliver a baby and, afterward, when they are nursing the baby.

It also turns out that oxytocin is related to commitment. Scientist Susan Carter, a friend of John's, studied two types of rodents, the prairie vole and the mountain vole. The prairie vole is monogamous; it mates for life. The mountain vole is promiscuous, and doesn't mate for life. However, if mountain voles' brains are injected with oxytocin, they suddenly become monogamous. It is also the case that oxytocin reduces the activity of the brain's fear centers, the amygdalae.

Paul Zak, in his brilliant book *The Moral Molecule*, studied the role of oxytocin in building trust. He used a lab method called the trust game. There are two players in this game. Let's call them John and Julie. Each player is given $10 at the start of the game. In this game, if John gives any amount of money to Julie, it automatically triples in value, and the next move is Julie's to give anything or nothing to John; whatever she gives also triples. Most people playing the trust game give about $5, which usually gets reciprocated. If John gives $5 of his $10 to Julie, then Julie will have $25 (triple John's gift of $5 = $15 plus Julie's original $10), and John will have $5. In the next move, if Julie gives $5 back to John, then John will have part of his original money (now $5), and his new $15, for a total of $20. Julie will also have $20 (25 − 5 = 20). They have each wound up gaining money. By trusting one another to reciprocate, they both gained. They began with $10 each, but now they each have $20. However, if John and Julie *team up* and John gives Julie all of his initial $10 (then she winds up having $40 = $30 + her original $10), and Julie then gives all of her $40 to John, John winds up with a whopping $120, and Julie is left with nothing. When they share, they both end up with $60, maximizing their gains. John gifting Julie with his entire original $10 requires John trusting that Julie will reciprocate his gift. It models commitment as well, because they have put all their eggs in one basket. It's smart to team up and to trust. The results prove highly equitable. Potentially. So, teaming up maximizes trust, commitment, and mutual gains.

As we mentioned, the average amount people actually give in this game is a little under $5. So, we can conclude that most people are fairly trusting. Notice that this is not at all logical, because they could potentially earn a lot more (proving that many economic decisions are often not rational). That fact has led to the emergence of a new, fascinating field called "behavioral economics." Here are some findings with the trust game. Women suffering from borderline personality disorder give nothing in the trust game, but only if they are playing with another person. If playing with a computer, they give an average of $5. For these women, no person is to be trusted, but a computer, maybe . . .

Now as to why it's called the "moral molecule." If you spray oxytocin up people's noses, they will give more money than $5, but not the entire $10. So, oxytocin makes people more generous and compassionate to the person they are playing with. They will be fair, and more just, more moral. By the way, Zak found that it's possible to accomplish this same effect with a 20-second hug. A former postdoc of John's, Guy Bodenmann, discovered that if one sprays oxytocin up the noses of couples before they have a conflict conversation, they will also become far more positive than couples whose noses are sprayed with neutral saline (harmless salt water). John keeps some bottles of oxytocin beside his therapy chair, but he has yet to use it. He's saving it for that couple who won't back down from their attack mode, like the couple in the film *War of the Roses*.

By the way, it's interesting that oxytocin is also the molecule of bad judgment. In a Swiss study, also by Guy Bodenmann, people who had oxytocin (versus saline) sprayed up their noses were more likely to give their money away to a well-dressed person posing as a banker who said, "If you give me your money, I will quadruple it, or, I may decide just to keep it and give you back nothing." Compared to the group that had saline sprayed up their noses, this seemed like a good deal to those who had oxytocin sprayed up their noses. John calls this the Bernie Madoff effect, after the psychopath who suckered his own friends and clients into his Ponzi scheme. Since we secrete oxytocin after every orgasm, these results also suggest that we might consider holding off on having orgasms early in a relationship, because it may cause us to ignore some of the red flag danger signs this potential partner is actually signaling. There's a warning totally based on physiology.

The Trust Metric

So, what does this all have to do with treating couples recovering from an affair? Well, the game-theory thinking that Paul Zak described helps us to be able to define and measure trust, and create a valid trust metric. What is trust? It's thinking for two. It means behaving in such a way that the choices one makes maximize the benefits of both people. It's thinking that gets us to the $60 per person in the trust game. And in John's research lab it means that when we use the rating dial as a measure of "payoff," or benefits, behavior coded with the SPAFF emotion codes line up with maximizing the positivity of the rating dials of both people. That leads to John's trust metric, which can be computed in any conversation for which we have both SPAFF and rating dial data. In the book *The Science of Trust*, John validated that trust metric.

However, understanding trust isn't enough. We also have to understand the role of commitment versus betrayal. Because an affair doesn't just destroy trust. It also destroys commitment and loyalty.

But how can we study things as elusive as commitment and betrayal in a laboratory? The brilliant researcher Caryl Rusbult provided us with an answer. She was a student of Harold Kelley, who had originally introduced game theory into psychology. Using a new questionnaire she created, Caryl measured a variable called Comparison Level for Alternative Relationships, abbreviated CL-ALT. How does this mighty CL-ALT variable work? Rusbult's idea was that we are always comparing the payoffs or benefits we receive in our relationship with the payoffs or benefits we might receive in other, real or imagined, alternative relationships. If we see this relationship of ours wanting, we then evaluate the investment we've already made in it, against the benefits and costs of leaving it and entering into a new relationship. Then we decide—to have an affair or not, how much to invest in this relationship, or whether or not to cross boundaries, like flirting with a stranger. Rusbult's investment model is the only research in the world that can reliably *predict* an affair in heterosexual couples. All other research on affairs has been post hoc, where people later try to recall why they had the affair. Post hoc accounts are clearly unreliable and notoriously biased. That's why Rusbult's model was such an outstanding accomplishment.

Rusbult also described some of the processes by which affairs are avoided, using her investment model. When couples describe their complaints to their partner, they are simultaneously building loyalty.

Rusbult's couples who build trust and commitment. Here's what these couples do: They cherish what they do have with this partner, while minimizing the importance of what they don't have. They therefore nurture gratitude for what they have with this partner. They proudly believe this relationship is superior to any other potential or actual alternative relationship. Like in ideal strategy in the trust game Paul Zak used, they have invested everything they have in this relationship. Commitment, Rusbult claimed, means putting all your eggs in one basket, the relationship. When an uncommitted couple has an argument, CL-ALT of course rears its head and they think, "Well, I believe that I can't do better. I have invested everything I have in this relationship. This is the love of my life. I will give voice to my complaints to my partner." Then they confide in their partner what they feel upset about and what they need. That kind of thinking builds trust, loyalty, and commitment.

Rusbult's couples who erode trust and commitment. On the other hand, when partners erode trust and commitment, and build toward betrayal, they have invested much less in the relationship. They minimize what they have with this partner and maximize what they don't have with this partner. In that case, after an argument with the spouse, CL-ALT rears its ugly head, and they think, "I *can* do better than this relationship. Who needs all this unpleasant conflict?" They've nurtured resentment for what's wrong with this partner, and think they can do better. They are then more likely to turn to someone other than their partner, and they then complain *about* their partner to someone else, not *to* their partner. By giving voice to their complaints to someone else, that person then might even become a possible alternative partner. While confiding to a sympathetic and available other alternative partner, in their mind they may tell this sympathetic other person how trivial is what they do have with their current partner, and in their complaints they might maximize what is missing for them. That kind of thinking erodes loyalty and commitment. Still, they now feel less lonely because someone else is actually genuinely interested in them and their plight, probably much more interested than their spouse. That thinking could give them permission to cross boundaries. They glumly think that their spousal relationship is probably inferior to other possible or actual relationships. In their mind, they are nurturing resentment for what is missing with their spouse, rather than nurturing gratitude for what they do have.

That very clear theoretical picture was Caryl Rusbult's huge contribution to our understanding of trust, commitment, loyalty, and betrayal. These ideas echo what Shirley Glass uncovered. John also helped the late Peggy Vaughan do an online survey of couples who had either stayed together or divorced after an affair. Vaughan discovered that couples who try to get past the affair and just move on are much more likely to divorce than couples who have thoroughly talked about the affair: when, where, and how it happened, why it happened, and how to strengthen and affair-proof their relationship in the future.

The Betrayal Metric

That prior research, plus the basic research on the trust metric, enables us to understand what couples do to build or erode trust over time. John also created and validated a "betrayal metric," which measures how couples build commitment and loyalty, versus betrayal, over time. John's betrayal metric measures the extent to which their lab conversations resemble a zero-sum game, defined as a near perfect negative correlation between partner rating dial numbers. In other words, one partner's high rating numbers are zeroed out by the other partner's low rating numbers, signifying that in the conversation, one person feels like they're winning while the other partner is losing. This zero-sum game obviously points to a power struggle. John's research found that affairs and other betrayals occur most commonly in relationships that have this zero-sum game, power-struggle dynamic.

Treating Affair Couples

All of this work on trust and betrayal led to a clinical intervention designed by the two of us for treating affair couples, which we are now testing in a national randomized clinical trial with Paul Peluso of Florida Atlantic University. The intervention is called the **atone–attune–attach model**. From here on out, we will refer to the betraying partner as the "involved partner" (meaning the partner involved with the affair), or IP, and the hurt partner's identity will be abbreviated as HP.

In general, the Gottman method couples therapy (GMCT) assessment always includes two individual sessions, in which one of the questions asked is whether or not this partner has had an affair in the past or is having one now. If there has been an affair, either past or present, this person is also asked whether or not they've disclosed it to their partner. If they haven't, the therapist tells them that the therapy cannot continue unless the partner is told. The therapist does NOT keep an affair secret; otherwise, the therapist is effectively colluding with the IP, the one who had the affair, against the more clueless partner, the HP, and contaminating the therapy with dishonesty. Therapy should be grounded in truth, not secrecy. Also, if the affair is ongoing, it must be stopped before the therapy can continue. If not stopped, the IP is working with one foot in the marriage and the other in the affair. Again, this is a setup for failure.

When the IP is first told these conditions (by the way, we include them in our disclosure statements but also remind the clients of these parameters in their individual session), there is often strong objection. Most of the time the IP is terrified that if the affair is disclosed, the IP will be rejected and abandoned. We empathize with the IP's fears. But we also state that affair recovery is indeed possible, that we've seen it accomplished many times. What is needed is to eventually rebuild trust with this same partner in order to create what we call "Marriage 2." But to rebuild trust there must be total honesty and transparency. Without it, you'll just be building a house of cards.

Most IPs agree to reveal the affair, but it may take two or three individual sessions to get there. If the IP absolutely refuses to disclose the affair, we tell the IP that therapy must be discontinued. If the IP doesn't want to terminate the therapy unilaterally, in a final session, we meet with both partners and tell them that at this stage, couples therapy appears to be "premature"; we suggest individual therapy for each person instead. Out of 25 years of treating affairs, this has happened only once for Julie. If the conditions have been met for continuing therapy—that is, any affair has been stopped and any and all affairs have been disclosed—the next conjoint session consists of explaining our atone–attune–attach therapy model for recovery. Now the real work of rebuilding can begin.

In the *atone* phase of therapy, analyzing the marriage itself is set aside for now (but not forever). Discussing the HP's contributions to the tone of the marriage risks the HP feeling blamed for the affair. It's one thing to be maritally unhappy; it's quite another to choose to have an affair. Instead, this phase of the therapy is more one-sided. The HP is given the opportunity to ask the IP any questions they wish, and the IP must answer them with absolute honesty and transparency. However, the HP is cautioned to not ask questions about the specifics of the affair's sexual activity, since the answers are bound to create more intrusive images in the mind of the HP, who presumably is suffering from PTSD. The HP is also supported to express whatever feelings the affair has caused, but without the use of criticism and contempt, since these two Horsemen will sabotage the IP's listening to the HP. The therapist needs to carefully monitor these conversations and support both partners, not just the one who has been hurt. Support for the IP can take the form of empathizing with how difficult it is for them to hear the HP's feelings, and checking in with them on how they're feeling throughout the process. Above all, the therapist must not stand at a pulpit and morally judge the IP. There's no place for judgment in affair recovery. Healing can begin only by the IP initially listening and offering empathy for the HP's pain. This phase of the therapy can take as long as needed—sometimes only a few sessions; other times, a few months or even a year.

Once the HP has had their questions answered and believes that the IP is truly remorseful, the *attune* phase can begin. In this phase the limitations of the relationship (often loneliness) are revealed and an alternative to conflict avoidance is taught using the three Gottman conflict blueprints (the Aftermath of a Regrettable Incident, the Gottman–Rapoport, and the Dreams Within Conflict With Compromise). Often there are many failures or attachment injuries that must be fully processed. Old gridlocks are also coaxed from beneath the rug into the open where they can be explored and understood. Extensively using the Dreams Within Conflict intervention is important here, for it deepens the understanding of each other's enduring vulnerabilities. Compassion can then warm the relationship. Methods of attunement are also taught for enhanced emotional connection, such as how to ask deeper questions, and how to express empathy. Recreating friendship is the goal. The couple may co-design new rituals of connection that include date nights, expressing appreciations daily, and engaging in stress-reducing conversations as needed. It's important to note that sometimes during this phase, the HP may get triggered again inadvertently (e.g., if the IP doesn't call the HP to say they're coming home late, due to their phone running out of juice). A repetition of the IP reassuring the HP that there is no affair, that the HP is the "only one" for them, and listening to the IP's remorse again may be needed. But gradually, as Marriage 2 grows stronger, the couple is ready for the third phase of treatment.

The goals of the *attach* phase of therapy are to solidify friendship, identify personal dreams, create shared meaning, and engage slowly in erotic intimacy. Most often, but not always, the HP avoids sex until they're good and sure the IP is now trustworthy, which often takes extensive time in the attune stage. Sexual intimacy should never be pushed. Otherwise, things may backfire. Sometimes, after the first intimate time or two, the HP's PTSD may again raise its hoary head, necessitating more work on reassurance and remorse. But eventually, sex again can resume more comfortably and naturally. Finally, in this phase, the couple makes a new commitment to their marriage. Many couples choose to honor their pledge with a ceremony they design together. Either private or with others present, this is often very meaningful for the couple—a symbol that their recovery is complete.

The atone–attune–attach model is manualized, and a workshop called Treating Affairs and Trauma is available from the Gottman Institute (TGI) an online learning program. It details the atone–attune–attach model and illustrates its phases with clinical films. We and many of our therapists have used this treatment method clinically for about 20 years. Initial results of our randomized clinical trial are promising. Please stay tuned for a more complete report in the future.

Case Example

Let's talk about a case now. Hal and Jillian had been married for 14 years. Together they owned a retail clothing boutique. Twice a year Hal traveled to different Asian countries to order their next round of textiles, styles, and manufacturing. Hal usually made these trips alone, as Jillian was a "homebody" and preferred staying home. Jillian also had a teenage son from a short-lived first marriage. She was reluctant to leave him for the weeks these trips lasted. As the years passed, Jillian and Hal's sex life had diminished slowly until it dwindled to a trickle. Jillian grew suspicious. Was Hal having "some fun on the side?" she wondered. She finally stepped up her courage and asked him if he was having affairs while traveling. He adamantly denied it. She asked again 3 months later, then again, 9 months later. Still, the answer was no.

In exasperation, Jillian hired a private detective, who followed Hal on the U.S. leg of his travels, and to the Asian countries he visited. Sure enough, Jillian was right. The detective reported that Hal was seeing prostitutes at each city stop. But in Tokyo, there was a woman designer he seemed to favor. He'd fly to her whenever he had a few spare days. This time, upon his return home, Jillian confronted Hal with tears, incriminations, yelling, and a few objects thrown his way. She told him about the detective she'd hired, and with no doubts now, there could be no denials. Swiftly she packed a large suitcase, told her son to pack one, too, and they flew out the door to stay in a hotel while she scanned ads for an apartment. Hal was devastated. And guilty. He begged her to return. "No way!" Over the next 6 months, this scene was repeated. Finally, Jillian agreed to at least try marriage counseling before filing the divorce papers she'd already had drawn up. She had no doubt it would fail. Hal had contacted Julie.

As they entered Julie's office for their first appointment, the tension was hot. At any moment, it might boil over and burn down the office. Julie had asked the couple to fill out the Gottman assessment questionnaires before their first session. She reviewed these, and—sure enough—every level of the Sound Relationship House (SRH) was broken and destroyed. The only level with above-average positive scores was love maps. The remaining friendship, conflict management, and shared meaning scores were abysmal. Julie had learned from Hal's initial phone call that affairs were the issue. So she had expected this. It was typical of couples with affairs, especially ones only recently discovered.

In their first session, Julie listened to their narratives and what they hoped therapy could do for them. Jillian had little hope that therapy would make any difference. But if she didn't at least try, she felt like she'd be running away too soon. This was her last-ditch effort to salvage some shreds of what they'd had. At a minimum, maybe therapy could aid them to decently co-parent their son if they divorced. She highly doubted the marriage could stand again after this knockout punch. Hal desperately hoped they could work it out. Their lives were so entwined together, in business, parenting, and land holdings, that a divorce would be awful and messy. He didn't want that. And besides, he really loved Jillian. He hated the thought of losing her.

"You should have thought of that before, buddy," mumbled Jillian. She gave a sardonic laugh.

Next, they detailed their history, individually and together. Jillian had been raised by a schizophrenic mother. Her father had abandoned the family when she was 5. Mom had good times and bad times. During the good times, things felt relatively normal. But when Mom stopped her meds, she would sink into paranoid fantasies. The characters on TV were planning her demise. People were whispering about her on the streets, outside her window, even in the apartment next door. She feared her food was poisoned, so she would eat only Saltine crackers. She'd soon dwindle to near nothing, an emaciated skeleton. Jillian fed herself, dressed herself, got herself to school. She told no one of her home life. When she was 10, there was a knock on the door. A woman from social services entered and scanned the filth all around. She'd been alerted to strange doings by the next-door neighbors. (Turned out they WERE talking about her.) Mom was taken away to a hospital, and Jillian wound up in foster care. At 18, many homes later, she had finally emancipated herself, gone to work, and never looked back.

Hal was raised in Lebanon, the son of a businessman and stay-at-home mom. His family had remained intact, despite his father's constant womanizing. "It was just part of the ordinary business world," Hal explained. Being the youngest of three sons, the "baby" of the family, he had been spoiled by Mom, given everything he wanted. All three sons were expected to join in the business. But Hal rebelled. He purposely did poorly in school, got into trouble, and occasionally dabbled in vandalizing buildings along with his best buddies. Dad would punish him with a stick and words of contempt. But it made no difference. Hal migrated to the United States for college, and then wrangled a green card to stay indefinitely.

The couple had met several years after college. Jillian was working as a barista, barely getting by. She had just left her first marriage to a marine, with whom she'd had her son. The marriage had turned violent after his return from the Gulf War. Meanwhile, Hal had inherited enough money from his grandfather to sustain him. Their courtship was passionate and short. They married 8 months after first meeting. They bought a boutique together, and soon developed a thriving retail clothing business. It specialized in exotic clothing made in various Asian countries. At first, Jillian had accompanied Hal on his trips to Asia with her son in tow. But soon the trips were timed for when the boy was in school. No more trips for Jillian. According to the detective's investigation, the affairs had started soon after.

It was time for Julie to offer feedback from their assessment and to describe a pathway forward. She delivered the bad news about the SRH scores by stating only what were challenges or strengths. She normalized the number of challenges facing them and noted many other affair couples she had treated that had successfully recovered. Even one with 57 affairs and counting! There was hope for this couple, too.

Now it was time to describe the atone–attune–attach model. Julie went into detail about how the atone phase worked. Jillian would be allowed to ask Hal any questions she had. He needed to answer them with absolute honesty and transparency. Otherwise, the therapy was guaranteed to fail. Marriage 2 could be built from the ashes of Marriage 1 (their pre-therapy marriage), but only on the solid ground of truth. Hal would also need to listen to Jillian's feelings about the affairs he'd had and to express profound remorse for them. There was no other way to heal from affairs than to go through them and all the pain they had wrought.

Julie also explained that Jillian was suffering from PTSD caused by the affairs. In her individual assessment session, she had reported suffering intrusive thoughts that were like fantasized flashbacks, nightmares, sleeplessness, severe depression, and hypervigilance every time they were together. If they had contact outside these sessions and Jillian wound up yelling and accusing him once more, it was likely that PTSD was in the driver's seat. Jillian didn't want these thoughts to come up and derail her. She just couldn't help it. This was normalized, too.

Once the atone stage was complete, the attune stage would follow. That would be the time to examine the marriage itself, and to reshape it into a much healthier relationship. Finally, in the attach phase, if the couple actually reached it, new commitments would be made to one another, loyalties proclaimed, and consequences defined if more affairs were to occur.

In the next session, Jillian brought in an entire thick notepad filled with questions. This was going to be a l-o-n-g atone phase. Jillian jumped in with question after question—where did this happen, when, for how long, how many women, how did they meet, did he ever pick up a sexually transmitted disease (STD), did he fall in love with any of them, how much money did he spend on them, what gifts did he buy them, and so on. Hal seemed to be answering each question honestly. (You never know for sure.) This process went on for 10 months! Much longer than usual, but then again, with so many different women Hal had slept with, that made sense. Jillian also zeroed in on the woman in Tokyo. She was a Japanese businesswoman—one of the suppliers for silk that he'd met. He liked her. And she obviously liked him. She'd pursued him all over the continent, flying to many of the cities he visited. Jillian cracked open when hearing about her. She cried and cried. Once she left the office halfway through the session. And did not return. Julie called her the next day to offer empathy and ensure that she was OK. She came back for the next week's session. She never missed one afterward. Julie described flooding to both of them. Jillian admitted she had definitely been flooded when she'd left the week before.

Jillian needed a lot of help to translate her accusations, criticisms, and contempt into expressions of her feelings. At first, Julie used the Dan Wile exercise to role model for her what feelings might sound like: "I was so devastated. What I was told by the investigator absolutely destroyed me. I wasn't sure I could go on. It was only thoughts of my son that kept me from jumping off a bridge. I'd given everything to you—my heart, my dreams, my bank account. . . . These betrayals have broken me—shattered me." With two episodes of Julie voicing for her, Jillian eventually was able to voice her own feelings. However, gentle redirection was needed when she'd slip into criticisms again. Julie also supported Hal with empathy about how hard it was to face Jillian 's feelings. At one point, Hal said he'd dreamed of being hung from a lamppost to die, just swinging there. Julie interpreted that perhaps the person who'd hung him up there was himself—the part of him that felt so guilty about hurting Jillian so badly. Hal repeatedly said how terrible he felt, so wrong were his betrayals. He voiced shame and apologies countless times.

Finally, Jillian was satisfied with his answers and his apologies, although it was hard for her to take them in. But her acceptance was good enough. It was time to put the marriage under a microscope in the attune phase. At first Hal was reluctant to attribute any fault to Jillian. Julie said that in this phase, the purpose wasn't to figure out who was to blame. It was to examine the dynamics between them, and to reformulate those in a healthier way to create a Marriage 2 that was satisfying for both of them. Hal finally admitted that he felt deeply criticized and unappreciated by Jillian. It seemed like he could never do enough to please her. When he finished one project at their home or in the store, there was never a thank-you. Just an "OK, here's what I want you to do next." Jillian was the boss, not something they'd agreed upon, but something she took on for herself. Hal had learned in childhood not to express any negative feelings, especially to an authority figure like his dad. And Jillian, it seemed, was just a fill-in for him. Over the years his resentment had grown into a smoldering fire. The trips he took were his only escape. He'd feel guilty when he got home but would rationalize to himself that he deserved the nice attention these women on the road gave him.

Jillian was shocked. She hadn't realized how critical she had sounded all this time. And at times, contemptuous, too. She acknowledged that she hadn't voiced gratitude to Hal for all he did—for the business and for her. She pointed out that she had carried the weight of caring for both herself and her mom when Mom was sick. And of course, no one ever thanked her, especially her mom. It hadn't occurred to her that Hal would need to even hear gratitude from her. And come to think of it, she never heard it from Hal either. But it didn't matter to her—she was used to that. Now, she thought, maybe they both needed to hear it.

At about this time, the couple decided to live together again. They had been having weekly dates for a few months now, and those had gone fairly well. Maybe they should try for more. No sex, mind you, but at least cohabitation. Jillian gave up her apartment and she and her son moved back home.

The couple had also had a long-standing gridlocked problem about how to parent Jillian's son. Julie introduced the conflict blueprint. Jillian wanted more emotion-focused gentle care and negotiation with her son. Hal thought he should have been far more disciplined all along, and needed much stricter consequences for negative behavior now, like a low GPA. In conducting the Dreams Within Conflict exercise, each partner's background showed up as deeply relevant. The boy had been 2 years old when Hal came on the scene.

Thus, Hal considered himself like the boy's father. He believed the child should receive much more discipline than what Jillian delivered. Spankings were a good idea. Hal had gotten plenty of them and had turned out just fine. But, Julie pointed out, perhaps he hadn't. After all, he never raised his marital complaints with Jillian, perhaps because he believed he'd be punished for daring to do so. His father had slapped him whenever he talked back or mentioned anything negative that he felt. So he'd learned to shut up and just go do what he wanted to do. Yes, he'd get badly punished for those actions. But it was worth it—at least those acting-out episodes gave him a way to vent his anger. Now, it was almost too late, the boy was about to turn 16. Hal considered him to be a part of his own legacy, his life purpose. He wanted his son to understand—the world is a tough place, and you wouldn't get away with lax behavior. It was an all-or-nothing world out there.

Jillian noted that no one had ever given her limits. And she'd wanted them. But more so, she just wanted a parent who cared enough about her to put her needs first. She had never felt that from anyone—her mom or any of her foster parents. It was a very lonely upbringing. At times she even felt like an orphan—sad and hopeless. There was no way she wanted her son to feel that way, nor, for that matter, to be raised with harshness. And to her, hitting a child, even giving a mild spanking, was dead-on wrong. She believed in listening, in understanding and empathizing with her son's feelings. And then redirecting him. Harsh punishments weren't necessary. And in fact, their son was doing well enough. Not perfectly, but well enough.

It turned out, both partners had similar goals for their son: to become a good citizen, to pursue a career he enjoyed, and to one day give them grandchildren. (They both laughed at that one.) Only, Jillian wanted him to learn how to be emotionally intelligent and sensitive. And Hal wanted him to be disciplined and tough enough to withstand the vagaries of the world. Both made sense, given their backgrounds.

Following this work, the couple focused on compromise. They actually had very similar wishes and dreams for their son, which were stated in both their inner circles. And there was lots of flexibility in what behaviors needed limits, and what the consequences would be if those limits and rules were violated. Once understanding and compassion entered in on how their backgrounds had shaped their beliefs, a reasonable compromise was much easier to achieve. Grounding him was OK, but not for months at a time. Taking away a phone was good, too. Curtailing attending a party? Fine. And remaining open to negotiating with their son on what limits made sense to all of them.

As conflict management was smoothed out, turning toward was stepped up, and fondness and admiration were vocalized more often, it was time to work on the attach phase. That meant the couple approaching a sexual relationship once more. (It had been 18 months by now.) Jillian was game to try. But after their first time having sex, Jillian suddenly grew more critical again. Julie pointed out that, in fact, beneath the criticism, Jillian was probably very afraid of the vulnerability she felt having sex with Hal again. And criticism was a powerful way to distance from him again. Jillian owned that, and described how she imagined Hal returning to his lovers and leaving her again. These were natural fears, probably exacerbated by Jillian's PTSD. And yes, it was a scary step to get intimate again. Hal needed to give Jillian lots of reassurance. And perhaps their erotic life should be taken more slowly. Simple explorations of each other's sensuality might feel good, before intercourse was attempted. Jillian liked that idea, and Hal agreed that would be OK with him. Two months later, intercourse was tried again. This time, they both agreed, it felt great. And a month after this step, they began to plan a recommitment ceremony, just for the two of them—no guests. Therapy finally ended. It had been a 2-year-long journey but, all agreed, definitely worth it.

The atone–attune–attach model has been manualized, and a workshop called Treating Affairs and Trauma has been made to portray the concepts and the therapy at work. Films include Julie's work with two highly distressed couples. The Gottman Institute has also made this workshop into an online learning program. Hopefully, final results of this study will underscore the effectiveness of this treatment model.

CHAPTER 18

Treating Situational Domestic Violence

This chapter talks about treating one of the greatest worldwide problems in relationships—domestic violence; and treating the most common form of it—situational domestic violence.

Treating the Major Form of Domestic Violence (DV)—Situational DV

Domestic violence (DV) is a worldwide problem. There is also great underreporting of DV. Yet, despite this underreporting, a UNESCO report concluded the following. The percentages of women who had been physically abused in romantic relationships: in Canada, 29%; Chile, 26%; Egypt, 35%; Japan, 59%; Kenya, 42%; Korea, 38%; Mexico, 30%; New Zealand, 20%; Nicaragua, 52%; Poland, 60%; Uganda, 41%; United Kingdom, 25%; United States, 28%; and Zimbabwe, 32%. Part of the problem involves cultural beliefs. In a UNICEF survey, the percentage of women ages 15–49 who say that a husband is justified in hitting or beating his wife were, in Ethiopia, 81%; Guinea, 85.6%; Jordan, 90%; Laos, 81.2%; and Zambia, 85.4%.

Unfortunately, domestic violence worsens when women are pregnant. A full 33% of DV is estimated to occur during the woman's pregnancy. The Centers for Disease Control and Prevention (CDC) estimates that 300,000 pregnant women are abused every year in the United States. Pregnant women who are physically abused are much more likely than other pregnant women to experience high blood pressure, miscarriage, stillborn birth, and premature birth; 12% of all maternal deaths are caused by physical battering. In the UK, 25% of babies are at high risk from infant abuse due to battering.

In our large international study of couples beginning couples therapy, over 60% of heterosexual couples reported some form of DV. But what type? Are all types of domestic violence the same?

No, they are not.

Researcher Michael Johnson (1995) identified two types of domestic violence: situational and characterological. In the following discussion, which largely addresses heterosexual relationships, the perpetrator is referred to as male, given this is true in a very high percentage of cases.

Two Types of Domestic Violence

In characterological DV, there is a clear victim and perpetrator. The perpetrator externalizes blame, and believes that his partner's harsh words justify his violence. The perpetrator may have antisocial or borderline personality disorder. Nothing the victim does either starts or terminates the violence. Also, in characterological DV, the victim fears the perpetrator, and is controlled, socially isolated, demeaned, humiliated, threatened, and sexually coerced by him. The violence in characterological DV creates serious harm and injury, and is more likely to involve a gun or knife. Compared to cases of situational DV, victims are more likely to wind up in shelters. On the other hand, in situational DV there is no clear victim or perpetrator. Both partners are equally likely to initiate and participate in the violence, and both partners think that the violence is wrong. Both partners take responsibility for their part in the violence, show remorse, and want to change. The violence causes only minor physical injury, with conflicts that do not escalate to the intensity or physical damage typical of characterological DV. Johnson pointed out that research on DV is highly biased. One set of writings comes from family survey research. Calls are randomly made to homes, and questions are asked about DV. These surveys mostly elicit information about situational DV. And about 40% of families hang up in response to these calls. The other set of writings comes from advocates who have experience with women in shelters, so this writing oversamples victims of characterological DV. Shelter advocates have had greater political power than family survey researchers. Jacobson and Gottman's (2007) data supported Johnson's typology of DV.

Characterological Domestic Violence. We prefer the term "battering" to describe characterological DV. Anne Ganley (1995) wrote that "battery is a form of abuse where the primary aggressor employs violence ranging from pushing to relationship rape, to homicide, to enhance the aggressor's *control* over the partner, leading the partner to modify their behaviors in daily life. It is meant to instill fear and intimidation." Battery is common only in characterological DV.

Eight myths persist about battery in characterological DV. These myths include:

Myth 1: Both men and women batter. The truth is that battery is overwhelmingly male, and women are more likely to be injured, tend to sustain greater injury, and are more often hospitalized, or killed.

Myth 2: All batterers are alike. Actually, they are not. Jacobson and Gottman discovered two types of characterologically violent perpetrators. The first we call the "pit bull." He is pathologically jealous, tends to have borderline personality disorder, is terrified of abandonment, is domineering in marital interactions, and is violent only toward the victim. He tends to lead with his forehead. He socially isolates his victim and gets physiologically flooded during their relationship interactions. The second type we call the "cobra." He is completely resistant to influence, is antisocial, is violent to others in addition to the victim, is belligerent in marital interactions, and is physiologically calm or even below baseline during marital interaction. He tends to lead with his chin. The cobra is also more likely to be physiologically calm when talking to law enforcement compared to the victim, and is more likely to elicit a benevolent response from police.

Myth 3: Battering is caused by alcohol and drugs. The truth is that although alcohol often plays a significant role, a great deal of battering does occur when the perpetrator is sober. Also, marijuana has an inhibiting rather than facilitative effect on violence (Leonard, 2007).

Myth 4: Batterers can't control their anger. The truth is that either domineering behavior or belligerence, rather than anger, characterizes batterers. There is no evidence that battering is an anger-management issue. This may be why anger-management groups fail at changing battering behavior. Instead, battering is triggered by a need to assert control.

Myth 5: Battering often stops on its own. The truth is that in our 9-year longitudinal study, battering did decrease in frequency, but this effect was illusory, because once total control and domination was established by the perpetrator, only vestiges of threat were now needed to elicit control through the victim's fear. Furthermore, psychological abuse continued unabated.

Myth 6: Psychotherapy is effective at treating batterers. The truth is that no therapy has ever been developed to end battering. Male batterers are often con artists, and therapists are notoriously poor at spotting liars.

Myth 7: Women provoke men into battering them. The truth is that in a sequence analysis of detailed reports of battering incidents there was nothing the victim did to either provoke or terminate the violence. This myth fundamentally blames the victim for the abuse; this is why couples therapy must be avoided for treating characterological DV.

Myth 8: Women who stay in abusive relationships must be crazy. The truth is that women do leave abusive relationships at a higher rate than the population average. Economic dependence is often a reason for staying. Our exit interviews showed that what needed to precede the victim's exit was a last-straw (usually near-death) incident, and the woman's contempt of the man, which indexed her renewed belief that the man would not ever change.

The Jacobson and Gottman 9-year longitudinal study had four groups of couples: happy and nonviolent, unhappy and nonviolent, unhappy situationally violent, and unhappy characterologically violent. One of our first findings was that no situationally violent couple ever graduated to become characterologically violent.

Most Domestic Violence Is Situational. In a second finding, using survey researchers to recruit couples, the percentage breakdown of situational and characterological violence was 80% situational and 20% characterological.

Situational Domestic Violence. Unlike characterological violence, which involves a clear perpetrator and victim and is marked by controlling and dominating behavior, situational violence is reciprocal in nature. Situational violence is characterized by mutual, low-level physical and psychological violence perpetrated by both partners that occurs somewhat infrequently (on average, every other month or so). It may take the form of pushing and shoving, for example, that is physical in nature but is not severe enough to cause injury. In addition, the intent with such behavior is not to control, dominate, or assume ownership over one's relationship or partner, as is the case with characterological violence. Also, situational violence has not been found to escalate into more severe forms of physical assault over time. It is believed that situational violence may occur between couples who lack conflict-management skills and thus resort to becoming psychologically and physically aggressive as a means of conflict resolution (Johnson, 1995, 2006; Straus & Smith, 1990). Thus, violent couples typically exhibit such behaviors during problem-solving interactions. In most situational violence, both partners take responsibility for their part in the violence, and the couple want to stay together, change their behavior, and improve their relationship.

As researchers and therapists, we had two problems to solve.

The first problem was a measurement problem. There is so much shame in reports of marital satisfaction that it cannot be used as an outcome measure by itself. Even with nonviolent couples, Tom Bradbury once wrote a paper titled "Why Do Happily Married Couples Divorce?" The answer he proposed is that measures of marital happiness are highly flawed. When he also used *observational measures* of marital interaction during conflict, these so-called happily married couples showed their unhappiness in their negative affect interaction patterns. This problem with shame in self-reporting an unhappy marriage is magnified when studying domestic violence. We had learned this from our 9-year longitudinal study. Thus, we knew that we had to use archival police records of violence as well as self-reports like the Straus Conflict Tactics Scale to more accurately measure the presence of situational violence. We also needed to measure physiology and gauge emotional behavior using the video-recall rating dial as well as relationship satisfaction self-report measures of violence. In the 1990s, to accomplish these goals we created what Robert Levenson calls a portable "lab in a suitcase." It included equipment designed by a local company called J&J Electronics. This lab in a suitcase accomplished with a laptop computer the synchronization of physiology with the video time code that John and Robert's original lab had accomplished with a large PDP-11 computer. In the mid-1970s the PDP-11 filled most of the control room. The observational coding in this more recent study was done using John's SPAFF together with computer-assisted Noldus Observer software.

The second problem we had to solve was creating the therapy. After having studied situational domestic violence and characterological violence for 9 years, we sought to develop and test a couples therapy for only situational domestic violence. Based on an extensive meta-analysis study done by John and Neil's former student, the eminent scholar Julia Babcock, we had a good idea that no intervention that separated the men from their partners in all-male groups was more effective than just one arrest. We also had the results of a solution-focused therapy study done by Sandra Stith and Eric McCollum with situationally violent couples. It had been highly effective. However, Stith's therapy was anti-emotion focused, and that made little sense to us. Stith and McCollum also had no systematic way of screening out characterologically violent couples nor a standardized manual for training therapists. To solve the screening problem, it was crucial to develop an accurate method to ferret out characterologically violent couples in order to exclude them from our subject base. Otherwise we risked women blaming themselves for the men's characterological violence and, most important, potentially rendering those women unsafe. Our screening tool included questionnaires that tapped the severity of previous violence, a woman's fear of her partner, and the amount of control a woman perceived her partner exerted over her. We carefully tested our screening method, and fortunately, it worked. Also, so did the Intimate Justice Scale (Jory, 2007), although it contained more bias in underreporting patterns of the characterological profile.

On to developing the therapy itself. We first theorized that in situational DV, the violence is caused by five variables: (1) physiological flooding, (2) no ritual for withdrawing from escalated conflict, (3) poor conflict-management skills, (4) poor skills for creating and maintaining intimacy, and (5) poor skills for sustaining shared meaning. Several years earlier, we had the good fortune of receiving funding from both Mathematica Policy Research, a think tank in Washington, DC, and the federal Administration for Children and Families. Our assignment was to develop and implement a therapy program for married and unmarried couples in poverty who were expecting a child. The goal was to create a program to help younger unmarried couples remain together—couples living in poverty who were less educated and were ethnically and racially diverse.

The design of the program, called Loving Couples Loving Children (LCLC), was completed in 2003. Julie took the program to some of the poorest regions in the country where community health centers still existed. State by state, she taught each center's staff members how to conduct the program, and in turn, they implemented it within their own communities, under the supervision of Julie and other Gottman-certified therapists. Some of the regional centers included ones in Broward County, Florida; Baton Rouge; Baltimore; the Bronx; Indianapolis; Huntsville, Alabama; and Decatur, Georgia. Fifteen hundred couples took the program, with another 1,500 serving as control subjects. The two groups were later compared by the DC think tank's methods, which proved to be sparse statistically. Still, LCLC showed promise, especially with people of color.

The Couples Together Against Violence (CTAV) intervention was based largely on LCLC, and on our previous psychoeducational interventions for couples. It was tailored to strengthen marriages by tackling low-level situational violence resulting from poor conflict-management skills. It was also geared to address issues related to responsible fatherhood: what being a father means, and the importance of father involvement. We describe the CTAV program in more detail now.

The CTAV intervention sessions used a manual available to all participants. The groups took a strengths-based approach, emphasizing skills for constructive conflict management, creating and maintaining emotional intimacy, coping with stress and depression, physiological self-soothing, and taking breaks to deal with flooding. It also included information about the importance of fathers and healthy marriage. The format of CTAV was the following: Small groups of five to seven couples met weekly for 2 hours. The meetings were facilitated by a male–female pair of masters-plus-level clinicians trained in GMCT. Given that many impoverished people have been shamed by peers and teachers in school settings, care needed to be taken to keep these meetings from feeling shaming, like a classroom. Instead, meetings were designed to highlight group discussion. Julie and John had videotaped and edited over 40 interviews in which Julie spoke with three or four couples at a time about topics related to strengthening relationships and avoiding or healing from situational DV. Filmed couples were all suffering from poverty and some from racism. They came from Georgia, Baltimore, Florida, and Seattle. The films were edited down to 10–12 minutes each. Twenty-two of these films were integrated into 22 core modules, and each week, one of the modules served as that week's focus.

Each couple's group meeting began with announcing the weekly topic and watching the relevant film. We figured if the group couples watched people like themselves talking truthfully about their own relationships, the couples in the meeting would feel more comfortable doing so, too. Following the short video, the group's facilitators encouraged discussion of the topic with understanding and social support in order to build group cohesion. Did they have life experiences like those described by the filmed couples? If so, how were their experiences similar or different? Had they already solved the problems discussed by the filmed couples or were they still struggling with them? The facilitators were urged not to chime in with their own knowledge or opinions, but rather to spotlight themes in common in order to create group cohesion. We believed that couples would return to the group week after week not because the facilitators were special in some way but because they felt a sense of community and connection with their fellow group members.

After the group's post-film conversation, the facilitators presented a 10-minute teaching about our knowledge of that week's topic and its importance in sustaining successful relationships. Then, the facilitators handed out to each group member an emWave2 biofeedback device made by HeartMath. This small cell-phone-sized instrument monitors heart rate synchronicity. Scientific studies have shown that the emWave2 can successfully teach users how to calm down and synchronize their heart rates, similar to a meditation practice. The instrument connects by wire to an ear clip where heart rate and synchronicity are measured. (These days, it is wireless and uses Bluetooth technology. It can also be purchased as an app.) On the device itself, there is a small bank of lights that guides the participant's breathing, plus another light that changes colors, from red to blue to green. The light shines red when the participant is physiologically aroused, but gradually shifts into what we call "the green zone," a calm and relaxed state, as the participant deeply breathes and focuses on a positive image. In every group session, after the film, discussion, and teaching, each group member received and worked with an emWave2 device for 5 minutes in order to help them learn the skill of self-soothing and self-calming. Finally, the facilitators instructed the group to do an exercise that would either deepen their topical discussion or teach them a research-based relationship skill, similar to what couples receive during a course of couples therapy. The various modules for each theme are named below:

Managing Conflict: preventing harmful fights; accepting influence; understanding two sides to every fight; compromising; what to do when endless fights turn harmful; how to have recovery conversations after a fight or failed bid; regulating physiology during conflicts; and avoiding and healing future violence.

Managing Stress: coping with stress as allies, not enemies; the stress-reducing conversation; dealing with depression.

Fathers, Marriage, and Parenting: the importance of fathers and positive connection with children; the benefits of marriage for children's well-being; guiding children by example; working with their partner to emotion-coach their children.

Maintaining Intimacy: maintaining affection and respect by knowing their partner; expressing and responding to their partner's bids for connection; learning about and showing support for their partner's past hurts; being proud of each other; preventing and recovering from infidelity; avoiding contempt, criticism, defensiveness, and stonewalling.

Creating Shared Meaning: the importance of listening to their partner's dreams and honoring and respecting them.

As with our most important interventions, we wanted to conduct a controlled and randomized study to test whether or not CTAV would work to strengthen the relationships of couples with situational domestic violence. Here are the research questions we wanted to answer:

1. Can a screening tool be developed that accurately identifies situationally violent couples (versus those who are nonviolent or experience characterological violence) so that only situationally violent couples can be invited to participate in the intervention?

2. Can a group-based intervention for low-income couples experiencing situational violence be effective in encouraging healthy relationship and conflict-management skills?

3. Can such a program be safely implemented and not increase violence in couples who participate? Can program completion directly reduce the incidence of situational violence?

4. If program completion can reduce instances of situational violence, what is the mechanism through which violence is reduced?

5. Can such a program lead to more responsible fatherhood, either directly through program completion, or indirectly through a healthier relationship with the children's mothers?

Hypotheses. To address these research questions, the following hypotheses were tested:

1. The screening instrument used in this study distinguished between characterological violence, situational violence, and no violence.

Self-reported conflict tactics in couples enrolled into the study would reflect only low levels of interpersonal violence (IPV) and would mirror those found in situationally violent couples from other studies. In addition, negative affect and hostility observed during conflict discussions would be within the acceptable range when compared to situationally and characterologically violent couples in previous observational studies.

2. CTAV would encourage healthy relationships. Compared to the control group, couples in the program group would experience less divorce and relationship breakup, and would report increased use of healthy relationship and conflict-management skills.

3. CTAV would be safely implemented in a sample of low-income, situationally violent couples. Both self-reported violence and behaviors that showed a susceptibility toward violence (i.e., negative affect and hostility) would not increase in the program group, and there would be less self-reported violence and observed conflict in the program group compared to the control group.

4. CTAV would result in lower levels of violence as a result of couples learning communication and conflict-management skills rather than in a change in men's attitudes toward violence.

5. CTAV would promote responsible fatherhood. Compared to the control group, fathers would exhibit more co-parenting and be more involved with their children; this would come about via improvements in couple relationship quality.

Participants. Using a new screening tool to distinguish between the two forms of violence, 128 low-income situationally violent adult couples were identified and invited to participate in the study. Final eligibility for the study was based on the following criteria: Couples had to (1) be romantically involved and in a committed relationship for at least 1 year; (2) be 18 years of age or older; (3) speak fluent English; (4) be experiencing situational violence; (5) have at least one child under age 12 living in the home; (6) have a combined income below the local county median for a family of three ($73,000); and (7) not be experiencing characterological violence, significant substance abuse issues, or carrying a positive screen for antisocial personality disorder.

Demographics. Average age of the participants was 35 years (±8) for males and 34 (±8) for females. Couples were romantically involved for an average of 7.9 years (±8 months) and had been living together for an average of 6.6 years (±7 months). Most couples had three to four family members living in the household (M = 3.76 ±.9) and an average combined household income of $53,664 (±$29,088); 73.2% of couples were married, 24.7% were unmarried but cohabiting, and 2.1% of couples had separated or divorced before the start of the study but were in the process of reconciling.

The racial and ethnic breakdown for males was 78.8% Caucasian, 16.2% African American, 4% Asian, 4.2% Latin American/Hispanic, 2% Pacific Islander, 2% Native American, and 2% endorsed another racial/ethnic background. Racial and ethnic breakdown for females was 87.4% Caucasian, 13% African American, 3.1% Asian, 6.8% Latin American/Hispanic, 4% Pacific Islander, 9% Native American, and 4% endorsed another racial/ethnic background. Many male participants (35.4%) reported completing high school and no further education; the majority of female participants (33.3%) had completed college but nothing further. Most of the males (69.7%) reported working full-time, although 10.1% were unemployed. Most of the females (52.5%) were unemployed homemakers, although 38% reported working full- or part-time, and 9.1% were unemployed.

Method. Couples were randomly assigned to the intervention or a control group (treatment group n = 63; control group n = 53) and followed for an 18-month period post-treatment. Couples were assessed through self-report, observational, and physiological data collection methods at four time points: baseline (Time 1), ~6 months after baseline (Time 2), ~12 months after baseline (Time 3), and ~18 months after baseline (Time 4). Couples assigned to the treatment group were offered the CTAV intervention program directly after baseline and prior to Time 2. Couples completed surveys on interpersonal violence, conflict-management and healthy relationship skills, relationship status, relationship satisfaction, co-parenting, and attitudes toward violence. During assessments, couples also participated in a 15-minute "conflict discussion" during which observable behaviors (e.g., anger, contempt, criticism, domineering, stonewalling, belligerence) were coded.

Physiological reactivity (e.g., heart rate, skin conductance) was also measured throughout the discussion.

Results. Analysis of the data showed the following results regarding the five primary hypotheses:

1. The screening instrument was able to successfully identify situationally violent, versus characterologically violent, versus nonviolent couples. Situationally violent couples enrolled into the study were found to report lower levels of IPV compared to characterologically violent couples from a previously collected sample, and comparable levels of IPV to situationally violent from the other sample. Enrolled couples did not report significantly higher levels of IPV compared to a sample of distressed nonviolent couples from the other sample, suggesting that the screener may have been sensitive enough to distinguish these two groups, but was better able to identify more divergent groups of couples (i.e., those who were situationally versus characterologically violent). Results suggest that the screener may be a useful tool within research and clinical contexts where discernment between these groups is necessary.

2. Although participation in CTAV did not lead to fewer instances of divorce and relationship dissolution, treatment couples did show significant improvements in relationship quality over time and in comparison to control couples. Specifically, self-reported relationship satisfaction and use of healthy relationship skills were higher and conflict was lower at Time 2 in comparison to control couples and in comparison to treatment couples at Time 1.

3. In addition, males in the treatment group were more successful in

their attempts to physiologically self-soothe at Time 2, as evidenced by a maintenance (over time) in heart rate during conflict, whereas control couples showed a significant *increase* in heart rate reactivity over time.

4. CTAV was safely implemented in this group of low-income situationally violent couples. Violence did not increase in the program group, although self-reported violence was not directly reduced over time based on program completion. Archival police records did show a significant decrease in IPV in the treatment compared to the control group. However, observed behaviors that show a propensity toward violence were reduced over time (across all four time points) and in comparison to controls.

5. Although CTAV did not prompt a direct reduction in self-reported violence, IPV was indirectly reduced via use of healthy relationship and conflict-management skills. In other words, treatment group status was associated with increased use of intervention skills, which was, in turn, associated with reduced IPV. In contrast, IPV was not reduced via changes in attitudes toward violence. Archival police records did show a significant reduction in IPV in the experimental compared to the control group.

6. CTAV promoted a stronger co-parenting alliance between partners, although this effect occurred as a function of improvements in couple relationships rather than directly as a result of program completion. Specifically, treatment group status was associated with improvements in friendship and shared meaning (facets of the SRH, the theoretical rationale that the intervention is based on), which were, in turn, associated with increased co-parenting reported by both males and females.

7. The figures below show the significant changes in hostility during conflict discussions for male (top figure) and female hostility for the control and treatment groups.

8. In conclusion, the CTAV program was shown to be effective in treating situational domestic violence.

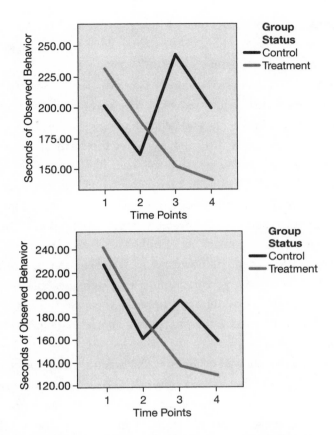

Given the positive results of CTAV, we have integrated the concepts and couple exercises into our couples therapy format. In other words, if not holding group meetings as in CTAV, we believe the precepts of CTAV can still be applied to couples therapy. Here is an example:

Case Study

Phillip and Sue were having terrible conflicts. They came in to see Julie. With two children under the age of 4, there was stress on top of stress. Phillip was a classical musician in a small symphony orchestra. Sue worked for a nonprofit. Money was tight. Phillip sought extra work in chamber music groups and churches to earn what extra he could. Phillip had come from a musical household. But his parents had divorced early, and Phillip was mostly raised by his mother, a piano teacher. Sue came from a rural family that owned a small farm. She and her siblings learned early to work hard, and that work took place daily.

The couple reported having one or two situationally violent episodes a month. Things hadn't begun that way. They had fallen deeply in love in their 20s, married after 2 years, and begun having kids almost immediately. At first, their fights were more calm, but after the birth of the kids, they began to escalate. Sue would get frustrated that Phillip wasn't finishing his home projects. He was still working on a bathroom he'd torn apart 6 months ago, which left all four in the family using only one tiny one. Phillip was also absent-minded, and would repeatedly forget other errands Sue begged him to do. Sue was now so angry with Phillip that she'd lob criticisms at him like curve balls. Only they'd hit him hard. He'd go defensive in return. Then they were off and running. Within minutes, they were pushing and slapping each other, with occasional objects thrown. Both would feel horrible afterward. They'd retreat for a day, then try to talk about what happened, which failed, too.

Their assessment showed no signs of characterological violence, but all the hallmarks of situational violence: use of the Four Horsemen, gridlocked conflicts, an inability to accept influence or compromise, failed repair efforts, and loneliness. Love maps were still strong, but fondness and admiration were declining. Shared meaning also remained satisfactory.

After their initial three sessions of assessment, Julie began the therapy by introducing the couple to the Aftermath of a Regrettable Incident intervention. They chose to process the most recent violent episode. They followed the format of the intervention booklet and, when listening, took notes. In abbreviated form, here is the gist of what they said:

Phillip: OK, I felt angry, sad, despair, hopeless, defensive, powerless, and exhausted.

Sue: Hmm, a lot of overlap . . . I felt angry, frustrated, sad, hopeless, defensive, ashamed, and culpable.

Phillip: Here's my narrative. I wanted to work on the kitchen. But I heard you say you needed me to watch the kids so you could visit a friend. I thought to myself, "I never get to see my friends," but I didn't say anything. I agreed to babysit. But inside I was fuming. I felt caught in a double bind, where you're wanting me to finish the bathroom, but when I have spare time I need to watch the kids instead of working on it. That kinda stuff drives me crazy. When you came back 2 hours later, the kids were both napping. We started to talk. I remember saying, "I wish I could see my friends, too. You get to play all the time." Then I heard you say something like "You get to see your friends in the orchestra all the time. What are you talking about?" I replied, "That's work, not play." Then I think I added, "It really pisses me off that you get so much playtime." I looked at your face and thought, "Uh oh, she's really angry. I better shut up." I walked into the kitchen. You followed me. I said, "Leave me alone." I remember you saying, "No! Let's finish this. You think I play all the time? You try taking care of these kids and going to work and cleaning and cooking and everything else I do around here." I replied, "Hah! Just try playing violin in three different groups where everybody expects you to be perfect. And never having time to practice cuz I have to watch the kids all the time." Then I think you said, "You're ridiculous. Poor baby, sitting and playing his little violin and doing nothing to help at home. You're just lazy!" Then I exploded. I picked up a plastic vase and threw it at you. Then you slapped me. I slapped you back. Then you started to cry. I went upstairs to our bedroom—that was it.

Therapist: OK, Sue, can you now summarize what you heard Phillip say, and add a few words of validation? Validation doesn't mean you agree with Phillip's point of view. It just means that if you could step into his shoes, you could see what he felt and thought—you could say something like "That makes sense to me."

(Sue summarized adequately and added a few words of validation. Then it was her turn to narrate her experience.)

Sue: I started out that day exhausted. I just wanted a break to see Cindy, who is going through a divorce. She's in a pretty bad state, and since I'm her best friend, it really felt important to me to go see her and talk and give her a hug. So I asked you to watch the kids. I thought I saw you grimace, but then you said, "OK." So I thought everything was OK. I went to

Cindy's. You know her husband had an affair, right? So she was horribly upset, talking about it, and devastated that he wanted to divorce and go be with this other woman who's half his age. When I was with her, I absorbed a lot of her feelings. It was hard. Then I came home. The first thing I remember you saying is that you wanted playtime, too. I imagined that you were trying to make me feel guilty. I felt defensive. I hadn't been playing. I'd been trying to support my poor hurting friend. So we bickered back and forth until you said that comment about me getting so much playtime. That made me furious! I said something back, I don't remember it but I know it was mean. The next thing I know, a vase is hurtling toward me. It freaked me out. But it made me even angrier. So I launched at you and slapped you. Then you slapped me back. It really hurt. I was so upset I started to sob. Then you left and I kept crying. The end. Ugh.

(Phillip then summarized Sue's point of view and added his words of validation.)

Therapist: Let's move on to triggers now. (Julie explained what triggers are and asked them, if they recognized any in themselves, to describe them plus a story from their past where the trigger originated.)

Sue: I know I got triggered. It was that comment about me having so much playtime that got me. It reminded me of my life on the farm. I really wanted to play with friends like everyone else around me did. But there was always some chore to do—clean out the stalls, fill the trough, feed the goats, milk Bessie, it never ended. I NEVER got to play. My friends all built these great friendships. But not me. How could I? And when I'd ask my folks if I could please go to somebody's slumber party, they'd just say, "No. You've got chores to do tomorrow. And you better start early because there's a lot of them. I expect ALL of them to get done before you do anything else." I'd work as fast as I could, but they always took all day, and that was that. There went my weekend. I guess I've built up a huge reservoir of resentment about that. So when you brought up that I always get playtime? I just went ballistic. I spent my entire childhood never having playtime. It went up from there.

(Phillip nodded and said he understood.)

Phillip: Well, I got triggered, too. From your comments, I imagined you were expecting me to be perfect—the perfect husband, the perfect father, the perfect provider. So when you made that last comment about me being a baby and never helping out, it hurt a lot. It reminded me of Mom, the perfectionist of all time. I would get criticized every time I turned around. "You're playing the wrong note, Phillip. What's the matter with you?" and "Why can't you keep your room clean? This room is a mess—it stinks in here!" and "Why are you so lazy? Get up and set the table, for God's sake. Do I have to do everything around here?" I could never ever please her. I don't think I heard one word of praise until I finally won that college music scholarship away. So I heard echoes of my mom when you spoke, I think. It made me furious. But I was probably more furious with Mom than you.

(Sue said now she understood why he'd gotten so upset.)

When the couple tackled owning responsibility for what happened, both acknowledged their contributions with great remorse, especially the violence. There were deep apologies, and tears.

Then they asked that the other partner listen better, and avoid going critical or defensive.

It was interesting that neither person raised the possibility of taking breaks when fights like these broke out. Julie described the behavior and physiology of flooding to them, then how to take a healthy break. She particularly emphasized how important it was to say when they'd return to talk before separating for the break, and to not think about the fight during their self-soothing time. She asked each partner to write down a list of ways they could each self-soothe. They should keep their lists easily accessible, so that during break times, they wouldn't have to think too hard about how to self-soothe. Julie also recommended downloading the emWave2 app, and practicing with it at least once a day. It would help them both to better down-regulate their anger so they could avoid their blow-ups. Phillip especially liked the latter suggestion, as he knew he had trouble calming down his anger. Anything he could try would be welcome.

In subsequent sessions, Julie shared with the couple the conflict blueprint exercises, including the Gottman–Rapoport exercise, the Dreams Within Conflict exercise, and the Two-Oval Compromise method. The couple worked on a big gridlocked conflict using those tools. The issue wasn't a big surprise: How do we get more playtime for us individually and as a couple? She also checked weekly on how their usage of the app was going, and whether they had any episodes that needed processing. There were two more episodes at home of violence, due to breaks being called for too late in the conflict discussion, after they were already fully flooded. Julie worked on helping the partners identify in their bodies the early warning signals that flooding was on the horizon. For Phillip, it was tightening of his jaw and tension in his hands. For Sue, it was shallow breathing and her stomach tightening as if she'd been kicked in the gut. It was hard for the couple to separate for breaks. Each wanted to get the last word in, which, of course, never worked. After 6 weeks of app practice, however, there were no more violent episodes. Breaks would be taken more regularly, before conflicts reached the boiling point.

As therapy progressed, other conflicts were dealt with as well. And more regrettable incidents from earlier in the relationship were processed. Gradually the couple drew closer to one another. Rituals of connection were explained, and they created several for just the two of them to practice, as well as several that involved the kids. One of those included going on a romantic weekend together once a quarter, just the two of them. This proved to be very popular! They loved their time alone, and they rekindled some of the romance they'd lost along the way. After 18 months of treatment, they felt ready to end their therapy. Julie suggested a gradual reduction in sessions to ensure that their new conflict-management skills and friendship rituals were firmly in place. For 1 month, they had sessions every other week, and for the last 2 months, they had one each month. We said goodbye with a smile.

CHAPTER 19

Treating Substance Abuse and Addiction

This chapter briefly explores current thinking and research on addiction, including symptoms and causes. A full research review on the latest neuroscientific findings and pharmacological treatments is not presented here, as these subjects are a separate field outside the purview of this book. However, some breakthroughs have been made in couples therapy for addiction, and these are introduced here. A case is described that details the Gottman method for treating an addiction.

Let us first try to understand the biological basis of substance abuse.

The Addicted Brain

All substance abuse and addictions hijack the brain's reward system. For that reason, all substance abuse disorders as well as behavioral addictions (e.g. gambling) are also brain disorders, since they reorganize the brain's anticipatory pleasure pathways, and can cause serious neuronal brain damage. We have to speak of three categories: (1) substance use, (2) substance abuse, and (3) substance dependence. Psychoactive drugs that are addictive include cocaine, heroin, caffeine, nicotine, opioids such as Oxycontin, alcohol, and other new pharmaceuticals now circulating on the streets.

The Diagnosis of Addiction and Substance Abuse

How shall we diagnose substance abuse and addiction in our clients? The *Diagnostic and Statistical Manual of Mental Disorders* (DSM) substance dependence criteria for addiction (termed "substance dependence" by the American Psychiatric Association) is defined as a maladaptive pattern of substance use leading to clinically significant impairment or distress, as manifested by three (or more) of the following, occurring anytime in the same 12-month period:

1. **Tolerance**, as defined by either of the following: (a) a need for markedly increased amounts of the substance to achieve intoxication or the desired effect, or (b) markedly diminished effect with continued use of the same amount of the substance.

2. **Withdrawal**, as manifested by either of the following: (a) the characteristic withdrawal syndrome for the substance, or (b) the same (or closely related) substance is taken to relieve or avoid withdrawal symptoms.

3. **The need for more**: the substance is often taken in larger amounts or over a longer period than intended.

4. There is a **persistent desire, and/or a history of unsuccessful efforts to cut down** or control substance use.

5. A **great deal of time is spent** in activities necessary **to obtain** the substance (such as visiting multiple doctors or driving long distances), in use of the substance (e.g., chain-smoking), or in recovery from its effects.

6. **Important social, occupational, or recreational activities are given up** or reduced because of substance use.

7. **The substance use is continued despite knowledge** of having a persistent physical or psychological problem that is likely to have been caused or exacerbated by the substance (e.g., current cocaine use despite recognition of cocaine-induced depression, or continued drinking despite recognition that an ulcer was made worse by alcohol consumption).

DSM criteria for substance dependence include several considerations, one of which is whether it occurs with physiologic dependence (evidence of tolerance or withdrawal) or not. In addition, remission categories are classified into four subtypes: (1) full, (2) early partial, (3) sustained, and (4) sustained partial; based on whether any of the criteria for abuse or dependence have been met and over what time frame. The remission category can also be used for patients receiving agonist therapy (such as methadone maintenance) or for those living in a controlled, drug-free environment. We should diagnose substance abuse only if it has significant negative life consequences, such as neglecting responsibilities or harming relationships (Polk, 2015). As a rough guide, look for three or more of the following features: (1) tolerance, (2) withdrawal, (3) compulsion and urge to use, (4) using more and more over time, (5) cravings, (6) obsession with the substance, (7) using the substance despite negative life consequences, and (8) the existence of significant environmental triggers. Note that it is possible to be addicted to a behavior or a process, like gambling, porn use, sex, video games, or any "supernormal" stimulus.

Brief History of Concern About Substance Abuse

In the early 1800s there was extensive use of opium, morphine, heroin, and cocaine. People at first had no idea of the harmful side effects of these substances, although it was a dark chapter in England's history. In particular, during the Opium Wars, the UK fought to get 25% of Chinese men addicted to opium. In 1906, across the waters, the Pure Food and Drug Act was passed in the United States. President Teddy Roosevelt signed into law the passage of Prohibition as the 18th Amendment to the U.S. Constitution, the only amendment ever repealed (in 1933). In 1970 Nixon passed the Controlled Substances Act, which started the Drug Enforcement Administration's (DEA's) War on Drugs and severely penalized both drug users and dealers. This act led to the mass incarceration of Black males in the United States. Since that time, there has been a movement to decriminalize drug use, to view substance dependence and abuse as treatable disorders, and to recommend community recovery services rather than punishment. In addition, although marijuana is still illegal on a federal level, a number of states have passed laws that allow limited amounts of possession for both recreational and medicinal use, making the farming and selling of marijuana into legitimate businesses.

The Psychology of All Addictions

Let's discuss some of the research on behavior, the brain, and substance addiction. Addiction involves the learning and reward systems. These systems were first studied by Ivan Pavlov in his research on classical conditioning, in which dogs learned to salivate to the sound of a bell by pairing the bell with food. Two hypotheses about addiction competed for prominence. Hypothesis 1 was the co-occurrence explanation of addiction, in which addiction results from the pairing of the drug with a pleasurable experience. This hypothesis turned out to be wrong, because if one adds another stimulus before the bell, thus causing the other stimulus to also closely co-occur with food, the new stimulus doesn't become associated with the food. This effect is called blocking. So, another hypothesis was needed, which led to Hypothesis 2: the breakthrough research by Bob Rescorla and Allan Wagner as an explanation of addiction. This hypothesis is based on surprise leading to learning. Theoretically, imbibing a substance would lead to a surprising, unpredictable effect, one that was pleasurable. Therefore, the anticipation of pleasure would become associated with the substance.

In neuroscientific research, Robert Heath discovered the septal region of the brain, which was initially labeled the brain's "reward" center. He and his colleagues discovered that animals would work to stimulate an electrode placed in this region, to the exclusion of food and sleep. James Olds and Peter Milner at McGill University also studied this septal self-stimulation center. They found that while an animal will not cross an electrified grid for food, it will do that for septal stimulation. It will even starve to death while pressing the lever that stimulates this center. Septal self-stimulation was even more powerful than the motives for sex, or the care of infants. Although initially called the reward center, Jaak Panksepp's research showed that the feeling induced by septal stimulation is the feeling that something wonderful is ABOUT to happen, which was also called the expectation of reward. In animals, including humans, it is a motive that is never sated. Animals can't ever get enough of it. In many ways it resembles falling in love. It is exciting, it is powerful, and it seems to be pure delight. In real life it is induced by falling in love and by curiosity, interest, exploration, play, and adventure.

Let's get a little more detailed. It turns out that this substance abuse brain region has three major parts. First is the nucleus accumbens (NA), the center for the anticipation of something wonderful (reward or pleasure). The NA lights up when heterosexual men look at naked women, when women look at babies, and when rats drink a sugar solution. It is a brain center for the secretion of the neurotransmitter of delight—namely, dopamine. The neurotransmitter dopamine is involved in all pleasure and excitement. The NA has been called the septal pleasure center, or the anticipation-of-reward center. As we noted, it generates that feeling that something wonderful is about to happen. Second is the prefrontal cortex (PFC). Damage to the PFC results in the disinhibition of impulses. So, the PFC actually controls one's impulses to take the substance responsible for lighting up the brain center of delight, the NA. Damage to the PFC, and therefore reduced impulse control, explains why trying to convince a substance abuser to stop using will not work very well. The PFC is just off-line. Third is the ventral tegmental area (VTA). The VTA was studied in monkeys by Wolfram Schultz at the University of Friborg in Switzerland. Schultz discovered that VTA activity reflects the occurrence of a surprising reward; the VTA is the center of all craving.

What explains addiction? For many years scientists preferred a _negative_ reinforcement model. That model suggests that addicts keep using the substance to avoid the negative withdrawal effects. The problem with this model was that some drugs are worse than others in withdrawal effects. For example, methamphetamine withdrawal is not so bad, whereas withdrawal from alcohol is life-threatening, yet methamphetamine is much more addictive than alcohol. Also, if withdrawal is the cause of addiction, the addiction should disappear once the withdrawal symptoms stop, but it doesn't. Hence, scientists went to a _positive_ reinforcement model of addiction and added the neural basis of addiction. The three parts were the VTA, the NA, and the PFC. This theory explains the three phenomena of addiction. Let's see how these neural functions of the addiction circuit explain the following three phenomena of addiction.

1. **The VTA creates a strong association** between a drug and the cues associated with the high, the pleasurable feeling that causes cravings. Cravings are not the same as liking. But how much the addict likes the drug causes increased craving over time.

2. **Substance abuse results in reduced pleasure and numbing.** The numbing of the NA is due to a homeostatic mechanism. The mechanism of numbing begins with overstimulation of the NA, which results in the secretion of dynorphin, a natural painkiller. Extra dynorphin in the system then inhibits and numbs the stimulation of the NA in order for the NA to not overproduce dynorphin. For the same reason, to correct a homeostatic imbalance, there is also a down-regulation of dopamine receptors. The results are that the addict needs more and more of the drug to get the same high; the addict eventually needs some of the drug just to feel normal. But now the addict is dependent on the drug to experience pleasure. And since the NA's activation and the number of dopamine receptors are all subnormal now, the addict becomes numb to all everyday pleasures (e.g., not liking normal sex because of a porn addiction). Finally, the drug is the only way the addict can ever feel good.

    In trying to understand the mechanism of cravings, we used to think that the VTA caused dopamine in the NA, and that was its only effect. Recent evidence shows that this is wrong. Actually, VTA neurons respond to *unexpected* stimuli. A light cueing the occurrence of delicious juice in a monkey's mouth doesn't become more pleasurable over time. Other evidence comes from Parkinson's patients. They get DA replacement therapy, so they have high levels of DA in the brain, but they still experience normal levels of pleasure. Instead, DA release in the VTA is associated with craving. This is a primitive impulsive desire. For example, most smokers don't want to smoke, but they have a primitive urge, making incentives more salient. Further evidence comes from DA-enriched mice. They move quickly to feed, but don't seem to enjoy it more. We know this from counting the mouse's facial expressions of pleasure (a tongue show). The conclusion is that DA release in the VTA is more about wanting than liking, which explains cravings. Two changes happen in the VTA: (a) incentive sensitization, which is the opposite of tolerance, because the VTA responds more with repeated use, so cravings get stronger; and (b) the DA release in the VTA means that an unexpected reward may soon arrive, or something wonderful is about to happen. It has evolutionary adaptive value. For example, if an animal in the desert comes upon unexpected water in an oasis, then the VTA $\rightarrow$ DA release sensitizes the animal to intensely recall any stimuli related to the unexpected reward, so the animal will remember how to get back to the oasis. Addictive drugs do this far more than normal rewards like unexpected water. They create more than normal release of DA in the presence of the drug; thus they become TRIGGERS in a highly remembered chain.

3. **Weakened inhibition**: When the number and effectiveness of PFC neurons taper down, the result is reduced self-control. This explains the mechanism of compulsions. Normally, the PFC inhibits undesirable behavior. It is the thinking part of the brain. It regulates what actions the individual should take. Addiction causes abnormalities in the PFC, and loss of functioning. This is part of why therapists find it hard to get through to the addict. The addict cannot hear the therapist, because the addict is brain damaged in the PFC. If one gives cocaine to rats, the result is that neurons and dendrites are misshapen in the PFC. Also, the volume of the PFC decreases. Addicts look and act just like patients that have sustained PFC brain injuries. There is also damage in the ability to maintain and focus attention.

The Genetics of Addiction

Gerald McClearn and David Rogers studied inbred strains of mice as they displayed a preference for alcohol over water. Studies comparing identical versus fraternal twins revealed the heritability of addiction: Heritability for alcohol is 50% to 70%; smoking, 50%; nicotine, 60%; and illegal drugs, 25% to 55%. These are polygenic phenomena, involving many genes.

Alcoholism as a Comorbidity

The substance abuse comorbidity we see most often is alcohol abuse. Alcohol is a real problem in couples' relationships, because even its mild or moderate use tends to lower the threshold for aggression. There is a great deal of research that supports this conclusion, including a massive review by the Gates Foundation. The review confirmed that alcohol abuse is widespread. It is estimated that there are 140 million alcoholics worldwide, and alcohol is involved in 50% of all traffic deaths. Alcohol affects glutamate, which is the major excitatory neurotransmitter in the brain. GABA is the major inhibitory neurotransmitter in the brain. Usually glutamate activates the NMDA receptor, which creates learning and memory. But alcohol diminishes this pathway's action. Also, there is an up-regulation of NMDA, in which alcohol binds to a different site on the NMDA receptor. This is called allosteric binding, and this in turn leads to a sedation effect. When combined, these mechanisms of alcohol suppress overall activity in the brain. That's why heavy drinking is often accompanied by amnesia and blackouts, in which memory functioning has been momentarily eliminated. Alcohol also affects GABA. It increases the activity of GABA, and more GABA leads to suppressed neural activity. It also makes GABA receptors easier for GABA to bind to, more so than they ordinarily would be. Alcohol also down-regulates GABA receptors. This effect mirrors what barbiturates do, and thus, we get the cross-tolerance effect between alcohol and barbiturates. Alcohol not only causes brain changes, it also alters the digestive system. With alcoholism, people produce more of the enzymes that, in turn, break down alcohol, so they have to drink more alcohol to get the same effect of the alcohol itself. But more enzymes of this kind damage the alcoholic's digestive system. Perhaps the best known effect is that alcoholics are likely to develop liver cirrhosis, and the least known effect? Brain shrinkage.

Finally, as if these effects weren't enough, when alcohol becomes unavailable, withdrawal symptoms from alcohol are potentially life-threatening. These include tremors, shakes, increased anxiety, increased blood pressure, sweating, nausea, seizures, delirium tremens, hallucinations, and massively increased neural activation.

What Is the Best Treatment?

For detox, a substitute may be given, usually benzodiazepines, although these in turn may result in more addiction if not carefully monitored. Injected once a month, Naltrexone, or Vivitrol, blocks the brain receptors that are linked to greater pleasure, and thus inhibits the pleasurable experience of alcohol. There is usually a component of psychosocial support. Some treatments use disulfiram, which inhibits the enzyme that breaks down alcohol—this causes an unpleasant reaction; or acamprosate, which acts on NMDA receptors, and reduces receptivity.

Of course, the most well-known treatment is attendance at self-led group meetings provided by Alcoholics Anonymous (AA). AA has broadened its reach into groups for every other kind of addiction, including behavioral addictions and drug addiction. (Each addiction is named with the first letter of the type of addiction plus "A" for anonymous, such as NA for narcotics addiction or SA for sex addiction.) In each program, self-disclosure and community support are folded into 12 steps to complete, and individual sponsorship by another AA member. AA was originally founded on Christian precepts, but over the last decades, it has embraced a broader spiritual viewpoint that includes belief in a "higher power." Probably the most powerful aspect of AA group attendance is community support. Plus there are groups worldwide, so the alcoholic or drug user can participate regardless of locale. Many hospital programs offer AA as a component of their treatment. It's important to know, though, that there is a large (estimated at 60%) dropout rate for AA. And the overall effectiveness of most alcohol treatments is around 5% complete remission.

The Case for a Couples' Treatment for Alcohol Addiction

The research of Barbara McCrady, and the separate research of Timothy O'Farrell using a behavioral couples' approach to both addiction and couples work, has a success rate of approximately 30% effectiveness. While this is still a long way from what we would hope for, it is an effect six times larger than other treatments. One strange result of their therapies is that the effect size of the couples therapy is also larger than it would have been treating a non-addicted group of couples.

The Navarra Couples Approach to Recovery

One of our Gottman master therapists and trainers, Robert Navarra, has developed a couples approach to recovery from any addiction. The approach is novel because partners are generally excluded intentionally from recovery programs or sequestered into allied groups like Al-Anon. When the recovering substance abuse patient returns home, typically the partner is totally in the dark about what the patient has experienced in recovery. Navarra argues that recovery requires the couple to build a new life not centered on the abused substance, and to establish a new sense of shared meaning together. He argues that therapy for addiction requires recovery for the addict, recovery for the co-addict or relationship partner, and recovery for the relationship itself. His specialized method is called couples addiction recovery (CAR). Navarra's therapeutic work is now being evaluated by the Gottman Institute. His program is available on the institute's online learning menu.

Can one be addicted to a behavior, or to just a stimulus? The idea of "supernormal stimuli" is based on the work of Nobel Prize–winning Norwegian ethologist Niko Tinbergen. Tinbergen studied how stimuli that were "larger" or more stimulating than normal in some way hyperelicit an evolutionarily adaptive behavior. He also states that a normal stimulus that usually elicited that particular behavior becomes inadequate at obtaining the usual expected response. A good example of a supernormal stimulus is pornography, which is supernormal in many ways, so much so that some people eventually lose interest in normal sex with their partner. Supernormal addictions are said to include:

1. **Fast food.** Two thirds of Americans are overweight, and one third are obese. Fast food has supernormal stimulus properties compared to unprocessed food. It contains more sugar and fat, which our bodies naturally seek for energy and sustenance.
2. **Cuteness.** Some people think that Walt Disney and the toy industry have overmanufactured and oversold neoteny (baby-like features) and cuteness so that we are overdosed on it.
3. **Sex by pornography.** The revenue of porn sites exceeds $20 billion

a year. One fMRI study of men who watch a lot of porn showed decreased dopamine activity when watching porn, suggesting a numbed NA, and the need to view more of it. Also, married male users of porn significantly decrease the amount of sex they have with their wives.

4. **Video games.** Hitting a target with a missile is an evolutionarily adaptive skill. Video games generate scenes where this happens once a second. The video game *Grand Theft Auto* earned $1 billion in its first 3 days, outclassing the earnings of any Hollywood movie.

5. **Television.** Visual stimuli change approximately once a second, especially for children's programming. This represents a supernormal stimulus.

6. **Cell phones, computers, and tablets.** These allow constant communication minute by minute all day, at any time. But they can result in far less face-to-face communication that allows for deeper communication. (See *Alone Together* by MIT professor Sherry Turkle, 2012.)

7. **The internet in general, which houses personal social media sites such as Facebook, Twitter, and TikTok, as well as instant messaging.** Users of these sites can spend entire days viewing messaging and videos shared there. (See the book *Supernormal Stimuli* by Diedre Barrett, 2010, and the book *The Shallows* by Nicholas Carr, 2010.) Clearly, more research needs doing on addiction treatment and the effects of supernormal stimuli, to which, in the United States, addiction is at an all-time high.

Case Example

Let's discuss a case of couples treatment for alcoholism. Julie conducted this case before Dr. Navarra's creation of CAR. Thus it demonstrates application of only GMCT to alcoholism and its effects on the relationship.

Cindy and Lilly came in for treatment due to Cindy's discovery of many hidden bottles in their garage. Upon being confronted by Cindy, Lilly confessed that prior to returning from work daily, she stopped at a corner store near her work and picked up a liter of scotch. She'd stop a block away from home, drink half of it, stash the bottle, and later walk in the door. This had been going on for years, with the time the bottle lasted lessening over time. Suddenly, many things made sense to Cindy. Lilly was now much quieter in the evenings after work than she ever had been before. Cindy would attempt to initiate conversation but, lately, to no avail. Whenever Cindy received invitations to attend parties or events, Lilly always insisted on staying home—alone, if necessary. Plus Lilly had gained much weight in the last few years—perhaps 30 pounds in all. Lilly felt terribly ashamed of her addiction, so it had become her secret pleasure. Cindy felt guilty that she'd not figured it out until now. Meanwhile, their relationship, which now numbered 20 years, had grown increasingly distant until barely a word passed between them day after day. Cindy knew almost nothing of Lilly's work life, nor her political views, future dreams, or relationship complaints. Lilly never asked. And because Cindy received only truncated responses to her questions of Lilly, she stopped asking, too. Now they felt miles apart, like diverging train tracks. Each was out of sight and mind of the other.

Their assessments followed suit. Friendship questionnaires were scored very low. Conflict-management questionnaires were mostly scored in the middle, because they never engaged in conflicts these days. And shared meaning between them had vanished. Cindy and Lilly had met at a political rally 25 years earlier. They were both adamant supporters of LGBTQ rights and, at the rally, ended up standing next to each other, cheering on the speakers. Afterward, coffee beckoned. There was a definite attraction. Their dating fired up. They discovered many of their political views and passions lined up beautifully. After three months, Cindy loaded up a U-Haul and moved into Lilly's place, a nice house Lilly had proudly purchased after years working in a high-paying job for a tech company. Since she made so much more than Cindy, they agreed that Cindy would take a break from her work as a restaurant server, which she'd paid for with aching wrists and shoulders. They'd lived together since then, and married as soon as they could after Obergefell v. Hodges (the Supreme Court decision that legalized gay and lesbian marriage). But somehow, over the years, the distance between them widened like a flooded river, and now was threatening to drown their relationship.

In their individual sessions, Lilly admitted to drinking half a fifth of scotch daily. She mumbled that she knew her drinking was out of control.

She hated that fact, had tried to stop from time to time, but had failed every time. When the possibility of joining AA was raised, she had adamantly refused. She would have none of that "higher power stuff." Once she'd tiptoed into a meeting, but she'd felt alienated from the start, and had rushed out as soon as the torture was over. She prided herself on being independent, a self-starter and a self-finisher. Julie gently explored, Was she ready to forgo the bottle yet? At this level of imbibing, she'd need a medically supervised detox, but could follow up in couples work together with Cindy afterward. Julie suggested that the bottle had risen up between Cindy and her like a rising sea, blocking them from even seeing one another, let alone deeply connecting. Lilly sadly nodded, "I know. But I refuse to go to AA." OK, Julie acknowledged, "we'll try it a different way."

Cindy's session began in tears. She sobbed over Lilly's illness of alcoholism. She'd banged her head against a wall, trying to figure out why their distance had grown so much, especially lately. Was she doing something wrong? Had Lilly fallen out of love with her? Was Lilly involved with someone else? What could she do to bridge that chasm? Like many partners of alcoholics (we'll call them co-alcoholics here), she blamed herself for all the signs that things were definitely bad and cruelly worsening. Even simple conversations had sunk underground. She wasn't sure she could make this relationship work. And without Lilly's quitting alcohol, there wasn't reason to. She didn't want to relate to a wife hidden behind an alcoholic wall.

In Julie's feedback session with the couple, alcoholism was the focus. Lilly admitted the extent of her drinking to Cindy—it was even more than she thought. Lilly had bottles stashed everywhere, in the garage, under some shrubs, in an air vent, behind a couch, everywhere. Anytime Cindy was in another room or away, Lilly would drink. Lilly cried, "I'm so sorry . . . " Her guilt and shame filled the room. Julie explained the mechanisms of alcoholism—how it worked in the brain to enslave the user, why the brain craved more continuously to get the same high, and how its toxicity damaged the GI tract, the liver, the lungs, the heart, the circulatory system, and the brain, even causing brain cell death. She showed the couple an MRI scan that compared the brain of an alcoholic to that of someone sober. Fully one third of the alcoholic brain was gone, leaving only black holes. Cindy shuddered.

Lilly shook her head. Julie also explained the effects of alcoholism on a relationship. Intoxication eventually produced so many personality changes in the drinker that a partner would think, "Who is this? Is this really who I married? Where did she go?" They would think they were talking to a stiff mask rather than a flesh-and-blood person. Eventually, the co-alcoholic who was kept in the dark would inevitably feel resentful, angry, and sad that connection was drifting away and being replaced with a cloud of smoke. Cindy added that she didn't know who Lilly was anymore. She'd tried for months to pull Lilly up and out of what she figured was depression. But it was no-go. Finally, she'd simply surrendered to the facts—there would be no intimacy, no loving warmth, and no endless talks. She'd tolerated this long enough— she couldn't take it anymore. Things had to change, or . . . Julie offered that alcohol was serving as a third party in the relationship, which walled them off from each other. It was sabotaging any of their efforts to touch again. It was a nasty enemy of their marriage. But if Lilly succeeded at ceasing to drink, in effect ridding the marriage of that intrusive toxin once and for all, their relationship could experience a renaissance, a rebirth of closeness. But with alcohol standing as a wall between them, that would be very difficult, if not impossible, to achieve. Lilly finally nodded, "OK, I'll try again."

Julie arranged for Lilly to go into detox at a hospital unit specializing in drug and alcohol treatment. Two weeks later, she emerged, shaky, but ready to begin therapy. In the hospital she had also been diagnosed as suffering from moderate depression, which would likely worsen as sobriety set in. The psychiatrist there had placed Lilly on a newer selective serotonin reuptake inhibitor (SSRI), which Lilly had tolerated well.

In our first treatment session, Julie encouraged Cindy to share with Lilly her feeling of looking in from outside Lilly's closed window. Her transparency had grown continually more opaque with time, like clear glasses that darken in the light until the outsider can only catch a reflection of themselves. Cindy's loneliness had steadily crept up on her. In the first few years, things had been fine. Cindy had loved living together, growing together, supporting each other. But in the last year, despair had visited Cindy and settled in to stay, emptying her heart of all hope. Lilly probably hadn't noticed, but Cindy in the past had initiated conversations—but now, there was nothing.

Just echoing empty silence. Cindy would occupy herself in other ways—more volunteer hours, more gardening, taking longer walks with friends. Cindy, in effect, had taken herself away from that painful ground between them. Now it was only cohabitation, not marriage.

Julie then asked Lilly to describe her last year and how her drinking had progressed. Lilly's manager at work made her miserable. He was white, racist (Lilly was Asian American), and a bully. But he had power, and was vital to Lilly's keeping her job, so she would swallow her anger and bear insult after insult. At some points, she had desperately wanted to quit, but a recession was on, and jobs were drying up. She had felt responsible to bring home the "big bucks." So she felt trapped, having to "endure this asshole." In the beginning, at the weekly two or three business lunch meetings, she'd have a beer, like everyone else. But soon it was two beers, then a scotch like her boss, who had two of those as well. Soon she was matching him glass for glass. But after a while, even that wasn't enough for Lilly. She wanted more, just to numb the rage that was building inside her, so she could actually concentrate on her work while blocking out her boss's ugly words. But after some months, more alcohol was needed to stay numb. She brought her first bottle home, and hid it. She worried now that Cindy would catch on and make her stop. She didn't want to stop. And she didn't want to complain about work all the time either—she thought Cindy would get bored with hearing her, so why even start. She got good at hiding, and covering the alcohol odor with snacks first thing after returning home. Smelly ones—like salami. Lilly also owned feeling a rising mountain of shame and guilt—hating herself that she was betraying Cindy with her nasty secret, and feeling so out of control. She knew she was addicted. She'd try to go two or three days with no drinking, only to make up for it with extra ounces the following day. She'd rationalize: It really wasn't that much. And it was the only way she could hold on to that job. Otherwise, she'd probably storm out in a rage and get thrown out on her ear.

Cindy was stunned, she'd had no idea about any of this. She softly said, "How can I help you?" Julie asked Lilly to think on that question. Cindy still loved her, even after all this. Her offer proved it. But Cindy also wanted entry into Lilly's world. Lilly would have to let her in if support was going to work.

In the next session, Cindy voiced more deeply her experiences—feeling shut out, and facing a towering wall of averted eye gaze, falling asleep early in the living room recliner, silent mealtimes, stony cold drives to do errands, and backs turned at bedtime. The loneliness she felt was surmounted only by her fear that Lilly couldn't stand her anymore. She'd lie awake at night reviewing everything that had happened that day, pondering how she could do better tomorrow. It must be her. Confusion, guilt, and frustration were feelings she bathed in daily. She recounted many of those times she'd reached out verbally or physically for connection with Lilly, only to be gruffly rebuffed. She'd finally given up. Lilly got it. And cried.

It was time now to introduce the couple to the Expressing Needs Card Deck. They split the deck and shuffled through their cards. They each picked three, then took turns saying each need in more detail. Lilly asked Cindy to please ask her about her day, and empathize with the stresses she voiced, but only that. She didn't want advice or solutions, just compassion and understanding from Cindy. Cindy eagerly agreed to do so, but only if Lilly would be truthful about what really transpired in her day. Cindy wanted that to include any cravings Lilly might have felt that day to drink again. She promised she would not chastise or criticize Lilly for any of it. She just wanted to better understand Lilly's internal world and the real thought that she was grappling with. Cindy said she'd be happy to ask Lilly about all the ups and downs of her day. And Lilly said, "Yes, I'll tell you all of it, even about my cravings." Cindy asked for Lilly to please give her a hug first thing once she'd walked through the door at night. She really missed their sharing physical affection, and a hug could feel really good as the beginning of rekindling their world of touch.

Lilly then asked Cindy to help her get rid of any and all bottles she may not have remembered hiding. Cindy promised; they'd do a thorough search of the house, garage, and yard—together this time, with only encouraging words spoken. This was the kind of help Lilly wanted—no criticism, doubts, or interrogations. Just words of comfort and support.

In the next session, Julie brought out instructions for the Gottman stress-reducing conversation, and had the couple practice it. First, Lilly was the speaker and described in strained, stuttering speech some of the worst things her boss had said to her: "You're built like a brick shithouse," "Why do you always have to wear pants—I want to see those legs," "Are you a Jap or a Chink?" "Your eyes too squinty to even read my memo? What's the matter with you?" And so on. He'd pile the work on Lilly, taking some of it from his pet protégés, then reprimand her for not getting it all done in time— sometimes four times what anyone else had to do. He was impossible! And never a word of praise, or even satisfaction. Cindy did a beautiful job of empathizing, questioning Lilly's deeper feelings, and touching her shoulder gently when Lilly would fall silent after some particularly torturous story. Then it was Lilly's turn to listen to Cindy's stress. Cindy commented about a neighbor who kept dumping branches onto their property, and who got angry and defensive every time Cindy asked him to move them. It had happened again yesterday. His anger was rather scary—he was a big guy, and would turn red as he counterattacked her by calling her stupid and petty for worrying about a few inches of stuff on her lawn (it was more like a dozen feet). Lilly at first had trouble asking Cindy questions to better understand the stress Cindy felt with this guy. But with the Gottman *Guide to Great Listening* in hand, she figured out some questions to ask that deepened her grasp of what Cindy was feeling. Then she empathized well with Cindy's feelings.

As therapy progressed, the couple began talking more to each other— but then one day, during their session, Lilly admitted that she'd had a glass of wine at lunch. Julie had supported her to bring up any slips she might have. There would be no judgment, just an examination of what had triggered her. Lilly mentioned that a young guy with far less experience had gotten an assignment she had really hoped she'd get. One that was fascinating and could lead to a promotion and a blessed transfer out of this manager's view. She knew she was the best qualified to handle it. But of course, her manager gave it to his pet employee, a white male who had only been working in the department for 6 months. So unfair. She'd gone out to lunch by herself, and had that drink. Then, with fear in the pit of her stomach, had stopped herself from having another.

We explored Lilly's world more deeply, and how she had gotten triggered to drink again. At first, Lilly had a hard time describing her earlier years. She'd been strictly taught growing up that it was wrong to ever complain about anything. That was not a useful tool for her survival. Julie gently countered this idea with the fact that actually, complaining was good, especially when not complaining converted her into a pressure cooker with no escape valve. Steam would keep building until finally the lid would blow off. That's what had happened at the bar that week. No wonder she had slipped. There had to be an escape valve somehow, and drinking was the only one Lilly knew of that could break open the cooker, release some steam, and return her to a calmer state.

Lilly finally poured out her history growing up in an all-white neighborhood, going to schools where often she was the only Asian American student there. How no one would sit with her at lunch. How she walked hallways alone. How she finally gained friends among the smartest kids in high school, who by then were outcasts, too. But lots of damage had already been done. Deep down, she had internalized the shame and feelings of inferiority sliced into her by the brutal remarks and exclusions of her peers. And her parents only pooh-poohed her reports home, saying that was nothing, she should hear what they went through, and blah, blah, blah.

Beneath the surface, there was a tributary of pain, anger, resentment, and shame that flowed steadily through her day-to-day life. And sometimes flooded her whole being. This boss was only the last in a series of bullies she'd encountered. It was as if, at work, she had to constantly walk down dark alleyways and be wary of any person approaching her. They could so easily hurt her with just one whispered word as they passed, like "Chink," a pejorative slang term for someone Chinese. Her boss handing that pipsqueak smug guy such a plum assignment curdled her stomach. She was so mad when he announced he'd gotten the assignment that she had to quietly run to the bathroom, lock herself in a stall, and cry. It was so unfair! She was such a mess, she didn't see how she could return to her office desk. She headed for the bar at the café she frequented. Down went the wine. Then up came the shame, the guilt, the despair—once again, she'd broken her vow to remain sober. She had initially thought, "I'll just lie about it." But by now she knew—that would only further cave in her sobriety, piling even more shame from her loss of integrity on the shame she already felt. She'd not give in to that compulsion. She'd tell Cindy the truth. Before going back to the office, she had called Cindy and admitted her slip. She'd begged Cindy's forgiveness. Cindy had responded, "It's OK. I'm not here to judge you. Come home as soon as you can and let's just talk about it. Sounds like you really need a hug." Lilly had done just that. Then promised to raise the episode in their next therapy session. And the session had proven fruitful, allowing Lilly to vent her rage at once again being passed over, and allowing Cindy to understand Lilly's suffering at an even deeper level.

The next piece of work took half a dozen sessions. Cindy and Lilly had had a big fight on work/life balance. They first used the Aftermath of a Regrettable Incident to process their fight. Then they embarked on discussing their central problem: Cindy wanted Lilly to work less and play more. Lilly was afraid to embrace that balance for fear of losing her job. As it was, she felt like she was teetering on the point of a precipice. At any moment her boss or someone else could just give her a little shove, and she'd tumble a thousand feet down into hopeless despair, not to mention the lack of income to feed and house the two of them. Cindy's argument was that this job was tearing Lilly up inside. She deserved to lead a better life, with a job where she could be really appreciated for the brilliance she brought to her work and still have time outside of work for loving, romance, fun, and adventure. She longed with all her being to just have hours spent reading together in their den in front of a crackling fire. That could make their lives really shine with quiet and serene joy. Throughout these sessions, the couple worked with the conflict blueprint, including the Gottman–Rapoport exercise, the Dreams Within Conflict intervention, and the Two-Oval Compromise method. Many Dan Wiles were added to the mix to help one partner understand the other. Eventually, they were able to speak more poetically and clearly about their own feelings without Julie's intervening. They finally arrived at a momentous decision. Lilly felt that she was about to get fired. So what? Just let it happen! Don't work so hard to avoid it! With being fired, she could collect unemployment checks and receive COBRA health benefits while looking for a much better fit. Lilly gulped and said, "Cindy, are you sure? There's no guarantee I'll get something else even if I find the perfect job." Cindy replied, "I don't care. You've got to get out of there just to save your sanity. I've got savings. If we have to, we can dip into that. I can't stand you being tortured in that job anymore!" Nodding slowly, Lilly said, "OK, I'll do it. Let's go to the beach this weekend!" "Right!" said Cindy.

Our final steps in therapy involved creating rituals of connection for this couple. They decided their first one would be sharing a cup of tea together every evening and discussing the ups and downs of their day together. Lilly loved that one. They planned out who would make the tea, and carry it into the living room, who would remove the dishes after they were done, and who would clean up. And they both decided to add just one little piece of chocolate each to sweeten up their talk. Lovely! Their therapist highly approved. Several more rituals followed this one. How to greet each other each morning; how to initiate and refuse lovemaking without crucifying their partner if it was a "no, thank you"; how to spend a weekend; whether or not to attend church as a weekly occurrence; and where they would go for their next vacation.

By now a year had passed. Lilly had maintained her sobriety ever since that first slip she took. Gradually we phased out the couple's therapy. By its end they had been working for 18 months on their relationship. It was indeed a new one. One uncontaminated by alcohol, one of mutual respect and kind-ness, and one with an open door on each partner's vulnerabilities. Now they had a relationship of human to human, not mask to mask. We said goodbye.

CHAPTER 20

Conclusion

This book is called *The New Marriage Clinic*. It will probably be our last revision because we are now really old. We've tried to give you a hand into our boat, as we navigate all the research and intervention work we've done over the last two and a half decades. We've docked at new relationship assessment processes, conflict interventions, and exercises to deepen friendship and shared meaning. Also, in an attempt to describe treatment for comorbidities as well as the relationship itself, we've presented strategies for working with three comorbidities, ones that cast the darkest shadows over couples' relationships. We've deeply enjoyed the journey, and we hope you have too.

We hope those who follow in our footsteps will be writing later versions, because we are fully aware of how many issues remain to be resolved in understanding and helping relationships. We are always eager to hear new ideas or errors we've made in our own work, in the hope that our efforts will continue, whether carried on by us or others. Both research and clinical work are a wonderful adventure. There is so much to learn. But we've learned that clinical applications and research must work in tandem to make real advances. As a married couple, a scientist (mostly) and a clinician (mostly) working together on the relationships of others as well as on our own relationship, we have hashed it out throughout our many years working together, so that there is no arrogance of a scientist toward clinical wisdom, or clinician's fear of research findings. We all need each other moving forward. Let's pledge ourselves to continue the adventure.

Bibliography

Abraham, L. (2010). *The husbands and wives club: A year in the life of a couples therapy group*. Touchstone.

Ackerman, N. W. (1966). Family psychotherapy—theory and practice. *American Journal of Psychotherapy*, *20*(3), 405–414. https://doi.org/10.1176/appi.psychotherapy.1966.20.3 .405

Agrawal, A., Verweij, K. J. H., Gillespie, N. A., Heath, A. C., Lessov-Schlaggar, C. N., Martin, N. G., Nelson, E. C., Slutske, W. S., Whitfield, J. B., & Lynskey, M. T. (2012). The genetics of addiction—a translational perspective. *Translational Psychiatry*, *2*(7), e140. https://doi.org/10.1038/tp.2012.54

Agronin, M. E. (2014). From Cicero to Cohen: Developmental theories of aging, from antiquity to the present. *The Gerontologist*, *54*(1), 30–39. https://doi.org/10.1093/geront/gnt032

Alonzo, D. J. (2018). "All that matters is that we know who we are": Multicultural considerations in brief sex therapy with same-sex couples. In S. Green & D. Flemons (Eds.), *Quickies: The handbook of brief sex therapy* (pp. 175–195). Norton.

APA (American Psychiatric Association). (2013). *Diagnostic and statistical manual of mental disorders* (5th ed.).

Azrin, N. H., Naster, B. J., & Jones, R. (1973). Reciprocity counseling: A rapid learning-based procedure for marital counseling. *Behaviour Research and Therapy*, *11*(4), 365–382. https://doi.org/10.1016/0005-7967(73)90095-8

Babcock, J. C., Green, C. E., & Robie, C. (2004). Does batterers' treatment work? A meta-analytic review of domestic violence treatment. *Clinical Psychology Review*, *23*(8), 1023–1053. https://doi.org/10.1016/j.cpr.2002.07.001

Babcock, J. C., Jacobson, N. S., Gottman, J., & Yerington, T. P. (2000). Attachment, emotional regulation, and the function of marital violence—differences between secure, preoccupied, and dismissing violent and nonviolent husbands. *Journal of Family Violence*, *15*(4), 391–409.

Bacchus, L., Mezey, G., & Bewley, S. (2004). Domestic violence: Prevalence in pregnant women and associations with physical and psychological health. *European Journal of Obstetrics and Gynecology and Reproductive Biology, 113*(1), 6–11. https://doi.org/10.1016/S0301-2115(03)00326-9

Bach, G. R., & Wyden, P. (1968). *The intimate enemy.* Avon.

Bakeman, R., & Gottman, J. M. (1997). *Observing interaction: An introduction to sequential analysis* (2nd ed.). Cambridge University Press.

Bakeman, R., & Quera, V. (2011). *Sequential analysis and observational methods for the behavioral sciences.* Cambridge University Press.

Bancroft, J., Long, J. S., & McCabe, J. (2011). Sexual well-being: A comparison of U.S. black and white women in heterosexual relationships. *Archives of Sexual Behavior, 40,* 725–740. https://doi.org/10.1007/s10508-010-9679-z

Barbach, L. (1982). *For each other: Sharing sexual intimacy.* Anchor.

Barrett, D. (2010). *Supernormal stimuli: How primal urges overran their evolutionary purpose.* Norton.

Basson, R. (2002). Women's sexual desire: Disordered or misunderstood? *Journal of Sex and Marital Therapy, 28*(Suppl. 1), 17–28. https://doi.org/10.1080/00926230252851168

Bateson, G., Jackson, D. D., Haley, J., & Weakland, J. (1956). Toward a theory of schizophrenia. *Behavioral Science, 1*(4), 251–264. https://doi.org/10.1002/bs.3830010402

Baucom, B. R., Atkins, D. C., Simpson, L. E., & Christensen, A. (2009). Prediction of response to treatment in a randomized clinical trial of couple therapy: A 2-year follow-up. *Journal of Consulting and Clinical Psychology, 77*(1), 160–173.

Baucom, D. H., & Epstein, N. (1990). *Cognitive-behavioral marital therapy.* Brunner/Mazel.

Baucom, D. H., Epstein, N., Rankin, L. A., & Burnett, C. K. (1996). Assessing relationship standards: The Inventory of Specific Relationship Standards. *Journal of Family Psychology, 10*(1), 72–88. https://doi.org/10.1037/0893-3200.10.1.72

Belsky, J., & Kelly, J. (1994). *The transition to parenthood: How a first child changes a marriage: Why some couples grow closer and others apart.* Dell.

Bergin, A. E., & Jasper, L. G. (1969). Correlates of empathy in psychotherapy: A replication. *Journal of Abnormal Psychology, 74*(4), 477–481. https://doi.org/10.1037/h0027815

Berkman, L. F., & Breslow, L. (1983). *Health and the ways of living: The Alameda County Study.* Wiley.

Berkman, L. F., Kawachi, I., & Glymour, M. M. (Eds.). (2014). *Social epidemiology.* Oxford University Press.

Berkman, L. F., & Syme, S. L. (1979). Social networks, host resistance, and mortality: A nine-year follow-up study of Alameda County residents. *American Journal of Epidemiology, 109*(2), 186–204.

Bernard, J. (1982). *The future of marriage.* Yale University Press.

Birchler, G. R., Weiss, R. L., & Vincent, J. P. (1975). Multimethod analysis of social reinforcement exchange between maritally distressed and nondistressed spouse and stranger dyads. *Journal of Personality and Social Psychology, 31*(2), 349–360.

Bloom, B., Asher, S., & White, S. (1978). Marital disruption as a stressor: A review and analysis. *Psychological Bulletin*, 85(4), 867–894.

Bodenmann, G. (2005). Dyadic coping and its significance for marital functioning. In T. A. Revenson, K. Kayser, & G. Bodenmann (Eds.), *Couples coping with stress: Emerging perspectives on dyadic coping* (pp. 33–49). American Psychological Association. https://doi.org/10.1037/11031-002

Bodenmann, G., Gottman, J. M., & Backman, H. (1997). A Swiss replication of Gottman's couple typology. *Swiss Journal of Psychology*, 56(4), 205–216.

Boiger, M., Kirchner-Häusler, A., Schouten, A., Uchida, Y., Mesquita, B. (2022). Different bumps in the road: The emotional dynamics of couple disagreements in Belgium and Japan. Emotion. 22(5):805-819. http://doi.org/ 10.1037/emo0000910

Boyce, W. T. (2019). *The orchid and the dandelion: Why some children struggle and how all can thrive*. Vintage.

Bradbury, T. N. (1998). *The developmental course of marital dysfunction*. Cambridge University Press.

Bradley, R. P. C., Drummey, K., Gottman, J. M., & Gottman, J. S. (2014). Treating couples who mutually exhibit violence or aggression: Reducing behaviors that show a susceptibility for violence. *Journal of Family Violence*, 29(5), 549–558. https://doi.org/10.1007/s10896-014-9615-4

Bradley, R. P. C., & Gottman, J. M. (2012). Reducing situational violence in low-income couples by fostering healthy relationships. *Journal of Marital and Family Therapy*, 38(1), 187–198. https://doi.org/10.1111/j.1752-0606.2012.00288.x

Bray, J. H., & Jouriles, E. N. (1995). Treatment of marital conflict and prevention of divorce. *Journal of Marital and Family Therapy*, 21(4), 461–473. https://doi.org/10.1111/j.1752-0606.1995.tb00175.x

Broderick, C. B. (1993). *Understanding family process*. Sage.

Brown, C. L., Chen, K.-H., Wells, J. L., Otero, M. C., McConnelly, D. E., Levenson, R. W., & Friedrickson, B. L. (2022). Shared emotions in shared lives: Moments of co-experienced affect, more than individually experienced affect, linked to relationship quality. *Emotion*, 22(6), 1387–1393. https://doi.org/10.1037/emo0000939

Brown, E. M. (1991). *Patterns of infidelity and their treatment*. Brunner/Mazel.

Bruner, J.S., and Taguiri, R. (1954) The perception of people. In G. Lindsey (Ed.), *Handbook of Social Psychology*. Wiley.

Buchanan, C. M., Maccoby, E. E., & Dornbusch, S. M. (1991). Caught between parents: Adolescents' experience in divorced homes. *Child Development*, 62(5), 1008–1029. https://doi.org/10.1111/j.1467-8624.1991.tb01586.x

Buehlman, K. T., Gottman, J. M., & Katz, L. F. (1992). How a couple views their past predicts their future: Predicting divorce from an Oral History Interview. *Journal of Family Psychology*, 5(3–4), 295–318.

Burgdorf, J., & Panksepp, J. (2006). The neurobiology of positive emotions. *Neuroscience and Biobehavioral Reviews*, 30(2), 173–187. https://doi.org/10.1016/j.neubiorev.2005.06 .001

Burgess, E. W., & Wallin, P. (1953). *Engagement and marriage*. Lippincott.

Burman, B., & Margolin, G. (1992). Analysis of the association between marital relationships and health problems. *Psychological Bulletin*, 112, 39–63.

Buss, D. M. (1989). Conflict between the sexes: Strategic interference and the evocation of anger and upset. *Journal of Personality and Social Psychology*, 56(5), 735–747. https:// doi.org/10.1037/0022-3514.56.5.735

Buss, D. M. (2016). *The evolution of desire: Strategies of human mating*. Basic Books.

Cacioppo, J. T., & Tassinary, L. G. (1990). *Principles of psychophysiology: Physical, social, and inferential elements*. Cambridge University Press.

Campbell, D. T., & Fiske, D. W. (1959). Convergent and discriminant validation by the multitrait–multimethod matrix. *Psychological Bulletin*, 56(2), 81–105. https://doi.org/10 .1037/h0046016

Campos, B., Graesch, A. P., Repetti, R., Bradbury, T., & Ochs, E. (2009). Opportunity for interaction? A naturalistic observation study of dual-earner families after work and school. *Journal of Family Psychology*, 23(6), 798–807. https://doi.org/10.1037 /a0015824

Campos, B., Wang, S.-w., Plaksina, T., Repetti, R. L., Schoebi, D., Ochs, E., & Beck, M. E. (2013). Positive and negative emotion in the daily life of dual-earner couples with children. *Journal of Family Psychology*, 27(1), 76–85. https://doi.org/10.1037/a0031413

Carr, N. (2010). *The shallows: How the internet is changing the way we think, read and remember*. Atlantic Books.

Carstensen, L. L. (1992). Social and emotional patterns in adulthood: Support for socioemotional selectivity theory. *Psychology and Aging*, 7(3), 331–338. https://doi.org/10 .1037//0882-7974.7.3.331

Carstensen, L. L. (1995). Evidence for a life-span theory of socioemotional selectivity. *Current Directions in Psychological Science*, 4(5), 151–156. https://doi.org/10.1111/1467 -8721.ep11512261

Carstensen, L. L., Gottman, J. M., & Levenson, R. W. (1995). Emotional behavior in long-term marriage. *Psychology and Aging*, 10(1), 140–149.

Carstensen, L. L., & Turk-Charles, S. (1994). The salience of emotion across the adult life span. *Psychology and Aging*, 9(2), 259–264. https://doi.org/10.1037/0882-7974.9.2.259

Chapman, G. M. (2015). *The 5 love languages: The secret to love that lasts*. Northfield.

Chen, K.-H., Brown, C. L., Wells, J. L., Rothwell, E. S., Otero, M. C., Levenson, R. W., & Frederickson, B. L. (2021). Physiological linkage during shared positive and shared negative emotion. *Journal of Personality and Social Psychology*, 121(5), 1029–1056. https://doi.org/10.1037/pspi0000337

Cherlin, A. (1981). *Marriage, divorce, remarriage*. Harvard University Press.

Cherlin, A. J. (1992). *The marriage go-round*. Vintage.

Christensen, A. (1987). Detection of conflict patterns in couples. In K. Hahlweg & M. J.

Goldstein (Eds.), *Understanding major mental disorder: The contribution of family interaction research* (pp. 250–265). Family Process Press.

Christensen, A. (1988). Dysfunctional interaction patterns in couples. In P. Noller & M. A. Fitzpatrick (Eds.), *Perspectives on marital interaction* (pp. 31–52). Multilingual Matters.

Christensen, A., Atkins, D. C., Baucom, B., & Yi, J. (2010). Marital status and satisfaction five years following a randomized clinical trial comparing traditional versus integrative behavioral couple therapy. *Journal of Consulting and Clinical Psychology, 78*(2), 225–235. https://doi.org/10.1037/a0018132

Christensen, A., & Heavey, C. L. (1990). Gender and social structure in the demand/withdraw pattern of marital conflict. *Journal of Personality and Social Psychology, 59*(1), 73–81.

Christensen, A., Sevier, M., Simpson, L. E., & Gattis, K. S. (2003). Acceptance, mindfulness, and change in couple therapy. In S. C. Hayes, V. M. Follette, & M. M. Linehan (Eds.), *Mindfulness and acceptance: Expanding the cognitive-behavioral tradition* (pp. 288–309). Guilford Press.

City of Seattle Planning Commission. (1990). *City of Seattle planning commission report.*

Cleek, M. G., & Pearson, T. A. (1985). Perceived causes of divorce: An analysis of interrelationships. *Journal of Marriage and Family, 47*(1), 179–183. https://doi.org/10.2307/352080

Coan, J., & Gottman, J. M. (2003). The Specific Affect Coding System. In J. A. Coan & J. J. B. Allen (Eds.), *The handbook of emotion elicitation and assessment.* Oxford University Press.

Coan, J., Gottman, J. M., Babcock, J., & Jacobson, N. (1997). Battering and the male rejection of influence from women. *Aggressive Behavior, 23*(5), 375–388. https://doi.org/10.1002/(SICI)1098-2337(1997)23:5<375::AID-AB6>3.0.CO;2-H

Cohen, R. S., & Christensen, A. (1980). A further examination of demand characteristics in marital interaction. *Journal of Consulting and Clinical Psychology, 48*(1), 121–123. https://doi.org/10.1037/0022-006X.48.1.121

Conger, R., Elder, G. H., Lorenz, F. O., Conger, K. J., Simons, R. L., Whitbeck, L. B., Huck, S., & Melby, J. N. (1990). Linking economic hardship to marital quality and instability. *Journal of Marriage and Family, 52*(3), 643–656. https://doi.org/10.2307/352931

Cookerly, J. R. (1980). Does marital therapy do any lasting good? *Journal of Marital and Family Therapy, 6*(4), 393–397. https://doi.org/10.1111/j.1752-0606.1980.tb01331.x

Cowan, P. A., & Cowan, C. P. (1990). Becoming a family: Research and intervention. In I. Sigel & A. Brody (Eds.), *Family research.* Erlbaum.

Cuber, J. F., & Haroff, P. B. (1965). Five kinds of relationships. In A. Editor (Ed.), *Sourcebook in marriage and the family* (4th ed., pp. 212–219). Houghton Mifflin.

Darwin, C. (1872). *The expression of the emotions in man and animals.* Murray.

Davidson, R. J. (1994). Asymmetric brain function, affective style, and psychopathology: The role of early experience and plasticity. *Development and Psychopathology, 6*(4), 741–758. https://doi.org/10.1017/S0954579400004764

Davidson, R. J., & Begley, S. (2012a). *The emotional life of your brain: How its unique patterns affect the way you think, feel, and live—and how you can change them. Hudson Street Press.

Davidson, R. J., & Begley, S. (2012b). Tired of feeling bad? The new science of feelings can help. *Newsweek*. https://www.newsweek.com/tired-feeling-bad-new-science-feelings-can-help-65743

Davis, D. (2013). *The compatibility gene: How our bodies fight disease, attract others, and define our selves*. Oxford University Press.

Davis, D. M., (2014). *The compatibility gene : How our bodies fight disease, attract others, and define our selves*. Oxford University Press.

Davoodvandi, M., Nejad, S. N., & Farzad, V. (2018). Examining the effectiveness of Gottman couple therapy on improving marital adjustment and couples' intimacy. *Iranian Journal of Psychiatry, 13*(2), 136–142.

Del Arco, A., Park, J., & Moghaddam, B. (2020). Unanticipated stressful and rewarding experiences engage the same prefrontal cortex and ventral tegmental area neuronal populations. *ENeuro, 7*(3). https://doi.org/10.1523/ENEURO.0029-20.2020

Denworth, L. (2020). *Friendship: The evolution, biology, and extraordinary power of life's fundamental bond*. Bloomsbury.

Derogatis, L. R., & Cleary, P. A. (1977). Confirmation of the dimensional structure of the SCL-90: A study in construct validation. *Journal of Clinical Psychology, 33*(4), 981–989. https://doi.org/10.1002/1097-4679(197710)33:4<981::AID-JCLP2270330412>3.0.CO;2-0

Derogatis, L. R., Lipman, R., & Covi, L. (1973). SCL-90: An outpatient psychiatric rating scale—preliminary report. *Psychopharmacology Bulletin, 9*(1), 13–28.

DeWall, C. N., Lambert, N. M., Slotter, E. B., Pond, R. S., Jr., Deckman, T., Finkel, E. J., Luchies, L. B., & Fincham, F. D. (2011). So far away from one's partner, yet so close to romantic alternatives: Avoidant attachment, interest in alternatives, and infidelity. *Journal of Personality and Social Psychology, 101*(6), 1302–1316. https://doi.org/10.1037/a0025497

Ditzen, B., Schaer, M., Gabriel, B., Bodenmann, G., Ehlert, U., & Heinrichs, M. (2009). Intranasal oxytocin increases positive communication and reduces cortisol levels during couple conflict. *Biological Psychology, 65*(9), 728–731. https://doi.org/10.1016/j.biopsych.2008.10.011

Dizzard, J. (1968). *Social change and the family*. University of Chicago, Family and Community Study Center.

Dreyfus, N. (2013). *Talk to me like I'm someone you love: Relationship repair in a flash*. Tarcher.

Driver, J. L., & Gottman, J. M. (2004a). Daily marital interactions and positive affect during marital conflict among newlywed couples. *Family Process, 43*(3), 301–314. https://doi.org/10.1111/j.1545-5300.2004.00024.x

Driver, J. L., & Gottman, J. M. (2004b). Turning toward versus turning away: A coding system of daily interactions. In P. K. Kerig & D. H. Baucom (Eds.), *Couple observational coding systems* (pp. 209–225). Erlbaum.

Dunn, G. (1989). *Design and analysis of reliability studies: The statistical evaluation of measurement errors.* Edward Arnold Publishers.

Ebling, R., & Levenson, R. W. (2003). Who are the marital experts? *Journal of Marriage and Family, 65*(1), 130–142. https://doi.org/10.1111/j.1741-3737.2003.00130.x

Edwards, S. D. (2016). Influence of HeartMath quick coherence technique on psychophysiological coherence and feeling states. *African Journal for Physical Activity and Health Sciences, 22*(41). https://hdl.handle.net/10520/EJC200070

Ekman, P. (1994). Strong evidence for universals in facial expressions: A reply to Russell's mistaken critique. *Psychological Bulletin, 115*(2), 268–287. https://doi.org/10.1037/0033-2909.115.2.268

Ekman, P., & Friesen, W. V. (1978). *Facial Action Coding System.* Consulting Psychologist Press.

Ekman, P., Friesen, W. V., O'Sullivan, M., Chan, A., Diacoyanni-Tariatzis, I., Heider, K., Krause, R., LeCompte, W. A., Pitcairn, T., Ricci-Bitti, P. E., Scherer, K., Tomita, M., & Tzavaras, A. (1987). Universals and cultural differences in the judgments of facial expressions of emotion. *Journal of Personality and Social Psychology, 53*(4), 712–717. https://doi.org/10.1037/0022-3514.53.4.712

Eldridge, K., Sevier, M., Jones, J., Atkins, D. C., & Christensen, A. (2007). Demand-withdraw communication in severely distressed, moderately distressed, and non-distressed couples: Rigidity and polarity during relationship and personal problem discussions. *Journal of Family Psychology, 21*(2), 218–226. https://doi.org/10.1037/0893-3200.21.2.218

Faulkner, W. (1951). *Requiem for a nun.* Random House.

Fisher, H. (1993). *Anatomy of love: A natural history of adultery, monogamy, and divorce.* Simon & Schuster.

Fiske, S. T. (2011). *Envy up, scorn down: How status divides us.* Russell Sage Foundation.

Fowers, B. J., & Olson, D. H. (1986). Predicting marital success with PREPARE: A predictive validity study. *Journal of Marital and Family Therapy, 12*(4), 403–413.

Frankl, V. E. (1985). *Man's search for meaning.* Simon & Schuster.

Friedly, J. L., Bauer, Z., Comstock, B. A., DiMango, E., Ferrara, A., Huang, S. S., … & Trontell, A. (2014). Challenges conducting comparative effectiveness research: The clinical and health outcomes initiative in comparative effectiveness (CHOICE) experience. *Comparative Effectiveness Research,* 1-12. https://doi.org/10.2147/CER.S59136

Friedman, H. S., Tucker, J. S., Schwartz, J. E., Tomlinson-Keasey, C., Martin, L. R., Wingard, D. L., & Criqui, M. H. (1995). Psychosocial and behavioral predictors of longevity: The aging and death of the "Termites." *American Psychologist, 50*(2), 69–78. https://doi.org/10.1037/0003-066X.50.2.69

Friend, D. J., Bradley, R. P. C., & Gottman, J. M. (2017). Displayed affective behavior between intimate partner violence types during non-violent conflict discussions. *Journal of Family Violence, 32*(3), 493–504. https://doi.org/10.1007/s10896-016-9870-7

Friend, D. J., Bradley, R. P. C., Thatcher, R., & Gottman, J. M. (2011). Typologies of intimate partner violence: Evaluation of a screening instrument for differentiation. *Journal of Family Violence, 26*(7), 551–563. https://doi.org/10.1007/s10896-011-9392-2

Froerer, A. S., Lucas, B. M., & Brown, T. B. (2012). Current practices of intimate partner violence assessment among marriage and family therapy trainees at a university clinic. *Journal of Couple and Relationship Therapy, 11*(1), 16–32. https://doi.org/10.1080/15332691.2012.639702

Ganley, A. L. (1995). Understanding domestic violence. In *Improving the health care response to domestic violence: A resource manual for health care providers* (pp. 15–42). Family Violence Prevention Fund.

Garanzini, S., Yee, A., Gottman, J., Gottman, J., Cole, C., Preciado, M., & Jasculca, C. (2017). Results of Gottman method couples therapy with gay and lesbian couples. *Journal of Marital and Family Therapy, 43*(4), 674–684. https://doi.org/10.1111/jmft.12276

Gendlin, E. T. (1978). *Focusing.* Bantum.

Gigy, L., & Kelly, J. B. (1993). Reasons for divorce: Perspectives of divorcing men and women. *Journal of Divorce and Remarriage, 18*(1–2), 169–188. https://doi.org/10.1300/J087v18n01_08

Glass, S. P., & Staeheli, J. C. (2003). *Not "just friends": Protect your relationship from infidelity and heal the trauma of betrayal.* Free Press.

Godek, G. (1991). *1001 ways to be romantic.* Casablanca Press.

Goffman, E. (1959). *The presentation of self in everyday life.* Anchor Books.

Goffman, E. (1981). *Forms of talk.* University of Pennsylvania Press.

Gola, M., Wordecha, M., Sescousse, G., Lew-Starowicz, M., Kossowski, B., Wypych, M., Makeig, S., Potenza, M. N., & Marchewka, A. (2017). Can pornography be addictive? An fMRI study of men seeking treatment for problematic pornography use. *Neuropsychopharmacology, 42,* 2021–2031. https://doi.org/10.1038/npp.2017.78

Goode, W. J. (1969). *Women in divorce.* Free Press. (Originally published as *Divorce and after,* 1956)

Gottman, J. M. (1979). *Marital interaction: Experimental investigations.* Academic Press.

Gottman, J. M. (1994). *What predicts divorce? The relationship between marital processes and marital outcomes.* Erlbaum.

Gottman, J. M. (1996). *What predicts divorce? The measures.* Erlbaum.

Gottman, J. M. (1998). Psychology and the study of marital processes. *Annual Review of Psychology, 49*(1), 169–197. https://doi.org/10.1146/annurev.psych.49.1.169

Gottman, J. M. (1999). *The marriage clinic: A scientifically based marital therapy.* Norton.

Gottman, J. M. (2001). Meta-emotion, children's emotional intelligence, and buffering children from marital conflict. In C. D. Ryff & B. Singer (Eds.), *Emotion, social relationships and health* (pp. 23–40). Oxford University Press.

Gottman, J. M. (2011). *The science of trust: Emotional attunement for couples.* Norton.

Gottman, J . M. (2014). *Principe amoris: The new science of love.* Routledge.

Gottman, J. M., Coan, J., Carrère, S., & Swanson, C. (1998). Predicting marital happiness and stability from newlywed interactions. *Journal of Marriage and Family, 60*(1), 5–22. https://doi.org/10.2307/353438

Gottman, J. M., & DeClaire, J. (1997). *The heart of parenting*. Simon & Schuster.

Gottman, J. M., & DeClaire, J. (2001). *The relationship cure*. Harmony Books.

Gottman, J. M., & DeClaire, J. (2011). *Raising an emotionally intelligent child: The heart of parenting*. Simon & Schuster.

Gottman, J. M., Driver, J., & Tabares, A. (2015). Repair during marital conflict in newlyweds: How couples move from attack–defend to collaboration. *Journal of Family Psychotherapy, 26*(2), 85–108. https://doi.org/10.1080/08975353.2015.1038962

Gottman, J. M., & Gottman, J. S. (2000a). *Assessment, intervention, and co-morbidities*. The Gottman Institute.

Gottman, J. M., & Gottman, J. S. (2000b). *Gottman method couples therapy: Bridging the couple chasm*. The Gottman Institute.

Gottman, J. M., & Gottman, J. S. (2007). *And baby makes three: The six-step plan for preserving marital intimacy and rekindling romance after baby arrives*. Three Rivers Press.

Gottman, J. M., & Gottman, J. S. (2017a). The natural principles of love. *Journal of Family Theory and Review, 9*(1), 7–26. https://doi.org/10.1111/jftr.12182

Gottman, J. M., & Gottman, J. S. (2017b). *Treating affairs and trauma: Helping couples heal and rebuild trust*. The Gottman Institute.

Gottman, J. M., & Gottman, J. S. (2018). *The science of couples and family therapy: Behind the scenes at the love lab*. Norton.

Gottman, J. M., Gottman, J. S., Abrams, D., & Abrams, R. C. (2018). *Eight dates: Essential conversations for a lifetime of love*. Workman.

Gottman, J. M., Gottman, J. S., Cole, C., & Preciado, M. (2020). Gay, lesbian, and heterosexual couples about to begin couples therapy: An online relationship assessment of 40,681 couples. *Journal of Marital and Family Therapy, 46*(2), 218–239. https://doi.org/10.1111/jmft.12395

Gottman, J. M., Jacobson, N. S., Rushe, R. H., Shortt, J. W., Babcock, J., Taillade, J. J. L., & Waltz, J. (1995). The relationship between heart rate reactivity, emotionally aggressive behavior, and general violence in batterers. *Journal of Family Psychology, 9*(3), 227–248.

Gottman, J. M., & Katz, L. F. (1989). Effects of marital discord on young children's peer interaction and health. *Developmental Psychology, 25*(3), 373–381.

Gottman, J. M., Katz, L. F., & Hooven, C. (1996). Parental meta-emotion philosophy and the emotional life of families: Theoretical models and preliminary data. *Journal of Family Psychology, 10*(3), 243–268. https://doi.org/10.1037/0893-3200.10.3.243

Gottman, J. M., Katz, L. F., & Hooven, C. (1997). *Meta-emotion: How families communicate emotionally*. Erlbaum.

Gottman, J. M., & Krokoff, L. J. (1989). Marital interaction and satisfaction: A longitudinal view. *Journal of Consulting and Clinical Psychology, 57*(1), 47–52. https://doi.org/10.1037/0022-006X.57.1.47

Gottman, J. M., & Levenson, R. W. (1985). A valid procedure for obtaining self-report of affect in marital interaction. *Journal of Consulting and Clinical Psychology*, *53*(2), 151–160.

Gottman, J. M., & Levenson, R. W. (1986). Assessing the role of emotion in marriage. *Behavioral Assessment*, *8*(1), 31–48.

Gottman, J. M., & Levenson, R. W. (1992). Marital processes predictive of later dissolution: Behavior, physiology, and health. *Journal of Personality and Social Psychology*, *63*(2), 221–233.

Gottman, J. M., & Levenson, R. W. (1999a). Dysfunctional marital conflict: Women are being unfairly blamed. *Journal of Divorce a Remarriage*, *31*(3–4), 1–17. https://doi.org/10 .1300/J087v31n03_01

Gottman, J. M., & Levenson, R. W. (1999b). How stable is marital interaction over time? *Family Process*, *38*(2), 159–165. https://doi.org/10.1111/j.1545-5300.1999.00159.x

Gottman, J. M., & Levenson, R. W. (1999c). Rebound from marital conflict and divorce prediction. *Family Process*, *38*(3), 287–292. https://doi.org/10.1111/j.1545-5300.1999 .00287.x

Gottman, J. M., & Levenson, R. W. (1999d). What predicts change in marital interaction over time? A study of alternative models. *Family Process*, *38*(2), 16.

Gottman, J. M., & Levenson, R. W. (2002). A two-factor model for predicting when a couple will divorce—exploratory analyses using 14-year longitudinal data. *Family Process*, *41*(4), 83–96.

Gottman, J. M., Levenson, R. W., Gross, J., Frederickson, B. L., McCoy, K., Rosenthal, L., Ruef, A., & Yoshimoto, D. (2003). Correlates of gay and lesbian couples' relationship satisfaction and relationship dissolution. *Journal of Homosexuality*, *45*(1), 23–43. https://doi.org/10.1300/J082v45n01_02

Gottman, J. M., Levenson, R. W., Swanson, C., Swanson, K., Tyson, R., & Yoshimoto, D. (2003b). Observing gay, lesbian, and heterosexual couples' relationships—Mathematical modeling of conflict interactions. *Journal of Homosexuality*, *45*(1), 65–91.

Gottman, J. M., Markman, H., & Notarius, C. (1977). The topography of marital conflict—a sequential analysis of verbal and nonverbal behavior. *Journal of Marriage and Family*, *39*(3), 461–477.

Gottman, J. M., Murray, J., Swanson, C., Tyson, R., & Swanson, K. (2002). *The mathematics of marriage: Dynamic nonlinear models*. Bradford Books.

Gottman, J. M., Notarius, C., Gonso, J., & Markman, H. (1976). *A couple's guide to communication*. Research Press.

Gottman, J. M., & Notarius, C. I. (2000). Decade review: Observing marital interaction. *Journal of Marriage and Family*, *62*(4), 927–947.

Gottman, J. M., & Parker, J. (1986). *Conversations of friends: Speculations on affective development*. Cambridge University Press.

Gottman, J. M., & Porterfield, A. (1981). Communicative competence in the nonverbal behavior of married couples. *Journal of Marriage and Family, 43*(4), 817–824.

Gottman, J. M., & Roy, A. K. (1990). *Sequential analysis: A guide for behavioral researchers.* Cambridge University Press.

Gottman, J. M., Ryan, K., Swanson, C., & Swanson, K. (2005). Proximal change experiments with couples: A methodology for empirically building a science of effective interventions for changing couples' interaction. *Journal of Family Communication, 5*(3), 163–190. https://doi.org/10.1207/s15327698jfc0503_1

Gottman, J. M., & Silver, N. (1994). *Why marriages succeed or fail: And how you can make yours last.* Simon & Schuster.

Gottman, J. M., & Silver, N. (2012). *What makes love last? How to build trust and avoid betrayal.* Simon & Schuster.

Gottman, J. M., & Silver, N. (2015). *The seven principles for making marriage work: A practical guide from the country's foremost relationship expert.* Harmony Books.

Gottman, J. M., & Tabares, A. (2018). The effects of briefly interrupting marital conflict. *Journal of Marital and Family Therapy, 44*(1), 61–72. https://doi.org/10.1111/jmft.12243

Gray, J. (1989). *Men are from Mars, women are from Venus.* HarperCollins.

Greenberg, L. S., & Johnson, S. M. (1988). *Emotionally focused therapy for couples.* Guilford Press.

Guerney, B. G. (1977). *Relationship enhancement.* Jossey-Bass.

Guerney, B. G., & Guerney, L. (1985). Marital and family problem prevention and enrichment programs. In L. L'Abate (Ed.), *Handbook of family psychology and therapy* (pp. 1179–1217). Dorsey Press.

Haavasi, N., Kaar, K. Z., & MohsenZadeh, F. (2018). Compare the efficacy of emotion focused couple therapy and Gottman couple therapy method in marital burnout and changing conflict resolution styles. *Journal of Fundamentals of Mental Health, 20*(1), 15–25.

Hahlweg, K., Schindler, L., Revenstorf, D., & Brengelmann, J. C. (1984). The Munich marital therapy study. In K. Hahlweg & N. S. Jacobson (Eds.), *Marital interaction: Analysis and modification* (pp. 3–26). Guilford Press.

Halford, W. K., Markman, H. J., Kling, G. H., & Stanley, S. M. (2003). Best practice in couple relationship education. *Journal of Marital and Family Therapy, 29*(3), 385–406. https://doi.org/10.1111/j.1752-0606.2003.tb01214.x

Hall, S. K., & Binik, Y. M. (2020). *Principles and practice of sex therapy.* Guilford Press.

Havighurst, S. S., Edvoll, M., Tidemann, I., Bølstad, E., Holme, H., Hansen, M. B., Eikseth, H. C., & Nygaard, E. (2022). A randomized controlled trial of an emotion socialization intervention in Norwegian kindergartens. *Early Education and Development.* https://doi.org/10.1080/10409289.2022.2160617

Havighurst, S. S., Wilson, K. R., Harley, A. E., Kehoe, C., Efron, D., & Prior, M. R. (2012). "Tuning into kids": Reducing young children's behavior problems using an emotion coaching parenting program. *Child Psychiatry and Human Development, 44*, 247–264. https://doi.org/10.1007/s10578-012-0322-1

Havighurst, S. S., Wilson, K. R., Harley, A. E., & Prior, M. R. (2009). Tuning in to kids: An emotion-focused parenting program—initial findings from a community trial. *Journal of Community Psychology, 37*(8), 1008–1023. https://doi.org/10.1002/jcop.20345

Havighurst, S. S., Wilson, K. R., Harley, A. E., Prior, M. R., & Kehoe, C. (2010). Tuning in to kids: Improving emotion socialization practices in parents of preschool children—Findings from a community trial. *Journal of Child Psychology and Psychiatry, 51*(12), 1342–1350. https://doi.org/10.1111/j.1469-7610.2010.02303.x

Hawkley, L. C., & Cacioppo, J. T. (2010). Loneliness matters: A theoretical and empirical review of consequences and mechanisms. *Annals of Behavioral Medicine, 40*(2), 218–227. https://doi.org/10.1007/s12160-010-9210-8

Heath, R. G. (1975). Brain function and behavior: I. Emotion and sensory phenomena in psychotic patients and in experimental animals. *Journal of Nervous and Mental Disease, 160*(3), 159–175.

Heavey, C. L., Layne, C., & Christensen, A. (1993). Gender and conflict structure in marital interaction: A replication and extension. *Journal of Consulting and Clinical Psychology, 61*(1), 16–27. https://doi.org/10.1037/0022-006X.61.1.16

Hendrix, H. (1988). *Getting the love you want: A guide for couples.* Holt.

Hetherington, E. M., & Clingempeel, W. G. (1992). Coping with marital transitions. *Monographs of the Society for Research in Child Development, 57*, 1–242.

Hite, S. (1987). *The Hite report: Women and love—A cultural revolution in progress.* Knopf.

Hochschild, A., & Machung, A. (2003). *The second shift.* Penguin Books.

Hoff, C. C., Beougher, S. C., Chakravarty, D., Darbes, L. A., & Neilands, T. B. (2010). Relationship characteristics and motivations behind agreements among gay male couples: Differences by agreement type and couple serostatus. *AIDS Care, 22*(7), 827–835. https://doi.org/10.1080/09540120903443384

Holt-Lunstad, J., Smith, T. B., & Layton, B. (2010). Social relationships and mortality risk: A meta-analytic review. *PLoS Medicine, 7*(7), e1000316.

Hooven, C., Gottman, J. M., & Katz, L. F. (1995). Parental meta-emotion structure predicts family and child outcomes. *Cognition and Emotion, 9*(2–3), 229–264.

Hochschild, A., & Machung, A. (2003). *The second shift.* Penguin Books.

House, J. S., Landis, K. R., & Umberson, D. (1988). Social relationships and health. *Science, 241*(4865), 540–545. https://doi.org/10.1126/science.3399889

Huston, T. L., & Houts, R. M. (1998). The psychological infrastructure of courtship and marriage: The role of personality and compatibility in romantic relationships. In T. N. Bradbury (Ed.), *The developmental course of marital dysfunction* (pp. 114–151). Cambridge University Press.

Izard, C. E. (Ed.). (1982). *Measuring emotions in infants and children.* Cambridge University Press.

Izard, C. E., Porges, S. W., Simons, R. F., Haynes, O. M., Hyde, C., Parisi, M., & Cohen, B. (1991). Infant cardiac activity: Developmental changes and relations with attachment. *Developmental Psychology, 27*(3), 432–439. https://doi.org/10.1037/0012-1649.27.3.432

Jacob, T. (Ed.). (1987). *Family interaction and psychopathology.* Plenum.

Jacobson, N. S. (1984). A component analysis of behavioral marital therapy: The relative effectiveness of behavior exchange and communication/problem-solving training. *Journal of Consulting and Clinical Psychology, 52*(2), 295–305. https://doi.org/10.1037/0022-006X.52.2.295

Jacobson, N. S., & Addis, M. E. (1993). Research on couples and couple therapy: What do we know? Where are we going? *Journal of Consulting and Clinical Psychology, 61*(1), 85–93. https://doi.org/10.1037/0022-006X.61.1.85

Jacobson, N. S., & Christensen, A. (1996). *Integrative couple therapy: Promoting acceptance and change.* Norton.

Jacobson, N. S., Christensen, A., Prince, S. E., Cordova, J., & Eldridge, K. (2000). Integrative behavioral couple therapy: An acceptance-based, promising new treatment for couple discord. *Journal of Consulting and Clinical Psychology, 68*(2), 351–355. https://doi.org/10.1037/0022-006X.68.2.351

Jacobson, N. S., Follette, W. C., & Revenstorf, D. (1984). Psychotherapy outcome research: Methods for reporting variability and evaluating clinical significance. *Behavior Therapy, 15*(4), 336–352. https://doi.org/10.1016/S0005-7894(84)80002-7

Jacobson, N. S., & Gottman, J. M. (2007). *When men batter women: New insights into ending abusive relationships.* Simon & Schuster.

Jacobson, N. S., Gottman, J. M., Waltz, J., Rushe, R., Babcock, J., & Holtzworth-Munroe, A. (1994). Affect, verbal content, and psychophysiology in the arguments of couples with a violent husband. *Journal of Consulting and Clinical Psychology, 62*(5), 982–988.

Jacobson, N. S., & Margolin, G. (1979). *Marital therapy: Strategies based on social learning and behavior exchange principles.* Brunner/Mazel.

Jacobson, N. S., & Revenstorf, D. (1988). Statistics for assessing the clinical significance of psychotherapy techniques: Issues, problems, and new developments. *Behavioral Assessment, 10*(2), 133–145.

Jacobson, N. S., Schmaling, K., & Holtzworth-Munroe, A. (1987). Component analysis of behavioral marital therapy: 2-year follow-up and prediction of relapse. *Journal of Marital and Family Therapy, 13*(2), 187–195. https://doi.org/10.1111/j.1752-0606.1987.tb00696.x

Joel, S., Eastwick, P. W., & Finkel, E. J. (2017). Is romantic desire predictable? Machine learning applied to initial romantic attraction. *Psychological Science, 28*(10), 1478–1489. https://doi.org/10.1177/0956797617714580

Johnson, M. P. (1995). Patriarchal terrorism and common couple violence: Two forms of violence against women. *Journal of Marriage and Family, 57*(2), 283–294. https://doi.org/10.2307/353683

Johnson, M. P. (2006). Conflict and control: Gender symmetry and asymmetry in domestic violence. *Violence Against Women, 12*(11), 1003–1018. https://doi.org/10.1177/1077801206293328

Johnson, M. P., & Ferraro, K. J. (2000). Research on domestic violence in the 1990s: Making distinctions. *Journal of Marriage and Family, 62*(4), 948–963. https://doi.org/10.1111/j.1741-3737.2000.00948.x

Johnson, S. M. (2004). *The practice of emotionally focused couple therapy: Creating connection* (3rd ed.). Routledge.

Johnson, S. M., & Greenberg, L. S. (1985). Differential effects of experiential and problem-solving interventions in resolving marital conflict. *Journal of Consulting and Clinical Psychology, 53*(2), 175–184. https://doi.org/10.1037/0022-006X.53.2.175

Johnson, S. M., Hunsley, J., Greenberg, L., & Schindler, D. (1999). Emotionally focused couples therapy: Status and challenges. *Clinical Psychology: Science and Practice, 6*(1), 67–79. https://doi.org/10.1093/clipsy.6.1.67

Johnson, S. M., Makinen, J. A., & Millikin, J. W. (2001). Attachment injuries in couple relationships: A new perspective on impasses in couples therapy. *Journal of Marital and Family Therapy, 27*(2), 145–155. https://doi.org/10.1111/j.1752-0606.2001.tb01152.x

Jones, A. C., Robinson, W. D., & Seedall, R. B. (2018). The role of sexual communication in couples' sexual outcomes: A dyadic path analysis. *Journal of Marital and Family Therapy, 44*(4), 606–623.

Jory, B. (2007). The Intimate Justice Scale: An instrument to screen for psychological abuse and physical violence in clinical practice. *Journal of Marital and Family Therapy.* Wiley.

Kahen-Johnson, V. J. (1998). *Intraparent inconsistencies across contexts: Implications for children's school adaptation* (Publication No. 9902113) [Doctoral dissertation, University of California, Berkeley]. ProQuest Dissertations and Theses Global.

Kahn, J. R., & London, K. A. (1991). Premarital sex and the risk of divorce. *Journal of Marriage and Family, 53*(4), 845–855. https://doi.org/10.2307/352992

Kamin, L. J. (1967). *"Attention-like" processes in classical conditioning* (Report No. 5). McMaster University.

Kaplan, H. B., Burch, N. R., & Bloom, S. W. (1964). Physiological covariation and sociometric relationships in small peer groups. In P. H. Leiderman & D. Shapiro (Eds.), *Psychobiological approaches to social behavior.* Stanford University Press.

Katkin, E. S. (1985). Blood, sweat, and tears: Individual differences in autonomic self-perception. *Psychophysiology, 22*(2), 125–137. https://doi.org/10.1111/j.1469-8986.1985.tb01573.x

Katz, L. F., & Gottman, J. M. (1986). *The meta-emotion interview* [Unpublished manuscript].

Katz, L. F., Wilson, B., & Gottman, J. M. (1999). Meta-emotion philosophy and family adjustment: Making an emotional connection. In M. J. Cox & J. Brooks-Gunn (Eds.), *Conflict and cohesion in families: Causes and consequences* (pp. 131–165). Psychology Press.

Kelley, H. H., & Thibaut, J. W. (1985). Self-interest, science, and cynicism. *Journal of Social and Clinical Psychology, 3*(1), 26–32. https://doi.org/10.1521/jscp.1985.3.1.26

Kelly, L. E., & Conley, J. J. (1987). Personality and compatibility: A prospective analysis of marital stability and marital satisfaction. *Journal of Personality and Social Psychology, 52,* 27–40.

Kenny, D. A., Kashy, D. A., & Cook, W. L. (2006). *Dyadic data analysis.* Guilford Press.

Kiecolt-Glaser, J. K., Bane, C., Glaser, R., & Malarkey, W. B. (2003). Love, marriage, and divorce: Newlyweds' stress hormones foreshadow relationship changes. *Journal of Consulting and Clinical Psychology, 7*(1), 176–188. https://doi.org/10.1037/0022-006X.71.1.176

Kiecolt-Glaser, J. K., Fisher, B. S., Ogrocki, P., Stout, J. C., Speicher, C. E., & Glaser, R. (1987). Marital quality, marital disruption and immune function. *Psychosomatic Medicine, 49,* 13–33.

Kiecolt-Glaser, J. K., Malarkey, W. B., Cacioppo, J., & Glaser, R. (1994). Stressful personal relationships: Immune and endocrine function. In M. R. Glaser & J. K. Kiecolt-Glaser (Eds.), *Human stress and immunity* (pp. 321–339). Academic Press.

Killeen, P. R. (2019). Predict, control, and replicate to understand: How statistics can foster the fundamental goals of science. *Perspectives on Behavior Science, 42*(1), 109–132. https://doi.org/10.1007/s40614-018-0171-8

Kitson, G. C., & Sussman, M. B. (1982). Marital complaints, demographic characteristics, and symptoms of mental distress in divorce. *Journal of Marriage and Family, 44*(1), 87–101. https://doi.org/10.2307/351265

Klein, W., Izquierdo, C., & Bradbury, T. N. (2007). Working relationships: Communicative patterns and strategies among couples in everyday life. *Qualitative Research in Psychology, 4*(1–2), 29–47. https://doi.org/10.1080/14780880701473391

Klostermann, K., & O'Farrell, T. J. (2013). Treating substance abuse: Partner and family approaches. *Social Work in Public Health, 28*(3–4), 234–247. https://doi.org/10.1080/19371918.2013.759014

Koch-Nielsen, I., & Gundlach, L. (1985). Women at divorce. In L. Cseh-Szombathy, I. Koch-Nielsen, J. Trost, & I. Weda (Eds.), *The aftermath of divorce: Coping and family change* (pp. 99–121). Akademiai Kiado.

Krokoff, L. J. (1989). Predictive validation of a telephone version of the Locke–Wallace Marital Adjustment Test. *Journal of Marriage and Family, 51*(3), 767–775. https://doi.org/10.2307/352175

Krokoff, L. J., Gottman, J. M., & Roy, A. K. (1988). Blue-collar and white-collar marital interaction and communication orientation. *Journal of Social and Personal Relationships, 5*(2), 201–221. https://doi.org/10.1177/026540758800500205

Kurdek, L. A. (2004). Are gay and lesbian cohabiting couples really different from heterosexual married couples? *Journal of Marriage and Family, 66*(4), 880–900. https://doi.org/10.1111/j.0022-2445.2004.00060.x

Kurdek, L. A. (2005). What do we know about gay and lesbian couples? *Current Directions in Psychological Science, 14*(5), 251–254. https://doi.org/10.1111/j.0963-7214.2005.00375.x

Langer, S. L., Ghosh, N., Todd, M., Randall, A. K., Romano, J. M., Bricker, J. B., Bolger, N., Burns, J. W., Hagan, R. C., & Porter, L. S. (2020). Usability and acceptability of a smartphone app to assess partner communication, closeness, mood, and relationship satisfaction: Mixed methods study. *JMIR Formative Research, 4*(7), e:14161. https://preprints.jmir.org/preprint/14161

Lavner, J. A., & Bradbury, T. N. (2012). Why do even satisfied newlyweds eventually go on to divorce? *Journal of Family Psychology, 26*(1), 1–10. https://doi.org/10.1037/a0025966

Lawson, A. (1988). *Adultery: An analysis of love and betrayal.* Basic Books.

Lederer, W. J., & Jackson, D. D. A. (1968). *The mirages of marriage.* Norton.

Leonard, K. E., & Eiden, R. D. (2007). Marital and family processes in the context of alcohol use and alcohol disorders. *Annual Reviews of Clinical Psychology, 3,* 285–310.

Levenson, R. W., Carstensen, L. L., & Gottman, J. M. (1993). Long-term marriage: Age, gender, and satisfaction. *Psychology and Aging, 8*(2), 301–313.

Levenson, R. W., Carstensen, L. L., & Gottman, J. M. (1994). The influence of age and gender on affect, physiology, and their interrelations: A study of long-term marriages. *Journal of Personality and Social Psychology, 67*(1), 56–68.

Levenson, R. W., Ekman, P., Heider, K., & Friesen, W. V. (1992). Emotion and autonomic nervous system activity in the Minangkabau of West Sumatra. *Journal of Personality and Social Psychology, 62*(6), 972–988. https://doi.org/10.1037/0022-3514.62.6.972

Levenson, R. W., & Gottman, J. M. (1983). Marital interaction: Physiological linkage and affective exchange. *Journal of Personality and Social Psychology, 45*(3), 587–597.

Levenson, R. W., & Gottman, J. M. (1985). Physiological and affective predictors of change in relationship satisfaction. *Journal of Personality and Social Psychology, 49*(1), 85–94.

Levenson, R. W., & Ruef, A. M. (1992). Empathy: A physiological substrate. *Journal of Personality and Social Psychology, 63*(2), 234–246.

Lewis, J. (1997). *Marriage as a search for healing.* Brunner/Mazel.

Locke, H. J., & Wallace, K. M. (1959). Short marital-adjustment and prediction tests: Their reliability and validity. *Marriage and Family Living, 21*(3), 251–255. https://doi.org/10.2307/348022

Markman, H. J. (1977). *A behavioral exchange model applied to the longitudinal study of couples planning to marry* [Unpublished doctoral dissertation]. Indiana University, Bloomington.

Markman, H. J., Stanley, S. M., & Blumberg, S. L. (2010). *Fighting for your marriage* (3rd ed.). Jossey-Bass.

Marmot, M. (2015). *The health gap: The challenge of an unequal world.* Bloomsbury Press.

Martin, T. C., & Bumpass, L. (1989). Recent trends in marital disruption. *Demography, 26*(1), 37–51. https://doi.org/10.2307/2061492

Masters, W. H., & Johnson, V. E. (1966). *Human sexual response.* Little, Brown.

Mauss, I. B., Levenson, R. W., McCarter, L., Wilhelm, F. H., & Gross, J. J. (2005). The tie that binds? Coherence among emotion experience, behavior, and physiology. *Emotion, 5*(2), 175–190. https://doi.org/10.1037/1528-3542.5.2.175

McClearn, G. E., & Rodgers, D. A. (1959). Differences in alcohol preference among inbred strains of mice. *Quarterly Journal of Studies on Alcohol, 20*(4), 691–695. https://doi .org/10.15288/qjsa.1959.20.691

McCrady, B. S., Wilson, A. D., Muñoz, R. E., Fink, B. C., Fokas, K., & Borders, A. (2016). Alcohol-focused behavioral couple therapy. *Family Process, 55*(3), 443–459. https://doi .org/10.1111/famp.12231

McManus, M. (1995). *Marriage savers*. Zondervan.

McWhirter, D. P., & Mattison, A. M. (1984). *The male couple: How relationships develop*. Prentice Hall.

Michael, R. T., Gagnon, J. H., Laumann, E. O., & Kolata, G. (1995). *Sex in America: A definitive survey*. Warner Books.

Mischel, W. (1968). *Personality and assessment*. Wiley.

Murstein, B. I., Cerreto, M., & McDonald, M. G. (1977). A theory and investigation of the effect of exchange-orientation on marriage and friendship. *Journal of Marriage and the Family, 39*, 543–548.

Nagoski, E. (2015). *Come as you are: The surprising new science that will transform your sex life*. Simon & Schuster.

Nahm, E. Y. (2006). *A cross-cultural comparison of Korean American and European American parental meta-emotion philosophy and its relationship to parent–child interaction* (Publication No. 3224266) [Doctoral dissertation, University of Washington]. ProQuest Dissertations and Theses Global.

Navarra, R. J. (2007). Family response to adults and alcohol. *Alcohol Treatment Quarterly, 25*(1–2), 85–104. https://doi.org/10.1300/J020v25n01_06

Navarra, R. J., Gottman, J. M., & Gottman, J. S. (2019). *Couples and addiction recovery: A Gottman approach for therapist, counselors, and addiction professionals*. The Gottman Institute.

Newcomb, M. D., & Bentler, P. M. (1980). Assessment of personality and demographic aspects of cohabitation and marital success. *Journal of Personality Assessment, 44*(1), 11–24. https://doi.org/10.1207/s15327752jpa4401_2

Newcomb, M. D., & Bentler, P. M. (1981). Marital breakdown. In S. Duck & R. Gilmour (Eds.), *Personal relationships* (Vol. 3, pp. 57–94). Academic Press.

Noller, P. (1980). Misunderstandings in marital communication: A study of couples' non-verbal communication. *Journal of Personality and Social Psychology, 39*(6), 1135–1148. https://doi.org/10.1037/h0077716

Noller, P. (1984). *Nonverbal communication and marital interaction*. Pergamon Press.

O'Farrell, T. J., & Fals-Stewart, W. (2006). *Behavioral couples therapy for alcoholism and drug abuse*. Guilford Press.

Olds, J., & Milner, P. (1954). Positive reinforcement produced by electrical stimulation of septal area and other regions of rat brain. *Journal of Comparative and Physiological Psychology, 47*(6), 419–427. https://doi.org/10.1037/h0058775

Ornish, D. (1998). *Love and survival: 8 pathways to intimacy and health*. HarperCollins.

Ortony, A., Clore, G. L., & Collins, A. (1988). *The cognitive structure of emotions*. Cambridge University Press.

Panksepp, J. (1998). *Affective neuroscience: The foundations of human and animal emotions*. Oxford University Press.

Panksepp, J., & Biven, L. (2012). *The archeology of mind*. Norton.

Parrott, L., & Parrott, L. (1995). *Becoming soul mates: Cultivating spiritual intimacy in the early years of marriage*. W Publishing Group.

Paterson, L. Q., Jin, E. S., Amsel, R., & Binik, Y. M. (2014). Gender similarities and differences in sexual arousal, desire, and orgasmic pleasure in the laboratory. *Journal of Sex Research, 51*(7), 801–813.

Patterson, G. R. (1982). *Coercive family process*. Castalia.

Pavlov, I. P. (1927). *Conditioned reflexes: An investigation of the physiological activity of the cerebral cortex*. Oxford University Press. https://psycnet.apa.org/record/1927-02531-000

Péloquin, K., Byers, E. S., Callaci, M., & Tremblay, N. (2019). Sexual portrait of couples seeking relationship therapy. *Journal of Marital and Family Therapy, 45*(1), 120–133. https://doi.org/10.1111/jmft.12328

Peluso, P. R., Freund, R., Gottman, J. M., Gottman, J. S., & Peluso, J. P. (2019). Validation of the Gottman Negative Comparisons for Alternatives Scale. *Family Journal, 27*(3), 261–267. https://doi.org/10.1177/1066480719843904

Pinsof, W. M., & Wynne, L. C. (1995). The efficacy of marital and family therapy: An empirical overview, conclusions, and recommendations. *Journal of Marital and Family Therapy, 21*(4), 585–613. https://doi.org/10.1111/j.1752-0606.1995.tb00179.x

Pinsof, W. M., Wynne, L. C., & Hambright, A. B. (1996). The outcomes of couple and family therapy: Findings, conclusions, and recommendations. *Psychotherapy: Theory, Research, Practice, Training, 33*(2), 321–331. https://doi.org/10.1037/0033-3204.33.2.321

Pittman, F. S. (1989). *Private lies: Infidelity and the betrayal of intimacy*. Norton.

Pittman, F. S., & Wagers, T. P. (1995). Crises of infidelity. In N. S. Jacobson & A. S. Gurman (Eds.), *Clinical handbook of couple therapy* (pp. 231–246). Guilford Press.

Polk, L. (2015). Integrating directive analytic systemic therapy and self-care for parents experiencing secondary trauma of sexually abused girls. *Mississippi College ProQuest Dissertations*, 10169649.

Porges, S. W. (2011). *The polyvagal theory: Neurophysiological foundations of emotions, attachment, communication, and self-regulation*. Norton.

Porges, S. W. (2015). Making the world safe for our children: Down-regulating defence and up-regulating social engagement to "optimise" the human experience. *Children Australia, 40*(2), 114–123. https://doi.org/10.1017/cha.2015.12

Potter, A. W., Santee, W. R., Clements, C. M., Brooks, K. A., & Hoyt, R. W. (2013). Comparative analysis of metabolic cost equations: A review. *Journal of Sport and Human Performance, 1*(3), 34-42. https: doi.org/10.12922/jshp.0009.2013

Putnam, R. D. (2000). *Bowling alone: The collapse and revival of American community.* Simon & Schuster.

Rapoport, A. (1974). *Fights, games, and debates.* University of Michigan Press. (Original work published 1960)

Raush, H. L., Barry, W. A., Hertel, R. K., & Swain, M. A. (1974). *Communication, conflict, and marriage.* Jossey-Bass.

Redford, R. (Director). (1980). *Ordinary people* [Film]. Wildwood Enterprises.

Rescorla, R. A., & Wagner, A. R. (1972). A theory of Pavlovian conditioning: Variations in the effectiveness of reinforcement and nonreinforcement. In A. H. Black & W. F. Prokasy (Eds.), *Classical conditioning II: Current research and theory* (pp. 64–99). Appleton-Century-Crofts.

Richtel, M. (2019). *An elegant defense.* HarperCollins.

Robinson, E. A., & Price, M. G. (1980). Pleasurable behavior in marital interaction: An observational study. *Journal of Consulting and Clinical Psychology, 48*(1), 117–118. https://doi.org/10.1037/0022-006X.48.1.117

Rose, J., Gilbert, L., & McGuire-Snieckus, R. (2015). Emotion coaching—a strategy for promoting behavioural self-regulation in children/young people in schools: A pilot study. *European Journal of Social and Behavioral Sciences, 13,* 1766–1790. http://dx.doi.org/10.15405/ejsbs.159

Rosenbaum, A., & O'Leary, K. D. (1981). Marital violence: Characteristics of abusive couples. *Journal of Consulting and Clinical Psychology, 49*(1), 63–71. https://doi.org/10.1037/0022-006X.49.1.63

Rossignac-Milon, M., Bolger, N., Zee, K. S., Boothby, E. J., & Higgins, E. T. (2021). Merged minds: Generalized shared reality in dyadic relationships. *Journal of Personality and Social Psychology, 120*(4), 882–911. https://doi.org/10.1037/pspi0000266

Rostosky, S. S., & Riggle, E. D. B. (2017). Same-sex couple relationship strengths: A review and synthesis of the empirical literature (2000–2016). *Psychology of Sexual Orientation and Gender Diversity, 4*(1), 1–13. https://doi.org/10.1037/sgd0000216

Rowell, L. B. (1993). *Human cardiovascular control.* Oxford University Press.

Rudder, C. (2014). *Dataclysm: Who we are (when we think no one's looking).* Crown.

Rusbult, C. E., Johnson, D. J., & Morrow, G. D. (1986a). Determinants and consequences of exit, voice, loyalty, and neglect: Responses to dissatisfaction in adult romantic involvements. *Human Relations, 39*(1), 45–63. https://doi.org/10.1177/001872678603900103

Rusbult, C. E., Johnson, D. J., & Morrow, G. D. (1986b). Predicting satisfaction and commitment in adult romantic involvements: An assessment of the generalizability of the investment model. *Social Psychology Quarterly, 49*(1), 81–89. https://doi.org/10.2307/2786859

Rusbult, C. E., Zembrodt, I. M., & Gunn, L. K. (1982). Exit, voice, loyalty, and neglect: Responses to dissatisfaction in romantic involvements. *Journal of Personality and Social Psychology*, 43(6), 1230–1242. https://doi.org/10.1037/0022-3514.43.6.1230

Russell, J. A. (1995). Facial expressions of emotion: What lies beyond minimal universality? *Psychological Bulletin*, 118(3), 379–391. https://doi.org/10.1037/0033-2909.118.3.379

Satir, V. (1983). *Conjoint family therapy*. Science and Behavior Books.

Scott, S. B., Whitton, S. W., & Buzzella, B. A. (2019). Providing relationship interventions to same-sex couples: Clinical considerations, program adaptations, and continuing education. *Cognitive and Behavioral Practice*, 26(2), 270–284. https://doi.org/10.1016/j.cbpra.2018.03.004

Seligman, M. E. P. (1995). The effectiveness of psychotherapy: The *Consumer Reports* study. *American Psychologist*, 50(2), 965–974. https://doi.org/10.1037/0003-066X.50.12.965

Shapiro, A. F., & Gottman, J. M. (2005). Effects on marriage of a psycho-communicative-educational intervention with couples undergoing the transition to parenthood, evaluation at 1-year post intervention. *Journal of Family Communication*, 5(1), 1–24. https://doi.org/10.1207/s15327698jfc0501_1

Shapiro, A. F., Gottman, J. M., & Carrère, S. (2000). The baby and the marriage: Identifying factors that buffer against decline in marital satisfaction after the first baby arrives. *Journal of Family Psychology*, 14(1), 59–70. https://doi.org/10.1037/0893-3200.14.1.59

Shapiro, A. F., Gottman, J. M., & Fink, B. C. (2015). Short-term change in couples' conflict following a transition to parenthood intervention. *Couple and Family Psychology: Research and Practice*, 4(4), 239–251. https://doi.org/10.1037/cfp0000051

Shortt, J. W., & Gottman, J. M. (1997). Closeness in young adult sibling relationships: Affective and physiological processes. *Social Development*, 6(2), 142–164.

Siegel, D. J. (2010a). *Mindsight: The new science of personal transformation*. Bantam.

Siegel, D. J. (2010b). *The mindful therapist: A clinician's guide to mindsight and neural integration*. Norton.

Siegel, J. P. (1992). *Repairing intimacy*. Aronson.

Simmons, D. S., & Doherty, W. J. (1995). Defining who we are and what we do: Clinical practice patterns of marriage and family therapists in Minnesota. *Journal of Marital and Family Therapy*, 21(1), 3–16. https://doi.org/10.1111/j.1752-0606.1995.tb00134.x

Smith, P. H., Homish, G. G., Collins, R. L., Giovino, G. A., White, H. R., & Leonard, K. E. (2014). Couples' marijuana use is inversely related to their intimate partner violence over the first 9 years of marriage. *Psychology of Addictive Behaviors*, 28(3), 734–742. https://doi.org/10.1037/a0037302

Spanier, G. B. (1988). Assessing the strengths of the Dyadic Adjustment Scale. *Journal of Family Psychology*, 2(1), 92–94. https://doi.org/10.1037/h0080477

Stith, S. M., McCollum, E. E., & Rosen, K. H. (2011). *Couples therapy for domestic vio-

lence: Finding safe solutions. American Psychological Association. https://doi.org/10.1037/12329-000

Straus, M. A. (1979). Measuring intrafamily conflict and violence: The Conflict Tactics (CT) Scales. *Journal of Marriage and Family, 41*(1), 75–88. https://doi.org/10.2307/351733

Straus, M. A., Hamby, S. L., Boney-McCoy, S., & Sugarman, D. B. (1996). The revised Conflict Tactics Scales (CTS2). *Journal of Family Issues, 17*(3), 286–316.

Straus, M. A., & Smith, C. (1990). Family patterns and child abuse. In M. A. Straus & R. J. Gelles (Eds.), *Physical violence in American families: Risk factors and adaptations to violence in 8,145 families* (pp. 245–262). Routledge.

Stuart, R. B. (1980). *Helping couples change.* Guilford Press.

Stulz, N., Hepp, U., Gosoniu, D. G., Grize, L., Muheim, F., Weiss, M. G., & Riecher-Rössler, A. (2017). Patient-identified priorities leading to attempted suicide. *Crisis, 39*(1). https://doi.org/10.1027/0227-5910/a000473

Swanson, J. M., Vigal, S. B., Udrea, D., & Lerner, M. (1998). Evaluation of individual subjects in the analog classroom setting: I. examples of graphical and statistical procedures for within-subject ranking of responses to different delivery patterns of methyl-phenidate. *Psychopharmacology Bulletin, 34*(4), 825-832.

Tabares, A. (2007). *How couples praise and complain: An examination of two brief marital interventions.* University of Washington.

Tannen, D. (2013). *You just don't understand.* Morrow.

Tavris, C. (1982). *Anger: The misunderstood emotion.* Simon & Schuster.

Terman, L. M., Buttenwieser, P., Ferguson, L. W., Johnson, W. B., & Wilson, D. P. (1938). *Psychological factors in marital happiness.* McGraw Hill.

Tharp, R. G. (1963). Psychological patterning in marriage. *Psychological Bulletin, 60*(2), 97–117. https://doi.org/10.1037/h0046726

Thibaut, J. W., & Kelley, H. H. (1959). *The social psychology of groups.* Wiley.

Thurner, M., Fenn, C. B., Melichar, J., & Chiriboga, D. A. (1983). Socio-demographic perspectives on reasons for divorce. *Journal of Divorce, 6*(1), 25–35.

Tinbergen, N. (1951). *The study of instinct.* Oxford University Press.

Tomer, R., Slagter, H. A., Christian, B. T., Fox, A. S., King, C. R., Dhanabalan, M., Gluck, M. A., & Davidson, R. J. (2014). Love to win or hate to lose? Asymmetry of dopamine D2 receptor binding predicts sensitivity to reward versus punishment. *Journal of Cognitive Neuroscience, 26*(5), 1039–1048. https://doi.org/10.1162/jocn_a_00544

Tomkins, S. (1962). *Affect imagery consciousness: Vol. 1. The positive affects.* Springer.

Tomkins, S. (1963). *Affect imagery consciousness: Vol. 2. The negative affects.* Springer.

Tronick, E., & Beeghly, M. (2011). Infants' meaning-making and the development of mental health problems. *American Psychologist, 66*(2), 107–119. https://doi.org/10.1037/a0021631

Tronick, E. Z., & Cohn, J. F. (1989). Infant–mother face-to-face interaction: Age and gender differences in coordination and the occurrence of miscoordination. *Child Development*, 60(1), 85–92. https://doi.org/10.2307/1131074

Tung, K. K. (2007). *Topics in mathematical modeling.* Princeton University Press.

Turkle, S. (2011). *Alone together: Why we expect more from technology and less from each other.* Basic Books.

Vaillant, G. E., Clark, W., Cyrus, C., Milofsky, E. S., Kopp, J., Wulsin, V. W., & Mogielnicki, N. P. (1983). Prospective study of alcoholism treatment: Eight-year follow-up. *American Journal of Medicine*, 75(3), 455–463. https://doi.org/10.1016/0002-9343(83)90349-2

Vaughan, P. (2010). *Help for therapists (and their clients) in dealing with affairs.* Dialog Press.

Verbrugge, L. M. (1979). Marital status and health. *Journal of Marriage and Family*, 41(2), 267–285. https://www.jstor.org/stable/351696

Verbrugge, L. M. (1986). Role burdens and physical health of women and men. *Women and Health*, 11(1), 47–77. https://doi.org/10.1300/J013v11n01_04

Veroff, J., Kulka, R. A., & Douvan, E. (1981). *Mental health in America: Patterns of help seeking from 1957 to 1976.* Basic Books.

von Neumann, J., & Morgenstern, O. (2007). *Theory of games and economic behavior* (60th anniversary ed.). Princeton University Press.

Watzlawick, P., Beavin, J. H., & Jackson, D. D. (1967). *Pragmatics of human communication: A study of interactional patterns, pathologies, and paradoxes.* Norton.

Wedekind, C., & Füri, S. (1997). Body odour preferences in men and women: Do they aim for specific MHC combinations or simply heterozygosity? *Proceedings of the Royal Society of London. Series B: Biological Sciences*, 264(1387), 1471–1479.

Weiner-Davis, M. (2003). *The sex-starved marriage: Boosting your marriage libido: A couple's guide.* Simon & Schuster.

Weiss, R. L. (1975). Contracts, cognition, and change: A behavioral approach to marriage therapy. *Counseling Psychologist*, 5(1), 15–26. https://doi.org/10.1177/001100007500500303

Weiss, R. L. (1980). Strategic behavioral marital therapy: Toward a model for assessment and intervention. In J. P. Vincent (Ed.), *Advances in family intervention, assessment and theory* (Vol. 1, pp. 229–271). JAI Press.

Weiss, R. L., & Cerreto, M. C. (1980). Development of a measure of dissolution potential. *American Journal of Family Therapy*, 8(2), 80–85. https://doi.org/10.1080/01926188008250358

Wiens, S., Mezzacappa, E. S., & Katkin, E. S. (2000). Heartbeat detection and the experience of emotions. *Cognition and Emotion*, 14(3), 417–427. https://doi.org/10.1080/026999300378905

Wile, D. B. (1988). In search of the curative principle in couples therapy. *Journal of Family Psychology*, 2(1), 24–27. https://doi.org/10.1037/h0080486

Wile, D. B. (1992). *Couples therapy: A nontraditional approach.* Wiley.

Wile, D. B. (1993). *After the fight: Using your disagreements to build a stronger relationship.* Guilford Press.

Wile, D. B. (2008). *After the honeymoon: How conflict can improve your relationship* (rev. ed.). Collaborative Couple Therapy Books. (Original work published 1988)

Wile, D. B., & Kaufmann, D. (2021). *Solving the moment: A collaborative couple therapy manual.*

Wilkinson, R., & Pickett, K. (2010). *The spirit level: Why greater equality makes societies stronger.* Bloomsbury.

Wilkinson, R. G., & Pickett, K. (2019). *The inner level: How more equal societies reduce stress, restore sanity and improve everyone's well-being.* Penguin.

Winch, R. F. (1958). *Mate-selection: A study of complementary needs.* Harper & Row.

Winkler, I., & Doherty, W. J. (1983). Communication styles and marital satisfaction in Israeli and American couples. *Family Process, 22*(2), 221–228. https://doi.org/10.1111/j .1545-5300.1983.00221.x

Witte, J., Northrup, C., & Schwartz, P. (2013). *The normal bar.* Harmony.

Yoshimoto, D. (2005). *Marital meta-emotion: Emotion coaching and dyadic interaction* [Doctoral dissertation]. University of Washington.

Zak, P. J. (2012). *The moral molecule: The source of love and prosperity.* Dutton.

Zak, P. J., & Fakhar, A. (2006). Neuroactive hormones and interpersonal trust: International evidence. *Economics and Human Biology, 4*(3), 412–429. https://doi.org/10.1016/j .ehb.2006.06.004

Zilbergeld, B., & Zilbergeld, G. (2010). *Sex and love at midlife: It's better than ever.* Crown House.

Zung, B. J. (1982). Screening alcohol problems in psychiatric inpatients. *Psychiatric Forum, 11*(1), 32–37.

Index

Note: Italicized page locators refer to figures; tables are noted with a *t*.